Ulrich Renz / Barbara Brinkn

Mirno spi, mali volk

Sleep Tight, Little Wolf

Slikanica v dveh jezikih

Prevod:

Jana Milovanović, Kostanjevica na Krki, Slovenia (slovenščina)

Pete Savill, Lübeck, Germany (angleščina)

Little Wolf would like to meet you at his home:

www.childrens-books-bilingual.com

"Lahko noč Tim, pa mirno spi!
Ga bova že jutri poiskala."

"Good night, Tim! We'll continue searching tomorrow.
Now sleep tight!"

Zunaj je že tema.

It is already dark outside.

Kaj počne Tim?

What is Tim doing?

Proti igrišču se je napotil.

Le kaj išče?

He is leaving for the playground.

What is he looking for there?

Mali volk!

Brez njega ne more zaspati.

The little wolf!

He can't sleep without it.

Še nekdo prihaja. Kdo je to?

Who's this coming?

Marija!

Prišla je iskat žogo.

Marie!

She's looking for her ball.

Kaj pa išče Tobi?

And what is Tobi looking for?

Svojo lopatko.

His digger.

In kaj išče Nala?

And what is Nala looking for?

Punčko.

Her doll.

Kaj ne bi morali biti ti otroci v posteljah?
Je zaskrbljena mačka.

Don't the children have to go to bed?
The cat is rather surprised.

Kdo pa zdaj prihaja?

Who's coming now?

Timova oče in mama.

Ne moreta zaspati brez njunega Tima.

Tim's mum and dad!

They can't sleep without their Tim.

Še več ljudi prihaja. Marijin oče.
Tobijev dedek. Nalina mama.

More of them are coming! Marie's dad.
Tobi's grandpa. And Nala's mum.

Zdaj pa hitro vsi v posteljo!

Now hurry to bed everyone!

"Lahko noč, Tim!
Jutri nam ne bo treba iskati."

"Good night, Tim!
Tomorrow we won't have to search any longer."

"Mirno spi, mali volk!"

"Sleep tight, little wolf!"

More about me ...

Que duermas bien, pequeño lobo
Schlaf gut, kleiner Wolf

Ulrich Renz / Barbara Brinkmann

| español | bilingüe | alemán |

Schlaf gut, kleiner Wolf
راحت بخواب، گرگ کوچک

Ulrich Renz / Barbara Brinkmann

| Deutsch | bilingual | Persisch (Farsi) |

Dors bien, petit loup
Sleep Tight, Little Wolf

Ulrich Renz / Barbara Brinkmann

| français | bilingue | anglais |

نم جيدا أيها الذئب الصغير
Sov gott, lilla vargen

Ulrich Renz / Barbara Brinkmann

| العربية | ثنائي اللغة | السويدية |

Sofðu rótt, litli úlfur
Όνειρα γλυκά, μικρέ λύκε

Ulrich Renz / Barbara Brinkmann

| Íslenska | tvímála | gríska |

Dorme bem, lobinho
Suaviter dormi, lupe parve

Ulrich Renz / Barbara Brinkmann

| português | bilingue | latino |

Schlaf gut, kleiner Wolf
おおかみくんも ぐっすり おやすみなさい

Ulrich Renz / Barbara Brinkmann

| Deutsch | bilingual | Japanisch |

잘 자, 꼬마 늑대야
Slaap lekker, kleine wolf

Ulrich Renz / Barbara Brinkmann

| 한국어 | 양국어 | 네덜란드어 |

Приятных снов, маленький волчёнок
Sleep Tight, Little Wolf

Ulrich Renz / Barbara Brinkmann

| русский | двуязычный | английский |

راحت بخواب، گرگ کوچک
Schlaf gut, kleiner Wolf

Ulrich Renz / Barbara Brinkmann

| فارسی | دوزبانی | کماني |

Que duermas bien, pequeño lobo
نم جيداً أيها الذئبُ الصغيرُ

Ulrich Renz / Barbara Brinkmann

| español | bilingüe | árabe |

സുഖമായി ഉറങ്ങൂ ചെന്നായി കുഞ്ഞേ
Dormi bene, piccolo lupo

Ulrich Renz / Barbara Brinkmann

| മലയാളം | ദ്വിഭാഷാ | ഇറ്റാലിയൻ |

Dormi bene, piccolo lupo
जम के सोना , छोटे भेड़िये

Ulrich Renz / Barbara Brinkmann

| italiano | bilinguale | hindi |

ፀብቅ ድቃስ፣ ንእሽቶይ ተኹላ
Selamat tidur, si serigala

Ulrich Renz / Barbara Brinkmann

| ትግርኛ | ብኽልተ ቋንቋ | Malaysian |

Śpij dobrze, mały wilku
ძილო ნებისა, პაწარა მგელო

Ulrich Renz / Barbara Brinkmann

| polski | Dwujęzyczna | gruziński |

Солодких снів, маленький вовчику
잘 자, 꼬마 늑대야

Ulrich Renz / Barbara Brinkmann

| українська | двомовний | корейська |

A Children's Book
for the Global Village

"Sleep Tight, Little Wolf" is a multilingual picture book for the ever growing number of children who face the challenge – and the opportunity – of living with different cultures and languages. Their families may have been displaced to another country as refugees. Or their parents may have chosen the life of expats, working for a global company or an NGO. Perhaps it may merely have been love that brought together two people from different world regions who don't even speak the same language.

Migration and ensuing multilingualism is a global megatrend of our days. Ever more children are born away from their parents' home countries, and are balancing between the languages of their mother, their father, their grandparents, and their peers. "Sleep Tight, Little Wolf" is meant to help bridge the language divides that cross more and more families, neighborhoods and kindergartens in the globalized world. This is a global picture book – coming to you in more than 50 languages and all conceivable bilingual combinations of them.

www.childrens-books-bilingual.com

Bilingual Children's Books - in any language you want

Home	Authors	The Little Wolf	About

Welcome to the **Little Wolf's Language Wizard!**

Tell me, first of all, in which language you want me to work for you. English or German?

English ▼ | Go!

Now just choose the two languages in which you want to read to your children:

Language 1:

Please choose... ▼

Language 2:

no 2nd language ▼

Go!

Learn more about the Little Wolf project at *www.childrens-books-bilingual.com*. At the heart of this website you will find what we call the "Little Wolf's Language Wizard". It contains more than 50 languages and any of their bilingual combinations: Just select, in a simple drop-down-menu, the two languages in which you'd like to read the story to your child – and the book is instantly made available, ready for order as an ebook download or as a printed edition.

As time goes by ...

... the little ones grow older, and start to read on their own. Here is Little Wolf's recommendation to them:

BO & FRIENDS

Smart detective stories for smart children

Reading age: 10 + - www.bo-and-friends.com

Wie die Zeit vergeht ...

Irgendwann sind aus den süßen Kleinen süße Große geworden – die jetzt sogar selber lesen können. Der kleine Wolf empfiehlt:

MOTTE & CO

Kinderkrimis zum Mitdenken

Lesealter ab 10 – www.motte-und-co.de

About the authors

Ulrich Renz was born in Stuttgart, Germany, in 1960. After studying French literature in Paris he graduated from medical school in Lübeck and worked as head of a scientific publishing company. He is now a writer of non-fiction books as well as children's fiction books. – www.ulrichrenz.de

Barbara Brinkmann was born in Munich, Germany, in 1969. She grew up in the foothills of the Alps and studied architecture and medicine for a while in Munich. She now works as a freelance graphic artist, illustrator and writer. – www.bcbrinkmann.com

© 2016 by Sefa Verlag Kirsten Bödeker, Lübeck, Germany
www.sefa-verlag.de

sefa

Database: Paul Bödeker, Hamburg, Germany
Font: Noto Sans

ISBN: 9783739946832

Version: 20160225

THE LEGION'S FIGHTING BULLDOG

There are many books about the Civil War era I treasure, but none more than *The Legion's Fighting Bulldog*. For sure, the letters of Will and Rosa Delony relate, in remarkable detail, the story of Cobb's Legion in language that, at once, stirs the blood and touches the heart. Reading the letters, one feels their patriotic fervor at the outset of the war, Will's horrid ordeal of fighting on the front lines, the equally painful and lonely trials of Rosa as wife and mother struggling to maintain home and children, and the disillusionment and then depression of Will and Rosa as they face the approaching reality that the world they loved was not going to last. The overarching story is not about the grim details of war, but of two noble and wonderful people, who are completely—and forever—in love with one another no matter the trials and tribulations. In an age where absolute devotion, fidelity, and commitment is so rarely eulogized, their tender letters, written as the world around them was disintegrating, are heartwarming and uplifting. I love this book and wholeheartedly recommend it to all who delight in great Civil War history and, moreover, in a real-life love story.

—Kent Masterson Brown, author of *Retreat From Gettysburg: Lee, Logistics, and the Pennsylvania Campaign*

This huge collection centers on the extraordinary correspondence between an Athens attorney-soldier and his wife. It highlights—as few previous works have done—the activities of Georgia soldiers in Lee's army, as well as tribulations ever present on the home front. Expertly annotated, with an easily flowing narrative, *The Legion's Fighting Bulldog* will hereafter be a basic reference tool for Georgia during its most traumatic years.

—James I. "Bud" Robertson, Jr.

The letters of W.G. Delony reveal the heart and heroism of a celebrated member of Cobb's Legion serving in Robert E. Lee's Army of Northern Virginia. Often in the thick of the fighting, the Georgian exhibited a fierce pride reflected in his views on friend and foe alike. Embracing letters from the Antebellum period to the end of Delony's service in 1863, this compilation reveals the essence of life, love, and war in a turbulent era.

—Brian S. Wills, director, Civil War Center, Kennesaw State University

Here is a book fully worthy of its protagonists—the passionate wife who concedes she's as "restive and impatient as a young unbroken colt" and the tender-hearted husband whose fascination with danger keeps dragging him, with all his affections, back to the battlefield. More than a collection of great letters, *The Legion's Fighting Bulldog* is a stellar biography of the Delonys, immersing us in one of the most dramatic periods in our history.

—Stephen Berry, Gregory Professor of the Civil War Era and co-director of the Center for Virtual History, University of Georgia

MERCER UNIVERSITY PRESS

Endowed by

TOM WATSON BROWN
and
THE WATSON-BROWN FOUNDATION, INC.

Love to Suadeen

— THE LEGION'S — FIGHTING BULLDOG

The Civil War Correspondence of William Gaston Delony,
Lieutenant Colonel of Cobb's Georgia Legion Cavalry,
and Rosa Delony, 1853–1863

Best Wishes —

Vince Dooley

VINCENT JOSEPH DOOLEY

and

SAMUEL NORMAN THOMAS, JR.

Mercer University Press | Macon, Georgia | 2017

Dedicated to the past, present, and future generations of the
Delony, Dooley, and Thomas families, and to the memory of
Samuel N. Thomas, Sr., and his great grandfather,
John Richard Miller, private, Co. I, 1ˢᵗ North Carolina Cavalry,
who fought alongside of William Gaston Delony.

MUP/ H927

© 2017 by Mercer University Press
Published by Mercer University Press
1501 Mercer University Drive
Macon, Georgia 31207
All rights reserved

9 8 7 6 5 4 3 2 1

Books published by Mercer University Press are printed on acid-free paper that
meets the requirements of the American National Standard for Information
Sciences—Permanence of Paper for Printed Library Materials.

ISBN   978-0-88146-604-1
Cataloging-in-Publication Data is available from the Library of Congress

Contents

"Do you think they will charge, Major?" asked Stuart.
"Charge, sir," indignantly responded Deloney,
"why they would charge so close to the gates of hell
as to singe their mustaches and eyebrows off.
We came here to charge, sir."

—Athens *Banner*, 30 April 1892

Foreword

The Legion's Fighting "Bulldog"

Congratulations, Gentle Reader. You have a genuine treat ahead of you. Whether you have bought, borrowed, or simply begun to browse this book, you are about to encounter two fascinating people.

One of the pleasures and perks of history is the opportunity to read other people's mail. Here are the letters of Rosa Eugenia Huguenin Delony and William Gaston Delony. Rosa and Will lived in exciting times and reflected those times in their correspondence. Both Rosa and Will were articulate and honest with each other. And both of them share important stories with us. They lived intently with the American Civil War—with challenges and hardships at home in Athens, Georgia, and with cavalry service and bloody combat in Robert E. Lee's Army of Northern Virginia.

In the beginning Rosa and Will wrote love letters to each other in intelligent, proper nineteenth-century prose. Beneath the surface, however, they offer intimate, possibly prurient feelings to each other.

On November 23, 1853, Will wrote about receiving a daguerreotype likeness of Rosa. He said, "When you read this letter you may think I can be almost as ridiculous with your picture *as with you after Sam had retired.* Would to Heaven I could make myself similarly ridiculous tonight, it is sort of ridiculousness I admire and love to indulge in and which by the way is the wisest thing we ever did in cherishing a love that is well worth preserving."

On February 11, 1854, Rosa wrote about a nightmare in which she had married another man. "I dreamed I was a loving maniac and woke up yelling and moaning most piteously. Now what say you to my dreams."

After their marriage in May of 1854, Rosa and Will lived apart for a time while Will oversaw the construction of a home for his family in Athens. During this period, Rosa wrote from Savannah in January 1855, "I miss you terribly Will, it's very lonely in the evenings. I often wonder Darling what would become of me without you. I wish I was not so dependent upon *certain* sources for my happiness."

The introduction of the book identifies Rosa and Will, and each of the fourteen chapters has a preface in which the editors place the Delonys in the context of the war. Appended to the text is a list of people mentioned and some identification as to who they were. Even many of the footnotes are fun; the discursive notes amplify issues and events mentioned in the letters.

Rosa's letters are especially important. In the summer of 1861, at age 29 with three small children, she became a single mother and a head of household. Will had left for the war in Virginia; Rosa was coping with the home front.

On December 22, 1861, she wrote, "I was busy all day yesterday and day before making soap and clarifying and hardening my tallow for candles.... Will have your clothes washed with soap of my manufacture when you come to see me and have one of my candles to see by and give you some sausages, and [pigs'] feet and tongues of my putting up. I am fattening the calves also. Feed them every day myself."

Rosa wrestled with taxes and money matters. On October 11, 1862, Will called Rosa "my poor little financier. I know you are in a peck of troubles."

Will Delony's letters described in great detail his battles and comrades. On one occasion, Will's metal flask stuffed into the pocket of his coat absorbed a saber slash and likely saved his life. He describes hand-to-hand combat and muses about colonels and generals. "Because I did not graduate at West Point I am to play second fiddle to a man who does nothing."[1]

Delony admires Wade Hampton and is proud to serve with him. Will portrays Hampton as Rod Andrew does in his splendid biography *Wade Hampton: Confederate Warrior and Southern Redeemer* (Chapel Hill: University of North Carolina Press, 2008). Will was critical of J. E. B. Stuart, who commanded all the cavalry in Robert E. Lee's army. He wrote about "Stuart's pets." "The Virginian Brigades are having fine times behind infantry lines.... We are doing the work [scouting and picketing], and they are reaping the rewards."[2] Delony admires Robert E. Lee but criticizes him for the failure at Gettysburg. In Delony's analysis, Lee was stymied in Pennsylvania because he depended upon capturing ammunition from his enemies.

Many of Will Delony's letters offer his thoughts about soldiers and soldiering. "I am very tired of being ordered about by a set of Jackasses," he wrote in May 1862. "Soldiers are like children," he proclaimed, "they lose everything, waste everything, and destroy everything." Delony thought often about home and family. In January 1863 he wrote, "I told the Genl. I was utterly demoralized and could do no more fighting until I saw my wife and children." In June 1863 Will wrote to Rosa, "The army doesn't suit me, and the truth is I have a feeling of contempt for men generally. I begin to think they are all alike and they are only redeemed from being devils by the influence exerted over them by the women."

And Will had more observations and conclusions; I have merely offered a sample. I ramble. My goal has been to introduce you, Gentle Reader, to two lively, intelligent, and articulate young people, and to point out how and how much these letters reveal about life on the home front and the war front during the America Civil War.

Enjoy. Editors Vince Dooley and Sam Thomas have done a fine job.

Emory M. Thomas
Regents Professor of History, Emeritus
University of Georgia

---

[1] William G. Delony to Rosa H. Delony, 16 November 1862, Delony Papers.
[2] William G. Delony to Rosa H. Delony, 6 December 1862, Delony Papers.

Acknowledgments

William Gaston Delony fought for about two and a half years during the war. Our work on his correspondence, and that of his wife, Rosa, has taken nearly twice as long. Along the way we have met many interesting characters who were touched by the life of William Delony, in particular Wylie Howard, a former member of Cobb's Georgia Legion Cavalry. To him, we are especially indebted, as his was the first concerted attempt to record this famous unit's history.

In this process, we have gathered together our own battalion of scholars without whom this work could not have properly progressed. Some broke down obstacles in our understanding while others furnished bits of additional information. All joyfully gave of their time, energy, expertise, and encouragement, and to them, we are deeply indebted. We apologize in advance if we have left anyone out.

First and foremost, we owe a debt of gratitude to the Hargrett Rare Book & Manuscript Library at the University of Georgia and to the Watson-Brown Foundation. Without the Hargrett's preservation of the original letters and the foundation's support and encouragement of this research, this work would have been a nonstarter. To Toby Graham and Tad Brown, we want to say a very special thank you.

One person in particular was instrumental in assisting us with references and logistical problems involving the legion cavalry. Cobb's Georgia Legion is a difficult group to follow for a couple of reasons. First, both the infantry and the cavalry components retained their original names throughout the war, which meant that when individuals or accounts referred to "Cobb's Legion" or the "Georgia Legion," it was often difficult to discern whether the subject dealt with the infantry or the cavalry. On top of that, Cobb's Georgia Legion, commanded by Thomas R. R. Cobb, was a part of Cobb's Brigade, commanded by Thomas's older brother, Howell, and many writers over the years have simply excluded mention of the legion when talking about the brigade. Gordon Blaker, a superb military historian, assisted us in sorting some of this out. Gordon furnished us with some of his early newspaper gleanings concerning the legion, which helped tremendously in our organization of events noted within the correspondence.

Three individuals deserve many thanks for their assistance at different points in our process. Kent Masterson Brown, a wonderful gentleman and a fine historian in his own right, was one of the first who brokered the idea to us about William Delony. Author of the acclaimed *Retreat from Gettysburg*, his work became critical in our understanding of some of Delony's lesser-known movements. Likewise, many thanks to David Rinehardt, a Delony enthusiast from Pensacola, Florida, who was helpful in sharing his personal notes with us on the family. We would also like to thank historian Clark "Bud" Hall, who happily gave of his time to acquaint us with the intricacies of the battle of Brandy Station. As one poster has mentioned of Bud on his "Rantings of the Civil War Historian" blog, "He probably knows more about this battle than the participants."

A special thanks goes out to Madison County, Virginia, historian Harold R. Woodward, who is the expert on the battle of Jack's Shop, where Will Delony was mortally wounded. His book on Madison County during the Civil War is the best to date on the battle and was cited often during the preparation for this work. Woodward was most generous with his time in providing a personal tour of the battlefield and willingly responding to several follow-up calls on the subject.

Most of the correspondence of William Delony and his wife, Rosa, is held at the Hargrett Rare Book & Manuscript Library at the University of Georgia. The daunting task of wading through not only the papers of the Delonys, but also of Thomas R. R. Cobb, was made much easier by the congenial staff at the Hargrett. Mazie Bowen, Chuck Barber, and Mary Linnemann were particularly helpful. These folks were constantly, and happily, pulling collections for our use. Another Hargrett stalwart we would like to single out for his great assistance is Steven Brown. Steven located photographs, including those of the Delony house. He also, on more than one occasion, answered questions on the spur of the moment whenever we were in need.

Several other individuals were instrumental in acquiring additional information needed to flesh our story out. Thanks to noted author, historian, and Gettysburg guide James A. "Jim" Hessler, who took us on a tour of the cavalry battle at Hunterstown, Pennsylvania; to Garry Adelman, a licensed Gettysburg battlefield guide and director of the Eastern Department of the Civil War Trust, which, along with Sam Smith, former education manager of the trust, gave of their research expertise in locating hard-to-find materials, including the photograph of Stanton Hospital in Washington, DC. And a special thanks to Lynette Stoudt, director of the Research Center of the Georgia Historical Society, and her fine staff for not only making available easy access to the society's library and archives, but also for furnishing information pertaining to Rosa.

Other scholars in the local community were of tremendous assistance. Gary Doster freely gave of his time, knowledge, and willingness to run down any question that arose about local events and people, enabling us to piece together parts of the puzzle. He is a great researcher and a wonderful friend. "Cousin" Charlotte Thomas Marshall was instrumental in our ability to identify much in terms of background on many of the individuals named in the correspondence. Whenever we asked Charlotte if she knew anything about an individual, we would inevitably get back two or three pages of information. Her own published work, *Oconee Hill Cemetery of Athens, Georgia* (vol. 1), was of immeasurable help. This work is truly exceptional and should be looked upon as the Holy Grail of cemetery publications. We would be remiss in not mentioning another work that helped us in piecing together a more complete picture of the Athens community. *The Tangible Past in Athens, Georgia* brought a number of diverse characters together as friends and colleagues in a massive project on Athens's past. This work was often referenced for an understanding of some of the relationships between individuals within the correspondence. Thank you Amy Andrews, Steven Brown, Janet Clark, Pat Cooper, Gary Doster, Lee Epting, Theresa Flynn, Mary Anne Hodgson, Marie Koenig, Milton Leathers, Charlotte Marshall, Hubert McAlexander, Henry Ramsey, Kenneth Storey, and Smith Wilson. You are truly deserving of the moniker "Dream Team."

A number of folks freely gave of their research and knowledge along the way. Colleagues Gordon Jones and Michelle Zupan made sure we were aware of anything coming across their desks dealing with the legion. Keith Bohannon and Bill Smedlund contributed some of their own research, including a few letters referenced within these pages. Ed Rowe furnished some of the first rosters and other relevant information used to identify some individuals. David Vaughan, that stalwart collector of Georgia Civil War soldier images, gave freely of his collection, not only with images of Will Delony, but also of other Georgia soldiers. Angela Elder gave us access to her work on the inner thoughts of women of the time, particularly of Rosa. Fran Thomas contributed to this work by answering questions early on and through her work as represented in *A Portrait of Historic Athens & Clarke County*. To each of you, many, many thanks.

People sometimes say that to be a historian, all you have to do is gather some facts together and then parrot them back. If that is true, then we'd like to thank several preeminent historical "parrots" for their knowledge of the events. Their assistance in reading sections, answering questions, and giving advice in the construction of this work was not only eagerly offered but also pleasantly and oftentimes humorously relayed. Most prominent among these parrots are Stephen Berry, Ron Coddington, Nash Boney, John Inscoe, and Emory Thomas. Not only is your knowledge of this period beyond measure, but your valued friendship is a true treasure.

We were extremely fortunate to have the services of an exceptional mapmaker. The battlefield maps in this work are the products of Julie Krick's painstaking work. Her eye for detail as well as her ability to take scribbled notes on crude, hand-drawn maps and turn them into something not only legible but works of art was astounding.

A very special thanks to Emily C. Carnes of Richmond Hill (Savannah), Georgia, great-great-granddaughter of Will Delony, who inherited the Carson Family Papers and willingly turned them over to us for research and safekeeping. The papers consist of Will and Rosa's genealogical material along with numerous family photographs and some original correspondence. Upon the completion of our research, the papers were turned over to the University of Georgia's Hargrett Rare Book & Manuscript Library, where they will be reunited with the bulk of the Delony's existing papers.

There are several other Delony family descendants who were very instrumental in furthering our work. Leigh Hull Steel, great-great-granddaughter of Delony, invited us to her home to meet with her husband, Mike, her mother, Barbara Smith

Hull, and her uncle, Charles C. Hull, to share information and to photograph Will's desk and little Rosa's silver cup. Uncle Charles Hull was especially helpful in sharing information and supplying numerous copies of research materials in his possession. Another direct descendant, Frank H. Maier of Atlanta, was helpful in directing us to Emily Carnes and the Carson papers as well as reviewing some genealogical information. To all, thank you for willingly sharing your family with us.

We'd also like to thank Chris Lloyd and the Hilltop Grille's congenial and pleasant staff. This became our common meeting place once or twice a month for the past couple of years as we chowed down on their delightful Friday BBQ as we discussed the latest editions and the next steps to take in this process. We were occasionally questioned as to whether we were ever going to finish the work or were simply dragging it out just to have more barbecue opportunities at Hilltop Grille. Thank you Bert Lumpkin and Brandon McDearis and the rest of your talented staff. The meals helped to sustain us through to the end.

Our greatest thanks, however, are extended to our wives. Sitting there with those glassy-eyed expressions while we described our latest incredible finds, or leaving us completely to our own world while we explored the ins and outs of Civil War cavalry life, or the seemingly endless trips to another battlefield or another repository just to come up with one small additional tidbit of information, especially when there was some other more important function going on. Barbara and Lynn know what it means to a marriage to allow their husbands room to share their enthusiasm with someone of like mind and understanding. Their support for us in this project never waned, and they never doubted that we would eventually finish this book. We owe our wives a tremendous thank you.

Finally, a word needs to be said of our editor, Marc Jolley, and Marsha Luttrell, and the fine staff at Mercer University Press. No work of this sort ever comes to fruition all on its own. Without a team of highly talented experts, this work and others like it would be very little more than a collection of letters. With the help of editors such as those at Mercer University Press, this collection not only adds to our growing knowledge of the Civil War participant, but also brings these interesting individuals to life as they begin to emerge from the following pages.

Editor's Note

The letters of William Gaston Delony and of his wife, Rosa Eugenia Huguenin, furnish us with a window into the lives of typical upper-level whites of the "master class" during the Civil War. They also offer the reader and researcher a window on one of the more famous cavalry units during the war, of which very little has been previously written. These are not the writings of the typical Confederate soldier or even the typical soldier of either side. Instead, they are the correspondence of well-educated and independent individuals who also happened to be well placed in society due to birth. From this standing, we can come to know something of what the common soldier thought and felt, something of what these families went through, both on the battlefield and at home, and why many Southerners were willing to give so much, especially as they began to see their numbers rapidly dwindle away. It is for this last reason that the following correspondence is most valuable.

Like all correspondents of the Civil War, letters from home were especially treasured, and Rosa's letters to Will were obviously no exception. Will treasured them and kept them with him, at least until he could send them home. It is much more common to find correspondence from the soldiers themselves. To have access to letters from home is more of the exception rather than the rule, so we are extremely indebted to Rosa, and subsequently, her children, who preserved the letters contained in the collection. Over generations, these letters were kept close to the heart and were highly prized for the information contained within.

As mentioned, most of the letters presented in these pages are contained in the William Gaston Delony Papers, housed at the Hargrett Rare Book & Manuscript Library at the University of Georgia. Some additional letters, still in the family's possession, were added late in the process when they were brought to light, and were quickly painstakingly transcribed by Lynn C. Thomas. These additional letters closed a number of holes that were evident in the chain of correspondence. However, as you read through the correspondence, you become aware that some letters are still absent. Either their location is not known or, most likely, they no longer exist. Many of Rosa's letters unfortunately fall into this category.

As we progressed through the editorial process, we kept two goals in mind: First, we have tried to maintain a consideration for the reader with the addition of some punctuation. Preserving the integrity of the letters as originally written proved to be more of a problem than one might think. The correspondence of both Will and Rosa, like that of their contemporaries, offers very little in the way of punctuation, which often leads to misunderstanding as the modern reader inadvertently places the wrong emphasis on different fractions of a sentence. In order to assist the reader, punctuation has been standardized throughout. Second, and most importantly, we have attempted to preserve the integrity of the original letters and let the writers talk for themselves. Many of the letters needed some context, so we introduce each chapter with some commentary and historical background.

Many Civil War-era soldiers used capitalization as a completely arbitrary literary function, and both of our writers here exhibit no exception to that rule. Capitalization, or lack thereof, was retained with the exception of the beginning of sentences. Abbreviations were left undisturbed, in keeping with the intention of the writers.

The letters of Will and Rosa, and later, of others, are presented chronologically with additional clarifying information, where appropriate, presented in the form of footnotes. Hopefully, this method will leave the reader unencumbered while still explaining some of the more puzzling statements within the writings and helping place the reader in the midst of the events as they were happening.

The legibility of the writings varies, making it often difficult to determine a word or in some cases making the word entirely illegible. When a word was determined to be indecipherable, it was replaced by a blank underlined space, and in some cases a suggested word was offered between brackets: [and].

Many of the individuals mentioned in the correspondence were family members and friends, but many more names simply cropped up here and there, sometimes repeating in later letters. These individuals have been identified, whenever possible, in the Biographical Roster printed at the end of the work. Prominent individuals, usually generals, have been furnished with only some brief information as to their involvement with the writer. Two appendices have been added, as both add some clarity to events in the correspondence but do not fit neatly within the commentaries: one concerns Delony's protest at being passed over for promotion in 1861, and the second relates to the Georgia Horse Infirmary.

We hope our efforts add to your enjoyment as you follow William and Rosa Delony through this turbulent period. We enjoyed getting to know this couple and appreciate their unintentional (as they certainly couldn't have dreamed their letters would one day be collected into a book) yet important and humanizing contribution to Civil War history.

Note: Camp locations were drawn primarily from William S. Smedlund, *Camp Fires of Georgia Troops, 1861–1865* (Lithonia, GA: Kennesaw Mountain Press, 1994).

William and Rosa Delony Timeline

1826   September 8: Birth of William Gaston Delony (St. Mary's, Camden County, Georgia).

1832   March 6: Birth of Rosa Eugenia Huguenin (Chatham County, Georgia).

1846   August 8: Will Delony graduates from Franklin College (University of Georgia).

1848   Will Delony appointed Instructor of Foreign Languages at Franklin College (University of Georgia)

1854   May 16: Will and Rosa marry in Savannah, Georgia.

1855   January 6: Will elected town warden of Athens, Georgia.
        June 29: Birth of first child, Eliza Huguenin Delony.

1856   January 5: Will again elected town warden of Athens.
        February: Will and Rosa move into newly constructed home adjacent to northeast corner of Broad and Lumpkin Street in Athens.
        June 20: Death of Eliza Huguenin Delony nine days before her first birthday.

1857   September 9: Birth of second child, Rosa Eugenia Delony.

1858   August 4: Will elected first lieutenant of Athens artillery company, the Flying Artillery.

1859   January 1: Will elected town warden of Athens for the third time.
        March 3: Birth of third child, Tom Cobb Delony.
        October 6: Will elected state representative from Athens.

1860   March 14: The Georgia House of Representatives meets at state capital in Milledgeville, Georgia, to select delegates to represent the state at the Democratic Convention in Charleston, South Carolina, the next month.
        September 2: Birth of fourth child, William Gaston Delony.
        November 6: Abraham Lincoln elected President of the United States.
        December 10: Will speaks in favor of secession to a group of Greene County, Georgia, residents.
        December 20: South Carolina secedes from the Union.

1861   January 9: Mississippi secedes from the Union.
        January 10: Florida secedes from the Union.
        January 11: Alabama secedes from the Union.
        January 19: Georgia secedes from the Union. Federal installations in Georgia
        are seized by the state.
        January 26: Louisiana secedes from the Union.
        February 1: Texas secedes from the Union.
        February 18: The Confederate States of America is formed in Montgomery,
        Alabama, consisting of Alabama, Florida, Georgia, Louisina, Mississippi,
        South Carolina, and Texas.
        April 12: South Carolina forces open fire on Fort Sumter in Charleston harbor.
        War begins. President Lincoln issues call to all states still loyal to the Union to
        supply a quota of 75,000 troops to put down the rebellion.
        April 17: Virginia secedes from the Union.
        May 6: Arkansas secedes from the Union.
        May 20: North Carolina secedes from the Union.
        June 8: Tennessee secedes from the Union.
        June 14: T. R. R. Cobb begins forming Cobb's Legion, a combined-arms force
        composed of infantry, cavalry, and artillery.
        June 21: Will Delony begins raising a cavalry company in Clarke and adjacent
        counties in Georgia.
        July 7: Delony elected captain of the cavalry company he raises; company en-
        camps on the Athens fairgrounds and begins training.
        August 21: Georgia Troopers (later Co. C, Delony's Company) organize for
        the war and begin arriving in camp outside Richmond, Virginia.
        September 1: Legion at Camp Washington, York County, Virginia.
        September 12: Cobb's Legion officially becomes part of the Army of the Pen-
        insula under Gen. John B. Magruder.
        October 10: Legion at Camp Marion, York County, Virginia.
        October 21: Legion establishes Camp Mud Hole, York County, Virginia, as a
        temporary camp while men build huts for winter quarters at Camp Marion.
        October 21: Delony leaves on twenty-five-day furlough.
        December 14: Delony arrives in Richmond, returning from furlough.
        December 20: Legion establishes a picket camp, Camp Disappointment, York
        County, Virginia, located on the peninsula below Camp Marion.

1862   January: Cobb's Georgia Legion, commanded by Col. T. R. R. Cobb, becomes
        part of McLaws's Division, Army of the Peninsula.
        January 15: Delony embarks on fifty-day furlough.
        January 18: Legion back at Camp Marion, York County, Virginia.
        March 7: Delony returns from fifty-day furlough.
        March 8: Legion at Camp Hunter, Suffolk County, Virginia.
        March 22: Legion at Camp Randolph, Wayne County, North Carolina.

April: The legion becomes part of Cobb's Brigade, commanded by Gen. Howell Cobb, McLaws's Division, Magruder's Command, Department of Northern Virginia. It serves in reserve capacity during the Siege of Yorktown.

May: The legion cavalry unofficially becomes a part of the Cavalry Brigade, Army of Northern Virginia.

May 25: Delony on sick furlough.

June 2: Will Delony returns from sick furlough to learn he has been appointed major of Cobb's Georgia Legion Cavalry.

June 8: Legion at Camp Meadow, Henrico County, Virginia.

June 25: Legion takes part in the Seven Days' Battles, but sees little action.

June 28: Delony leads his first charge of Cobb's Georgia Legion Cavalry at Dispatch Station.

June 29: Legion cavalry under Wade Hampton's command proceed to White House Plantation on the Pamunkey River near West Point, Virginia, to ascertain possible Union withdrawal.

July 3: Legion at Camp Hardtimes, Henrico County, Virginia.

July 3: Legion cavalry attack a Union gunboat on Haxall's and Herring creeks.

July 4: Legion cavalry again attack a Union gunboat on Haxall's and Herring creeks.

July 5: Legion at Camp Meadow, Henrico County, Virginia.

July 21: Legion cavalry headquarters moves to Hanover Court House.

July 25: J. E. B. Stuart promoted to major general and cavalry reorganized into two brigades: first brigade commanded by Wade Hampton and second brigade commanded by Fitzhugh Lee.

July 28: Cobb's Legion Cavalry raised to regimental strength and officially becomes part of Hampton's Brigade, Cavalry Division, Army of Northern Virginia.

August 2–8: Elements of the legion have numerous brief clashes with Federal scouts from Harrison's Landing at Thornburg, or Massaponax Church, Virginia.

August 22: Legion captures more than 300, including many of Pope's staff officers at Catlett's Station.

August 30: Legion covers Stonewall Jackson's right flank at Groveton Heights during battle of Second Manassas.

September 1: Legion is attacked by Union infantry at Chantilly, or Ox Hill, while driving Federal cavalry before them. The legion beats off the attack with support of Jackson's Infantry.

September 12: Legion cavalry enters Frederick City, Maryland, while under fire.

September 13: Following an attack at Crampton's Gap and the rapid pullback of Confederate infantry, the legion cavalry makes a brief stand east of Middletown and then west at the Catoctin Creek bridge. Later in the day, fighting

takes place at Quebec Schoolhouse, or Burkittsville, Maryland, with Delony leading a sabre and pistol charge as the legion cavalry rout the Federal cavalry.
September 14: Battle of South Mountain, part of the Antietam Campaign.
September 17: Battle of Sharpsburg, part of the Antietam Campaign.
September 30: Legion at Camp Tom, Frederick County, Virginia.
October 9: J. E. B. Stuart and most of his cavalry conduct a circuitous raid through Maryland and Pennsylvania as they encircle the Union army.
October 10: Action near Chambersburg, Pennsylvania.
October 13: Following the Maryland/Pennsylvania raid, the legion is at Camp Rapidan, Orange County, Virginia (near Raccoon Ford on the Rapidan River).
November 1: Thomas R. R. Cobb promoted to brigadier general and given command of the newly reformulated all-Georgia Brigade. With Cobb's promotion, Young becomes colonel of Cobb's Georgia Legion Cavalry while Delony becomes the new lieutenant colonel of the legion cavalry.
November 5: Action at Barbee's Cross Roads, Virginia.
November 8: Engagement at Little Washington, Virginia.
November 28: Skirmish between pickets at Hartwood Church, Virginia.
December 12–15: Legion is scouting and picketing near Fredericksburg, Virginia.
December 13: Battle of Fredericksburg; death of T. R. R. Cobb.
December 17: Hampton's raid begins with Delony leading seventy-five men from Cobb's Georgia Legion Cavalry.
December 19: Skirmish near Occoquan Bridge, Virginia.
December 20: Skirmishing near Occoquan and Dumfries, Virginia. Delony returns after successful raid begun on December 17.
December 27 and 28: Skirmishing near Occoquan, Virginia, with Delony commanding Legion Cavalry.

1863   January 6: Legion at Camp Georgia, Culpeper County, Virginia, near Raccoon Ford of Rapidan River.
January 26: Legion at Camp Stevensburg, Culpeper County, Virginia.
January 31: Georgia Troopers (Co. B) at Camp Fannie, Culpeper County, Virginia.
February 1–May 1: Delony on extended furlough and recruiting assignment in Georgia.
February 5–7: Legion involved in operations at Rappahannock Bridge and Grove Church, Virginia.
February 15: Co. K establishes picket camp, Camp Maynard, Culpeper County, Virginia, near Stevensburg.
March 30: Confederate Order No. 104 officially designates the legion cavalry as the 9th Georgia Cavalry Regiment. The legion cavalry's members refuse to be so designated and continue to refer to themselves as Cobb's Georgia Legion Cavalry. They never adopted the official designation.

April 27: Legion involved in Chancellorsville Campaign.

April 29: Legion involved in operations against Stoneman's Raiders.

May 8: Legion ends its operations against Stoneman's Raiders.

May 20: Legion camped near Culpeper, Virginia.

May 22: First "Grand Review" of J. E. B. Stuart's Confederate cavalry, including Cobb's Georgia Legion Cavalry.

June 3: Legion begins involvement in Gettysburg Campaign.

June 5: Second "Grand Review" of J. E. B. Stuart's Confederate cavalry, including Cobb's Georgia Legion Cavalry.

June 8: Third "Grand Review" of J. E. B. Stuart's Confederate cavalry, including Cobb's Georgia Legion Cavalry. Robert E. Lee in attendance.

June 9: In the largest cavalry battle ever fought in North America, Cobb's Legion Cavalry distinguishes itself in the Battle of Brandy Station.

June 10: Legion in camp near Stevensburg, Virginia.

June 17: Action at Aldie, Virginia, as the legion screens the Army of Northern Virginia as it begins its northward thrust.

June 21: Action at Upperville, Virginia.

June 23: Legion in camp near Asbury's Gap.

June 28: Skirmish near Rockville, Maryland.

June 30: Action at Hanover, Pennsylvania.

July 1–3: Battle of Gettysburg.

July 2: Most of the legion cavalry battles Custer's cavalry at Hunterstown just northeast of Gettysburg. Delony is seriously wounded from a deep sabre cut to his head.

July 4: Delony is part of Imboden's 17-mile-long wagon train.

July 5–24: Legion operates in a number of rear-guard actions near Manassas Gap, Virginia.

July 5: Skirmishes near Fairfield, Pennsylvania.

July 6: Actions near Hagerstown and Williamsport, Maryland; Delony leads wounded and wagoners in defense of Williamsport.

July 7–12: Delony and injured Barrington King are cared for in Williamsport, the home of an undercover Confederate sympathizer.

July 10: Skirmish near Williamsport, Virginia.

July 16–August 5: Delony and King are cared for in the home of King's sister and her husband, the Rev. William Baker, in Staunton, Virginia.

July 24: Engagement near Wapping Heights, Manassas Gap, Virginia.

August 8: Delony rejoins regiment camped on the railroad between Brandy Station and Stevensburg.

August 17–29: Legion at Camp Stevensburg, Culpeper County, Virginia.

August 30: Legion at Camp Gordon, Orange County, Virginia.

September 9–11: Legion involved in skirmishes near Stevensburg, Virginia.

September 11: Skirmish near Raccoon Ford, Virginia.

September 13: Action near Culpeper Court House, sometimes known as 2nd Battle of Brandy Station.
September 14–16: Legion in number of actions near Raccoon Ford and Rapidan Station, Virginia.
September 15: Skirmish near Robertson's Ford, Virginia.
September 17: Skirmish near Raccoon Ford, Virginia.
September 18–25: Legion encamped near Orange County Court House.
September 19: Skirmish near Raccoon Ford, Virginia.
September 21: Skirmish near Madison Court House, Virginia.
September 22: Action at Jack's Shop, near Madison Court House, Virginia. Delony mortally wounded, captured, and taken to Stanton USA Hospital in Washington, DC.
October 2: Delony dies and is buried in a marker grave in the Soldiers' Home Cemetery in DC.
November 8: Birth of fifth child, Martha Roberta Delony.

1866   July 21: Martha Roberta dies of whooping cough.
September 24: Delony's body is disinterred from Washington, DC, cemetery and reinterred in the Oconee Hill Cemetery in Athens.

1871   September 21: Death of William Gaston Delony Jr. ("Willie"), 11 years of age.

1897   September 3: Rosa E. Delony dies at age 65 and is buried in Oconee Hill Cemetery next to her husband.

1912   May 24: Death of Tom Cobb Delony, who "dropped dead on Broad Street [Athens] age 53."[3]

1915   April 25: On Confederate Memorial Day, a monument in memory of Delony is unveiled in Oconee Hill Cemetery.

1937   September 19: Death of Rosa Eugenia Hull, age 80 years, daughter of William and Rosa Delony.

---

[3] Carson Family Papers.

William Gaston Delony prior to his marriage.
Hargrett Rare Book & Manuscript Library, University of Georgia.

Rosa Eugenia Huguenin around the time
of her marriage to William G. Delony.
Carson Family Papers.

William Gaston Delony, Lieutenant Colonel,
Cobb's Georgia Legion Cavalry.
David Wynn Vaughan Collection.

Eliza Valard Huguenin (Rosa's grandmother).
Rosa lived with her in Savannah.
Carson Family Papers.

Home of William G. and Rosa Delony, Athens, Georgia.

Hargrett Rare Book & Manuscript Library, University of Georgia.

"Little Rosa," about age two.
Carson Family Papers.

"Willie," about age five.
Carson Family Papers.

Presentation cup from Robert Taylor, uncle of William Delony,
upon the birth of his daughter Rosa.
Carson Family Collection.

Thomas Reade Rootes Cobb, commander of Cobb's Georgia Legion.
T. R. R. Cobb House Collection.

James Ewell Brown "Jeb" Stuart.
National Archives.

Wade Hampton, commander of Hampton's Brigade.
T. R. R. Cobb House Collection.

Pierce Manning Butler Young.
Colonel and commanding officer of Cobb's Georgia Legion Cavalry.
David Wynn Vaughan Collection.

Matthew Calbraith Butler.
Commander of the 2nd South Carolina Cavalry in Hampton's Brigade.
T. R. R. Cobb House Collection.

Gilbert Jefferson Wright.
Captain of Co. D, Albany Hussars, Cobb's Georgia Legion Cavalry.
Hargrett Rare Book & Manuscript Library, University of Georgia.

Barrington Simeral King, Captain of Co. C, Fulton Dragoons, Cobb's Georgia Legion Cavalry. King took over as Lieutenant-Colonel of the Legion following Delony's death at Jack's Shop.

William Henry Fitzhugh "Rooney" Lee (oldest son of Robert E. Lee)
originally commanded the 9th Virginia Cavalry and later was promoted
to command Stuart's Third Division of Cavalry. The White House on the
Pamunkey River, Virginia, was the home of Rooney Lee.

Library of Congress.

Beverly H. Robertson.
Commanded North Carolina cavalry during the Gettysburg Campaign.
Library of Congress.

The first flag of Independence raised in the South
by the citizens of Savannah, Georgia, November 8, 1860.
Library of Congress.

Georgia Cavalry in camp.
Missouri Historical Museum.

Pvt. John Stapler Dozier, Cobb's Georgia Legion Cavalry.
Georgia Archives.

The Picket, Rappahannock River near Beverly Ford.
Library of Congress.

White House on the Pamunkey River, home of Rooney Lee,
prior to the war. *Library of Congress.*

White House after the Federal visit in June 1862.
Library of Congress.

Catlett's Station prior to Stuart's 1862 raid.
Library of Congress.

Destruction of the Orange and Alexandria railroad
following the 1862 Confederate cavalry raid.
Library of Congress.

Catlett's Station about the time of Stuart's 1862 raid.
Library of Congress.

Confederate cavalry attack on a Federal supply train.
New York Public Library.

Confederate cavalry under Stuart crossing the Potomac in 1862.
Library of Congress.

Confederate signal station along the Rappahannock River.
Library of Congress.

"Culpepper [sic] from the North West" ca. 1863.
Library of Congress.

Scouting in the Blue Ridge, Loudoun Valley, Virginia.
Library of Congress.

Cavalry clash near Aldie, Virginia, 1863.
Library of Congress.

Brandy Station, 1863.
The largest battle of cavalry ever seen in North America.
Library of Congress.

Rappahannock Station, Virginia, was a major observation point and
crossing for cavalry on both sides in 1862 and 1863.
Library of Congress.

Cavalry crossing Ely's Ford on the Rappahannock River.
Library of Congress.

Presbyterian Manse, Staunton, Virginia.
This is the house where Delony and King recuperated in 1863
as well as the birthplace of President Woodrow Wilson.
Vincent J. Dooley.

Douglas and Stanton Hospitals, Washington, D.C.
William G. Delony died at the Stanton Hospital.
Stanton Hospital is the wooden barracks in the foreground.
Library of Congress.

William G. Delony on Marmion. It is believed that this was the
image of Delony on Marmion that was painted on a flag presented to
"Little Rosa" on Confederate Memorial Day in April 1915.

—THE LEGION'S —
FIGHTING BULLDOG

Introduction

Veterans landing on the beaches of Normandy in France on 6 June 1944, talk of the tremendous bloodshed and carnage that took place that day. Folks who have seen Steven Spielberg's *Saving Private Ryan* and its scenes of the storming of Omaha Beach come away with images of the great butchery that took place over a five-mile-wide beach as 43,000 Americans swarmed ashore under a monstrous barrage of artillery and small-arms fire. For fifteen hours they fought for that tiny beach-head, suffering an incredible 4,500 casualties in killed and wounded.

As horrendous as the fighting on Omaha Beach was that day, it was not the first time Americans had suffered so. On 13 December 1862, at the town of Fredericksburg in northern Virginia, two great armies, both American, assembled for what was to become a tremendous confrontation. The fighting that took place that day was many times more intense and the carnage more severe than it would be eighty-two years later on that French beach. On that December day in 1862, over a period of less than nine hours, Americans fought over a parcel of ground that was only about 400 yards wide. When the fighting ended that day, there were nearly 10,000 casualties. The Irish Brigade of Ambrose Burnside's Army of the Potomac began their charge with 1,600 men; they came out with 256. The next day, as the field of battle was examined, bodies were found to be piled three deep in many areas.

America's Civil War was the most terrible and costly conflict in the country's history. In 1941, as the United States entered World War II, the population stood at just over 131 million people; nearly 417,000 of these Americans lost their lives during that three-and-half-year conflict. Compare that to the four-and-half-year conflict of the American Civil War, when 620,000 died out of a total population (in 1860) of only about 31 million.

Cobb's Georgia Legion

"The best regiment of either army, North or South." This was South Carolina Lieutenant General and Corps Commander of the Army of Northern Virginia Wade Hampton's assessment of Cobb's Legion Cavalry shortly after the war.[1] Cobb's Georgia Legion is one of the more famous Confederate cavalry units of the war, made even more famous in the twentieth century by Margaret Mitchell in *Gone with the Wind*. Some will remember the scene in which Melanie asks a returning

---

[1] Edward L. Wells, "Hampton & His Cavalry in '64" (Richmond, VA: B. F. Johnson Publishing Co., 1899) 82.

soldier if he knows anything of her officer husband, Ashley Wilkes, who is a member of Cobb's Legion.

Although Cobb's Legion is one of the more famous Civil War units, outside of Wiley Howard's *Sketch of Cobb Legion Cavalry and Some Incidents and Scenes Remembered*, published in newspaper form in the early 1900s, and Harriet Bey Mesic's more recent *Cobb's Legion Cavalry: A History and Roster of the Ninth Georgia Volunteers in the Civil War* (Jefferson, NC: McFarland, 2009), little has been published over the years on the unit, or, for that matter, on the various units of Wade Hampton's Cavalry Brigade. Cobb's Georgia Legion Cavalry formed the core of Wade Hampton's Cavalry Brigade and then Corps during much of 1862 and 1863, although, as Thomas Reade Rootes Cobb, the unit's namesake and originator of the legion, confided to his wife, the legion did most of the fighting and "Hampton's Cavalry" got most of the credit.[2]

Wiley Howard produced his account of the legion in 1901, and although a member of the legion cavalry who served directly under William Gaston Delony wrote the work, it is a memoir written many years after the actual events and in some cases does not follow the chronological path of the legion. Various works have been completed on other units within Hampton's Cavalry, namely Richard Coffman's *Going Back the Way They Came: The Phillips Georgia Legion Cavalry Battalion* (Macon, GA: Mercer University Press, 2011); Donald Hopkins's *The Little Jeff: The Jeff Davis Legion, Cavalry, Army of Northern Virginia* (Shippensburg, PA: White Mane Books, 1999); Chris Hartley's *Stuart's Tarheels: James B. Gordon and His North Carolina Cavalry in the Civil War* (Jefferson, NC: McFarland, 2011); and Sheridan Barringer's *Fighting for Lee: Confederate General Rufus Barringer and the North Carolina Cavalry Brigade* (El Dorado Hills, CA: Savas Beatie, 2015). Although there have been a great number of works done on Wade Hampton and Hampton's Cavalry in the years since the end of the conflict, very few are anything more than biographical sketches of this very prominent nineteenth-century leader, who, along with Nathan Bedford Forrest, was the only individual to achieve the rank of lieutenant general in the Confederate army without any previous military experience.

Three men were responsible for Hampton's apt description of the legion cavalry besides Hampton himself: General Thomas R. R. Cobb, who originally organized and led the unit; Colonel Pierce M. B. Young, the unit's first colonel; and William Gaston Delony, who gave all his energy, his courage, and his decisive determination for three and a half years in molding Cobb's Georgia Legion Cavalry into an efficient and dependable fighting force. Greatly loved by those who served under him, William Delony possessed, in the eyes of members of his legion, three

---

[2] Thomas R. R. Cobb to Marion Cobb, 10 November 1862, T. R. R. Cobb Papers, Hargrett Rare Book & Manuscript Library, University of Georgia, hereafter cited as T. R. R. Cobb Papers.

attributes that were greatly admired: "commanding presence, bull dog courage and superb generalship."[3] Delony allied himself with like-minded individuals such as Thomas Reade Rootes Cobb, who aside from being a personal friend also became Delony's commanding officer in the Confederate army. Taking such a prominent part in Hampton's cavalry command in 1862–1865. *The Legion's Fighting Bulldog* seeks to rectify the dearth of information on this significant body.

The letters reproduced in these pages relay the story of a young man on the cusp of a promising law career in the 1850s who comes to the conclusion that his way of life, and that of his neighbors, is about to change forever. The 167 letters of William Gaston Delony, interwoven with those of his wife, Rosa Eugenia Huguenin, furnish us with a window into the lives of typical upper-level land-holding whites prior to and during the Civil War. Delony doesn't just write about his movements or the battles he participated in, however, although he does a very good job of relaying information on that front. He also writes about his views and concerns on events and activities taking place, both military and domestic, as well as some of his innermost feelings. Delony expresses concern for his wife's struggles with her pregnancy as well as his own woundings, even though he attempts to downplay the latter. As the correspondence progresses, Delony's sense of nationalism gradually gives way to disillusionment in the workings of the army, in the favoritism shown to those with West Point backgrounds, and, finally, to a sense of waning support shown by "chimney corner patriots."[4] By the summer of 1863, a sense of depression begins to take hold of the man, a melancholy so strong that he begins to talk of resigning from the service. Yet his sense of duty always prevails. Rosa's correspondence, written in response, gives us an insight into the conditions and activities of the Civil War home front and concerns about the children's well-being and that of their "Papa."

These are not the writings of the typical Confederate soldier, or even those of the typical soldier of either side. Instead, they are the correspondence of well-educated and independent individuals who also happened to be well placed in society due to birth. From this standing, however, we can come to know something of what soldiers thought and felt, and something of what their families went through, both on the battlefield and at home. Together, the couple's correspondence offers the reader and researcher a window on this critical period in our shared history. It is for these reasons that the correspondence is most valuable.

---

[3] Wiley C. Howard, "Sketch of Cobb Legion Cavalry and Some Incidents and Scenes remembered" (Atlanta: Camp 159, published talk given at U.C.V. meeting) 19 August 1901, 24–25.

[4] This was a term given to those back home who were constantly complaining about how the war was being waged and about the military leaders conducting that war yet were not willing to enlist and take part personally.

William Gaston Delony and Rosa Eugenia Huguenin

William Gaston Delony and Rosa E. Huguenin were married on 16 May 1854 by Rev. Willard Preston at the Independent Presbyterian Church in Savannah.[5] This marriage represented a classic union of two families from the emerging elite planter class of Georgia.

Both William, called "Will," and Rosa were descendants of French Huguenot ancestors. William Deloney's third great-grandfather, John Deloney, was born in 1632 near Birmingham in Nuneaten, Warwickshire County, England. He immigrated to James City, Virginia, where his wife gave birth to a son, Louis Henry Deloney, in 1670. Louis's son, Henry Deloney, became a member of the House of Burgesses in the Assembly of Mecklenburg County, Virginia, in 1765–1766 and 1768. Henry and his wife, Rebecca (Bradnax), lived in Brunswick, Virginia, with their five children, the youngest being William, the grandfather of William Gaston Delony. Grandfather William was a "wealthy gentleman living in Richmond Virginia," who married his first cousin, Martha R. Montfort, in 1786 in Amelia County.[6] In 1800, the couple moved first to McIntosh County and then Camden County, Georgia, where they settled on a 1,000-acre plantation called "Bolingbrook," deeded to Martha in 1803.[7] The plantation was located along Crooked River 7 miles north of St. Mary's.[8]

Three children were born here: Martha M. Deloney, Robert James (William G. Delony's father), and Elizabeth (Eliza) Bolling Deloney. Aunt Eliza remained close to her nephew for the rest of her life. Delony's grandfather William died in 1805, followed by his grandmother Martha in 1820. In 1826, Sheriff James Scott

---

[5] Chatham County Marriage Book 1830, 1844, 1849, 1852, "Georgia's Virtual Vault," Georgia State Archives, Georgia Historical Society, Savannah, GA. Independent refers to the Savannah church not officially being a part of any organized Presbyterian denomination, adhering more closely to the Church of Scotland. Interview with retired Presbyterian minister G. Daniel McCall of Augusta, GA, 14 June 2014.

[6] "Henry Deloney," "William Delony," www.ancestry.com. Deloney and Huguenin family genealogical papers in possession of Emily C. Carnes, daughter of the late Gordon Carson Jr., Richmond Hill, (Savannah) Georgia, and great-great-granddaughter of William G. Delony; hereafter cited as Carson Family Papers. All of Delony's ancestors' names were spelled with an 'e' (i.e., "Deloney"); William G. Delony was the first to exclude the 'e' except on rare occasions. The nameplate on his pew, which remains today in the First Presbyterian Church in Athens, is spelled "Deloney."

[7] Marguerite Reddick, *Camden's Challenge: A History of Camden County, Georgia* (Camden, GA: Camden County Historical Commission, 1976) 35.

[8] St. Mary's and Jeffersonton were the only two towns in Camden County before the Civil War. Bolingbrook was one of the several large plantations in the county. Most of the planters were wealthy slave owners. Carson Family Papers. James T. Voccelle, *History of Camden County, Georgia* (Kingsland, GA: Southeastern Georgian, 1914, reprinted 1967).

4

sold Bolingbrook Plantation, including "fourteen negroes," cattle, and tools at auction to Robert J. Deloney, who served as the executor of Martha's will. Robert Deloney obtained the deed to the property the following year. Three children were born to Robert and his recent wife, Maria O. Baird: Martha A., the oldest, born in 1824; Will, born in 1826; and their youngest, Robert James Jr., born in 1829.[9]

Robert became highly successful growing Sea Island cotton on the plantation for several years. The shipment reports in the Savannah *Georgian* paper speak to the business operation of his enterprise. The cotton, at times as much as sixty bales, was shipped by boat from St. Mary's to Savannah on the schooner *Betsy and Maria* and distributed to "Sundry Persons." [10] Since the trip could take three to six days, Robert on occasion brought his entire family on the excursion.

The tenth child of David Huguenin Jr., John Huguenin, Rosa's grandfather, married Eliza Vallard, and the couple moved from Beaufort to Savannah in 1824, shortly thereafter purchasing at auction "1400 acres for $3,560 in southwest Chatham County known as the Queensberry and Ashton Plantation." By 1830, John Huguenin owned eight slaves and employed three "free whites." [11] John Huguenin died in 1835, and his wife, Eliza, lived on the plantation until 1848, when she moved to Savannah and bought a house on 34 Liberty Street.[12] Rosa, who lost her mother at age 4, was raised at this house in Savannah by her grandmother Eliza. Rosa spent her time alternating between the Queensberry and Ashton Plantation and the Liberty Street house in Savannah. It was probably during this time when young Will was visiting his aunt in Savannah that the couple first came in contact.

---

[9] Carson Family Papers list one other child, Eliza, who died at a very early age.

[10] *Georgian* (Savannah) 24 June 1826; 2 February 1828; Reddick, *Camden's Challenge*, 5–6.

[11] The Huguenins migrated to Switzerland from France around 1580 to escape the religious persecution of Louis XIV. Will's wife, Rosa Eugenia Huguenin's family can be traced to Moyse Huguenin of LeLocie Neuchatel, Switzerland, a French Huguenot who died in 1630. Moyse Huguenin's son, David Hugenunin Sr. (Rosa's great-great-grandfather) married Susanna Jacot, and the couple set sail with a Huguenot group for Charles Town (Charleston), South Carolina. The colony, led by Col. John Purry, obtained a royal grant from King Charles II from England and established the town of Purrysburg, South Carolina, 10 miles up the Savannah River in 1732. Rosa's great-grandfather, David Huguenin Jr., though born in Switzerland, arrived in South Carolina at age 7, and after a long life with two wives and eleven children, died in 1796. "Moyse Huguenin," "David Huguenin Jr.," "John Huguenin" www.ancestry.com; Carson Family Papers; Nancy Birkheimer, "Eliza Vallard Huguenin: A Genealogy," unpublished paper in Lane Library, Armstrong State University, Savannah, GA; Henry A. P. Smith, "Purrysburg," unpublished paper paper in Lane Library, Armstrong State University, Savannah, GA; 1830 United Federal Census.

[12] Birkheimer, "Eliza Vallard Huguenin." The 1858 Savannah city directory has Mrs. Eliza V. Huguenin living at 34 Liberty Street. The 1870 Directory lists her residence as 140 Liberty Street.

Rosa's father, Edward David Huguenin, enjoyed the privileges of a planter's son and entered Franklin College in Athens, "matriculating in 1829."[13] A few years after leaving college, he married Amanda Louisa Baker, the daughter of Captain Bright and Jane Baker.[14] Amanda was stricken with tuberculosis at an early age, and the affliction became chronic after Rosa was born in the summer of 1832. When Rosa was 3 years old, Amanda's mother, Jane Baker, kept Rosa in Athens while Amanda and her husband, Edward Huguenin, traveled to Warm Springs (Asheville) in the North Carolina mountains, seeking relief from the disease. While there, Amanda penned a very sad letter to her aunt Eugenia in Savannah, describing her declining health. She ended the letter on a cheerful note, however, about soon joining "my dear Rosa and mother" in Athens in September. She also took the opportunity to mention that Rosa was "healthy but very saucy."[15]

Rosa's mother died in October 1836 at the age of 32. Shortly thereafter, her father took Rosa to live with her grandmother Eliza in Savannah. Rosa's father often visited her in Savannah while he was assisting with the Chatham County plantation after the death of his father. Following Amanda's death, Edward inherited land and slaves. He married a second time to Martha Forte and the couple moved to Martha's plantation in Sumter County, Georgia. This union produced five half-siblings to Rosa.[16] At this time, Rosa's father began selling off several tracts of land and some of the slaves he had inherited from Amanda. This action eventually led to a legal dispute with his daughter, who believed she was entitled to some of her late mother's estate.

We know very little about young Will's and Rosa's formative years or as young adults. After his aunt Eliza passed away in 1840, Will ended up staying in her home in Athens with his step-uncle, Gen. Robert G. Taylor, and his three cousins while

---

[13] Carson Family Papers has Edward D. Huguenin graduating in 1829, but the University of Georgia *Catalogue* has him matriculating in 1829 (with Robert Toombs) but not graduating. University of Georgia Alumni 1785–1806. *Catalogue of Trustees and Alumni and of the Matriculates of the University of Georgia, Athens, Georgia* (Athens, GA: E. D. Stone Press, 1906) 27.

[14] The Bakers held extensive land holdings in McIntosh County, Georgia, where at one time, they owned a 488-acre plantation known as "Mosquito" as well as land south of the plantation between Marengo and Harris Neck, known as the "Baker Plantation." This plantation consisted of two properties of 140 acres with thirty-four slaves at Harris Neck and 900 acres and fourteen slaves located southeast of Lebanon. Ironically, the "Mosquito" plantation was later acquired by Jonathan Thomas, Captain Baker's son-in-law, who married the Baker's second daughter, Mary Jane. Bright Baker to Jane Baker, 28 May 1829, Delony Papers, Hargrett Rare Books & Manuscript Library, University of Georgia, hereafter cited as Delony Papers; Buddy Sullivan, *Early Days of the Georgia Tidewater: The Story of McIntosh County and Sapelo* (McIntosh County Board of Commissioners, 1990) 254.

[15] Amanda Baker Huguenin to Eugenia Huguenin Rose, 26 July 1835, Delony Papers.

[16] Birkheimer, "Eliza Vallard Huguenin"; "Edward D. Huguenin," www.ancestry.com.

attending Franklin College.[17] The Taylors built a summer home in Athens (Taylor-Grady House)[18] and moved there permanently to put their three sons through the college. Admitted to Franklin College in 1842, Will enjoyed excellent accommodations off campus while attending school in the Classic City.[19] The catalogue of the officers and students of Franklin College's junior class of 1844–1845 list him as living in "General Taylor's" house.[20] More than likely, he lived there throughout his college career. Will Delony was only slightly older than his three first cousins, Richard D. B. (two years younger), Robert G. (three years younger), and Thomas (who died as a young boy).[21] Lucy Ann Barnes, an older cousin of Mrs. Taylor's, became the homemaker for the Taylor household "to tend to W. G. Delony's needs."[22]

By Delony's junior year in school the studious scholar developed a passion for politics and patriotism. During the annual three-day commencement exercises in 1845, which attracted the most "prominent men of the state" and "a solid mass of human beings," selected students displayed their gifts of elocution. The third day, during "the junior exhibition," Delony gave his oration on "party spirit." He acquitted himself, as some other speakers had done, "to the gratification of a numerous and attentive auditory."[23]

---

[17] The University of Georgia was founded in 1785 and was the first state-chartered university in the United States. The first classes were conducted at Franklin College in 1801, and the school officially became a university in 1859.

[18] Maj. William S. Grady, home on leave from the Confederate Army of Northern Virginia in 1863, purchased the house where his soon-to-be-famous son, Henry, lived for a short period of time while attending the university. Maj. Grady, head of the Highland Guards, was wounded at Petersburg in 1865 and died of the wound while traveling back to Athens. John F. Stegeman, *These Men She Gave* (Athens: University of Georgia Press, 1964) 129.

[19] His aunt, Elizabeth (Eliza) Bolling, lost her first husband, Dr. Richard McAllister Berrin, of McIntosh County, Georgia, to yellow fever in 1820 shortly after their first child was born. Several years later, in July 1827, she married, in Savannah, Gen. Robert G. Taylor, an Irish immigrant who became a very wealthy planter and merchant in Chatham County. Carson Family Papers; "Robert G. Taylor," www.ancestry.com.

[20] *Southern Banner*, 10 April 1845.

[21] "Robert G. Taylor," www.ancestry.com.

[22] Lucy Ann Barnes was the niece of Will's grandmother Martha Munford Deloney, and she eventually moved in with Will and Rosa in their new home in 1857 to help with the many chores of the house and the children. Charlotte Thomas Marshall and Sam Thomas, e-mail message, 20 February 2013; Last Will and Testament of Martha Munford Deloney, Carson Family Papers.

[23] Augustus Longstreet Hull, *Annals of Athens, Georgia, 1801–1901* (Athens, GA: Banner Job Office, 1906) 169; *Augusta Chronicle*, 9 August 1845.

Will graduated from Franklin College in 1846 with a Bachelor of Arts degree and "with the highest honors in his class."[24] After graduation, he left Athens and moved to southwest Georgia to engage in planting. A few years later, he was "called by the trustees of his alma mater to a tutorship...a position he filled for a number of years."[25] Historian F. Nash Boney, however, in his book *A Pictorial History of the University of Georgia*, writes that Delony "served briefly as a tutor in Ancient Language at the University"[26] and at some point also tutored in math.[27] Perhaps he did both. Delony is listed in the annual college catalogue in 1851–1852 as a "tutor in Ancient Language and an instructor in French."[28] The following year, in the 1852–1853 catalogue, he was again listed as a tutor in "Ancient Language."[29] To further complicate the question of Delony's service to the university, Thomas Reed, in his extensive history of the University of Georgia, wrote that Delony "served only one year as a tutor."[30]

During the time he was serving the university, Delony studied law under William L. Mitchell, a trustee of the university who held the position of secretary and treasurer. Mitchell also served as a professor of law and for a time as head of the Lumpkin Law School. Mitchell was described as an "intense...warm friend, a bitter enemy, a hard fighter, a devoted partisan." He also was portrayed as "hating the Yankees" and "despising every church but the Presbyterian."[31] Perhaps some of the intensity and passion of Will's mentor rubbed off on him. Following Will's death in 1863, the Bench and Bar of Clarke Superior Court eulogized the Confederate colo-

---

[24] "Confederate Necrology," *The Georgia Historical Quarterly* 19/4 (December 1935): 334–36. Thomas Reed wrote that "James G. Collier and William G. Deloney [were] first honor men" among the twenty-four graduates of the 1846 class; "Confederate Necrology," 456, 457.

[25] *Georgia Historical Quarterly*, 334–36.

[26] F. Nash Boney, *A Pictorial History of the University of Georgia* (Athens: University of Georgia Press, 1984) 45.

[27] Delony's descendant Gordon Carson writes that Will Delony "was mistaken for a professor disliked by students and was hit on the head by a brick and he spent two years on a plantation to recuperate." This appears to coincide with the time Delony spent in southwest Georgia working as a planter after graduation and prior to his return to Athens in 1851 as a tutor at the university; Carson Family Papers.

[28] Of interest, there were a total of nine faculty members listed in the catalogue with the tutor Delony listed as the last one of the nine; "Catalogue of the Offices and Students (1851–1852) Franklin College (University of Georgia) Athens, Georgia," Hargrett Rare Book & Manuscript Library, University of Georgia.

[29] "Catalogue of the Offices and Students (1852–1853)," Hargrett Rare Book & Manuscript Library, University of Georgia.

[30] Thomas Reed, *The History of the University of Georgia*, http://dlg.galileo.usg.edu/reed/ Accessed 13 April 2015: 494.

[31] Hull, *Annals of Athens*, 143.

nel as a "professional in the practice of law." He was also praised for "his eloquent manners and his genial temper, and noble bearing."[32]

While Will Delony was starting his law practice, his affection for Rosa grew. At the same time, Rosa's rift with her father widened. By 1853, Will and Rosa were so in love they vowed to get married and set a date for the wedding. Rosa, however, was "not of age" (apparently 21) and had to seek her father's permission, but her father denied the appeal.[33] Both Will and Rosa were distraught over having to postpone the wedding. It was especially hard on Rosa, who was forced to remain in Savannah idle and insecure while Will was busy in Athens starting up his law practice. They exchanged affectionate letters during this time of separation. Will's romantic letters were aimed not only at reassuring Rosa of his love, but also the love and acceptance of her by his family. On 13 December 1853, Will wrote reminding Rosa of their "sweet memories of the past and the bright visions of futurity," and imploring her to know of "the depth of my love." He further wanted Rosa to know that his sister, Martha, thought Rosa a "noble girl," and that she and her mother, who, having just arrived in Athens for the holidays, sent "much love." He encouraged Rosa to look for "the hidden good under the postponement of our marriage." Will reassured her that he would "forever strive to merit dear Rosa's love."[34] This outpouring of affection kept Rosa's spirits high until they were able to consummate the marriage several months later after Rosa came of age.

The relationship between Rosa and her father, Edward Huguenin, was further strained when he refused to attend the wedding in May 1854. To further exacerbate the relationship, Rosa's father cut her and "her children" out of his will, stating she was "amply provided for and has a sufficient estate in her own right."[35] Rosa's father's attention was focused more on providing for his second wife and their five younger children.

Later, Will Delony and Thomas R. R. Cobb represented Rosa in her legal battle against her father over her inheritance. There were two meetings in Macon with her father, who in the first meeting in 1853 "wanted to settle the dispute."[36] The records of a second hearing in 1854, preserved in the Hargrett Rare Book & Manuscript Library at the University of Georgia, give insight into Rosa's father's argument in opposition to the marriage. Her father was accused of not favoring the marriage because it would give William G. Delony a legal claim to some of the inheritance. The complaint filed by Thomas R. R. Cobb cited as evidence Rosa's fa-

---

[32] *Georgia Historical Quarterly* (December 1935) 334–41.
[33] Delony Papers.
[34] William G. Delony to Rosa H. Delony, 11 December 1853, Delony Papers.
[35] Delony Papers.
[36] Ibid.

ther's refusal to give her permission to marry due to her age and later his refusal to attend the wedding.[37] Rosa's father argued he was against the marriage because Delony was "afflicted by epilepsy" and he was "concerned for his daughter."[38] There was no evidence of Delony denying the affliction, but his father-in-law's accusation is questionable since the issue never appeared again in any further research. Neither meeting produced a resolution to the controversy.

During the controversy, Rosa's stepmother, Martha Forte Huguenin, admitted an injustice had been done and proposed a good-will gesture from her former husband in the sum of $5,000. Rosa refused the offer.[39] The passage of time and a crisis can help heal family wounds, and several years later, Rosa visited her father, who was on his deathbed, in Atlanta. She wrote Will on 8 January 1862 explaining that Mrs. Baxter advised her to visit her father and wrote that her "grandmother and Aunt Mell are both there."[40] After Rosa's visit, her father rallied and lived for another year before dying in March 1863, at age 57.[41]

---

[37] Complaint filed by T. R. R. Cobb to the Superior Court, Bibb County, Georgia. Delony Papers.

[38] Response filed by Edward D. Huguenin to the Bibb County Superior Court. Delony Papers.

[39] Delony Papers.

[40] Rosa to Will Delony, 8 January 1862, Delony Papers. After her father's death, Rosa secured $5,576 in three payments.

[41] Carson Family Papers.

Chapter 1

Setting Up House:
November 1853–July 1859

The soil you see is not ordinary soil—
it is the dust of the blood, the flesh,
and the bones of our ancestors.
                                   —Curly, Crow Indian[1]

We begin the correspondence in the prewar years with the Delonys just after their marriage and their time "setting up house." While Rosa was with her husband intermittently in Athens while he was practicing law and serving the community, she did not join him permanently until 1856, almost two years after they were married. The temporary separation was necessary in order to build their home, which was constructed on property they acquired adjacent to the northeast corner of Broad and Lumpkin streets. During the separation, Rosa and their first child, Eliza Huguenin Delony,[2] lived with Rosa's grandmother in Savannah.

Delony traveled the long distance to Savannah when practical; however, most of the time he was busy with his law practice and overseeing the construction of their Athens home. On New Years Eve 1855, he wrote Rosa that he was "intolerably lonesome at my hovel of a home."[3] Rosa responded a few days after New Year's wishing her "darling Will...a Happy New Year." However, she was soon chastising the homebuilder, a Mr. Whitman, for being so slow in finishing the house. "Confound old Whitman...what's the old rascal about?" she complained to her husband. Frustrated, she expressed that she could not wait any longer to come to Athens and wanted to know "why I can't sleep in the out house with you" until the home is ready. She vowed that would be the "last time I'll ever leave you...my dear dear

---

[1] Speech before congressional committee, 1912, http://lib.lbhc.edu/index.php?q=node/144.
[2] Tragically, Eliza, named after her great-grandmother, lived less than a year, dying just nine days shy of her first birthday (29 June 1855–20 June 1856). Charlotte Marshall, *Oconee Hill Cemetery of Athens Georgia* (Athens, GA: Athens Historical Society, 2009) 285.
[3] Will Delony to Rosa Delony, 31 December 1855, Delony Papers.

Will."[4] She never did, although Will did continue to leave her from time to time as events unfolded.

By the time Rosa was finally able to move into their Athens home, Will had already entered politics. He served as town warden (commissioner) in 1855, 1856 and 1859, representing the second ward. In 1859, he was elected state representative (1859–1860), the first Democrat to be elected to that office "from the Whig-dominated town." Delony soon gained notoriety by his work on the committee to examine and approve the law code of the state preparatory to its final adoption.[5]

Will Delony began gathering influential friends, including Benjamin Harvey Hill, a state senator from LaGrange, Georgia, who at the time was involved in the adoption of the state code. They obviously knew each other at the university, as there were barely 100 students there when they attended. Hill was first honor graduate in the class of 1844 while Delony was first honor graduate two years later, in 1846. They both entered the field of law and their paths undoubtedly crossed many times in the profession.[6]

In addition, Hill married an Athens lady, Carolyn E. Holt, whom he "wooed and won while in college." The "marriage connected him with one of the oldest and best known families in the state."[7] Her father was the solicitor general in Athens, and her brother was a physician and later surgeon during the Civil War. Carolyn Holt's father died when she was young, and her stepfather, John I. Huggins, another prominent Athenian, lived just three blocks from the Delonys.[8]

Before the Civil War, Will immersed himself in his law practice and in his service to the Athens community. He was a partner in a successful law practice with

---

[4] Rosa to Will, 12 January 1856, Delony Papers.

[5] Ernest C. Hynads, *Antebellum Athens and Clarke County, Georgia* (Athens: University of Georgia Press, 1974) 163–65; John F. Stegeman, *These Men She Gave* (Athens: University of Georgia Press, 1964) 87; *The Georgia History Quarterly* (December 1935) 334, 335.

[6] In 1861, Hill was elected a Confederate senator from Georgia. Due to his friendship and respect for Will Delony, Hill presented him with a very handsome lawyer's desk before leaving for Richmond to assume his senatorial duties. The desk was passed on to the descendants of Delony and now is in the possession of Leigh Hull Steele of Madison, Georgia. Leigh Hull Steele, the great-great-granddaughter of William Gaston and Rosa Delony, received the desk from her mother, Barbara Smith Hull, upon the death of Mrs. Steele's father, William Delony Hull, great-grandson of Col. W. G. Delony. Barbara Smith Hull received the desk from her husband's mother, Mrs. W. D. Hull, as a wedding present on 3 August 1949. Leigh is married to Retired US Army Ranger Col. Michael D. Steele, who played on the University of Georgia's 1980 national championship football team. *Atlanta Journal*, Peachtree Parade (August 1949) 17.

[7] See Benjamin H. Hill Jr., *Senator Benjamin H. Hill of Georgia: His Life, Speeches and Writings* (Atlanta: H. C. Hudgins & Company, 1891).

[8] Kenneth Coleman, "Map of Confederate Athens," in *Confederate Athens* (Athens: University of Georgia Press, 1967).

Samuel L. Thurmond, who later became solicitor general of the Athens circuit during the war.[9] Delony served on several civic committees and boards in Athens as well as a member of the towns' militia. He also served on the Oconee Hill Cemetery board in 1856 to address the issues of the newly opened cemetery.[10] In 1859, he was a committee member who proposed the official names of the streets in Athens, many of which still exist today, and a year later became a member of the board of directors of the Branch Bank in 1860.[11]

In July 1858, with sectional tensions in the nation on the rise, Delony was elected first lieutenant of a newly formed artillery company known as the "Flying Artillery."[12] The following year, outfitted in the "old continental uniform with blue coats...knee britches and top boots," the company made its first appearance, firing their newly acquired brass six-pounder, which aroused the military spirit of many of the Athens citizens.[13]

The following prewar romantic letters cover the period both prior to and following Will and Rosa's marriage. During that period, they were separated first while their home was under construction and afterwards while Will was on the circuit practicing law in nearby districts.

* * *

Athens Nov 23rd 1853

My Own Dear Rosa

Tonight I was greeted with your daguerreotype and if you could see within "Will's" heart, you might feel vain of the impression you have there made, and your little self that I am now looking at & that is looking at me too makes my heart overflow with love to my precious Rosa and seems to be animated with something of her sweet spirit. The likeness is lifelike and I think you must have thought of Will and sent something of your soul to animate the picture and make it more dear to him. Dear Rosa if you knew how much of my time was devoted to sweet thoughts of you and how entirely my heart & life were yours I think you would come to Athens at all hazard in Jan. It is perfectly delicious to love you as I do and when I see the other side of the picture & feel that I am "pair en _____." It wanders often to Savannah when we are separated & brings back to me sweet thoughts that tell of Rosa & her truthful noble heart. I have been sad since I left you but not unhappy, and shall look

---

[9] Frank A. Holden, *History of Athens and Clarke County* (Athens, GA: Legal Profession of Athens, 1923).

[10] The cemetery opened in 1855. See Marshall, *Oconee Hill Cemetery*, 485–86.

[11] Hynads, *Antebellum Athens*, 48, 49, 52; *Augusta Chronicle* (9 June 1859).

[12] *Southern Banner* (5 August 1858).

[13] Ibid., 24 March 1859.

forward with great anxiety until you have heard from your father. I do hope that Providence may put it into his heart to accede to our wishes and make us both happy. I think if he but knew how grateful to him we should feel and how much of happiness he would afford to us by relaxing his objections he would not hesitate long to allow us to have our own way. It seems to me Dear Rosa every hour that passes increases my affection for you. It is a gushing spring of love within my heart the waters of affection welling out ever pure ever fresh & sparkling giving joy to us both, at some future trial to unite with all other stream from a hundred heart & flow on to Eternity & beach us both to a happy home here after when pain & disappointment & sorrow shall be human no more. Oh believe it. There is something in human love to purify the spirit of man to elevate & ennoble his nature. No one can love a noble lovely woman with such devotion and not be a pure noble being. Worlds of wealth in the scale of Eternity would weigh but lightly with such a love as mine to Dear precious Rosa. That impression my heart will carry with it to another world and God grant it may carry me to a better one than this. "To have loved her was a liberal Education" said one of the old English writers. To love you is almost piety say I. I cannot think of Rosa and not feel some thing of the spirit of religion within me. Is not mine the better love. And here you are before me Dear Rosa reminding me so mindly of the delightful evenings of the past week, evenings never to be forgotten, feelings never to be effaced, words never to be forgotten, all now crowding upon me. Dear girl, you ought to know and appreciate the feeling. I do not believe that such a love is an ordinary one. I cannot think so, and a life service will prove it so. You'll think me sentimental—wont you—well I am willing. It seems to me that when with you or thinking of you, I can say but one thing, but Rosa says it is pleasant to hear the ofttold tale and it is more than pleasant for me to tell it. You must excuse all incoherences & blunders tonight for here is your daguerreotype right before me and looks so precisely like you that my eyes are constantly wandering from the papers to it & remember I have just received it and have not yet a real good long satisfactory look at it. There is the ring however and the arm too bathe in the right place, but your figure is not displayed to full advantage. It is perfectly charming however and if you could see me now you might almost be jealous of your own picture. What do you think I would part with it for. The more I look at it the more it looks like Rosa and I can almost imagine you are here. I guess to when you read this letter you may think I can be almost as ridiculous with your picture as with you after Sam had retired. Would to Heaven I could make myself similarly ridiculous tonight it is a sort of ridiculeousness I admire & love to indulge in & which by the way is the wisest thing we ever did in cherishing a love that is well worth preserving and which I feel has the sanction of Heaven, this man may deserve. Well I shall have to write another sheet as this is but the prelude to my song, and in that I shall talk more sober sense tho' you must not expect the other sheet to be not a love letter—simply because I shall still be writing to my scrap. I pity you in the perusal but hope it may afford the reader a tithe the pleasure it has given me to write it & you will not quarrel with "Will."

Perhaps I ought to obey Rosa's instructions and retire at 11 oclock but I am very sure she will forgive me this time if I should be by chance a little later tonight in finishing my first Epistle to my sweetheart. If my inclinations were to be consulted alone I am inclined to think that a much later hour would still find me here, writing and looking at your daguerreotype alternately. It is very delightful employment I assure you this. I talk nonsense perhaps. The fact is Rosa, your picture pleases me so, and looks so sweetly, and so like you, I can think well of nothing else and it looks as if perfectly conscious that I am talking to it. I feel that it ought to talk to me. It might say "Do you love me much" or how much do you love me or something else the original can say so sweetly. I must confess it I am a happy man, and Rosa is the cause of all my happiness. May I soon be the happiest man, and you'll say so too wont you. I wish I could take one of old Rip Van Winkle snoozes and wake up the night before the middle of January. No I dont either. It is to made be appraised to be awake and conscious of the possession of my treasure. What that treasure is I leave you to imagine. Well all this is to say that I arrived here yesterday quite well, and after a journey up with nothing to call an incident, unless that one of the cars ran off the track frightening nobody I believe and did no damage. Sister and the children I found well but mother was half sick and last night had an attack of sick headache. She is now better however, having spent the evening in chess playing, and seems cheerful. She loves her "other daughter" and I rather think is pretty well satisfied that there is somebody she knows quite good enough for her son "Will." She says she will certainly occupy your man a portion of her time when in Savannah, and anticipates a pleasant time with Rosa & Mrs Starke. I do not think she will leave Athens before the 10th or 13th of December. Mother is unselfish enough to be perfectly devoted to those among her and I think on Sister's account will remain here till then. She will return with us in January and protect you against me and the Athenians. I have just been in to see her & she sends much love to you and says, Oh yes tell her I'll come back and take good care of her too. Sister also sends love. I saw Uncle today he was perfectly delighted to see me again and have some one to ride & talk with & we have been going all day—this morning over his fields and this afternoon "trying horses." The old gentleman feels lonely in the world and an agreeable companion who will quarrel with him occasionally is always welcome. Lulah is sick with chills & fever—poor girl she has a hard time of it. Bob & Dick & Jane have all gone to Early. Aunty is as usual. Mrs. Maxwell unwell & looking badly. She was taken quite sick yesterday at Uncle's & was compelled to spend the night there. All send love & inquired kindly after you. Every one I meet inquires after you and I answer all their impertinent questions. I told Uncle that I went to Sumter & was treated cordially by your father, but that he wishes to defer the wedding and that I did not know when I would be married. He says we ought to have it over at once, and is decidedly of the opinion I think that I will be getting the best of the bargain. You know not how great a pleasure it gives me that you are so well appreciated by my immediate friends. He has a high regard for Rosa and I hope you will be good friends [for] ever. He has a kind heart tho' under a determined manner. He & mother had it hot & heavy a day or two ago about my not paying Court to the Bencens Laws & McAllisters of Savannah. "The world was made for Mothers' sons" not they for the world. He has said nothing to me as yet, he was too well pleased to have some one to talk politics & plantation & cotton today. Sister's movements are still uncertain. Mother is about to make a fortune from her mining operations and I hope will make us all rich. The fortune is already made on paper in New York City. Perhaps posterity may realize it. I have seen no one to tell me the news & prospects of Athenian Society but all I have met are surprised to see me return a single man and to the question. Is yr lady at the Newton House. In several instances I have replied in the affirmative so look out when I come again. I must steal the hand or take the hand as well as the heart.

Savannah Feby 11th 1854

My Dear Will

To night, I procured myself the pleasure of retiring at an early hour to my room, and there enjoy to my satisfaction the writing of a lone letter to my absent sweet-heart, but after ten, who should walk in, as usual, but John Guerrard and a few moments after Mr Basinger. Away went all my plans and it is too late now to do more then begin a reply to your last two, which have duly arrived and their perusal been as ever productive of more pleasure than any thing else could except your own arrival Dear Will. So you think Grandmother must have encouraged John Guerrard. You are indebted to an unruly imagination for that suggestion, for the old lady would make a terrible fuss if I were to propose him, for her Grand-son. She thinks a great deal of you and will love you very dearly when we are married, provided you are attentive and affectionate, which I know you will surely be. She has treated John with a great deal of politeness to make up for my rudeness, for at one time I actually disliked him so much that I failed to treat him with civility, and as for your feeling jealousy, I dont believe one word of it. Have you not my promise my ring my daguerreotype, and if I am not Mrs William G Delony shortly it will be because the fates are strongly adverse and not from a lack of inclination or effort on my part.

16

Don't let your imagination run away with you. Do you recollect the last time I told you that? Things have changed vastly since then thanks to a kind providence Sunday 12th. Your little note of the 8th was received yesterday and I cant tell you how well pleased I am that your prospects of law practice are growing so much brighter. Did I not prophesy they would? And my predictions are being verified. You must be happy contented and grateful and try not to forget the Great Giver of every good gift because it is He who ordains success as well as any thing else. We fail too frequently being grateful for small matters, and thus ourselves prevent greater one's succeeding. Dont you think so? Just as long as we regard God as our Kind and merciful Heavenly Father, "acknowledging him in all our way, and making known all our request to him." Just so long may we expect to be blessed. And we must ever teach each other to do that, that we may be among those whose God is the Lord. I wont preach you a sermon then, if it is Sunday, but I cant avoid a few of those remarks once in a while. I am delighted that there is a chance of you coming down soon. I will welcome you with gladness, but don't intend to let you remain long Will because I know you should be in Athens to meet the clients if any come. I am very cruel am I not? To myself then. I woke up in the middle of last night very much distressed, had dreamed that I was married to one of our store-keepers and my great grief was that I would never see Will again. Strange conceit. Marcia Champion gives a large party this week. I rather think I will not go. I am tired of parties. Mary McLaw wrote me that if we were in Athens next summer, she was coming up to board at the same hotel.

Grandmother and Mrs Starke have both had a hen-party this week. What is your case about? Be sure and gain it if possible. I cant write any more for I have been taking some homeopathic medicine for my throat and it makes me so sleepy that I can scarcely keep my eyes open. Love to your Mother and Sister from us all and Grandmother sends hers also. I am going to dine tomorrow with Mrs. Starke. I am there half of my time.

Ever yours

Rosa

Aunty sends Love and says write to her.

I wrote Dear Will the proceeding pages before I went to church this morning. Went and heard a very uninteresting sermon from Mr Rogers of Savannah so I won & go again this afternoon, but will add a word or two more to Will. Dr. Preston has gone up to Elbert to marry Miss Rucker. Let me tell you of a dream I had night before last, a very romantic one. I dreamed you had neglected me and days and weeks had sped by and not a line of love or explanation for long silence. In the mean while Richard Guerrard had paid his addresses and in a fit of desperation I had accepted him and married him. I had been but three days a bride when a yellow envelope was handed in the old and familiar hand of Dear Will filled with satisfactory reasons for silence and abundant with words of kindness and affection and assurances of undying fidelity I dreamed I was a loving maniac and woke up yelling and moaning most piteously. Now what say you to my dreams. What does it portend if taken courtesy wise as dreams ever are. It speaks of happiness as great in proportion. I hope as the misery so sensibly experienced.

Sarah has recovered her blue attack and is humming a lively tune very merrily. She thinks I doubt not that she is chanting in Methodist measure a psalm. She says Rosa well Mr. Delony he was given to me but he fled the track, but its not too late amen has not yet been said. I wish you had her problem for she is rummaging in my jewelry boxes much to my discomfort. I will write again as soon as I can but I cant do so often for I am very busy.

Affect. R

Athens April 14/54

My Dearest Rosa,

I have not had time today to write you a letter but will dispatch a little note to say all are well and on Sunday will devote a sacred hour or two to my sweet good angel. I had written two letters this morning and had intended writing you but one of my friends wanted a legal opinion and I have been at work ever since racking my brain to give it. The letters were to Aunty & Mrs McLaws, the latter wished my escort as far as Savannah and Aunty, I invited to the wedding and told her that you as well as myself desired the presence of herself, cousin Martha & the Doctor which I presume will all be right. You must not let Mother feel neglected at my not writing her. I shall do so on Sabbath but as she has been staying with you heretofore I did not write as often as I could. Sister is now unable to write at all, the window sash yesterday having fallen on her right hand bruised it considerably, it is swollen & sore. The children are pretty well with the exception of colds. I wish in addition to the names mentioned in my Early Co. letter you would write Col. & Mrs. Billups, Dr. & Miss Billups, Col. Thos Caenah & Mrs. Craig and Mr. John Thomas & lady & Miss Ella Thomas of this place & Mr. & Mrs. Lucius Ferry of Danburry Connecticut, Mr. & Mrs. Jno. Thomas are staying at the Newton House and she is a stout little woman whom you will like also Mr. & Mrs. Edgeworth Bird Sparta, Georgia & Benj. Wolfe (Judge) Blakely Ga, and Dr. A. S. Hill of this place. These names complete my list I believe. Two weeks from Monday will be the first of May and we Dear Rosa will soon meet again. Never again I trust to be separated so long. It seems an age since I have seen you and the inclination toward Liberty street is at most irresistible. You must write me often. I am hard at work now trying to make spare time for the summer months and your letters are a solace whose value none can estimate. I must now say good bye. Sister sends love. Give my regards to Grandmother and to Mother also when you see her. With much love

Yr own
Will

Savannah, April 23rd 1854

My Dear Will

I have just received and read your letter of the 20th Cousin Mary was sitting by my side and tried very hard to coax me into letting her see, and Sarah P_____ looked right jealous because her sweet heart had not been as good as mine and greeted her bright and early this beautiful Sabbath morning with a nice long sweet message of love. Between you and I, judging from divers little thing I think Sarah is decidedly in love. I hear she has a clever beau. I hope so at any rate for she is a good girl. I have promised her whenever she is married that we will certainly attend the wedding. I received a very kind affectionate note from Mrs. Nesbitt full of good wishes for our happiness, also regrets at her inability to be in Savannah on the 16th. She says Dr. Nesbitt wants very much for them to come, but she cannot persuade Aunty to stay and take charge of her children. The latter sends much love to me, and says when I come to Athens she will do all she can to make me happy. I think with you tis best for us to invite Mrs. Maxwell. The wisest plan in this world, is to be as blind as possible to the imperfections and follies of those around us, unless they directly interfere with us, for there is "good in all and none all good."

Sarah has just had a letter handed her, and has thrown herself on the bed, and is weeping most bitterly. Why or wherefore I cannot divine. Poor poor girl, every heart knoweth its own bitterness. I some times imagine I have a multitude of troubles to annoy me, but its an ungrateful bad spirit. Where we have a home Dear Will, and even before lots always try to be contented and cheerful I do not wonder great evils befall us some times, and great blessings are with held. We magnify our little crosses and murmurs, and depreciate our innumerable blessings almost because they are so constant and so common. This is a beautiful world full of warm kind hearts and noble generous impulses and if we would only "cast out first the beam out of our own eye before casting the mote from the eye of others" we would be far happier and far more perfect imitators of our great example. We all spent last evening with Mrs. Starke and enjoyed a strawberry feast. I am so sorry the frost has killed all the fruit in upper Georgia, for that is all I live on in the summer. I have only three more Sabbaths to sit under the sound of Dear old Dr. Prestons voice. He has been a kind fatherly friend to me and I shall ever love venerate and respect him. People may say what they will I know him to be a good man, and his influence over me has ever been for good. How odd it does appear to me when I think of leaving home for good, but I hope our new home will be our little Paradise, where love, charity, gentleness and mutual lenity and forbearance shall reign perfect and supreme, fitting and preparing us for our heavenly and eternal home. Such my imagination has pictured it, and such may we both realize it, will be our constant prayer. Sarah and Grandmother send their love, mine to Sister—affectionately. Dont study any more at night please Will.

Rosa

Athens April 24th 1854

My Own Dearest Rosa

Your sweet letter of the 23rd I have just read. Yesterday Dear Rosa was the first Sabbath for months I have not written you when at home and yesterday I commenced a letter and tries to write but could not. Ever since my trip to Apalachicola I have been sick and for several days last week you could not hear me speak from cold & sore throat, the cold has left me but the effects are worse than it and I am now half sick & how long I am to remain so God only knows. I go about but feel miserably and my physician Dr. Hill has advised to remain quietly at home & lay everything aside and now when I ought to be at Watkinsville attending court I am here at home doing nothing. I would not Dear Rosa have told you this but I cannot write cheerfully and it is so natural to unburden my mind to you. I cannot help it. It does seem hard to hear some times & yet I feel how wrong to complain, for all other blessings aside your love Dearest Rosa is sufficient with me to atone & compensate for all my suffering and sorrows. Every spring since I left Early County I have been sick & whether this is to be the last I know not, but it does seem hard to be this unfortunate just before being married. You cannot tell how I have wished to see you Dear Rosa and how much good one of Rosas sweet smiles would have done me, and I have sometimes been strongly tempted to come & see you in Savannah, but still hoped in that the worst was past. I should soon be myself again. I shall now let books and business go until I get entirely well, this is my most important business. I must neglect myself no longer. I sincerely hope that my next Sabbath days letter will tell my sweet ladylove that Will is entirely well again and not as now depressed and gloomy. I cannot take care of myself—too restless—too impulsive and I hope Rosa will when she gets Will into her possession make him obedient & prudent. But I will promise now for her sake to take good care of him for her till I present him in May, so you must not be sad about me Rosa. I am sure my ailments are but temporary with a moderate cure of myself and I shall be careful for Rosa's sake. I received a beautiful letter from Col. Johnson this afternoon and have half a notion to send it to you but I guess will wait till you come up. It was upon my marriage with you and his thoughts are just and beautiful, his is a noble nature, trammeled and soured by an unfortunate alliance. I admire his character, and doubtless you too will be a good friend of his when well known to you. I am glad to hear that Miss Pyuchion [?] has a beau and hope with you he is worthy of her affection. I some times think that few men are worthy to love of a pure & noble womans heart, and if ever man lived who pair a heartfelt homage to the superior worth of woman that man Dear Rosa is your own Will. Were that idea & feeling eradicated from my notion I should be as miserable as I would be devilish. You are far, far better than we, and each passing day makes this opinion the more confirmed. Miss Pyuchin [?] is no doubt a sweet girl, one of positive not negative worth, and one I should imagine who must admire before she loves. If she has a beau worthy of a pure woman's love, tell her to cherish his love as the only true fountain of human happiness. I understand Miss Rucker had the reputation with the Savannah gentry of being worth half a million of dollars, hope McAlpin is not marrying under that impression. Do you know him. Three more weeks from tomorrow night Dear Rosa and we will bid adieu to the miseries of a life of single blessedness. I hope there will be opened to us both a world of continued & pure enjoyment and that our love and our life will both reflect the purity & happiness of heaven. I began this morning to write my speech for commencement. I was terribly blue and when thinking over the past and the happy hours past in the hall of the Phi Kappa Society, you cannot tell how sad I felt. I wrote only an introduction and then left my office. My subject will be the Influence of Southern Slavery on Modern Civilization. What think you of it. If there be any you prefer suggest it to me and if I am equal to it I shall write upon it. You must pardon Dear Rosa this sad and selfish letter. I cannot with any other hand tonight, but will overcome the blues soon and when I do my song of love shall be more cheerful than it is at present. Do not dream tho that Will neglects you, this he cannot do. He may neglect himself but his love for his sweet good angel is too strong not to give his heart a right. Think of me often Dear Rosa and true we will. I shall I trust be well in a week devoted to my health entirely and you must anxious about me. Give a kiss to Miss Pyuchin [?] for me and my kind love to Grandmother & cousin May.

Affectionately
Yr own
Will

Athens Dec 30, 1855

My Own Precious Rosa

Here I am all by myself at our dear little house in Athens but as homesick and desolate as ever poor mortal man ever was in this world before. I havent felt so since I have been married and if ever again I leave my poor little Scrap and our dear little Darling in Savannah, & I in Athens you may apply at once for a commission of lunacy for me. You cant imagine my feelings when I arrived here last night and came here to meet only Henry & Sarah instead of a sweet kiss from my own dear little wife. I got here about dark & found no fire no supper awaiting me. Sarah informed me that there was no coffee in the house & I concluded to go to an eating house & get my supper, but I have now things put to rights and going on well & smoothly. My room is very comfortable, considering you are away & it is a bachelor establishment but I am most intolerable lonesome. I am more dependent on my little Scrap for happiness than I thought and I last night for the first time since my marriage had the heartsick desolate dont-know-what-to-do-with-yourself feeling of a bachelor. I vow we shall never separate again upon the same terms. My journey up was very unpleasant, rained all the time & when we arrived in Augusta, it was within five minutes of the time for the cars to leave for Athens, so I hurried the Cabman & went immediately to the Depot at full speed and after arriving there waited nearly two hours before starting an acct of an accident to the Engine, so you perceive we were behind time all the way up & got nothing to eat until one oclock yesterday as the cars could not stop at the breakfast house. Last night I made up all assuages however both in eating & sleeping. I found here a letter from sister to you which I will forward to you tomorrow. One also from your mother to me & several others I found awaiting me. I will send you the measure of the room also. I was afraid to measure it today particularly as I heard one of the old Doctors best sermons this evening telling us why we should [be] good and grateful. Sarah tells me that old Whitman has been taking Christmas this past week and had done nothing on the house. He is a lazy creature & I will worry him enough this week for I am determined matters must go on faster or we will part. He has no such idea of energy than a jackass, and about as little sense. I am going to have the house well enough fixed to have you & baby here in two weeks for I dont think my patience will hold out longer than that without you. You are both ever present to my mind and I almost feel that you are with me some times thinking so constantly. In fact I have only been out today to go to the Presbyterian Church this morning & the rest of the time I have been mourning in my little hovel of a house, wishing for you and our precious sweet little baby. There is some difference between a sweetheart and a wife after all,

& I find the party of a lover's life isnt half equal to the realities of married, the fashionable world to the contrary.

I saw Fleming last night and he was very profuse in compliments to you and myself. I think he is tired of his new neighbors already. He thinks I have a much cleverer wife than Goodman, & I think so too. What says my little Scrap. Bob Pittard came to see me this afternoon & there are all of Athens I have seen as yet, so I cant tell you what is going on in our town.

You must write to me often Dear Rosa and tell me all you are doing & thinking of and all our sweet little one does and says for I am very lonely without you and your letters will be all I shall have to comfort me till I see you again. I shall go to work in earnest tomorrow and forward my business as fast as possible, in order to be able to come down for you shortly.

I will go around and pay up some of my accts tomorrow and send on Mothers money & write you tomorrow night all I will have done. Sister has sent me a Bill of sale to Dolly, which I am afraid will hardly suit Uncle. You ladies are curious business people. Give my love to Grandmother, Aunt Mell & all the young people. Kiss our little treasure over & over for me & make it write a little letter to Papa. Bless its little heart & my own Precious Rosa.

Your own Dear Will

Sav Jan 1st 1856

A Happy New Year to you my Darling Will and a great many returns is the ardent prayer of your little wife. Every body has gone to bed, little baby fast asleep too, but I could not sleep without writing you a line or two. I guess you are in the land of dreams yourself, for its quite late. I wonder if you are dreaming of me. I was dreadfully disappointed this afternoon not receiving your letter. Every time I sent to the office it was closed so I'll have to wait till tomorrow. Ever since you left it has been pouring down rain till this morning. So after breakfast I went round to Morrells[14] and exchanged the furniture. Darling Will please write me the earliest you think you can come for me. I am half crazy to see you. I'll not be caught again in a hurry visiting without you. You have spoiled your "little Scrap." Will, she is fit for nothing without you, but that's all right isn't it? Good night Darling. After I get your letter tomorrow I'll assess some more. Had a mighty nice dinner to-day thought of you. Good night.

---

[14] Morrell's was I. W. Morrell, a cabinetmaker who operated his business at 132 and 134 Broughton Street in Savannah in 1850. *Directory of the City of Savannah for the Year 1850* (Savannah, GA: David H. Galloway, 1849).

Wednesday Morning. My own dear Will, your letter came this morning and I'm real unhappy I want so much to see you. Confound old Whitman. What's the old Rascal about. I don't see why I cant sleep in the out-house with you. My poor fellow I think I see you now all by yourself, It's the last time I'll leave you. I've got Eliza in my lap while I'm writing you. I believe she knows the letter is to Papa for she is as still as a mouse and is cooing a sweet little love message to you. I haven't been able to go out any-where. It has rained every day since you left. As soon as we have fair weather I'm going out visiting. Do Darling make old Whitman finish the up-stairs and the dining room immediately, and have them painted, make him finish them entirely, for after they are painted I don't want a thorofare up there. It will spoil the looks of the paint. Come for me just as soon as you can possibly close. Did Sarah finish the lard I left for her. If you don't watch her she will be very extravagant with the lard she uses for you. A table-spoon full is as much as she ought to have for any one dish she may chance to make for you. Did you send Mrs. Manly her note? I hope the letter I wrote you on Sunday went safely. Take good care of yourself my dear dear Will. I didn't know how dearly I loved my old Fell before those who prate about the diminution of love after marriage never knew aught of it before eighteen months has not in the least cured me of any of the romance poetry or sentiment that mingled with mine, nor will the same no [number] of years do it either. God bless you my Darling Will. Well as spontaneously from my heart as it ever did in the days when I used to be your sweet heart and not your owned dear little wife.

Rosa

Athens Jany 2, 1856

My Dearest Rosa

Your letter of last Saturday I have just received and was dreadfully disappointed that I did not hear from my poor little heart last night. How I wish I was with you now, or rather you with me in Athens in our cozy little nest. My room I find to be really comfortable upon trial and if you & our little dearest baby were with me we could be right happy here. It is raining terribly and has been all day so I have a good occasion to test the cosiness of my batchelor home. My only companions are Buck and Trip who are playing & fighting & sleeping by turns. It's a glorious time for them for they have undisturbed possession of the hearth. The Shanghaes too are doing well having taken up their abode with Sarah in the Kitchen & one of the hens is laying in her room. The cow is giving more than two gallons of milk per day, so you see, we are all doing as well as could be expected except poor Will & the Turkeys one of whom was unfortunately stolen during the holidays. I have been endeavoring to clean up &c, but we have so much rain we can do but little, indeed unless we can soon have better weather I am afraid we will not be able to have our house ready this winter. It is impossible for the flooring to be put down now and indeed it is a bad time for the Doors & windows to be put together. I find old Whitman always at work when I go to his shop but he is awfully slow. If the house is not ready in time I shall have to write you & the baby to live with me for I cant live without you much longer. I didn't know how much I loved my poor little heart before. She is indeed all the world to me and without her life would be blank indeed.

Eelsy has come, but none of them are doing much, waiting for my little Scrap to lay out there work. I send you a letter from Mary McLaws which came tonight also one from Sister which I before mentioned. Mrs Andersons Breast Pin I presume Tom Cobb will bring down when he comes. Suppose you come up to Augusta with Basinger on the 11th Feb we meet you at McLaws' & spend a day or two with them, or you stay there while I go to the Democratic Convention at Milledgeville on the 13th. I guess I shall have to be there. Some of my friends want me to be the Elector for President from this Congressional Dist. Tho' you must say nothing of this to any one. I have been you don't know how busy, with the Town business & my own since my return. Give much love to Laura, Aunt Nelle & other young folks for me & kiss our little one over & over again for poor Papa. I forgot all about the reasons for the rooms but will attend to it tomorrow you must excuse me I have been so busy. Good night my poor little heart.

Your own Dear
Will

Thursday the 4. I wrote the above yesterday, but Mr Sledge was detained in consequence of the hacks breaking down. He will send my buggy around to my house tonight and the young man who brings him to Athens will bring my buggy back tomorrow. I am better of my Cold but still hoarse. Our Court is getting on slowly & will consume the week I think with the Criminal docket, much to my regret. With much kind love to Dear Rosa & our little one, I am Your Own

Will

Still later. Ned Lumpkin has determined to go down with Sledge so you can send George up on Saturday morning with my buggy to take me home. How cold it has been this week. I am afraid too cold for planting.

25

Wednesday night

Dearest Will

I intended writing you last night, but I dont know what made me think it was Monday instead of Tuesday. I hope you are well Darling. I am not feeling as well as I did last week. Our little Precious pet is quite well and as lively as she can be, slept the whole of last, and the night before. I think she will walk very soon. While I am writing the Boys are eating supper. I have not eaten any since you left, but I can scarcely refrain. No letters have come since you left. I dont know why Dr. Schley dont write. All the afternoons have been unpleasant, so I have not been to make any more visits. I miss you terribly Will, its very lonely in the evenings. I often wonder Darling what would become of me without you. I wish I was not so dependent upon certain sources for my happiness. I hope you will be able to leave for home on Friday. Take good care of yourself. Good night. God protect and bless you Darling.

Affectionately your own

Rosa

Athens Jany 6, 1856

My Own Precious Rosa

I recd your letter of the 2nd yesterday and owe you & myself an apology for my neglect to send you the measure of our parlor—it is 30 feet & 8 inches long by 12 feet & 8 inches wide—so that it will take 6 headtles 30 ft 8 inches or 10 yds 8 inches long making in all 61 1/ 5 yds of carpeting. You had best order 6 headtles cut those 8 inches in length & get a receipt guaranteeing that where cut they will match. You must forgive my forgetting this matter. I have been very busy & there is some excuse for your poor fellow. My poor poor little Scrap. How much I would like to see you & our poor little baby tonight. You don't know half how lonesome it is here all by myself. I will try and come for you as soon as I can. Mr. Whitman has just got ready for the plastering & if the weather will only moderate a little so it can be done. Mr. Crane will soon finish it. We had a beautiful clear morning today but very cold & now the skies are all overcast again & before morning I would not be surprised if it rained again. We have hit upon an unlucky time for repairing certainly, but my little home will do for us both until the "Big House" is finished—won't it? I think I will return as many cases to this as many cases to this Court as any in Athens, which is sure comfort any how. I got their new ones yesterday, & by the way our election for town officers is over and I am elected again notwithstanding the trickery of the know nothings. My vote was 1/3 larger than last year & two democrats were elected in an Ward. Dr. Sutter/Sutler was beaten, which we all regret & Dorsey was elected Marshall. I called on Mrs. Ferry last evening & dined with her today. She says she is very anxious to see you & the Baby about both of whom I boasted very much. She says she knows my choice must be pretty & I told her the prettiest in Ga. Wasn't I right? My poor little Darling Scrap, she is the prettiest in Georgia to me and every day that passes but make me love her dearer & appreciate her more. If she was only now here with me how happy I could be. Nobody can tell but my sweet little wife. If I can only succeed in thinking of her & making her happy, poor Will will be content in this world & his life shall be spent in trying to do so. Kiss our sweet little baby over & over for poor Papa & remember poor Will & think of him often. God bless my Dear Rosa.

Sunday night Jan 6th [1856]

My Darling Will

This has been a beautiful right sunny day and I have been thinking of you and longing for you. Actually pining to see you. I would have written to you this afternoon and have sent the letter by tonights mail to Augusta but I was waiting to see Mr. Basinger and see if I could arrange it so as to leave with him. I will tell you my plans and you must write me immediately upon receiving this if they meet your approval. I will leave next Saturday at twelve in the morning for Augusta and reach there Saturday night and go round to Mary McLaws'es if you decide upon attending the democratic convention (on the 15th I believe). I'd stay in Augusta and on your return from Milledgeville you can carry me home. If you are not going to Milledgeville you can meet me in Augusta and spend Sunday with Mary or if that don't suit, you come for me on Monday or Tuesday. I cant stand it away from you darling. It really makes me un happy. I can live in the out house very well I'd rather live in a pen with my own dear Will, than in a palace without him. Now be sure and write me immediately so that I can receive it time enough to let Mary know. I leave here with Mr. Basinger in the Saturday morning train. Twelve o'clock I think? Write me how long you will be in Milledgeville I would not attend the Convention were I in your place unless I knew it would be of some benefit. I would not go simply to gratify my friends, but if you know it to your advantage don't let what I say influence you. Its to nominate the President isn't it? It seems to me it would not advantage you much—especially during this session, or after this session but don't mind my thoughts for they may be very nonsensical. My Darling Will I am almost crazy to see you, how I wish I could put my arms around your own dear neck and hug and kiss you to my hearts content to night, and our precious little baby wants to see you too. I say Papa to her and she smiles as though she understands me. Now be sure and write me. I am going to buy some Salmon and tea. My cold is better but

I'm still very hoarse. My poor darling, I know you have written me to night. Oh I do want to see you. All send love. Eliza sends Papa a very sweet kiss.

God bless you my
Own dear Will
Rosa

Be sure and bring your trunk and dear Will if you buy some 5 or 6 dozen eggs have a little box packed with them and bring them to Grandmother she cant get any. Put cotton inbetween them Now don't forget

Sav Jan 6th [1856] Monday

My Darling Will,

I wrote you a letter this morning saying that I would leave on Saturday with Mr. Basinger for Augusta and stop at Mary McLawses where you could meet me, but since I wrote dear little Eliza has been right sick affected just as she was the time we sent for Dr. Smith. I think she is cutting another tooth she is a great deal better now tho and I guess by tomorrow will be quite well, but I cant help thinking that with the baby teething and the weather as cold, going about visiting with her unadvisable. Grandmother says she thinks so too and that when I start for home I had better go straight there without stopping. So dear Will do carry out your original intention of coming to Sav for me and do come just as soon as you possibly can for I'm real un happy I want so much to see you. My poor fellow I am afraid you thought your poor little wife closed about the measure of the room which you have neglected sending. I did not mean to be, tho you ought to get a scolding. Come for me soon, very soon. Little precious Eliza sends a sweet kiss. She laughed out very merrily just now at some of Lollies antics so I think she must be a great deal better but I tell you she was real sick this morning and I real uneasy I can very well live in the room with you. Do make old Whitman take advantage of this fine weather to lay the floors etc. I can't write any more or this will not be in time for the mail. Good bye my own Darling take good care of yourself for your own affectionate

Rosa

Savannah Jan 18th 1856

My Dear Will

You are a mean fellow to treat me in the way you do. You wrote me you were coming for me the last of this week and just when I am looking for you, here comes a letter saying that you cant come till next week. Now I don't blame you for staying till Return day is over, but I do for disappointing me so badly. Now you must come for me next week for I am not going to stay here any longer. I am heartily sick of being cooped up in the house with nothing to do. I have been out but three times since you left, for it has rained day and night, besides I ought to be at home attending to my own affairs. If I had known there was more than one Return day I should have carried out my intention of going to Augusta, but as you offered to meet me there the last of the week, I presumed of course you could leave Athens. You havn't written me a line about what's going on, on our premises now answered a single question and if you were not so far away I don't think I could well resist giving a little scolding. I shall look for you Thursday next. If you could possibly so arrange it as to leave on Tuesday for Sav would be better, for there you could stay a day and we could leave for Athens on Friday. I hope sincerely the upstairs of our house and the dining room may be finished before you go off to attend court so that I may have George Smith with me. I shall not relish much staying in the out-house alone.

Dear little Eliza is too sweet. She is very busy helping Sarah make some starch. She sends a kiss to dear absent Papa and says he must make haste and come. She has another little tooth peeping out, bless her little soul. Dear Will I want to see you more than you want to see me I know. I havn't enjoyed my visit to Sav I have missed you so. I have done nothing but think of you and eat these gloomy rainey days. Don't expect to see much of your $5000 when you come for I have eaten it most all up. Good bye my own Darling this is the last letter I shall write, for another would not reach you. Do wrap yourself up well travelling down. Be sure and bring the cloak and don't forget the eggs.

Affectionately your own dear
Rosa

Athens Sunday Night [1856]

My Darling Will

I went into my writing desk just now and the first thing that met my eye was an old letter of mine written to you while you were off at Court the September after we were married—written the night of the day that you left. A disconsolate wail for my departed spouse so lover-like that it has put me in the humor of writing this little note. I want to see by comparison the alteration 18 months make in the affections and tone of the letters etc. My poor darling I feel your absence just as much to-night as I did then, only more. I wonder if you have thought of me to-day. Once I know you did when you untied the biscuits and cake. I thought of you and wondered if you had any thing to drink from. I miss you terribly when you leave me to spend a solitary Sabbath but little Eliza beguiles me by her sweetness of some of my loneliness, bless her precious little soul, she is fast wrapt in her peaceful rosy slumbers. She stood up alone this morning and took two or three steps without any assistance and jabbered papa. My theme has slightly changed since last September hasn't it? Tomorrow I am going to commence putting to-rights. How glad I will be when you are home for good. Think of your little wife and baby darling Will (wife first) and do your best, and make haste and come home and we'll give you a sweet kiss and nestle close to you and welcome you as joyfully as 18 months ago.

Affectionately your own

Rosa

Athens Feby 19, 1857

My Dear Rosa,

As Mr. Sledge has just informed me that he is going to Athens I send this note to say that I am well and will not be able to be at home until Saturday.

My cases will not be up until tomorrow probably and it is possible that one of them will not be tried until Saturday morning.

Why haven't you written me. There is a daily mail here. I hope my little Scrap is quite well & getting on better than when I was at home. It is time for her to improve a little. God bless you all.

Very affectionately

W. G. Delony

Athens March 16th [1857]

My Own Darling Will,

I have just finished copying your bill in Equity for you and am going to send it off tonight. How I wish you were here Darling for I feel gloomy. Bob and myself had a flare up to day at dinner, and he left the house in a great passion and said he would not come into it again. I hate to write you all this, for I know it greaves you. When I came down to dinner I found Bob preparing to have a fight between his little game cock and our large black and yellow shanghai. He had tied one of those long pointed spurs or gaffs on his fowl. I did not wish the shanghai injured and I had never seen you allow one of them to fight that way, so I told him he must not fight the shanghai. I did not wish it. He paid no attention whatsoever to me, but thro dinner I felt no help when he came back. I did not wish my shanghai fought, that he might do what he pleased with his chicken, but that the shanghai were mine for I had raised them and besides that I knew you did not wish them fought. He said if you said so, you were a great story-teller for you told him differently. He was so extremely insolent that I said Bob you do not treat me with a particle of respect. I surely have a right to say I do not wish my fouls fought. He was in such a passion he jumped up from the table, said the next time he came to my house I would think he treated me with respect, then seized hold of his gun and killed his game chicken. Dear Will am I to bear all this, as your wife, whom no man would be allowed by you, the insult without being made account for it. Am I to bear this insult from him simply because he is your brother and could not broach an insult from my father because he was my father neither did I expect you to, and can more be expected of me. Dear Will I can't do it no woman of my temperament could. None by God knows what your family have caused me to feel, and I have no patience or charity left. Dear Will dont blame poor Rosa, nature never made her able to rise above some things, little they may seem to you but better annoyances to her. Darling you know I love you, and would do any thing on earth for you, and I am grieved now because I know I am grieving you, but I cannot consent to be the object upon which Bob Delony is to give vent to his evil and bitter feelings. Good night my poor fellow dont feel unhappy and dont blame your little wife. She only wants a _____.

Affectionately your own
Rosa
Make haste and come.

Lexington April 23, 1857

My Dear Rosa,

I received yesterday your welcome letter of the night before and was glad to learn that all were well. I am here doing nothing, none of my cases have as yet been reached. The Court has been disposing of old cases of its docket and we have had some fine speaking & an interesting time. Yesterday the Criminal docket was taken up and the first case has not yet been disposed of. None of my cases will come up in all probability before morning and I have no idea that I shall be in Athens before Saturday night. Mr Cobb will give me a seat in his buggy should I not get through in time for the Cars. Our old Judge is very slow and the business is protracted un-necessarily. I took tea at Gov. Gilmers night before last, the only time I have seen the ladies. I have dined out twice, yesterday & the day before & continue quite well. Lexington is indeed a pleasant little place & I wish my little Scrap was here with me. Our tavern however is execrable & you would pity the lawyers could you see us here.

God bless my little Scrap. Keep well & think often of her own dear

Will

Athens Feb 16th 1858

My Darling Will

I do hope you have received my little note I wrote you Sunday evening and that you are quite well, prospering in your business and enjoying yourself with Brother's Tom & Hope in Col Grant's hospitable mansion. I have just finished writing two long letters one to Mrs Ferry and the other to Mary McLaws, the letter in reply to a very sweet one received yesterday. We are missing you very much, but I am trying to beguile the time by being very busy. I went out yesterday afternoon visiting, to see Mrs. Ester Church and Mrs. Henry Hull. "Miss Ella" is expected to morrow to be here till May. I spent a very pleasant afternoon and am going out again to-morrow. Alek hauled a large load of wood here early Monday and as the day was very clear I told him he need not haul any more. George is still hauling. I think he can haul enough this week to do me some time and he can then get a chance to work in the garden. Old Mr. Sledge was round here yesterday for a few minutes to say that when he went to planting his potatoes he would take great pleasure in coming here and showing George how to plant yours. Dr. Reese called to-day after dinner and sat awhile. His object was to collect missionary donations. I told the old gentleman that we were dead broke and had suspended payment but that I would give him three dollars, two for me and one for the Baby. Only two letters have come for you one from Mrs. J. Taylor acknowledging the receipt of a check you sent her and the other from New Orleans from Girardey. I will tell you below what he says. Little precious Rosa sends dear Papa a sweet kiss and I send one too to my old fellow

Affectionately your little wife

Rosa E. Delony

The letter is dated 8th. Acknowledges yours of the 2nd. I don't know Darling after reading Girardeys letter whether he wants you to compromise or not. He says first "If in your opinion a favorable compromise can be made I fully authorize you to make it." Then he speaks of Wrightmens being able to obtain testimony in August of his excellent moral character. Then he says "If this will strengthen the case in your opinion sufficiently to hazard the matter against threats of establishing complicity, I am not willing to have our claim reduced to nothing or only one half, unless the company pays all cost of Suit with interest from the day same was one." Then he wants to know the net amount coming to him in event of a compromise, and your news as to the above testimony. Then follows a long rigmaroll about his transferring the claim in payment to some firm and of the $200 offered you of which he says he has heard nothing from you. Wants to know if they have written you and your reply. Then he says he will send them your letter and if they take the claim in payment and want to compromise you will hear from them. Then after that he signs his name and add a P.S. Since writing the above "I lost sight of the last proposal to settle according to testimony. This as it stands is satisfactory to you, and I now authorize you to do so." Then he adds a P.S. which he says he has sent to the agent of the other company Mr. G. G. Wilbun and says if you do not hear from him in a week, proceed with the case as lastly instructed. Darling I did not send the letter because you told me not to, but as well as I could I have tried to tell you all in it.

Danielsville Mch 3, 1858

My Dear Rosa,

Your little note with the pipe stems enclosed I recd yesterday & am sincerely obliged to my little Scrap for her kind remembrance of her old fellow. I had a terrible time coming up here on Monday. It was very cold and windy and when I arrived Court was in session. The consequence was that I had to go to the Court house and did not get warm until dinner, and now have a cold and am very hoarse. There is a case being tried this afternoon in which I am not interested & I shall stay by the fire and endeavor to get rid of my cold. The Judge was sick yesterday & we had no Court. All of which I attribute to the fact then there is no stove in the Court house & you have no idea how uncomfortable it is.

I have collected about forty dollars with a promise of as much more & another chance of Fifty more, but I can only count safely upon the cash in hand.

Give a sweet kiss to our little one for me and remember me kindly to the boys. With much love to my own Rosa I am

Very affectionately
W. G. Delony

[June 1859]

My Own Dear Will

How disappointed I was when your letter was handed me saying you would not be home till Thursday, you well know. The tears would come all I could do. Friday morning Cousin and the girls came and I was going to see them in the afternoon but company called and prevented me so Saturday morning I walked all the way in the hot sun to see them in order to be at home in the afternoon to welcome my old fellow so judge of my disappointment to hear that you were not coming. Judge Jackson came over in the afternoon to tell me how you were. Do be prudent especially in exposing yourself to the hot sun. We are all well except my old complaint. I went to church this morning, heard a good sermon from the old Dr. Mr.

Witherspoon had his little Baby baptized.[15] I felt so sorry for him when he present-ed it alone poor little motherless thing. The Dr. as usual made himself ridiculous. John Thomas says he is on a begging expedition for money enough to let the old man go north and recover his health. I promised to help but will have to wait till the old fellow gets back as funds are low at present. He has got 200 already.

Mr. White's youngest child has died from hooping-cough. I fear we will soon have it on our lot. Catherine carried Hannah and Andrew to Mrs. Georgous who has a child with it the other night when I sent her to Mrs. G with Tonk altho she has been expressly forbidden to do so. There was a circus in town yesterday. One of the tents was pitched in front of the Baptist Church. I do really think the Authori-ties ought to appropriate some place for such purposes. I never heard any thing to equal the hurrah and noise. Darling I hope you are spending a quiet day at Mrs. Pattersons and not doing any work, and thinking sweetly of your wife and precious little children and feeling grateful for your recovering health and prosperity and in-numerable blessing and mercies.

Cousin says she is coming to tea to go with us to church to night if she can get the carriage. She looks thin from her recent sickness. I got a letter from Sister yes-terday, all well and ready for a start to see old Mrs. Gunnison.

Judge Jackson says you had an idea of coming home to spend Sunday. I am glad you did not, the weather is too warm to travel much. Oh Darling I miss you so much and am jealous of this week which I was counting on as mine and a Sunday without you is a broken day, for I am sure of you all to myself then. Come just as soon as you can and be sure of a welcome to Dear Papa from little Rosa and Tom and your poor

Old Scrap
R

Athens Tuesday Night July 1859

My Dear Will

Here I am in the Driving rain writing to you, Rosa and Buddie asleep up stairs. I do hope that I may hear from you in the morning and learn that you are getting better.

About an hour after you left Rosa came to me and said Mama! Papa gone to buy little baby a pretty dress. You recollect you told her you were going away to make some money for her to buy dresses with. A letter came for you on Monday with checks from Mr. Collier, and then from your friend Moss reminding you of

---

[15] Robert L. Witherspoon lost his wife, Mary C. Witherspoon, on 11 May 1859, probably during childbirth, as he raised "a living infant." *Southern Watchman* (2 June 1859).

your promise to make the speech, his exhibition is to be the week before commencement 25th I thinks, and he invites you to stay at his House. Darling do take care of yourself this hot weather, and dont drink too much water when you are heated and keep out of the hot. So Do Will be prudent for your Rosa's sake, for life would be a blank to me without you. Dear Will, I do hate you to be absent from me when you are sick, as I know I can take better care of the old fellow than any one else, and I think he would rather feel her hand on his head than any one else. It is very warm. I went this afternoon to see Mrs. Childs. She was too unwell to see me, but I saw the Baby a fine child. Went to see Mrs. Hunter and Smiths. The Dr. has gone to Gainesville. Rosa and Tommy send dear Papa sweet kisses and Mama sends a sweet kiss too

Your Own Rosa

Chapter 2

A Coming Storm:
January 1860–August 1861

We are a band of brothers and native to the soil
Fighting for the property we gained by honest toil
And when our rights were threatened, the cry rose near and far
Hurrah for the Bonnie Blue Flag that bears a single star!
—"The Bonnie Blue Flag" 1861

Despite the storm clouds then gathering in the country, the start of a new decade in 1860 found the Delony family living a prosperous and happy family life in the Classic City. The couple had been married for four years, and though they had lost their first child Eliza after only one year, they had two other children: Rosa Eugenia, born in 1857, and Tom Cobb, born 1859.[1] When "little Rosa" was born, Gen. Robert Taylor presented Rosa and Will with an engraved silver cup.[2] By late 1859, the couple were also busy moving into their newly built home in downtown Athens, adjacent to the corner of Lumpkin and Broad Street, across the street[3] from the Franklin College and a block from the Arch, the university's most prominent symbol today. The Arch was at the time the gate of the newly constructed ornamental fence that encompassed the small campus.[4] Rosa was also pregnant with William Gaston Delony Jr.

---

[1] Eliza Huguenin was born 29 June 1855 and died 20 June 1856, Charlotte Marshall, *Oconee Hill Cemetery of Athens Georgia* (Athens, GA: Athens Historical Society, 2009) 285. Rosa Eugunia, born 9 September 1857; Tom Cobb, born 3 March 1859; Bible records of William G. and Rosa E. (Huguenin) Delony, Family History Library Catalogue, The Church of the Latter Day Saints.

[2] The silver presentation cup presented by Gen. Robert Taylor is in the possession of Leigh Hull Steele, great-great-granddaughter of William G. Delony. See footnote 50.

[3] The northeast corner is a parking lot for the Bank of America building. From 1844 to 1932, the lot was the site of the Anthenaeun Building (a social club) that later housed the university law school from 1919 to 1932 before it was demolished. The Delony House site today is the high-rise senior-living building called Denny Towers adjacent to the corner parking lot.

[4] 1860 Census. Living in the Delony house in addition to Will, Rosa, "Little Rosa," and "Little Tom" was Lucy A. Barnes, the older first cousin of Elizabeth Bolling Taylor, who helped Delony while he was a student living in the Greek Revival Taylor (Grady) House that Delony

The Delonys were well established as respected, highly regarded members of the upper-class elite of Athens society.[5] From his mother, Will Delony received 400 acres in Houston County shortly before his marriage to Rosa, which represented the estate of his deceased father. The transfer of the property was drawn up in Kent, Michigan, where Delony's mother moved to be with her daughter Martha following the death of Martha's husband.[6] In addition to the Houston County property, the Delonys possessed $10,000 in real estate and $35,000 in personal estate.[7] Despite a more than sufficient number of lawyers in the city, Delony established a thriving practice and was hailed as a "good lawyer, a cultivated gentleman and a true patriot."[8] The Delonys were also active and respected members of Athens Presbyterian Church.[9]

By 1860, Athens, "with a corporate limit of a two-mile radius from the college chapel," had grown to a population of nearly 4,000, almost equally divided between whites (1,955) and enslaved (1,892) plus one free person of color.[10] Franklin College

---

describes as the "big house" in a letter to Rosa, 13 December 1853, Delony Papers. The Delony house site today is the high-rise senior-living building called Denny Towers. Kenneth Coleman, "Map of Confederate Athens," in *Confederate Athens* (Athens: University of Georgia Press, 1967).

[5] Angela Esco Elder, "A Community of Condolences: The Civil War Experience of Rosa Delony," unpublished paper, History Department, University of Georgia, 2012.

[6] Indenture from Maria B. Delony to William G. Delony, 6 June 1853, Delony Papers. "John W. Gunnison," www.ancestry.com. Martha's husband, Capt. John W. Gunnison, a West Point graduate, and several soldiers were tragically murdered on 26 October 1853 in Utah by a band of Indians while on military duty against the Mormons. The event became known as the "Gunnison Massacre." Gunnison is honored with seven places named in his honor, including cities of Gunnison in Colorado and Utah.

[7] 1860 Clarke County Census; converting this to the 2009 standards shows an equivalency of $266,000 in real estate and $998,000 in personal estate, Elder, "A Community of Condolences."

[8] *The Georgia Historical Quarterly* (December 1935) 335.

[9] Now First Presbyterian Church of Athens. The original church was founded in 1823. In 1855, a new Presbyterian church, described as a grandiose building of worship, was built on Hancock Street, where it stands today. The Delony home was located just three blocks from the church. The historic church had private pews and the Delony seats were directly behind Thomas R. R. Cobb's, an elder in the church. After Will's death, Rosa remained a member of the church for over fifty years until her death in 1896. Delony Papers. *The Georgia Historical Quarterly* (December 1935) 335. Thomas R. R. Cobb's nameplate is located on the right front pew while the "W. G. Deloney" (note the 'e' is included) nameplate is located in the third pew from the right middle front. The same pews with some of the original nameplates (Cobb and Delony) remain today, although they have been relocated and recently refurbished, working through several layers of paint. History of the First Presbyterian Church of Athens from an interview with senior pastor Dr. W. Glenn Doak (28 March 2013). Interview with Superior Court Judge Lawton E. Stephens (10 April 2013); Marshall, *Oconee Hill Cemetery*, 285.

[10] Kenneth Coleman, *Athens, 1861–1865: As Seen through Letters in the University of Georgia Libraries* (Athens: University of Georgia Press, 1969) 1

had an enrollment of 113 and another 47 more enrolled in the new law school. In addition to its uniqueness of being a college town, the Classic City was also an important center of industry, transportation, and communication.[11] Athens had a railroad spur that connected the city to the south at Union Point on the Georgia railroad that ran between Augusta and Atlanta.

In those early months of 1860, there resided within Clarke County pockets of "rabble-rousers" over secession in the county. Most of the leading citizens and populace, however, favored preserving the Union. As the November 1860 election drew closer and it was apparent that support for Abraham Lincoln was growing stronger in the North, many citizens in Georgia, and particularly those in Clarke County, became very disturbed, even bordering on hysteria.[12] The controversy split the national Democratic Party. The northern Democrats nominated Stephen A. Douglas and Johnson County, Georgia's, Herschel V. Johnson, while the southern Democrats nominated John Breckinridge and Joseph Lane. In addition to Lincoln and his Republican running mate, Hannibal Hamlin, a new party emerged, the Constitutional Union Party, which nominated Tennessean John Bell and Edward Everett.[13]

A group of prominent Georgians, led by Thomas R. R. Cobb, began emerging in the late 1850s pushing for secession if the government refused to address their concerns. In his efforts, Thomas Cobb was supported not only by others such as William Delony, but also Cobb's brother, Howell, who was at the time serving as the secretary of the treasury in the James Buchanan administration. Members of the "Cobb faction" were opposed in their efforts by the "Stephens faction," led by Alexander Stephens and his half-brother, Linton. The latter faction promoted an attitude of "wait and see" in relation to the necessity of immediate secession to resolve the state's grievances. Cobb, Delony, and others began crisscrossing the state giving speeches in support of their positions.

The first effort in their overall plan was to create a voting block supportive of their goals at the forthcoming Democratic Convention in Charleston, South Carolina. In May 1860, members of the Georgia House of Representatives met in

---

[11] Coleman, *Athens*, 6, 2. Michael Gagnon, *Transition to an Industrial South: Athens, Georgia, 1830–1870* (Baton Rouge: Louisiana State University Press, 2012).

[12] "The news of the success of the Black Republicans in Pennsylvania on the 9th reached us yesterday and I confess it sounded to me as the death-knell of the Republic. I can see no earthly hope of defeating them in November and their success then, whether we will it or not, is *inevitable disunion*. And calmly and coolly, my dear wife, is it not best? These people hate us.... They are a different people from us, whether better or worse and *there is no love* between us. Why then continue together? No outside pressure demands it, no internal policy or public interest requires it." Thomas R. R. Cobb to Marion Cobb, 11 October 1860, T. R. R. Cobb Papers.

[13] Coleman, *Athens*, 14.

Milledgeville, Georgia, to select delegates representing their state's position in the convention. Thomas Cobb wrote his brother in March 1860,

> Your letter was recd yesterday astounding me with the intelligence of Henry Jackson's curious freak. We have all been relying here on his presence. I saw Deloney at once & he immediately agreed to go. He left this morning. Hope is at Gwinnett. I don't know his final determination. Barrow was here & would have left this morning, but his little girls have the measles & he dislikes to leave them. He gave Deloney a proxy for Oglethorpe.[14]

During the 1860 political campaign, Delony supported Breckinridge for president and traversed the state making several speaking stops for the candidate in the summer before the election,[15] including in Watkinsville, the county seat of Clarke County,[16] and in Columbus, in the western part of the state. The patriotic Delony was committed to secession and Southern independence.

The month prior to the presidential election saw members of the state legislature meeting to determine their party's delegates. Delony, as a member of the Georgia House, traveled to Milledgeville to cast his vote. "There are present only *eight* members out of the *fifteen*," wrote Thomas R. R. Cobb. "Poor Irwin was one—and his untimely end leaves only *fourteen*. Those present are—of the Senate—*Holt* and *Printup*, of the House—*Lester, Fannin, Williams, Lewis, Delony,* and *Broiles.* Lawton I hear will be here today."[17]

Three days later, Thomas Cobb reported to his brother,

> I found that a *large* majority of the meeting were anxious to endorse strongly the action of the Seceders. While a few thought they saw Brown's (of Miss) Slave Code in the Majority Platform all were willing to endorse fully *your suggestions* in your letter. So we reported strongly against Squatter Sovereignty & endorsed your suggestions about Baltimore & Richmond. Our Report was adopted *unanimously.* I found Mitchell & Delony both *doubting* about the propriety of the Secession. They are both fighting on your side & I deprecated a division in our own ranks. *Hope Hull* is more determined than any one. But he would not go to the meeting as he says he does not wish to come in conflict with you or your friends. You will find

---

[14] Oglethorpe County, Georgia. Thomas R. R. Cobb to Howell Cobb, 15 March 1860, T. R. R. Cobb Papers.

[15] *Southern Banner* (23 August 1861).

[16] Clarke County was organized in 1801 from Jackson County with Watkinsville as the county seat. The area included most all of present-day Clarke, Oconee, and Green counties. The county remained as such until Oconee was created from Clarke in 1875. *The Counties of the State of Georgia* (Savannah: The Georgia Historical Society, 1974) 6, 22.

[17] Thomas R. R. Cobb to Marion Cobb, 11 October 1860, T. R. R. Cobb Papers.

the Convention overwhelmingly on your line, as against Douglas. *The diffi-culty will be to control the ultra fire-eaters.* You will stand as a middle man & can then direct. You & Jim were to be appointed Delegates from this County. J Lamar is also a Delegate.[18]

Thomas Cobb also expressed the views of many in late 1860 in a letter he penned to his brother, Howell: "Tomorrow is the day of Election & before you re-ceive this you will have known the fate of the Union or the South one or the other is irretrievably gone if Lincoln is elected. I confess I feel very sad. The forebodings of my mind are of the most depressing character & my soul is 'disgusted within me.' I would that I had the faith to trust like David & say to my soul 'Hope thou in God!' It is our only trust. He may save us. Human effort is vain."[19]

Activities in the state were rushing forward and Delony was working as active-ly as any in efforts to consolidate Georgians behind the movement for secession. In December 1860 he spoke to the assembled citizens of Greene County who were nominating delegates to attend the state convention in January at the capital in Milledgeville, Georgia. His message "to explain the views and principles of what is called the secession party" and to urge "the people of Greene County who had a common origin, interest and destiny to have a record which their posterity would read with pride, and not with shame...and to make known by resolutions and acts that they will not submit to black republican rule."[20]

As the election drew near, members of the Cobb faction began canvassing for their candidates and looking for any information about the coming vote. "I shall leave for Milledgeville on Saturday," wrote Thomas Cobb to his brother. "I have given Deloney, Barrow & Ed Lumpkin your views & position. They leave tomor-row & promise me to spend the three last days of this week in posting themselves so as to post me on my arrival. By that time we shall know the result of the election."[21]

Breckinridge carried the state, although Clarke County went for the Unionist Bell, with 695 votes, while Breckinridge gathered 451 and Douglas 57. Lincoln, whose name was not even on the ballot, carried the national electoral vote and thus the election.

In October 1860, Cobb wrote his wife Marion, "*Separation is desirable,* peacea-bly if we can, forcible if we must. If all the South would unanimously say 'we sepa-rate,' it would be as peaceably done as a summer's morn."[22] Delony's "trust that the people of Georgia will endorse the policy of the secessionists" was apparently well

[18] Thomas R. R. Cobb to Howell Cobb, 28 May 1860, T. R. R. Cobb Papers.
[19] Ibid., 5 November 1860.
[20] *Daily Constitutionalist* Augusta, GA (20 December 1860).
[21] Thomas R. R. Cobb to Howell Cobb, 5 November 1860, T. R. R. Cobb Papers.
[22] Thomas R. R. Cobb to Marion Cobb, 11 October 1860, T. R. R. Cobb Papers.

founded, although his views to Rosa concerning the South's prospects to a peaceable split from the Union is quite interesting in that it was an opinion not shared by most Southerners, including his personal friend, Thomas R. R. Cobb. Writing to Rosa, he confided, "My opinion is that we are on the verge of revolution, not a peaceful one, but a bloody war."[23]

With the election of Lincoln, South Carolina seceded from the Union on 20 December 1860. Taking South Carolina's lead, the other Southern states began to move like a set of dominoes. South Carolina was followed by Mississippi on 9 January in declaring its secession, then Florida on the 10th, and Alabama on the 11th. On the first day of the Georgia convention on 16 January 1861, a resolution declaring Georgia's "Right and Duty" to secede from the Union passed by a slim margin of 166 to 130. Two days later, on 18 January, "The Ordinance of Secession" passed with 208 yeas and 89 nays, a majority of 119. Seeing that opposition was probably pointless, "Most of the cooperationists...folded and went with the secessionists."[24] Patriotism exploded in Athens with students celebrating with a torch-light parade as Georgia became the fifth state to secede. Delony's friend, Thomas R. R. Cobb, who led the secession movement in Milledgeville, returned to Athens a hero.[25] For his part, Delony was praised for taking "a bold and independent stand in favor of the secession of Georgia."[26]

Determined not to be left out of the growing nationalistic movement swirling about the South in late 1860, Delony set out to form his own military unit, something he was very successful in doing, and despite Rosa's feelings on the subject, he was determined to be an active and enthusiastic (at least at first) participant in the conflict. Delony's summary of his personal performance and that of his unit, as well as his concerns for the tribulations of his wife and family at home, make this an interesting and potentially valuable collection of letters. The consistent written exchange between the two during the war show a degree of affection between husband and wife and an attention to detail seldom found in Civil War letters.

The five Southern states were soon followed by Louisiana, which seceded on 26 January, and Texas, which followed suit on 1 February. Three days later, these seven states met together in Montgomery, Alabama, and formed the Confederate States of America.

---

[23] Will Delony to Rosa Delony, 10 December 1860, Delony Papers.

[24] Mark Scroggins, *Robert Toombs: The Civil Wars of a United States Senator and Confederate General* (Jefferson, NC: McFarland, 2011) 124, 125.

[25] John F. Stegeman, *These Men She Gave: The Civil War Diary of Athens, Georgia* (Athens: University of Georgia Press, 1964) 12–13.

[26] *The Georgia History Quarterly* (December 1935) 335.

The country quickly began preparations for war, and Delony busily set about raising a cavalry company for the "brief affair" that was to follow. Rosa, however, was not ready for her new husband to be all that eager to leave her and take to the field of battle. In May 1861, Mary Ann Cobb wrote to her husband, Howell,

At Sister M's[27] I saw Mrs. W. G. Deloney. She is rebellious at the thought of *her* husband going in to the Army. Bad as my trial is and heavy as the crosses I have to bear, I could not exchange lots with her because she cannot *see* her *duty* for the selfishness that stands between and she cannot bring her *will* (tho strong in other things) to bear upon this one painful duty. She says "she has no patriotism when it comes to parting with *her husband* when *he* goes her all goes, having no near relations to look to." I made a broadside thrust at her in my usually abrupt & decided manner, "You could not have him stay at home and be *disgraced*?" Oh no said she, but she could *not* part with him. Well said I, the trial will come sooner or later. The longer postponed the greater the trial. She remarked that what she hated was that such a vile crew was first formed to fight against the *very flower* of *our* country. Yes, said I, "and *you intend* to keep *your flower* at home." She could not help laughing heartily over the idea. For ridiculous it is, indeed.[28]

Events now began careening seemingly out of control. On 12 April, South Carolina forces in Charleston Harbor opened up a thirty-four-hour bombardment on US forces at Fort Sumter. Just two days after the bombardment began, Lincoln called on the states still loyal to the Union to supply a quota of 75,000 men each to suppress the rebellion. With that, Virginia seceded on 17 April, followed by Arkansas on 6 May, North Carolina on 20 May, and finally Tennessee on 8 June. The opposing sides were finally set and both began their preparations.

Over the next four months, as the opposing sides organized and prepared, so too did the individuals who would fight this war. Thomas Cobb began his preparations from Richmond, where he was serving as a Georgia representative in the Confederate legislature.[29] Cobb started making preparations in May to form a legion, a combined-arms force of infantry, cavalry, and artillery.[30] In June, Cobb wrote Geor-

---

[27] Marion Cobb, wife of Thomas R. R. Cobb.

[28] Mary Ann Cobb to Howell Cobb, 17 May 1861, Howell Cobb Papers.

[29] Cobb served as the chairman of the Judiciary Committee, and due to his previous experience in authoring the new Georgia State Constitution in 1860, he became the main author of the Confederate Constitution. See William B. McCash, *Thomas R. R. Cobb: The Making of a Southern Nationalist* (Macon, GA: Mercer University Press, 2004).

[30] The term "Legion" and how T. R. R. Cobb came to decide upon that particular unit designation is open to speculation, but since Cobb was such a student of the classics and ancient history, he was very familiar with Roman history. The legion was the basic military unit of the ancient

gia governor Joseph Brown, "Mr. Hodgson goes to Milledgeville to get an order from you for accoutrements &c. I have said nothing to him, but the idea struck me that I should be very glad if you would allow me to order from him the necessary equipment for my Regt of Voltigeurs."[31] A few days later, Cobb wrote his brother to push President Jefferson Davis for arms for his legion: "If Prest Davis decides in favor of a Legion rather than a Regt. of Voltigeurs I should like to have Stanley's Artillery Co attached as a part of the Legion. I can get enough of them to go *for the war* to keep the Corps organized. If Mr Davis refuses Cavalry altogether from me, see if you can secure arms for a Regt of Foot from me."[32] A few days later, Cobb's plan for his legion began to crystallize in a letter to his brother: "I am 'on thorns' to hear from the Prest. Brown has placed me so that I can get only 300 carbines from him. My idea *now* is for a *Legion*, 300 horse 600 foot & 100 Artillery. I hope to get arms *for all* from Brown. Is not Georgia entitled to 'a Legion'? I propose to call it the 'Georgia Legion.'"[33]

Over the next couple of weeks, men throughout Athens and the surrounding region rushed to the recruiting tables to sign up. Both of the Athens newspapers ran notices for the recruiting of various units. Because of Thomas Cobb's notoriety within the state, his legion was a popular unit. Many in Athens, Augusta, and other closely surrounding areas flocked to his call for men.

The Southern Watchman
Delony's Cavalry

Wm. G. Delony, Esq., is now raising a Cavalry company in this and adjoining counties, to form a part of Cobb's Legion. As Gov. Brown has promised to arm and equip the Legion, there will be no difficulty on that

---

Roman army, and because of the tremendous military successes of the Roman Republic and later Empire, the legion was held by many military experts of the mid-nineteenth century as the model of military efficiency and ability. The Roman Legion typically consisted of three components: infantry, cavalry, and auxiliaries. One of the strengths of the legion was that it was self-contained, able to operate either in conjunction with other legions or on their own as a "mini" army. A single, integrated command gave them this strength.

[31] Thomas R. R. Cobb to Gov. Joseph Brown, 8 June 1861, T. R. R. Cobb Papers. In 1804, Napoleon created military units called "Voltigeurs." These lightly armed infantry units were designed to proceed to a battle as cavalry and then dismount to fight on foot. This creation enabled more troops to be moved faster and to be brought to bear on a weakened portion of an opponent's line at a much quicker moment, thus giving the attacker an advantage.

[32] Thomas R. R. Cobb to Howell Cobb, 14 June 1861, T. R. R. Cobb Papers. Cobb's "Regiment of Foot" was a British military designation for heavy infantry (more heavily armed than Voltigeurs). The strength of an army during this period lay in the army's heavy infantry.

[33] Thomas R. R. Cobb to Howell Cobb, 15 June 1861, T. R. R. Cobb Papers.

score. Let those who wish to join a Cavalry company report to Mr. Delony at once.[34]

The Southern Watchman

Cobb's Legion: The Chronicle & Sentinel says: A letter has just shown us from T. R. R. Cobb, in which he modestly prefers that the Regiment of Voltigeurs now organizing for service, be called the "Georgia Legion." We beg leave to differ with Mr. Cobb, and, in common with many others, had rather stick to the original title. Why not? We have: "Hampton's Legion" in South Carolina, "Wise's Legion" in Virginia, &c.

"Cobb's Legion" has been accepted by President Davis, and will be mustered into service very soon. It will contain four companies of horse. Our spirited corps, the Richard Hussars, Capt. Stovall, have been awarded the first position. They will do honorable and gallant service in the field.[35]

Southern Banner

Hon. T. R. R. Cobb's Legion: Mr. Delony, of our town, is endeavoring to raise a Cavalry company from this and surrounding counties, with a fair prospect of success—for the purpose of joining Mr. Cobb's Legion. As there is no doubt of his company being armed by Gov. Brown, it gives an opportunity to every man, desiring to join a cavalry company, to go into immediate service. We hope that the company will be immediately made out of the fine material to be found in this and the neighboring counties, and we doubt not that the gallant boys of this section of our State will promptly rally to the call.[36]

Augusta Daily Chronicle & Sentinel

We are glad to hear Tom Cobb's Legion is rapidly organized. It will be composed of four cavalry companies and one artillery and six or eight infantries. Gov. Brown will arm the entire legion. The government will furnish saddles, bridles, housing, martingales, etc., but each member must furnish his own horse, the government paying hire monthly, and also for the horse, if killed. This is a first rate chance for our hardy and fearless riders and good shots in Richmond, Columbia and adjoining counties to secure one of the best places in the picture. The Legion will doubtless be at

---

[34] *The Southern Watchman* (26 June 1861).
[35] Ibid.
[36] Ibid.

the seat of war in some six or seven weeks, and should be drilling every day.[37]

Augusta Daily Chronicle & Sentinel

The Richmond Hussars are enlisting mounted men for the war, to go in Col. Thos. R. R. Cobb's Legion. Monthly compensation for the hire of horses will be given, and if horses are lost, will be paid for by the government. Each member will be furnished with a Sharpe's carbine, revolver, sabre, belt, saddle, bridle, martingale, bit and canteen. Pay for privates, $12 per month. All applications must be made up forthwith. Thomas P. Stovall, Captain, Commanding Richmond Hussars[38]

The Southern Watchman

"Tom Cobb's Legion" will be composed of four cavalry companies, six or eight infantry companies, and one artillery. Delony's cavalry, raised in Clarke and surrounding counties, the "Richmond Hussars," Capt. Stovall of Augusta, will be two of the cavalry companies. We have not learned where the others are from.

The Legion will serve during the war, and we learn from the Chronicle & Sentinel will be commanded as follows: T. R. R. Cobb, Colonel, Maj. Smith, formerly of the U.S.A. Lieut. Col., and _____ Cross, also a late U.S. Officer, Major.[39]

Delony worked feverishly, scouting through Clarke, Madison, Jackson, and Hall counties for "good men and mounts to join his cavalry unit." At a public meeting "held at Parker's Store" in Hart County, Georgia, Delony delivered an "eloquent and patriotic address" to the Poole Volunteers "upon the platform of the Depot, just before their departure."[40] As men hurried to sign up for the cavalry, by 4 July, Delony had enough recruits to advertise for company elections for officers. As reported in the Athens *Southern Banner*, the new recruits were ordered to turn out at the Athens Town Hall for the elections.[41]

[37] *Augusta Daily Chronicle & Sentinel* (27 June 1861).
[38] Ibid. (28 June 1861).
[39] *Southern Watchman* (3 July 1861).
[40] Ibid. (31 July 1861).
[41] Stegeman, *These Men She Gave*, 27–28; *Southern Watchman* (3 July 1861); *Southern Banner* (3 July 1861).

Southern Banner

The Cavalry Company now forming in this place and the adjoining counties, held an election for commissioned officers last Thursday, with the following result:

W. G. Delony, Captain

James B. Lyle, 1st Lieut.

Thomas Williams, of Jackson, 2d Lieut.

The other officers will not be elected until the company's ranks are full. Those wishing to join have but little time to spare, as it is rapidly filling up.[42]

Back in Richmond, Thomas Cobb, taking his seat in the Confederate legislature, awaited the men as they proceeded to Virginia to join his Legion Infantry and Cavalry. In the meantime, "the soldiers are pouring in here," he wrote his wife in late July. "I came from Petersburg with 600 and left 2,000 waiting for cars to come."[43]

The cavalry companies began arriving quickly. "The Richmond Hussars is now a full company, as regards to men, but about fifteen more horses are required. Let those who are able to step forward and supply the deficiency, so that the Hussars may take the field, a pride and an honor to Augusta."[44]

At the same time, Delony's Georgia Troopers were also coming together under his spirited leadership. On 1 August, the men assembled at the fairgrounds in Athens, where they established their initial camp. The *Southern Banner* described Delony as a strikingly handsome lawyer and "as gallant a man as ever bestrode a horse."[45] At the same time, *The Southern Watchman* also ran a notice asking for additional recruits to fill the ranks: "There are a few vacancies in this company. Men are furnished everything except a horse, 1 pr. wool pants, 1 jacket or coat, 3 pr. woolen socks...1 pr. coarse boots, 1 pr. shoes, 1 blanket for horse, or overcoat, 2 woolen shirts, cotton shirts, curry-comb and brush."[46]

---

[42] *Southern Banner* (10 July 1861).
[43] Thomas R. R. Cobb to Marion Cobb, 21 July 1861, T. R. R. Cobb Papers.
[44] *Augusta Daily Chronicle & Sentinel* (16 July 1861).
[45] *Southern Banner* (24 July 1861).
[46] *Southern Watchman* (24 July 1861).

The Southern Watchman

Delony's Cavalry" This fine company, belonging to "Tom Cobb's Legion," is now encamped at the Fair Grounds in the neighborhood of this town, and drilling daily. Numbers of citizens go out every evening to witness their drilling, as cavalry drill is rather a novelty here. They will go on to Virginia shortly.[47]

For the next two weeks the Georgia Troopers camped, organized, and drilled as they prepared for their departure for Virginia and what was sure to be a quick war. On the 8th, a request was made to the Augusta paper for "competent musicians [who] are invited to join in organizing a full Brass Band to go into immediate service with Cobb's famous legion." Two days later, the paper announced that "Hon. T. R. R. Cobb arrived in town yesterday. His 'Legion' will soon be in readiness for duty in the field."[48] There was just one more item that needed to be carried out for Thomas Cobb's Legion. "We are requested by the Chaplain of Cobb's Georgia Legion," wrote another newspaper a few days later, "to ask contributions of pocket bibles, Sunday School Union Hymn books, and tracts for the Legion. It is impossible to buy these now, and yet nearly every family can spare a Bible for the knapsack, one or more hymn books, and loose or unused tracts, in various numbers. Anything will be greatly appreciated; it will be bread cast upon the waters." [49]

A few days later, Cobb wrote to his wife, "It is now midnight and for the first time since I got into my room have I been free from company.... I have made the Circuit of the City again today while visiting the wounded Georgians,[50] and receive every hour telegrams from anxious friends which I am compelled to attend to. You can well imagine that these duties in addition to my Congressional labors in the fixing up of my Legion, keep me engaged every hour."[51]

On 14 August, the Georgia Troopers left on the 11 o'clock train bound for Virginia and their awaiting commander. Upon arrival, each man was mustered into Confederate service and, at the age of 34, William G. Delony was made a captain "for the war" in Cobb's Legion Cavalry.[52] "I am very much pleased with my cap-

---

[47] Ibid. (7 August 1861).

[48] *Augusta Daily Chronicle & Sentinel* (8, 10, and 14 August 1861).

[49] *Southern Banner* (8 August 1861).

[50] The "wounded Georgians" Cobb is referring to are those men in the 7th and 8th Georgia Infantry who took part in the Battle of Bull Run on 21 July.

[51] Thomas R. R. Cobb to Marion Cobb, 24 July 1861, T. R. R. Cobb Papers.

[52] *Southern Watchman* (14 August 1861). The cavalry of Cobb's Georgia Legion was originally composed of four, then six, companies originating from the counties of Richmond, Fulton, Clarke, Hall, Jackson, Lumpkin, Dougherty, Cobb, Gwinnett, and Burke. Five more companies were added later. From July 1862 until the end of the war, the legion cavalry fought under the

tains," wrote Cobb to his wife on the 19th. "Every one seems to do his best to aid me in all my plans."[53]

The Southern Watchman

"Georgia Troopers" This fine cavalry company, under command of our townsman, Capt. Wm. G. Delony, left this place on an extra train on Thursday morning last, on their way to Virginia. We expect to hear a good account of them as soon as they have an opportunity to show the stuff they are made of. They had been encamped some two weeks at the Fair Grounds in the vicinity of this place; and their good conduct had won the admiration of all our citizens.[54]

While away from each other for the war, Will and Rosa remained faithful letter writers. The Georgia Troopers, or "Delony's Company," as it was known, was absorbed into the legion and redesignated "Company C." The legion cavalry was originally organized with four well-equipped companies. Eventually, the number of companies in the legion cavalry was increased to eleven.

* * *

Athens Nov 23rd 1860

Dearest Will,

I suppose while I am writing you, you are on your way to Columbus or already there ready for the speech making tomorrow. I hope you will make a good speech, but if all come who are invited you will not have time to say very much. We are all quite well. Tom was lively as usual gotten over his temporary indisposition. Little Willie is very sweet, begins to notice and coo a great deal, but is a little fat. It is turning very cold and the wind blowing a perfect gale, but very cosy and warm it is in our little dining room and if the old fellow was only in it with us I could even

---

command of Wade Hampton. In July 1864, the cavalry was reorganized with one company transferred to the Phillips's Legion Cavalry and Cobb's Legion Cavalry being redesignated as the Georgia 9th Cavalry Regiment. The new designation, however, did not sit well with the men, and they continued to refer to themselves as "Cobb's Legion Cavalry." The cavalry participated in over twenty actions, including Antietam, Fredericksburg, Brandy Station, Gettysburg, the Wilderness, Spotsylvania Court House, Petersburg, the Carolinas Campaign, and Bentonville (March 1865). At Brandy Station in 1863, the legion cavalry's reputation rose to even greater heights as they swept down the hill to save J. E. B. Stuart's headquarters, which was about to be captured in some of the hardest hand-to-hand combat by cavalry during the war. Brandy Station remains the greatest cavalry fight ever fought in North America. The legion cavalry was surrendered by Joseph E. Johnston at Durham Station, North Carolina, on 26 April 1865.

[53] T. R. R. Cobb to Marion, 19 August 1861, T. R. R. Cobb Papers.

[54] *Southern Watchman* (21 August 1861).

enjoy the wind. George got his left hand mashed last week and instead of coming to me went to Mrs. White, she gave him some salve but he did not take the care of it he should and although it is not a very serious bruise, yet enough so to take care of the joints of three fingers. I made him stay home yesterday and today and do nothing and keep it polticed, he can't cut any more wood till it has healed.

Addie Moore's Intended arrived today and I think the wedding will be tomorrow night, she has been in bed ever since she heard that he was sick, an unfortunate occurrence truly and short somewhat of the usual romance. It will be cold enough tomorrow, elegant weather for meat if any comes. I have very little that is new to tell you and you must excuse a short letter after so many long ones. I wish you would all make haste and adjourn at Milledgeville for I am so anxious to see you. All write in love to you. Little Rosa, Tom, and Willie send much love, and lots of sweet kisses to dear Papa, and me too, Darling.

Good night
Your own Rosa

Milledgeville
December 10, 1860

My Dear Rosa,

I wrote you by Mr Cobb which letter I hope reached you this morning. I have not heard a word from home since I left you and feel great anxiety about all of you and especially yourself. I do most sincerely hope that [all] are well and that I shall hear by this days mail. I do not think that we shall be able to adjourn before Wednesday week. We are very far behind and even at that time I do not think we shall have gotten through with the business of the session. We get on slowly.

I could not go as Early as I wrote you much to my regret as matters of importance are coming up and my friends pretested against my leaving. Tomorrow the Legislature are going over to Macon to attend the Cotton planters Convention.[55] I shall not go but remain here to prepare a speech to deliver in Greensboro on Friday night. I am invited to come over there on that day by our friends to address a meeting to be then held. I wish I could come up to Athens, but it will be impossible as I must be here on Saturday so that you must write to me to Greensboro on Friday morning. Be sure to do it, so that I can hear from home. I am very anxious to come

---

[55] The "Cotton Planters Convention" was a type of fair held in different locations in different Southern states at this time. The convention brought together manufacturers from across the region to discuss items of mutual interest, such as finance, tariffs, currency regulations, and direct trade with Europe. The convention displayed many items domestically produced within the region, along with "Secession Bonnets" and "Secession Badges" for the patriotic man and woman.

home, and it is all important for the members to return home. My opinion is that we are on the verge of revolution, not a peaceful one, but a bloody war. I see no hope for any other course, the Black Republicans seem determined to pursue their ruinous policy and I trust that the people of Georgia will endorse the policy of the secessionists as we are called. I will not close this until the mail opens.

Monday night: Today's mail has brot me no letter. What has become of you?
Your own
Will

GEORGIA TROOPERS—MUSTER ROLL[56]

OFFICERS

Colonel—Thomas R. R. Cobb

W. G. Delony, Captain, Clarke County

J. R. Lyle, 1st Lieutenant, Clarke County

T. C. Williams, 2d Lieutenant,
Jackson County

J. E. Rich, 3d Lieutenant, Clarke County

John A. Wimpy, 1st Sergeant,
Lumpkin County

J. C. Rutherford, 2d Sergeant,
Clarke County

Quartermaster—F. Watkins

D. E. Smith, 3d Sergeant, Hall County

M. Simmons, 4th Sergeant, Hall County

E. D. Cowan, 1st Corporal,
Jackson County

W. D. Simmons, 2d Corporal,
Jackson County

S. T. Whelchel, 3d Corporal,
Hall County

Willie E. Church, 4th Corporal,
Clarke County

PRIVATES

Geo. G. Bowman	Hall	W. J. Helton	Lumpkin
J. J. Bishop	Hall	J. J. Turner	Lumpkin
J. J. Head	Hall	M. M. Bell	Lumpkin
F. M. Whelchel	Hall	F. Chandler	Jackson
A. R. Thompson	Hall	John H. Cowan	Jackson
W. H. Read	Hall	N. B. Nash	Jackson
B. T. Gundle	Hall	J. W. David	Jackson
J. T. Glenn	Hall	R. L. Nash	Jackson
R. W. Goudelock	Hall	C. T. Cash	Jackson
N. M. Anderson	Hall	J. R. Nash	Jackson
M. W. Anderson	Hall	J. G. Sharp	Jackson
J. H. Garner	Hall	F. J. Whitehead	Jackson

---

[56] *Southern Watchman* (14 August 1861).

J. M. Cooper	Hall	H. S. Bradley	Madison
A. S. Whelchel	Hall	S. J. Johnson	Madison
E. P. Bedell	Hall	M. D. L. Pitman	Madison
E. S. House	Hall	S. Bailey	Clarke
M. V. B. House	Hall	W. C. Bone	Clarke
T. Gower	Hall	C. R. A. Harris	Clarke
D. O. Connor	Hall	Richard More	Clarke
J. S. Blackwell	Lumpkin	M. W. Riden	Clarke
J. T. Fields	Lumpkin	Phillip Wray	Clarke
J. Blackburn	Lumpkin	Walter Wray	Clarke
R. Barrett	Lumpkin	J. P. Cherry	Clarke
W. T. Barrett	Lumpkin	A. L. Harper	Clarke
Wm. H. Earley	Lumpkin	W. C. Howard	Oglethorpe
Wm. F. Earley	Lumpkin	W. R. Lord	Oglethorpe
A. W. Earley	Lumpkin	T. R. Tuck	Oglethorpe
J. M. Anderson	Lumpkin	Madison Bell	Banks
W. E. Anderson	Lumpkin	J. B. Riley	Banks
T. J. McCurray	Lumpkin	H. F. Jones	Thomas
S. M. McCurray	Lumpkin	L. P. Thomas	Greene
D. R. Parks	Lumpkin	O. H. Prince	Cass
A.B.C. Densmore	Lumpkin	B. R. Moseley	Madison, Fla.
A. D. Bruce	Lumpkin		

BATTALION STAFF

Lieut. Colonel—R. H. Garnett	Commissary—T. M. Lampkin
Major—E. F. Bagley	Surgeon—S. G. White, M.D.
Adjutant—P. M. B. Young	Assist Surgeon—Jos. Hatton, M.D.
Sergeant Major—J. C. Floyd	Chaplain—R. K. Porter

Chapter 3

Learning the Trade:
August 1861–December 1861

When you go out to war against your enemies,
and see horses and chariots and an army larger than your own,
you shall not be afraid of them, for the Lord your God is with you.
            —Deuteronomy 20:1

He sat on his charger grandly, his fine physique and full mahogany beard flowing, he looked a very Titan war god, flushed with the exhuberance and exhiliration of victory.... He was a symmetrically built, distinctively handsome man, of commanding mien in any company of commanding characters; his full brown or mahogany beard and high massive forehead, intellectual face and eagle eyes, marked him as a man among men, resembling the finer full bearded engravings I have seen of Stonewall Jackson. The world never produced a better, braver soldier, truer patriot or grander hero than William G. DeLoney.[1]

Wylie Howard enlisted in the legion's Georgia Troopers as a private during the creation of the unit in August 1861. Twenty-two years old, he was typical of most of the early enlistees: young, energetic, and well educated. Like his commanding officers, Howard was a lawyer and served in the legion throughout the war, rising to the rank of lieutenant by the time the unit surrendered at Greensboro, North Carolina, in April 1865. Howard penned the best account of Cobb's Georgia Legion in 1901.[2]

Thomas Cobb kept his wife, Marion, informed of the goings and comings of his legion. It took the Georgia Troopers six days to arrive in Richmond, where they were eagerly met by their commander. "Tuesday Morning: Delony's company came yesterday and are all well. Stovall's and Yancey's will be here today or tomorrow.

---

[1] See Wiley C. Howard, "Sketch of Cobb Legion Cavalry and Some Incidents and Scenes remembered" (Atlanta: Camp 159, published talk given at U.C.V. meeting) 19 August 1901, 24–25. and Harriet Bey Mesic, *Cobb's Legion Cavalry: A History and Roster of the Ninth Georgia Volunteers in the Civil War* (Jefferson, NC: McFarland, 2009).

[2] Ibid.

The want of saddles alone will keep me from reporting ready for service."[3] The Richmond Hussars arrived in Petersburg from Augusta later that evening.[4] Col. Cobb wrote his wife the following day: "Capt. Yancey came today. Stovall will come over tomorrow. Congress will not adjourn before next Wednesday. I cannot move until I get my saddles. They may furnish them to me here.... Deloney's Company are all well with slight exceptions." "Stovall's company is here," he wrote her on the 25th, "and my legion is now complete as to numbers."[5]

The legion cavalry became Thomas Cobb's pride and joy, which he expressed regularly to his wife. "My Cavalry companies are the admiration of the city. They do make a very fine appearance. My companies are all doing very well and I think I shall be proud of them." The following day, he again wrote Marion that "I am proud of my Legion. I held the election yesterday for officers. Not a vote was cast against me.... Deloney is very well and doing *excellently*. He has a fine company."[6] Two weeks later, Cobb wrote his wife, "I had my first review today of my entire corps. I confess to you I was proud of my command as I rode down the line. They did excellently well. A goodly number of ladies and gentlemen were out to see them."[7]

Cobb was hard at work during the last two weeks of August organizing his legion and making arrangements for family members. "Miller[8] requested me to have him transferred to my Legion to join Deloney's company," he wrote his wife. "By hard begging I succeeded in getting it done today. He goes down to Portsmouth tomorrow to get up his goods and chattels and will return in a few days. I am very glad that I shall have all the boys with me. I can do some good in that way if in no other."[9]

Cobb's Legion, including both infantry and cavalry, were brigaded together in what would become "Cobb's Brigade," under overall command of Howell Cobb, Thomas Cobb's older brother. The brigade camp, known as Camp Cobb, was located on the racetrack of the old Richmond fairgrounds about a mile from the statehouse.[10] The men within the various regiments brigaded there complained of the filth and lack of sanitation. With so many men in such close quarters, it was a

---

[3] Thomas R. R. Cobb to Marion, 22 August 1861, T. R. R. Cobb Papers.

[4] *Augusta Daily Chronicle & Sentinel* (22 August 1861).

[5] Thomas R. R. Cobb to Marion, 23, 25 August 1861, T. R. R. Cobb Papers. For more on Benjamin C. Yancy and Thomas P. Stovall see Biographical Roster.

[6] Thomas R. R. Cobb to Marion, 25, 26, 27 August 1861, T. R. R. Cobb Papers.

[7] Ibid., 2 September 1861.

[8] Miller Lumpkin was Thomas Cobb's brother-in-law. See Biographical Roster.

[9] Thomas R. R. Cobb to Marion, 22 August 1861, T. R. R. Cobb Papers.

[10] William S. Smedlund, *Camp Fires of Georgia Troops, 1861–1865* (Lithonia, GA: Kennesaw Mountain Press, 1994) 92.

simply a matter of time before disease began to run rampant within the ranks. On the 29th, Cobb wrote his wife that "the measles are extending in my camp. I have 57 reported sick this morning. Howell has more than double that number. None of Deloney's men are sick enough to be called to my attention."[11] Cobb later wrote his wife, "I have noticed one thing in my short experience: The Cavalry service does not seem to induce sickness like the infantry. There are three of the latter sick to one of the former. It is attributed partly to the proximity of the horses and partly to the nature of the exercise taken by them. My observation confirms also what I have heard from others about the health of town and country boys. The latter suffer much more from sickness. One of my companies, entirely from the country, has more than half sick."[12] Cobb anticipated the adverse conditions of camp life on his men, appointing Dr. Joseph Hatton as the legion's assistant surgeon.[13]

Thomas Cobb's next difficulties came as he pondered the decision of who to select as his lieutenant colonel, his second-in-command. This position needed to be filled by an officer of experience and good judgement, something Cobb believed he had found when he wrote his wife,

> I am writing in my tent after a hard days work, but it has relieved me of several troubles and I feel compensated. I have a Lt. Col. at last and one 'that was offered a Colonel's commission but said he preferred being Lt. Col. under me to commanding a Regt. himself. He is Capt. Thomas E. Jackson of South Carolina and has been fourteen years in the U.S. Service, since his graduation at West point. The commissions were ordered to day to him, Maj. Bagley and myself. So we are getting organized.[14]

His selection of Jackson as lieutenant colonel did not work out as he hoped, though, as ten days later he was again writing Marion of his distress: "To my great regret I discovered last night that the gentleman selected as my Lt. Colonel (Jackson of So. Ca.) had been drunk for *five days*. He had not yet been appointed, so I went to see him this morning and frankly told him I could not receive him. I am again at sea for an officer. What a terrible curse liquor is! I had no conception how prevalent the voice of drunkenness was in the army."[15]

It didn't take long for Cobb to find a replacement for Jackson. "I am now regularly installing in command of my legion," wrote Cobb.

---

[11] Thomas R. R. Cobb to Marion, 29 August 1861, T. R. R. Cobb Papers.

[12] Ibid., 25 September 1861.

[13] *Augusta Daily Chronicle & Sentinel* (24 August 1861).

[14] Thomas R. R. Cobb to Marion, 22 August 1861, T. R. R. Cobb Papers.

[15] Ibid., 31 August 1861.

My Congressional labors closed last night near midnight. This morning I put on my uniform and took entire command of my camp. I have had Capt. Garnett (cousin of B. T. Hunter) appointed Lt. Col. of my regiment, and he will be out in a few days to assist me. Prest. Davis has consented to give me a Major of Cavalry, but I have not as yet selected him. My adjutant (Young) has been elected Lt. Colonel to Benning's regiment and thus I shall lose him. This puts me at sea again for a very important officer.[16]

Two days later, determined not to lose an experienced officer, Cobb made an offer to his adjutant, Pierce M. B. Young: "I have determined to keep my adjutant (Young) by appointing him Major of my Cavalry. He is a fine young officer, and commands the admiration of all the men. I am well pleased with my new Lt. Col. Garnett. He is a perfect gentleman. I apprehend no trouble from any of them."[17] According to Young's memoirs, "I accepted on the condition that the captains of the cavalry companies would request me in person to accept the position. These gentlemen...were Ben Yancey, Wm. Lawton, Thos. P. Stovall and Wm. G. Delony. After a long consultation with Colonel Cobb they came to my quarters and made the request."[18]

The legion spent the first two weeks of September 1861 honing their skills in drilling. Their preparations were cut short when the legion was ordered to the Williamsburg area as part of the Army of the Peninsula under Gen. John B. "Prince John" Magruder on 12 September. "Today I started my cavalry to march to Yorktown formed in line, with 19 baggage wagons," wrote Cobb. "It made a very imposing spectacle. I went with them four miles to get them under way. The sun was boiling hot, but I perspired freely and felt no bad effects from it. I regretted much that I was compelled to violate the Sabbath. Today has been far from a day of rest."[19]

Cobb's new camp, Camp Washington, was established 2 miles southeast of Williamsburg, just beside the Temple farm in York County, Virginia,[20] but he had to wait on the arrival of the cavalry after Magruder had them stopped at Williamsburg. For the next several days, the legion cavalry floundered in Williamsburg. Cobb reported to his wife the evening of the 19th, "My cavalry has not come in, and

---

[16] Ibid., 1 September 1861.

[17] Ibid., 3 September 1861.

[18] Lynwood M. Holland, *Pierce M. B. Young: The Warwick of the South* (Athens: University of Georgia Press, 1964) 54–55.

[19] Thomas R. R. Cobb to Marion, 15 September 1861, T. R. R. Cobb Papers.

[20] Smedlund, *Camp Fires*, 284.

I am satisfied from rumors that I hear that Genl. Magruder has stopped it at Williamsburg and ordered it into camp."[21]

Early the next morning, as Cobb wrote Marion,

> I ordered my horse, elected Capt. Knight as my escort, loaded all my pistols and with Jesse[22] behind bade farewell to my camp to hunt for my cavalry. We had not gone a mile before we met the advance guard of the cavalry coming in. Genl. Magruder stopped them in Williamsburg for two days and then without assigning a cause ordered them to proceed this morning. All came in in good health and fine spirits, after a long pleasant trip.... Genl. Magruder has promised to give my cavalry a tour through the Peninsula and I intend to make it with them. I suppose he will let them recruit for a few days. The officers were very much pleased with him. They say he is perfectly sober (does not touch a drop) and a perfect gentleman. He told them the "Cobb Legion" had a great reputation to sustain, and that the Cavalry came fully up to that reputation.[23]

While the cavalry were in the process of relocating to Williamsburg, recruiting was going on back at home for additional troopers for the legion:

Georgia Troopers! Recruits Wanted

> The Georgia Troopers, Capt. Wm. G. Delony, now in service in Virginia, attached to Cobb's Legion, are in need of about 20 more men. Persons desiring to join will please report their names to James A. Sledge, at the Southern Banner office, or to the undersigned. Recruits must furnish themselves with a good horse, saddle, bridle, three hickory shirts, two or three pair drawers, socks, and a suit of clothes, such as they may have on hand. Uniforms will be furnished.

> Thomas House. Sept. 18, 1861[24]

Meanwhile, back on the peninsula, the legion was busy reconnoitering the area. On 25 September, Cobb sent captains Delony and Lawton with a detachment of eighty men to survey from their camp down to the beach area. Two days later, Cobb reported, "My scouting expedition returned today all safe and sound, having been in sight of Hampton. They stayed two nights at Bethel Church." During their stay, Delony's men had their first encounter with a new enemy: "The Yankees had occu-

---

[21] Thomas R. R. Cobb to Marion, 19 September 1861, T. R. R. Cobb Papers.

[22] Jesse was a slave of Thomas R. R. Cobb. See Biographical Roster.

[23] Thomas R. R. Cobb to Marion, 20 September 1861, T. R. R. Cobb Papers.

[24] *Southern Watchman* (18 September 1861); *Southern Banner* (18 September 1861).

pied [the place] previously and had left so many fleas that my men say they would rather have fought the Yankees than the fleas."[25]

Delony was quickly becoming the person on whom Cobb relied to get things done within the legion. On the 28th, Cobb dispatched Delony and Stovall, with twelve men and a wagon, to a nearby house, which was suspected by Col. Cobb as the source of some liquor recently discovered in the camp. According to Cobb, "It came from four men living in houses in the neighborhood." Delony seized all he could find, reported Cobb, and the men made no resistance, but "two strapping fat women gave him a terrible tongue-lashing."[26] The detachment seized about thirty gallons of the "genuine poisoned stuff." Being a former leader of the Temperance Society in Georgia, Cobb kept a close eye out for spirits, continuing to police his camp of all liquors and sending out detachments periodically whenever he caught wind of any in camp.

Thomas Cobb reported the position of his Legion to Marion in a letter on 1 October. "I hear tonight that we will be ordered to 'Cockletown' in a day or two. This is about seven miles below here and about five miles this side of Bethel. It is in a line drawn from ship's Point on York River to Mulberry point on James River and on which line the General proposes to post several regiments. General McLaws will command on the James River. Col. Colquitt on the York and my Legion is to be stationed in the centre as an independent command."[27]

As plans were being made, back at Camp Washington, the officers seemed to be enjoying themselves.

> This morning two of the neighbors came in their fishing boats and invited me to sail out into the river and fish a while. Deloney, Stovall, Yancey and John Rutherford went with me.... We stayed about three hours and caught about one hundred and fifty nice fish. Spots, Flounders, Perch, Blackfish, Tailors, Hog fish, etc. etc. besides any quantity of crabs and oysters. Among other things drawn up was an oyster shell from which was growing a beautiful sea-weed. The latter was covered with little measuring worms, which soon perished away. I have preserved the shell and weed and hope to get a chance to send it to you. The flounder is a very curious fish. It looks precisely like a fish split in two, except that both eyes are on one side of it. I must believe the species to be a monstrosity. Nature does not thus her

---

[25] Thomas R. R. Cobb to Marion, 27 September 1861, T. R. R. Cobb Papers.

[26] Ibid., 6 October 1861.

[27] Ibid., 1 October 1861. "I am anxious to provide them [winter quarters] for my men. In a few days the cold nights here will give them pneumonia and other catarrhal affections. I want huts or houses to shelter them.... The prospect of a winter at 'Cockletown' (a miserable little cross roads with a few dilapidated houses) is far from pleasant to me. We can get no comforts, no supplies." Thomas R. R. Cobb to Marion, 5 October 1861, T. R. R. Cobb Papers.

work generally. Why two eyes? On different sides of the head, visibly for protection. On the same side, it is a monstrosity. The spider and fly may have a thousand fixed eyes, but these eyes are movable.[28]

During the early part of October, the men of the legion were busily building huts for their winter quarters at Camp Marion. While the construction went on, they stayed in a temporary camp known as Camp Mud Hole.[29] Writing from Camp Washington, Cobb reported,

> This morning was wet and blustery but as I had appointed to reconnoiter Cockletown for a camp, and the wind was from the N.W. I started my cavalcade at 8 o'clock. I took with me the officers commanding all of my companies and ten dragoons. The rain soon ceased though the sheltering clouds protected us all day. We were in the saddle until 1/2 past four this afternoon travelling over a little more than twenty miles. I selected a camp between 7 and 8 miles from Yorktown in the midst of a pine grove, where I knew I could build huts easily, and about one mile from the line across the Peninsula which Genl. Magruder has laid out as his fighting line. Cockletown is a miserable little hole with four or five mean houses, interspersed with marshy ponds, a black smith shop, a store and a bakery for the troops. My camp is two miles off. I shall have the use of a brick church near by as a hospital for my sick.[30]

The following day he again wrote his wife,

> I shall leave behind me about three hundred men, the sick and convalescent, whom I shall be afraid to expose to this weather. Major Young is sick and will remain with them. Mr. Porter is still in bed and will remain also. Dr. Hatton will remain to attend them. So this is my last letter from Camp Washington. My next camp will have a nobler name. It shall be Camp "Marion" and when the men ask me after whom I shall tell them the story of my noble wife.[31]

The legion began settling into their new camp about mid-October and developing their guard-duty routine. Always on the alert, the legion was finally roused on 14 October. Thomas Cobb reported,

> Night before last I was awoke by a courier with an order from Genl. Magruder. Two of my Cavalry companies were ordered to leave at daylight to

---

[28] Thomas R. R. Cobb to Marion, 2 October 1861, T. R. R. Cobb Papers.

[29] Ibid., 9 October 1861.

[30] Ibid., 8 October 1861. "Camp Washington" was named for George Washington, of whom Thomas Cobb was a descendant. See Smedlund, *Camp Fires*, 284.

[31] Thomas R. R. Cobb to Marion, 9 October 1861, T. R. R. Cobb Papers.

join an expedition towards Newport News, and the rest of the legion directed to take post on the line of defence four miles below our camp. I detailed Stovall's and Yancey's companies. The rest of us took position as ordered, remained there all day and bivouacked in the open air last night, returning to our camp this morning. Capt. Stovall was a little more lucky or unlucky. His company went down within seven miles of Newport News. With a detachment of eight men he went five miles farther and while reconnoitering found himself within one hundred yards of one hundred Yankees. He was on foot but got to his horse quickly and had to ride 150 yards with the whole body firing at him and his little squad. Fortunately none of them were injured. One ball passed through the coat sleeve of one of his men and another went through the cantle of the saddle of another. Col. Levy (of La.) who commanded the party would not pursue them and thus ended a skirmish which has been magnified into the "cutting up of Cobb's legion." It is wonderful how these stories grow.[32]

The following night was much the same as the previous.

About 3 o'clock a courier passed by and told some one that the enemy was on the march in force, and only about seven miles off. I scouted the idea and ordered a battalion drill of the Cavalry. We had been on the field about an hour when I heard volley after volley of musketry at Col. Winston's[33] camp about a mile on our left. I had agreed with the Col. this morning that we could mutually support each other. So I stopped the drill instantly, ordered the cavalry to get to their camp and prepare to leave at once, gave a similar order to the Infantry and sent a courier to Col. Winston to find out if he was really attacked. In ten minutes he returned telling me they were only shooting off their guns, which had been loaded under a mistake. So ended our second alarm in three days.[34]

One of Thomas Cobb's major concerns at this time had to do with the welfare of his men, and especially with regard to the care for the sick. In November, a request was made for the procurement of male nurses for the legion. In a letter to the Augusta newspaper, the editor, J. A. Ansley, wrote,

I am in receipt of a letter from the Chaplain of Col. T. R. R. Cobb's Legion, requesting assistance in the securement of six efficient male nurses for the relief and comfort of the suffering soldiery of the legion. He informs me that the average number of sick is about two hundred, and that with

---

[32] Ibid., 14 October 1861.
[33] Col. John Anthony Winston of Alabama. See Biographical Roster.
[34] Thomas R. R. Cobb to Marion, 15 October 1861, T. R. R. Cobb Papers.

only two surgeons it is impossible to give the requisite attention to them, such as administering medicine, nursing, etc. He refers to the labors of such nurses as likely to be arduous. These nurses will be regularly commissioned and paid by the Government. I am authorized to receive application for this service.[35]

With the exception of an occasional call to arms to meet the expected enemy, the legion continued to drill and build their winter quarter huts for the rest of October.[36] As they did so, the sicknesses within the legion began to diminish and so too did the deaths. Writing to Marion, Cobb reported, "Another death in camp last night, Chandler of Deloney's Co., one of the largest and heartiest men in the legion. He refused to take medicine from the first and his own imprudence in drinking too much water was at last the cause of his death. The sickness in my Legion is diminishing sensibly and my sick men generally are improving."[37]

The rather dullness of October was broken by two major events in November, which occurred on the 9th and 10th. The first involved the legion's initial military excursion as a coordinated unit, along with two regiments of infantry, additional companies of cavalry (in addition to the legion), and six pieces of artillery. Their foraging expedition headed toward Big Bethel Church. As Cobb reported in a letter to his wife,

> Two columns started off today from this point, one towards Newport News—the other toward Fortress Monroe. In the latter commanded by Genl. Magruder himself, my Legion occupied the post of honor. Two other regiments, besides several detached companies of cavalry, infantry and artillery made up the column. I took my post in the centre of the Legion, but the old Genl. sent for me to take the head of the column by his side. We had fifty wagons and went some four miles below where we soon pulled and filled the wagons with corn and returned to our camp. The men started off full of the idea that we would have a brush with the enemy, but when they found it was merely a corn-pulling, they were much discouraged. This operation I suppose we will repeat for four days to come, except that it is highly probable we shall not return every night. We will thus provide some six or eight thousand bushels of corn for our horses and shall keep the Yankees from getting it.[38]

The other event, a much more serious one, was the loss of both of Cobb's majors at the same time: one through death and one through promotion. This double-

---

[35] *Augusta Daily Chronicle & Sentinel* (2 November 1861).
[36] Thomas R. R. Cobb to Marion, 16, 21 October 1861. T. R. R. Cobb Papers.
[37] Ibid., 31 October 1861.
[38] Ibid., 9, 10 November 1861.

pronged event undoubtedly sent the legion into a state of uneasiness, and their commander into turmoil. "The death of Bagley[39] raised a stew about his successor, almost every Captain aspiring to the place," Cobb wrote his wife. He continued,

> I determined to get rid of it, by not filling the place at all. But yesterday when I had arranged all my matters to leave for Richmond, Col. Garnett received to his surprise and *my astonishment* a commission as Brigadier General.... I am without a single field officer. I have never been so troubled. I called together my officers and told them to recommend to me two from their own body and I would make them Major, promoting Young to be Lt. Colonel. They have been hammering at it for two days and have done nothing as yet. I notified them that if they did not recommend before I left, I should select for myself as soon as I reached Richmond and *outside of the Legion*. The officers of cavalry have just come in and announced they could not agree, but begged me to select for myself from the four Captains.[40]

One of the Captains, Z. A. Rice, penned a request and submitted it to Colonel Cobb on 22 November. "After meeting of 2 hours, failed to nominate for your appointment anyone voted & all Captains recvd. different ballots one vote short of an election 6 votes each—vote tied at 6 each—Capts Lawton and Yancey 'We therefore respectfully solicit that you appoint, for the sake of harmony one of our four Captains of the Cavalry.'"[41] That night Cobb confided to Marion, "If the infantry men agree as I think they will on *Knight* for their Major I shall take Yancey for the cavalry."[42]

The following day Thomas Cobb received a message from Will Delony:

> From our conversation this morning and your remarks tonight to the Cavalry Captains I feel constrained to believe that my name is embarrassing to you in the consideration of the vacant Majority in the Legion. Permit me to withdraw entirely from your consideration. After mature reflection I am well assured that the appointment or election of a senior Major for the cavalry battalion is essentially necessary to the well being of your Legion, and I am unwilling that my name should any longer embarrass your final decision.[43]

---

[39] Edward F. Bagley was major of Cobb's Legion Infantry. See Biographical Roster.

[40] Thomas R. R. Cobb to Marion, 22 November 1861, T. R. R. Cobb Papers.

[41] Z.A. Rice to Col. Cobb, 22 November 1861, "Letters Received," C. S. Sec. of War, M437, Roll 24, NARS.

[42] Thomas R. R. Cobb to Marion, 22 November 1861, T. R. R. Cobb Papers.

[43] W. G. Delony to Col. Cobb, 23 November 1861, "Letters Received," C. S. Sec. of War, M437, Roll 24, NARS.

The course of action that Cobb outlined to Marion came to fruition. Cobb appointed Capt. Benjamin C. Yancey of the Fulton Dragoons to major and Lt. Zachariah A. Rice succeeded Yancey as captain of the company. Cobb responded to Delony as he made his decision:

> You divined rightly my troubles. I *wanted to appoint* you as Major for your own sake and mine. I believe you to be the most military man, and eventually to make the best officer. On the contrary, Yancey has treated me with a great want of confidence in this matter, which I feel *deeply*. Still I was, after most mature and earnest thoughts impressed with the conviction that the place was due, to his age, position, and attainments, *taken all together*. Your note to me was most generous, such as I expected from you. Still, I have since crossed the matter over and over in my mind, for fear I was doing you injustice. If at last I have done it Captain, I beg you to remember how earnestly, I sought to avoid it. I write in haste, I find that my troubles are but begun. I fear that dissensions will arise in spite of all my care.[44]

"The cavalry officers failed and I selected Yancey," Thomas Cobb wrote Marion immediately after responding to Delony. "I hesitated between him and Deloney. The latter had all my personal preferences and I hated much not to give it to him."[45]

About the third week of November, Delony received a twenty-five day furlough to Georgia. During the time he was away from the legion a number of changes took place. The legion established a picket camp, known as "Camp Disappointment," on the peninsula below Camp Marion,[46] and various companies of the legion alternated back and forth between the two camps.

Thomas Cobb was greatly surprised by the state of the unit when he returned from a trip to Richmond. He wrote to Marion,

> I found my Legion in a much worse condition than even my fears had suggested. Nothing done since I left, no drills, no work, no discipline, no cordiality. The men were all depressed by Genl. Magruder's stampede from his line of defense and some few were ready to growl at me for the appointment of Majors. I regret to say that the man most petted and indulged by me in the Legion (Captain Knight) was at the bottom of the dis-

---

[44] Thomas R. R. Cobb to Delony, 26 November 1861, "Letters Received," C. S. Sec. of War, M437, Roll 24, NARS. See Appendix A.

[45] Thomas R. R. Cobb to Marion, 26 November 1861, T. R. R. Cobb Papers. Benjamin H. Yancey was the commander of Fulton Dragoons. See Biographical Roster.

[46] Smedlund, *Camp Fires*, 113; Tammy Harden Galloway, *Dear Old Roswell: The Civil War Letters of the King Family of Roswell, Georgia* (Macon, GA: Mercer University Press, 2003) 19.

satisfaction. Two Cavalry companies had been ordered off.... Yancey has done his best, but he is a slow coach.[47]

With the couple's absence from one another, the two tried to stay in touch as much as possible in order to ease their separation, if only until the next letter. Failing the arrival of the next letter, the anxieties that both felt tended to gnaw at their peace of mind. This situation would continue for the next two years.

* * *

Athens Oct 3rd 1861

My Dearest Will,

I received your letter of the 24th yesterday and shall feel truly thankful when I get another telling me that you have returned safe and well into Camp. I cant help feeling uneasy till I hear from you tho you say you are not going beyond our pickets. Darling dont eat oysters yet, and do be very prudent till frost which I hope may be soon about my coming to spend the winter with you, you know Darling it would be delightful to me. I can love any home in any kind of place with my old fellow and if you can get a place to put the children where they can have plenty of fire and be comfortable just let me know and whenever its practicable I am ready to come. When will you go into winter quarters and what do you call going into winter quarters, and about what time do you suppose you will want me? Darling a hovel with him is better than a palace without and that you know. I am sorry you cant get any thing good whenever I get an opportunity. I'll always send you something good. I could have sent you butter in your package if I had have known it was so scarce. Don't you want me to send you some sugar and coffee and the like. Darling will you have to go often on those expeditions? Where is the nearest point the enemy is to you? Will the children be in any danger of measles if I bring them on. Do many of the officers talk of having their families with them? All of us are well. The children send you a very sweet kiss. I will send you some ink by the first opportunity. Good bye Dear Darling. I cant write more now, wrote you yesterday. Jennie[48] sends love. A heart full from your own

Rosa

Dont your mother lose Dick by the sequestration act?[49]

---

[47] Thomas R. R. Cobb to Marion, 14 December 1861, T. R. R. Cobb Papers.

[48] Delony's sister-in-law, married to his brother, Robert. See Biographical Roster.

[49] Approved by the Confederate legislature on 31 August 1861, the Sequestration Act created a legal instrument by which property in the Confederacy belonging to Northern citizens could be confiscated by the government in payment to properties of Southern citizens seized by the United States government.

Athens Oct 6th 1861

My Dearest Will

I have just finished hearing dear little Rosa say her hymns and then she said her spelling lesson. You would be surprised to hear her spell, both in, and out of the book. She has learned some new hymns. We talk very often about dear absent Papa and I dont think they will forget you. Sunday is the hardest day to bear your absence and I sit and think of you until it seems as tho I could not get along without my own darling Will any more. I hope the trial may be shortened. I went out yesterday and got you an over-coat from Bloomfields[50] very much like your other. I saw no cloth that could make a better one so got that and will send it the very earliest opportunity for I am anxious you should have it. I asked Dick about the sash, he says he will need his and there are none to be had here. I sent to Mr. Henry Hull to see if I could get his, but he had given it to Harvey. If one is to be had here, or any where else I will get it. Did they steal your India Rubber[51] one too? I am truly sorry my letters reach you so irregularly, but it is not that they are not written and whenever they don't come you must know and not doubt it is the least that your little Scrap has certainly written you for I would not grieve your heart for any thing Darling and letters are the only comforting things these trying times. I have not failed to mail you a letter every other day since you left except in the case of the one sent by Mr. House and I explained in that why it was not sent when written. I hope you have received your comfort. Write me when you answer this, whether I shall send you any blankets. The stores here are almost empty of stuff for clothing so you must take good care of your things. I do hope Darling you will not have to go many times on those scouting parties just think of your being as near as 4 1/2 miles of the enemy. It frightens me just to think of it. How does John get along? And is he tired yet of military life? And what kind of bread does he make you? Dont you want me to send you some Yeast cakes? George always enquires about you and seems much interested. He is still cutting peas but he has had bad weather. (Sunday night) I have just come down from hearing Rosa say her prayers she called after me, "Mama dont forget to tell Papa to bring a true fine pony for Bubber Tom." Sometimes Hannah goes to the window and says I see Papa and such a scampering "me tee pa too," and Tom's little fat legs fly to the window. Willie says something that sounds very like "gone" when I say where is Papa Willie? He is perfectly beautiful and his little head is a mass of curls, he falls down without crying just like Tom, answers when he is called and says what he intends for yes when he is asked any questions. Jennie had a letter from Boston came thru Mr. Philips whose has recently left

---

[50] A clothing store in Athens owned by Robert Lee Bloomfield. See Biographical Roster.

[51] Boots or overcoats made of natural rubber.

Washington and had been read in one of the Gov departments, it had a likeness of Jennie in it very pretty but not equal to our Willie, one of those made to look at thru a stereoscope. You must take great care of yourself this fall weather especially at night. Have your cot in a comfortable place where the wind cant blow on you for pneumonia will be very common among you on the sea coast this fall and winter. Why dont you have a board platform made for your cot to rest on. Do Darling use every precaution that you possibly can to ward off disease and dont let your good health send you into security for cold weather will be hard on you. I hope it will be so that I can be with you to take care of you. Good night my own dear Will. All send love. Hal and Jennie send their very sweet kisses from little ones and a heart full of love from your own

Rosa

Athens Oct 31st (Thursday) 1861

My Dearest Will

I had my first trial to day attending to business, never knew till last night that to-day was the last day for receiving returns for the war tax and as I knew nothing at all about the valuation of things I sent for Mr. Mitchell and told him everything that I knew of that we had and what it cost when we bought them, and he valued them, and promised to attend to it. Just think your watch and mine, all the silver, piano, Carriage etc. I think it is an imposition myself.

Hue is two inefficient and I could not help telling him so last night. I returned $13,500 of Bonds, $9,375 owed by Father, House and lot, Shop and tract of land, Wood land, Up town lot, the servants, Silver, Carriage, Watches, piano. I could not tell him any thing about your notes, but he said he would fix it. I hope I have done every thing right. Havnt you paid your Co tax for the support of the Volunteers families, be sure and write me if you have. Mr. Carlton was here this morning to know about the receiving of your note in bank and if you had left a blank with me and says you must send it next time you write. If the Yankees are going to be taxed as we are, to carry on this war it will not last long. I think it an imposition upon a people who have given so freely voluntarily. I am trying to be as economical as possible but the high rates take every thing as fast as it comes, seems to me. I bought a small can of lard from Mr. Johnson who is going away and had to pay 10.62 1/2 for it. I thought I had better give that now, than run the risk of its rising still higher at the stores. We are all well Darling and having beautiful weather which the children are enjoying. Geo says he will get the wood house filled this week and is going to plant wheat next week and then haul wood for market. I have pickled two quarters of Beef and saved enough tallow to make a hundred pounds of soap. I am going to mould some Candles too. So you see I am trying to do something myself these hard times. Dick Taylor came to say good bye yesterday, leaves to day with the other Taylor for the Coast, he says he wrote you a business letter which you have never answered he would not tell me what he was going to be said it was a secret so I suppose he is going to be an officer, Field Officer possibly. The children are all playing in the yard and I can hear their merry little voices and wish you could too, little Willie as busy as any, does just what they do, comes every day for his sugar like Tom. Tom put a bench the other day to climb up to get something off the beaureau, first thing I know Willie had climbed up on the same bench, and was tipping up to get something, dont mind a knock at all. All send sweet kisses to you, they have not forgotten you, and shall not. The moment Willie sees your picture he says Pa. Good bye my dearest. Will, think often and sweetly of me and accept your own large share of love

From your own
Rosa

Athens Dec 13th 1861

My Darling Will

Only a line to-night. I have been interrupted, but my next shall be a long one. I can hardly believe you have been, and gone, such a delight anticipated and so short a realization. I have thought of you every mile of your journey, and hope the cold wind did not increase that cough.

All of us missed you dreadfully and the one theme is Papa, a most important character in our little home is that same dear Papa. I hope soon to hear from you and it is too late to say more. God bless you my own dear Will is my sweet prayer.

Rosa

Richmond Dec. 15, 1861

My Dear Rosa

I arrived here last night after a very fatiguing journey and will leave in the morning for the peninsula. Bob and Jenny are well. The baby tho' has a bad cold and cough. My own cough is better, have no soreness at all in my chest or throat, but my eyes are so sore I can scarcely see. Couldnt open either eye this morning until after I washed. Took a nap this afternoon and woke up in the same fix.

Bob received a letter from Ritch today. All is quiet on the peninsula and there is no movements on either side indicative of a fight.

Kiss the little ones for me and excuse a short letter. I can hardly see to write my eyes are so inflamed with cold and rail road travelling. I came within an ace of turning back at Kingsville with Judge Thomas[52] but finally concluded to come on and get a new furlough.

Ever yours
Will

Camp Marion Dec. 17, 1861

My Dear Rosa,

I have at last returned to camp much better of my cough but still with a bad cold affecting my eyes especially. In fact, I am troubled beyond measure with my right eye it is so badly inflamed. I cant open either of them in the morning until I wash my face and I can scarcely see half my time. Otherwise, I am very well, with a good appetite and I can honestly say to you that I see no chances for a fight on the peninsula though Gen. Magruder is about blocking up all the roads to prevent their coming up by land at all. Tomorrow my company and Capt. Lawton's go to Young's mill to report to Gen. McLaws. We go reluctantly, dislike to leave our cabins, but must obey orders. Excuse a very short note. It is very painful for me to write. Kiss the dear little ones for me. You can never know the desolate feeling of my camp after leaving you and them. God bless you all, Darling, & think often & sweetly of me.

Ever your own,
Will

Athens, Georgia
December 17, 1861

My own Dearest Will,

I have just come from our comfortable room, putting away our Darlings for the night. Every thing looks so snug and cheerful up there that a feeling of gratitude involuntarily comes to my heart for so many blessings and only one sorrow to mar my happiness and that is separation from you, yet that only comprehends so much and covers so much ground, that I am half afraid I regret more what I have not, than enjoy what I have. I am glad to say our dear little Willie is much better, eat chicken soup today with as much relish as Tom used to and as each meal was accompanied with a dose of my never failing antidote—lime water. I hope will be well

---

[52] Thomas W. Thomas. See Biographical Roster.

digested. Old Tom fell down in the street yesterday and is to-day almost as good a specimen of a boy as his Papa could desire, nose and face all scratched up. He has been playing marbles all day before the door "tooting" as he expresses it. Your summons to return to Camp came by last nights mail. Its well you went when you did. It is always well to do our duty at the right time and place and I believe my old fellow always tries to follow that principle. I hope too it may prove a false alarm. I feel much depressed at the prospect. I pray that you may be protected but its fearful any how. I have made a good many calculations and fear several days must elapse before I can hear from you and I am anxious to know about the cough. That letter of Mr. Cobb to you I put in the top of your trunk, be discreet in all you say and do in that matter. Be sure and let Maj Yancy know that you are not dissatisfied with his appointment but with Col Cobbs personal dealings with yourself short of that explanation I do not think he could recognize your right to object or even to do more than condemn Col Cobbs cause and dont forget you and Mr. C have been friends.

I have bought 29 bushels of Corn and some peas and am going to fatten the calves my self. I am going to trade the old black Cow for a sow, that idea is like my "improvements" you wont like, till you experience the benefits which makes my mouth water just to think of. I dont mean that I am going to fatten the calves on the 29 bushels of Corn, I mean I have that much of the supply bought. You must take good care of yourself and follow all my directions and read the Bible, and go to prayer meeting and every thing that you know I want you to do. Good night, Darling. All would send sweet kisses if awake to dear Papa, for aught I know they may be dreaming of you. Aunty sends love. God bless you, Darling.

Your own
Rosa

Chapter 4

Yorktown and the Peninsula: December 1861–January 1862

It paws fiercely, rejoicing in its strength,
And charges into the fray.
It laughs at fear, afraid of nothing;
It does not shy away from the sword.
—Job 39:22

John Bankhead Magruder was a man of flamboyant manners and dress. Those who knew him referred to him derisively as "Prince John" due to his aristocratic airs. He dressed in a uniform that he fashioned for himself, including a black felt hat and black overcoat with cape. Resigning his command in the US Army when Virginia seceded, he joined the Confederacy and became the third highest-ranking officer in the Virginia forces, behind Robert E. Lee and Joseph E. Johnson. Generally thought to possess a good military mind, Magruder was, nevertheless, known to be a rather nervous individual who always believed he was outnumbered and saw constant enemy threats from all directions.

In September 1861, Magruder was placed in command of the newly created Army of the Peninsula, an army of 13,600. Ordered to defend the Virginia peninsula from Federal invasion from Fort Monroe in October, he immediately set to work constructing earthworks roughly north to south across the peninsula between the York and James rivers. His defensive line resembled somewhat the old Revolutionary War defenses around Yorktown. Here, Magruder very skillfully held his position against George B. McClellan's Federal force of more than 105,000 men for a month.[1]

Much of November and December 1861 saw cold, wet days, common weather for Virginia during that time of year.[2] The weather gave rise to the growing number of sicknesses being reported within the regiments. During this time, Cobb's Legion

---

[1] See Thomas M. Settles, *John Bankhead Magruder: A Military Reappraisal* (Baton Rouge: Louisiana State University Press, 2009).

[2] See Robert K. Krick, *Civil War Weather in Virginia* (Tuscaloosa: University of Alabama Press, 2007).

Cavalry was camped at Camp Washington along with the infantry of the legion.[3] The cavalry was detailed for service doing vidette duty, with companies alternating between Camp Washington and a vidette camp called "Camp Disappointment" further down the peninsula.[4]

During December, the Federals constantly tested the Confederate defenders by sending small reconnaissance raids up the peninsula, probing the Confederate defenses in anticipation of a grand push on Richmond. Thomas Cobb mentioned one of the reconnaissance probes in a letter to his wife just a couple of days prior to Christmas. From his "Bethel Bivouac (Bethel Church)" he wrote, "At one o'clock that night came an order for the Legion Artillery, Cavalry and Infantry to go to Bethel to the support of Col. Winston, who was skirmishing with the enemy. We came down yesterday and made quite an imposing appearance when the whole body got into line. It was fully a half mile in length."[5] Aside from their normal picket duty, the legion cavalry settled into a relatively quiet period for the remainder of the year.

As the new year dawned, Americans realized that the Confederacy had survived its first year and wondered what 1862 would hold. It was a time of great uncertainty. Although some still held out hope, the one realization that now began to come to everyone's attention was that this war was not going to be a quick affair.

Despite his earlier communication with Thomas Cobb in which he said otherwise, the recent selection of Yancey as major did not sit well with Will Delony and became a topic of continuing discussion in his letters to Rosa. On 30 December, he submitted a formal letter of protest to Thomas Cobb.[6] By early January, the recent unsettling events over promotion and the hard feelings among some of the officers, especially Delony, were coming to an end. Thomas Cobb wrote his wife from Camp Marion giving her an update on the situation within the regiment among the officers, many of whom she knew personally.

Don't be worried about my troubles. They have very much disappeared. Even Deloney has become very agreeable & every thing seems to be as harmonious as ever. I am sorry Tommy has been worrying you with his

---

[3] Camp Washington was located "about two miles southeast of Yorktown, within one hundred yards of the house on the Temple Farm" and 1 mile from where Cornwallis surrendered to George Washington. The Temple house was Washington's headquarters during the Siege of Yorktown. William S. Smedlund, *Camp Fires of Georgia Troops, 1861–1865* (Lithonia, GA: Kennesaw Mountain Press, 1994) 284.

[4] Videttes were those men, usually cavalry, detailed to act as sentinels or guards and posted forward of the main body. They were the first to raise the alarm of enemy movement or impending attack.

[5] Thomas R. R. Cobb to Marion, 23 December 1861, T. R. R. Cobb Papers.

[6] See Appendix A for Delony's letter of protest and Thomas Cobb's response.

stories about the Legion, & I am surprised at some of them. The tale about Major Lamar not speaking to me & my not speaking to Major Yancy is pure fabrication. The most cordial good feeling prevails in all the Legion among the officers. Capt Deloney was the last with the "pouts" & he has become very agreeable. As to my appointments I am satisfied I did right & have no reason to regret my action in regard to anyone of them.[7]

* * *

Camp Disappointment
Dec. 20, 1861

My Dear Rosa

I just find an opportunity to send a note to the Post Office to say that since I have come to the woods again into the open air strange to say my cold is getting well. This morning for the first time I saw daylight upon awaking without the assistance of cold water. Dr. King insists it is homeopathy. I think it is the open air, what say you? At any rate I feel well again and very thankful I am for it. We have delightful weather, such as you had when I was in Athens, and a pleasant camping ground. Still no sign of the Yankees approaching and the time appointed by Magruder spies has expired so I hope that very soon we will be again sent to our cabins. Gen McLaws says as long as the weather continues so fine however we may have to remain, but when the winter sets in in earnest we will certainly [be] sent back so you need not be anxious about me.

Yours of the 13th I received today, many thanks for it. I hope to be with you again in January. Kiss the little darlings for me and don't [let] little Addie wait too long for that bed & bedstead. A merry Christmas to all my treasures at home.

Ever yours
WGD

Athens Dec 21st 1861

Dear Darling

I cannot tell you how much gratified I was at receiving last night your letter saying your eyes were better. I wrote you the night before, and send enclosed your blue spectacles, and some of my prescriptions which I imagine would excite the merriment of your homeopathic Dr. I am sorry that you are not in your comfortable Cabins. I think Gen Magruder might make your situation much more tolerable if

---

[7] Thomas R. R. Cobb to Marion, 7 January 1862, T. R. R. Cobb Papers.

THE LEGION'S FIGHTING BULLDOG

he desired. I shall be truly thankful when I learn that you have left Young's Mills[8] which is too near the enemy for my use. I send you by Mr. Stovall a vest I have had made for you, and some sassafras pills. If your eyes are well you can put it away for future use.

Don't forget to write a note acknowledging the receipt of the Cap Mrs. Stovall sends you. The Children are all well and enjoying their Christmas gifts. Little Rosa will write you a letter and give you an assessment. I cannot wish you a Merry Christmas. I hope tho' you will have, or are having a pleasant day. Aunty and myself are going to eat a Turkey and apple Dumplings. I prey [*sic*] God that this day the coming year will find us reunited. What a Glorious thought it is. I cannot tell you how eagerly I am looking forward to your coming. Do get a long furlough. Judge Thomas I learn got one for thirty days, cant you too? Every thing else I will leave for Rosa to tell. A heart full of love to my own dear Will from his own

Rosa

You must put that knit cap in your over-Coat pocket and always have it ready to sleep in when you go out at night. It will keep you nice and warm. About a Tea spoon full of sassafras pills will thicken a tumbler of water.

Camp Marion Dec. 22 1861

My Dear Rosa

We arrived at camp yesterday and I have only time before taking breakfast and leaving to write a short note saying I am very much better of my cold and cough tho' I am not yet entirely free from either.

We are ordered to Bethel to reinforce Col Winston, not that "the command-ing General thinks that the enemy will attack him but as a precautionary measure" and thus we are moved about, this time we will be gone three days. I think that Genl. Magruder is now fully satisfied that there is no prospect here for a fight and I hope soon that Col Winston will be convinced of the same fact, then we may hope to remain quietly in our winter quarters or better still go home for a while to see our wives and children. Mr Bell of my company arrived last night about ten oclock and says I have the three prettiest children he ever saw and that the "old lady" herself is hard to beat. I don't know whether he admired, Mother or children most. I have

---

[8] Young's Mill stood on Deep Creek and was a crossing point of the Great Warwick Road that connected Williamsburg with Hampton, Newport News, and Warwick Court House. The mill was the apex in the western section of Magruder's first line of defense on the peninsula. Young's Mill became the forward staging point in operations against Union forces at Camp Butler. See "The Historical Marker Database," www.hmdb.org.

not yet recd the letter you sent by him as his trunk is still in Yorktown. I must close this as it is time to be off. Kiss our precious little ones for me.

Ever your own
Will

Athens Dec 22 1861

My Dear Will,

Today is a gloomy unpleasant rainy Sunday. I have just been hearing little Rosa [say] her hymns and catechism. They are all well and are writing you a letter and Tom and Willie making a great noise in the other room. I wish you were here by the nice comfortable fire. I wrote you only a short note the last time, was feeling too sick for more. I had fever all that night with nausea and purging but next day was better and am quite well again.

I was busy all day yesterday and day before making soap, and clarifying and hardening my tallow for Candles. My soap is splendid. I shant have to buy any for washing purposes this coming year. I made it from my lard cracklings. Will have your clothes washed with soap of my manufacture when you come to see me and have one of my candles to see by and give you some sausages and feet and corned beef and tongues of my putting up. I am fattening the calves also. Feed them every day myself.

Cousin was married last Wednesday morning. Aunty heard from her from Macon. Mrs. Duncan made Bobby a present of a likely negro girl the day of the marriage. They are going to New Orleans and then to see Ellie and then to Savannah.

How soon will you be able to get another furlough? Embrace the earliest opportunity and dont put off coming till spring for then you may be hurried back as before. I am busy fixing up a doll house for Rosa for Christmas. I hope the poor little things will enjoy Christmas. I cannot feel "merry" at such times, will kill my only turkey and dispose of a slice or so in consideration of the day, but that's all. A long rainy spell has begun. I think by the looks of the clouds and such days I feel like Noah must have done on the Ark as tho all vestiges of humanity were extinct except me and my family. I was amused the other day hearing about the letters your man Friday has been writing to his sweetheart, Mrs. Camack's [sic] girl. He says when he returns from the war he will be "covered with glory" his pistol is to do infinite dispatch it seems. I hope when he sees the Yankees for the sake of his matrimonial negotiations the trumpet wont blow an uncertain sound and make him mistake "Dixie Land" for "Get out the way old Dan Tucker." Do write very often to me for I assure you it's a hard matter to drive away dull care and to wait with any show of patience for the first faint streak of dawn in such a night as this.

Do take care of yourself, Will, for our sakes. Your share of love from us all.

Your own
Rosa

Camp Marion Dec. 25, 1861

My Dear Rosa

We returned to camp today from Bethel and I sincerely trust that you are having a merrier Christmas than I, notwithstanding. I have recd two invitations since dark, one to an Eggnog party and the other to an oyster supper, the latter invitation I have accepted and will undoubtedly enjoy both the oysters and the company. Your letter of the 17th I received last night and I am truly relieved to hear that dear little Willie is well again. I feel very anxious about the little fellow and will feel so until he has his teeth, but from the manner he is teething I think we have reason to hope that he will teeth like Rosa and not hardly as Tom. I long for the time to come when I can return home and be with you all once more permanently. You did not send me the cap from Mrs Stovall but when it comes be assured I shall thank her for there is no one for whom I entertain a more sincere respect or higher regard. The truth is the ladies of Athens have been so kind to me and my company I feel that I cannot say too much for them collectively and especially for Mrs Stovall, Mrs Howell Cobb and a few others.

I am not yet entirely well of my cold and cough, and again have some pain in my chest. I have put on the plaster tonight & will take some of Dr Kings little pills and as I am again in comfortable quarters and excused from night duty, will make it my business to get well and as my appetite is fine I think that in a few days I will be entirely relieved. My cough indeed is much less troublesome than it was but I have been so much exposed since my return to camp it was impossible to get well so soon. I have been in my cabin but one day since I returned and we have had some very cold unpleasant weather. As to the danger of a fight on the Peninsula you need have no apprehensions. Our officers are exceedingly prudent, more so indeed than the Yankees. We went down below Bethel yesterday with the Legion and Col Winston's Alabama regiment and some Virginia artillery and Cavalry, set fire to three houses & came back promptly, notwithstanding, we received intelligence that within 1 1/4 miles there were three Yankee companies who might have been cut off with skillful management. The Yankees, it is reported, came up after we left and burned the houses on our side of the creek & the day before Old Winston retreated in double quick from a large imaginary force at the same place, and no one has yet been able to say they saw or fought against more than 40 of them. So many are coming in you must excuse this scrawl. God bless you all Darling, think often & sweetly of me. I hope soon to see you all again.

Ever your own
Will

Camp Marion Dec 28th [1861]

My Dear Rosa

Your two letters of the 18th & 22nd reached me this afternoon and I regret to learn that my poor little scrap has been sick, but glad that you are better. The meals are so irregular that sometimes when your letters do not come I have the blues terribly particularly since dear little Nellie has been sick. I sincerely hope that you will all continue well and that I shall again soon have the pleasure of being with you. Gen Magruder says I can certainly come home again so that all doubt is now removed as to a new leave of absence being granted. Williams will leave within a few days probably by the last day of this month or the first of next and when he returns I shall come immediately on. If I can get off before he returns I shall certainly do so but I think it just to him that he shall now have the preference particularly as he has behaved very gentlemanly about it and would yield if I insisted. I am pretty well again. My cold is well my cough nearly gone and the soreness of my chest disappeared entirely. Gen Magruder says that the Legion can now secure in their winter quarters unless the Yankees advance and if they do he will take Fortress Monroe and Newport News and winter his troops very comfortably there. As you will perceive that we are bound to be well provided, so able as the General says. I congratulate you upon your success in soap making and hope the candles will turn out as well and congratulate myself upon having such a wife and will enjoy the good things you have in store for me as you know I can enjoy them. I thought of you today at dinner and instead you could have enjoyed with me the oyster pie which John had made. He is a first rate cook & I think under your tutor he would be very soon quite equal to Catherine and I am not sure but that you had better keep him at it if ever this abominable war is over and we can return home safe and sound. I to my wife and he to his lady love where his valor is to immortalize. He has her ambrotype and is almost as proud of that as of his courage and pistol. The "Nigger" is a great institution indeed. I can yet see no gleam of hope for peace except the bankruptcy of both parties. Gen Magruder remarked I learn he didnt care if the war lasted 20 years but for them at home & leave out his qualification and he but expressed the feeling of too many of our leaders. There are too many in power who are making a good thing out of the war and its continuance is their gain. Kiss the little folks for Papa. I hope the precious little things are enjoying a merry Christmas. Tell little Rosa that she must learn some more hymns and to try to read for Papa when he comes home again. Bill and Wimpy expatiate eloquently upon my wife and children and indeed they are hard to beat. So Cousin is married & Bobby bribed and I suppose all now satisfied but Aunty. Tell her to go and do likewise. My love to her. God bless you Darling. With much love

Ever Yr own
Will

Athens Dec 31st 1861

My Dear Will

I feel much troubled at learning from your letter of the 25th that you are again troubled with that pain in your Chest. You must be extremely careful and refuse to expose yourself, until you are well for you have gone thru enough to teach you that your chest and lungs are constitutionally weak and only careful and regular living has over come that tendency. I dont think you have any idea of how much constant solicitude I feel for you my dear Will. You happy Mortals who live in the present not subject to anxieties about the future cant understand and indeed I shant think men ever were made to feel like women, however just recollect one of that unfortunate class is worried to death about you. Our little ones are all well—asleep. I heard Rosa ask Aunty to night to let her fix her cap and make her look pretty, if she was old—she is sweet and smart. Old Tom had a big tale to tell of what he saw down town, bless his little fat self. Dear little Willie wakes me up every morning jabbering calls over every ones name and among them is Papa always. Aunty and myself have been taking advantage of the fine weather to visit, went to see Mrs. Howell Cobb yesterday, found her all packed to leave this morning for Macon to be gone till warm weather. Libby was complaining of head ache—significant. All enquire kindly of you where ever I go. I heard this afternoon that Dr. Mell was married to his sister in law, it may only be a rumor, and I hope it is for it troubles me such things as that, his wife the mother of a large family was buried last July. Capt Dorsey called yesterday to see if I wanted any thing and says he comes in the yard constantly, he gave a dinner on Christmas to some of the Guards on a visit here. Mr. Adams who married Miss Lisson asked me this afternoon to pay your subscription to the church singing $25.00 he said, I told him I know nothing about it, had no money to pay it with and thought there must be some mistake about the amount. $5 I should think would have been an ample donation from you. We will have to retrench in subscriptions or I shall have no heart to practice economy. I paid Bishops Bill to-day $150.00 for the last two months of this year, and a greater portion of our supply for meat coffee and candles, Rice etc, our bill for the quarter before was the same so you will be able to see that I must have economized a good deal in order to make the same amount buy for another year. I shall have no account even with Bishop for 1862 and will be able to save a good deal if you will only deny yourself the luxury of giving the same amount that men of twice your means give. When we shall have paid all we owe, I will never lecture about your giving. Dr. Hoyt is welcome to all we give and I wish it was more, but Mr. Adams is not to have the amount the Preacher gets, not from us, and if he had not been a Yankee he would never have dunned me for it. Aunty had a letter from Eliza, enjoying herself very much in Savannah. Darling when are you coming? Do try and come soon for I am afraid something will turn up to keep you, and I do want to see you so much. Tomorrow is the new Year. A sad old year it has been to me, but one full of blessings, the priceless one of health to us all and our dear little children should be gratefully remembered, and God's kind fatherly care of you in the far off Camp surrounded by sickness and hunger. Dont overlook it all my dearest Will and forget to be thankful. Aunty says I must tell you old Willingham is going to marry Joe Newtons widow, she says she tamed one man and is going to try her skill on another. Aunty says she is getting in the notion of marrying herself and if you see any military fellow with plenty of money and a few honorable scars send him along. Dr. Smith is expected to-morrow night. I wish it was you. Do my Dear Will be prudent with that cold of yours. It troubles me beyond measure your constant exposure. Write often to your little Scrap Darling. A happy New Year to you, happier than the old and may God continue to protect and bless you and our dear little children is my constant prayer. Aunty send love. Your own large share from us.

Affectionately
Rosa

Do take care of that pain and if it gets any worse come home and let me cure you.

Camp Marion Dec 31st, 1861

My Dear Rosa

I have just learned that Goodman is about leaving for Athens and I cannot miss so good an opportunity of sending by him messages of love for my little wife and children. I hope sincerely that upon this the last day of the year that all are well and happy and that the next year to us all are prosperous and happy. I was deeply disappointed today in not hearing from you all. The mails are very irregular and your letters come to me two or three at a time & then not a word sometimes for a week. I shall rejoice when I can return home for good and dispense with letter writing also great and intervening distance. I am glad to say to you that my colors well and the cough and pain in my chest have disappeared entirely. The plaster still sticks to me hard ever closer than a brother as is becoming very annoying. You told me to wear it. I believe to wear it until it dropped off and I am as you know always obedient. Yesterday Col. Cobb sent for me to know the reason I did not appear at drill with my company. I replied because my company had been placed by him in a position which I was unwilling to occupy. He said I had better submit my objections to him in writing which I promptly said I would do immediately and that I would further submit in my communication any protest to his course in relation to the late promotions in the Legion which I have done respectfully but firmly. The whole question will go up to the War Department for final decision. I care but little as to what the decision may be. I so have expressed myself in my letter to him and that I protest because I think the names assigned for the promotion of Yancey might not to have anything to do with military promotions and that all I desire is that there shall be some Rule of Promotion. I care not what if impartially adhered to. We have not discussed the question at all. He is "surprised" that I am not satisfied. I am surprised that he is surprised which is about the sum & substance of our conservation. We have both been very polite—extremely so indeed. I think he will discover before the war is ended that his officers are to be controlled in a different mode from the one he has adopted. Kiss the little folks for me and give my love to Aunty. I am going in the morning to see Genl Magruder with Williams to see if we can both get off but I think I shall have to wait until Williams returns. All is quiet on the peninsula, no movements at all. The weather continues cold, clear & delightful.

Ever Yours, Will

Camp Marion Jan 1 1861 [1862]

My Dear Rosa

Lieut. Williams leaves tonight for home and though I think he will not go through Athens he promises to send this to you from Union Point.[9] A happy New Year to you, Darling, and to our precious little children. I did not know how hard it was to stay in Camp and let Williams go home, nor how badly I wanted to see you all till tonight. I saw the Genl. today he says Williams can go now and I can come on subsequently. Rather indefinite but I think as soon as the Federal fleet at Annapolis leaves & don't come to Yorktown as everybody is now pretty well satisfied it will not that he will let me off, which I hope will not now be long. At furtherest, however, I shall be with you by the last of this month and we ought to be satisfied

---

[9] Union Point, south of Athens, connected the railroad from Athens to the Georgia Railroad.

with that. I am quite well again, have gained four pounds since I left Athens and have a voracious appetite, so don't have any apprehensions about me. I am not sure this will reach you and Dr Carlton will take another note tomorrow so good night Darling, with many kisses for our dear little ones and warm love for yourself. I have not heard from you in several days and cannot but fear that you or one of our little children may be sick. I hope to hear tomorrow. God bless you all.

Ever your own
Will

Athens Jan 1st 1862

A Happy New Year to you my Dearest Will. I wrote you a long letter last night, but I have been thinking of you all day and your cough and sore chest and I must send you a little love message to night and tell you over again how constantly you are in my thoughts and also to beg you to come home and get cured of that cold. It will never do for you to trifle in the least with yourself and I feel so wretched about you. I do hope the plaster helped you. I heard a most beautiful lecture from Dr. Lipscomb this morning at the Soldiers prayer meeting. The more frequently I hear him the better I like him. I have been busy all day at my old trade putting to rights all the holes and corners of the little house clean for a new year and wish my heart could be purified and fresh for its beginning too. I am glad your commanding officers are proving themselves prudent men. Those little skirmishes cannot affect the cause much either our way or the other one or two should hurried into Eternity and nothing accomplished by it. I feel profoundly grateful that you have been spared a fight so far. Tom Hoyt I mean William called to see us yesterday he looks quite foreign and distinguished enough to be a lion among the ladies. He enquired very kindly about you and seems to feel quite satisfied that he is once again safe on terra firma and beyond the Yankee clutches. I saw Mr. Adams to day fresh from Legislative halls. He enquired very kindly about you. His wife they tell me has left him, cant agree. I dont know whether it is true or not. I bought some Turkeys to day for you when you come. You must feel very much complimented at that because we only have Turkey on extra occasions and dear darling its the most "extra occasion" that could possibly happen to us the arrival of the "old fellow." I wonder if the time will ever come when you will come home to remain. God grant it may. I ought to take courage for the future from the wonderful kindness to us in the past and I would were I sure we were grateful enough. Eight years of almost uninterrupted prosperity and yet hoping for more and wondering, sinning and straying all that time. God is very good to us Darling and we cannot acknowledge it too often or keep it too constantly in remembrance. I hope you will soon come. The little pills are very good doubtless, but tell Dr. King I think the little wife better. All our Darlings well. The children dressed up Willie this afternoon in a pair of pants and I wish you could have seen him strutting with his hands in his pockets, he is too sweet. All send sweet kisses to dear Papa. Good night, God bless you Will is the prayer of your own

Rosa

Do come home to stay till you are entirely well for I am wretched about you and the pain in your chest, yet have to stay till you are well.

Camp Marion Jan 2 1861 [1862]

My Dear Rosa

Dr Carlton has to leave earlier than I expected and is now waiting on me for this note. I can only say that I am well and hope when the mail comes in today to learn that my little Scrap is also well and our precious little children. I will be with you the last of the month not before I fear.

We are doing but little now, building stables and drilling, no appearances of a fight. The weather is threatening and if we have snow and rain now you may feel that there is no possibility of a fight so don't be weary about me. God bless you all Darling, think often of me & write whenever you can. Kiss the little folks for me & tell little Rosa that if she learns to read for me, I will bring her a "heap of things." My love to Aunty.

Ever your own
Will

Athens Jan 3rd 1861 [1862]

My Dearest Will

I cannot tell you how much pleasure your letter sent by Mr. Glenn gave me. He delivered it himself and paid me quite a visit. What a smart little fellow he is, and as much like his uncle _____ as it is possible for him to be and a most enthusiastic adviser of Capt. Delony. The old fellow seems to have a winning way about him the same way that entrapped a poor little woman some years ago. I am glad you have so many friends Darling and I am always glad to hear your praises sung. I am delighted that you are nearly rid of your cold. How many blessings you have to be grateful for. I hope old Magruder will stop that incessant guarding you have been doing so much of. I hope soon to see you and look anxiously every evening for the arrival of Lieut Williams. I have been busy to day with candle making and they are not to be sneered at I can tell you. I expect to make about 40 lbs. I wrote to the Editors of the Columbus Times and Federal Union and stopped the papers and paid the Bills the last been owing for three years $80 in all. I told them whenever you returned home you would probably renew your subscription. Our Darlings are all well and while I write, I hear the pattering of their little feet and their little mess up stairs, all going to bed. Rosa is very smart and well raised will make a sensible woman if she is spared.[10] A mighty responsibility and I don't often feel equal to it. I pray I may be aided. They are all self willed chips from the old block. Poor little things I hope they may have a sunny childhood, nothing like that after all. A happy home and kindred spirits. I hope you wont have to wait for Lieut Williams thirty days to expire. I am glad now you had to go back coming again. Dr. Mell arrived this evening with his new wife, his wifes sister she was, what wont a man do and reluctantly I'll have to add in this instance a woman too, but its awful to think of. I write you so often and so little happens to write about that you must excuse a rather shorter letter than usual to night. Aunty sends love and do Darling take care of yourself and don't give up your time for coming to any one. All the children send dear Papa sweet kisses and say bring some candy for them. Good night my Darling. A heart full of love from

Your own
Rosa

Athens Jan 5th 1862

My Own Dearest Will

Yours of 31st by Mr. Goodman reached me last night. It was quite late, and the man who brought it made such a loud knocking at the door at the same time turning the knob coupled with the fact of there having been considerable attention in the streets, a tiny excitement over the newly elected Marshall that Aunty and my self thought that one of the disciples of Bacchus[11] had stopped to pay us a visit. We beat a retreat in double quick, she to the back piazzi and I upstairs so you may judge how pleased I was to welcome my old fellow's letter in place of an intruder. Today is disagreeable and rainy, how I wish you could be spending it with me. I cannot help hoping a little that Gen Magruder will let you come with Lieut Williams. I am grateful to learn that you have got rid of your cough, even if you cannot of the Plaster. You will have to wear till it gets tired of you as an attempt to forcibly remove it would be worse I imagine than pulling out gray whiskers. I cannot tell you Darling

---

[10] Although spared many of the common childhood diseases of the time, Rosa had a troubled married life. See Biographical Roster.

[11] The Roman god of wine and intoxication. Followers were noted for their boisterous and loud celebrations.

how much I regret the difficulty you have been forced into with Col Cobb. I think tho, you are right to maintain your ground in a firm respectful manner. I fear Maj Yancy tho, will not understand your movement, and attribute it to chagrin or disappointment at you not obtaining the place. The whole ground of your complaint to my mind is in Col Cobbs personal dealing with you in his telling you, you were the most competent officer to fill the place and then appointing Maj Yancy upon the score of "age, position, and other attainments," rather than military qualifications. The fact of your superiority you need not expect Maj Yancy to be sensible of and unless he knows what Col C's private opinion, expresses to you was how is he to understand your dissatisfaction at the choice of the Col which you all agreed to abide by. I hope that you will not feel called upon to leave the place you are at, you are now acclimated which is half the battle. I don't know how the Southern Coast would treat you in warm weather and for Heaven's sake don't go any farther off. I hope it will all yet be settled satisfactorily to you. In the mean while my Dearest Will don't permit any feeling of bitterness at the falsity of friends to fill your heart. You have only learned that your own honest nature make it hard to understand that a man is a very mortal thing to depend upon. God is the only one "with whom there is no variableness or shadow of turning." Our Darlings are all well. I enclose you a specimen of your Son's penmanship. The crooked lines if we could read them alright would mean some thing very sweet to dear Papa I doubt not. Little Willie gets sweeter every day and dreadfully spoilt last night in the night I attempted to cover his little feet, "Toes mom" he said. Rosa is hard at work at her hymns to learn for Papa and learn one in a very little time. I love to teach them to her, good seed for the little heart which may spring up some of these days and bear fruit. Good bye my own dear Will. Try and be prudent and have as little strife as possible about that matter and Heaven protect and bless you, and bring you soon to us all.

Camp Marion Jany 6, 1861 [1862]

My Dear Rosa,

Your two letters of the 27th & 29th I recd by Saturdays mail and I would have written you by the last mail but for marches and counter marches.[12] I am really glad

---

[12] Thomas Cobb referred to these movements in his correspondence with his wife: "Camp Marion, Jany 3rd 1862 (Night), I have just returned from Bethel. We heard today that the Yankees were there burning the houses &c, & hurried down to meet them. The cavalry got there just in time to see their retreat. There were about three hundred of them, all mounted, & they got out of the way rapidly. The cavalry reached Winston's camp sometime before his line was formed & the artillery were there before the column moved." Thomas R. R. Cobb to Marion, 1 January 1862, T. R. R. Cobb Papers.

to hear that you are all well. I have been very anxious about you. I hope Darling that our dear little Willie will not teeth as hard as Tom and from the fact that he is teething like Rosa have reason to think he will get through like her.

On Friday last the Yankees with about 300 cavalry came up as far as Bethel Church which Genl Magruder about a mile or before had evacuated and they burned several barns along the road & stacks of fodder &c. and set fire to the church in three different places. They then left immediately. Maj. Philips who was at half way house about 2 miles off with a Company of ten of Va cavalry went immediately down & put out the fire in the church & followed the Yankees down, came in sight but did not have force enough to attack them. As soon as we recd the intelligence our cavalry went down in a gallop under my command, but Col Winston overtook us & stopped us at Bethel as I think we could have driven the rascals in double quick into Newport News. Our Cols are too prudent & it makes the Yankees all the more imprudent and distracters on our men & does us no good. If the videttes had come at once to our cause I could have reached Bethel by the time the Yankees did as in ten minutes. After the order was given our men were on the march down & ready for a fight. As were not allowed to go far enough down that road to learn what the enemy intended, we had to be up at two oclock Saturday morning and go below again. It was sleeting at the time, dark as Erebus[13] and as cold as the Yankees could have wished. I was sent to Brohu Bridge on the Bethel stream with my company & Stovalls and verily let alone. I sent out pickets from there & obtained information as far as the James River to the effect that no Yankees were out & that their expectation the day before was simply a rear raiding party which we could have beaten easily. I don't think the exposure to a fight is any more dangerous than this continued exposure to wet and cold. I am very tired of such a policy. The trees and ground are soon all covered with sleet. It is cloudy & I think we may now look for winter in earnest. It is very cold and no army can serve here and accomplish anything, so I hope Magruder will let us stay in our houses for a time yet. I am now satisfied we will never have a fight here unless the enemy advances with an army to Yorktown. Providence thru the waking clear of lustre of our officers. God bless you all Darling. I will have to remain here until Williams returns but will be with you the last of the month. Kiss the little folks for me. My love to Aunty, with a heart full for yourself from

Yr own
Will

---

[13] The Greek personification of darkness.

Atlanta, Georgia
January 8, 1862

My own precious Will,

I know you will be much surprised at receiving a letter from me written from this place. I last night received a letter from Fathers wife stating that Father was very ill with only a doubtful hope of his recovery and was willing to see me if I desired it. I took the letter immediately round to Mrs. Baxter who advised me by all means to go. Dr. Smith very kindly offered to go with me and take me back and here I am tonight feeling lone and desolate enough and wanting you, my own precious one, worse than I ever wanted you in my life. Oh! Will, you know what a trial it must be to me to go there. Our precious little children Mrs. Hunter assured me she would take entire charge of till my return. I do not now propose staying longer than a day. Grandmother and Aunt Mell are both there. It will take nearly two days to get from Athens to Macon.

Darling, there is no place on earth like our quiet little home and nothing to me like our blessed little children and a thousand times dearer than all are you, my dearest Will, and if I could only see you to-night. It seems a long time to have to wait to hear from you till I get back home. I haven't any thing to write you about, only a sweet little love message to send. May God spare you to me Darling.

Your own affectionate
Rosa
I will write you the earliest chance.

Camp Marion Jany 9, 1861 [1862]

My Dear Rosa,

Today I have recd three letters from you and one from precious little Rosa, and tonight the old fellow is almost a happy man. If instead of letters I could be at home and hear from you all that the letters contain I would be a happy man, but fate seems against my coming until the return of Lieut Williams. We are having alarm after alarm and are marching & countermarching on horses until there is almost nothing left of them. My fine black is used up and I have now to rely upon my bay, which is certainly one of the very best of horses. Night before last I was called out of bed at twelve oclock before getting to sleep to take supper at Capt. Glenn's. As I had been in bed since ten and could not sleep thinking of my wife and little ones I went to the supper, and before we were through the dispatches commenced coming in that the enemy were certainly advancing and I and my orderly Sergt. were kept up till about four. I slept till daylight, was waked up with the order to leave in 15 minutes, took a "hasty" cup of Coffee but had no time to eat, and from that time until dark I was in the saddle, having eaten my breakfast of biscuit & fat bacon about 3 oclock in the afternoon and this is the life we lead. It was a clear cold day however and we called it a pleasant trip. Since I have come back from home I am so restless and so anxious to return that positively I cannot sleep without great fatigue compelling it. I wish the confounded Yankee fleet would sail off to its destination, and give me a chance for a furlough, while it remains at Old Point I have no hope for one. Magruder's spies keep him excited and in hurrily expectation of a great battle at Yorktown, which I have no idea the Yankees have the slightest notion of offering him.

I am really sorry to hear of the marriage of Dr. Mell, tho' it is none of my business and as the lady was the sister of his former wife, I suppose its no body's business, but nevertheless it's a heartless act and ought to damn them both. There is no religion in that truly.

Many thanks to you for the vest and sassafras pulp. My eyes are well & I will keep the latter for future contingencies. The vest came in good time as my old friend is fast falling to pieces. The plaster still sticks to me closer than a brother & I am inclined to think it has taken quarters for the winter. I recd also the gift from Mrs Stovall & have written her tonight.

Bless our precious little children. How I should like to be with you all tonight, Darling you can never know. I don't think I was ever as homesick in my life. Gen Magruder will not permit Leave for John Cobb to meet their wives in Petersburg to be gone only for two days until the Yankee fleet leave Old Point.

God bless you all Darling. Tell Aunty all the "rich old fellows" are at home not in the Army. Kiss the babies for me.

Ever Yr own
Will

Camp Marion Jany 12, 1861 [1862]

My Dear Rosa,

Yesterday I recd two more letters from you one in reply to the one I wrote by Mr Goodman, which is by far the most expeditious mail carriage that the Southern Confederacy has been guilty of since I have been in the service. I hope you and Aunty have recovered from your fright and that you will both be more courageous in the future one, a soldiers wife, and the other hoping to be. I wrote you night before last and since then I have learned that the long looked for fleet from Annapolis has arrived in Hampton Roads and if the Yankees do not drive us out of the Peninsula before this letter reaches you they will have probably left for some point on the Southern Coast and furloughs will be again granted to our soldiers. I shall leave just as soon as Gen Magruder feels it right to grant furloughs to my men. I hope he will begin this week as I learn that he feels able to resist any force the enemy may bring against him. He says he has the best army in the Confederate service and I doubt not thinks the army has the best Commanding General. They certainly have great confidence in him and the Yankees will find it a hard road to travel any farther than Yorktown, if ever they succeed in getting that far which is extremely doubtful. I am becoming so homesick I scarcely know what to do with myself, and unless I can manage some to see my little Scrap and our precious little children I shall die of the blues. I am living by myself and at night my Cabin is as lonely & desolate as my Early County palace of former days, much more so indeed for then I did not have you and the little ones to attract me elsewhere. Little Rosa's letter was quite a treat and Tom's was perfect of its kind. I shall certainly not forget to bring them and Dear little Willie their full share of candy, not forgetting that others of the household are also fond of indulging sometimes in a childish taste for sweet things. Tell Aunty I have picked out for her a beau, precisely such as she wants with but one imperfection. He is old, ugly & rich, a General to book, but I am afraid hasnt brains enough to find his way to Athens without an escort and for this reason I have hesitated to propose on her behalf until I hear further from her. He is only one of a larger class which are a curse to our country and who of themselves are enough to call down the curse of Heaven upon the officers of our Government and one Henry Wayne of Ga is added to the list. It is enough to make a patriot tremble for the Cause of our country. Wayne is one General and his wife and children, father and brothers all with the enemy. I wouldnt trust him with a company, much less a brigade. I am going to try and leave here by tomorrow week and shall use every effort in my power to get off. One of my men Hilton from Lumpkin County was brought to Camp today from his picket post very sick with pneumonia. He was truly sick yesterday. An ignorant Virginia officer forbid his coming home and the poor fellow was exposed all last night. He is very sick and I feel very anxious about him. He is one of our best soldiers and cleverest men. Kiss the dear little ones for me and give my love to Aunty, reserving a large share for your own dear little self.

Will

Camp Marion Jany 14, 1861 [1862]

My Dear Rosa,

I have just finished paying off my Company and before retiring must say a few words to my precious little wife and children. Yours of the 7th inst was recd today and I am sure you are not more anxious for me to come home than I am to get there. I was never so homesick and anxious to see you in my life. I am wearied with the Camp and yet I scarcely know when Gen Magruder will be willing for me to leave. The Yankees keep him in a state of constant expectation and excitement with their fleets and rumors of fleets and he will not grant our furloughs except in very urgent cases. I have been waiting with the hope that the time would come when affairs on the Peninsula would be quiet and that even the Genls would not be in expectation of an attack so that I might wait at home enjoying myself with you in peace and quiet without the fear of being recalled to camp. I am now pretty well satisfied however that no such time is coming and I shall in a day or two go to see the Genl. and get off if I can and let the war take care of itself until my furlough is out. If I succeed I shall be with you very soon and if I do not you will know in my next letter. When I wrote you last the weather was unseasonably and oppressively warmer. Now the ground is covered with snow and sleet with a fair prospect of a continuance of wet weather. Sometimes I wish we could have a forty days rain, and make the roads impassable for Yankee Artillery. Then I might reasonably hope for the enjoyment of a pleasant & peaceful furlough.

You think the war cannot last long. Unless we meet with some terrible reverse at some important point within the next month or two, I think you are right. The Yankees cannot keep up this sort of game much longer without a better run of luck. They are growing uneasy at their want of success, and the Administration is losing its popularity. Dissensions are rife among them and nothing but unexpected victories can keep up the war on their part much longer. They whistle loudly to keep their courage up but I am satisfied that the Northern people are opening their eyes to the fact that they have attempted an impossibility. I never felt so hopeful before.

Gen Magruder says that the advices to our Government from all parts of [the] country and from all our armies are favorable in the extreme, and unless Burnsides' Expedition is more successful than its forerunner I think we may all have reason soon to hope for peace.[14]

If Lincoln don't fight his Administration is gone and if he does fight I am very sure we will whip them so that in either event I am very hopeful and hopeful too for the first time. I count upon no aid from Englands advance in my calculations of the United States while these powers are fast becoming serious and very interesting to us. For me however I want no foreign aid as I believe we are fully equal to the task we have undertaken as the sequel will show. But here I am writing you a political letter for which you will probably read me a lecture so I must desist.

---

[14] The "Burnside Expedition," commanded by Ambrose E. Burnside, was a joint army and naval expedition to Roanoke Island, North Carolina. Rumors abounded when the expedition got underway 10 January from the Potomac River headed south; *The Daily Journal* Wilmington, NC (10 January 1862). For more, see Richard A. Sauers, *"A Succession of Honorable Victories": The Burnside Expedition in North Carolina* (Dayton, OH: Morningside House, Inc., 1996).

Kiss our dear little ones for me and tell my precious little Rosa that Papa says she must grow and soon be a big girl to see for him and to sing for him too. Give my love to Aunty and reserve a goodly share for your own dear self.

From Yr own

Will

Chapter 5

Turmoil:
January 1862–June 1862

Harness the horses; mount, O horsemen!
Take your stations with your helmets,
polish your spears, put on your armor!
—Jeremiah 46:4

Around the middle of January, Will Delony was finally able to have his much-deserved rest. About the 16th, he embarked upon a fifty-day furlough to Georgia to be with his family. While he was gone the legion cavalry continued to drill and make ready for their first encounters with the enemy. The legion, however, was never far from his mind, as he continued to recruit for its ranks, something the legion would need many more of in the days ahead.

Delony enjoyed his lengthy furlough at home in Athens. Between the middle of January and the first week of March, while he was absent from the legion cavalry, the cavalry was busily settling into the normal routine of military camp life—drilling, doing vidette duty, and trying to pass the time. During Delony's absence, the cavalry took up its main camp at Camp Marion in York County, just 7 miles below Yorktown.[1] A letter penned from Camp Marion to *The Southern Watchman* newspaper in Athens the end of January gave folks back home an update on the legion cavalry's present activities.

> Mr. Editor:—Supposing your numerous readers would be pleased to hear from the Legion, and the "Georgia Troopers," I take the occasion, by your permission, to say something of our brave soldiers. Camp Marion has become quite a little town, since we all have got into our cabins. We are very

---

[1] Cobb wrote his wife about the drilling being undertaken: "Today has been a spring day, beautiful warm sunshine. All the Legion were out on the parade ground and made quite a show.... Tomorrow afternoon I am going to have a grand drill, and shall undertake to drill all three (Artillery, Cavalry and Infantry) at the same time. I don't know how I will succeed and I doubt if it ever was tried before, but there is nothing like trying and I shall make the effort. I have a beautiful parade horse now and I don't think you would be ashamed of me, at the head of my Legion." Thomas R. R. Cobb to Marion, 12 February 1862, T. R. R. Cobb Papers.

comfortably situated, and have no reason to complain. We have had an immense amount of rain and bad weather this month, and have been almost unable to do anything, except perform our camp duties. We have, every Sunday morning, a company inspection, and sometimes a general inspection of the whole Battalion of Cavalry; but those inspections have not been so frequent here of late. The hardest and heaviest duty we have to perform, is that of "videtting." Every morning at 8 o'clock, twenty-five mounted men are sent from the Battalion of Cavalry "on vidette," whose duty it is, after being posted on our lines and every point available for the observation and approaches of the enemy, to keep watch and report to headquarters everything that transpires. For those who are quietly sheltered in warm bedding, and who know not what it is to be without three hot meals daily, it is difficult to realize what privations these men undergo. Without tents or shelter—in some positions dispensing with fires, for fear of being observed by the enemy—they do their duty unostentatiously, and none but those in the advance are aware of their sacrifices and dangers. Perhaps there is no arm of the service which calls for so many manly qualities as are required by the mounted men of an army. Separated from their Regiment or Legion, they must be brave and watchful, and withal be possessed with good judgement. We have never heard of our men being found napping on their post. On the contrary, they are complained of as being too watchful, by reporting things trivial in their character. The health of the Legion and of the company, is very good, with a slight exception of mumps and colds. None, however, have been dangerously ill with the mumps. We lost another member of our company with the pneumonia— Wm. J. Helton. He was a good soldier and a brave man, ready at all times to perform the duties devolving upon him. His remains were sent home to his father, who lives in Lumpkin county. We are waiting patiently for the advance of the enemy—feet able and willing to give the Yankees another lesson like that of Great Bethel, and convince them that we are not only a Legion, but Legions.

Yours, &c.

J. A. W.[2]

Delony did not fritter his time away while at home on furlough, but kept himself busy continually recruiting for the cavalry as was common for most officers of the period.

---

[2] The letter-writer was John A. Wimpy, a private in Co. C. See Biographical Roster. Although written on 31 January, the letter was not published in the *Southern Watchman* until the following month. *Southern Watchman* (12 February 1862).

Volunteers WANTED!

Being authorized to increase the number of my Company, I will take on with me, the first week of March, all who desire to join. For particulars, apply to me at my residence in Athens.

W. G. Delony. Feb. 12, 1862.[3]

Arms Wanted!

The undersigned is authorized to purchase double-barreled Shot-Guns for the Confederate Government. A fair price will be paid for good guns, and patriots at home cannot do their country a better service than to furnish arms to the soldiers in the field. Bring up your guns.

W. G. Delony[4]

Delony's recruiting efforts were tremendously successful, as *The Southern Watchman* reported in its 12 March issue that "Capt. Delony had no difficulty whatever last week in raising a second company of cavalry. Indeed, we learn he had to refuse many applicants. He has since received authority to raise a third company."[5] This second company became Company H of the legion cavalry, also known as the "Georgia Troopers."

Meanwhile in Virginia, on 5 March, the cavalry crossed the James River near old Jamestown and went into camp the following day. Named Camp Hunter, this camp in Suffolk County, Virginia, became the cavalry's new home for several weeks.[6]

Within the next few days, Delony was on his way back to Virginia to rejoin the cavalry. Taking the train in Athens, he proceeded to Union Point, where the Athens spur connected up with the Georgia railroad to Augusta. After overnighting in Augusta, it was onto the South Carolina railroad to Branchville, South Carolina, where he changed trains onto the Charlotte and South Carolina railroad. In Charlotte, he was again forced to change trains to the North Carolina railroad and pro-

---

[3] *Southern Watchman* (12 February 1862).

[4] Ibid., 5 March 1862.

[5] Ibid., 12 March 1862.

[6] Camp Hunter was located "a little over one mile from the center of Suffolk, on the Norfolk & Petersburg Railroad"; Tammy Harden Galloway, *Dear Old Roswell: The Civil War Letters of the King Family of Roswell, Georgia* (Macon, GA: Mercer University Press, 2003) 20; see also, Athens *Southern Banner* (26 March 1862); William S. Smedlund, *Camp Fires of Georgia Troops, 1861–1865* (Lithonia, GA: Kennesaw Mountain Press, 1994) 160.

ceeded to Greensboro, North Carolina, where, once more, he changed to the North Carolina and Richmond railroad.[7]

Federal troops under Ambrose Burnside captured Roanoke Island off the coast of North Carolina on 14 March, establishing a base from which they could advance up the Neuse River into the interior of the state and cut the Weldon Railroad, a major supply line of the Confederacy. To meet this perceived threat, the legion cavalry was ordered first to Suffolk, Virginia, then on 20 March to Goldsboro, North Carolina, to bolster the Confederate inland defenses. On the very day the cavalry received their order to move, Federal forces moved on the town of Washington, North Carolina, capturing it the following day.[8]   ·

During Will's time of absence from home, Rosa was dutifully showing her support for the Confederate cause and Georgia's common defense. After the great naval battle between the *USS Monitor* and the *CSS Virginia* at Hampton Roads, Virginia, on 9 March, women throughout the South began clamoring for the building of more gunboats. Throughout the Confederacy women began forming societies to raise money for the construction of gunboats similar to the *Virginia*. Women put on "gunboat fairs" to raise the necessary $80,000+ through raffles and donations. In Georgia, two women from Macon prompted a statewide campaign to create the "Ladies Gun Boat Fund" to build an ironclad vessel for the protection of the state's coast. Led by the ladies of Savannah, women from across the state contributed to the fund. The 19 March issue of *The Southern Watchman* ran an article about the local efforts toward construction of such a vessel: "Mrs. W. G. Delony donated $5.00 to the Ladies' Gunboat Fund sufficient to build and equip a gunboat for the protection of our coast and rivers."[9]

---

[7] Many historians consider the inability of the South's railroad system to support a large-scale war effort as one of the region's greatest weaknesses during the Civil War. See John Elwood Clark Jr., *Railroads in the Civil War: The Impact of Management on Victory and Defeat* (Baton Rouge: Louisiana State University Press, 2004).

[8] A Union report in March stated that Cobb's Legion consisted of about 400 cavalry, armed with Maynard's rifles. *War of the Rebellion: Official Records of the Union and Confederate Armies.* Series 1, vol. 11, pt. 1 (Harrisburg, PA: The National Historical Society, 1971) 267. Hereafter cited as *OR.*

[9] *Southern Watchman* (19 March 1862). The Ladies Gun Boat Fund raised over $115,000 for construction of the *CSS Georgia* for the defensive naval squadron in Savannah. The vessel was about 150 feet long and 60 feet wide, designed to carry ten guns. Due to the shortage of iron for its armor, the *CSS Georgia* was covered with overlapping railroad ties, which added tremendous weight to the boat, causing its engines to be too weak to propel the vessel in the strong current of the Savannah River. The *CSS Georgia* was then anchored near Fort Jackson and designated a floating battery. It was scuttled by her crew on 20 December 1864 as Sherman's forces approached the city. The *CSS Georgia* was also referred to as the "Georgia Ladies Ironclad" and the "floating battery with propellers." *Macon Daily Telegraph* (25 April 1862 and 10 July 1862). The *CSS Georgia*

Back in Virginia, the legion cavalry was making preparations for their change of base to Goldsboro. Their move to North Carolina almost did not happen. "This morning came an order for all of Howell's Brigade to go to Goldsboro, sans tents, sans everything, except knapsacks and cooking utensils," Thomas Cobb wrote his wife. "My cavalry had to go by land of course and I was preparing them to leave when I heard that [by] Genl. Magruder's special request the Legion had been ordered back to Yorktown. My men would rather have been drafted and every tenth man hung, so I hurried them up and before the order reached the camp, I had the cavalry on the road and the artillery horses with them."[10]

Once in the Goldsboro vicinity, the cavalry established Camp Randolph in Wayne County "in a pine grove beside the railroad 4 miles below Goldsboro."[11] Thomas Cobb described the location to his wife: "We have a beautiful camp here about 2 1/2 miles from the town and on the rail road leading to Newbern. I have named it after our new Secretary of War, who, you know, is a favorite with me."[12] The legion cavalry remained in camp here until 4 April, when they were once again on the move.

A week after the legion cavalry left for Goldsboro, E. J. Allen (Allen Pinkerton) submitted in his report to Maj. Gen. George B. McClellan on 29 Mar 1862 "Cobb's Legion, 5 or 6 miles from Big Bethel Church, 2 1/2 miles west of the road to Hampton and opposite Little Bethel. This Legion consists of about 400 cavalry, armed with Maynard's rifles."[13] Although correct as to the arming of the cavalry with Maynard carbines, Allen was of course wrong as to the presence of the cavalry still in the defenses of the peninsula. This faulty intelligence is often cited as one reason that McClellan moved so sluggishly up the peninsula in the summer of 1862.

During this time, the infantry of Cobb's Legion was brigaded in Cobb's Brigade, McLaws's Division, Magruder's Command, Department of Northern Virginia. Thomas Cobb, in command of the legion infantry, went into the Yorktown defenses at Dam No. 2, while the cavalry spent its time recruiting to increase its size

---

was rediscovered during dredging operations in 1968. Beginning in November 2013, the US Corps of Engineers raised the first pieces of the hull in what is expected to be a $14.2-million-dollar effort to recover what is left of the boat—forward and aft casements, remnants of the engines, including boilers, shafts, and propellers, as well as several cannon and ordinance scattered around the wreck.

[10] Thomas R. R. Cobb to Marion, 20 March 1862, T. R. R. Cobb Papers.

[11] Smedlund, *Camp Fires*, 234.

[12] Thomas R. R. Cobb to Marion, 24 March 1862, T. R. R. Cobb Papers. Appointed in March, George W. Randolph was Davis's third secretary of war. Known as a meticulous organizer with a strong work ethic, Randolph continued his predecessor's difficulties with Davis. Coupled with ongoing health problems, Randolph was replaced in November 1862 with James Seddon.

[13] *OR*, ser. 1, vol. 11, pt. 1, 267.

from battalion to regimental strength. The addition of new recruits and their drilling apparently led to some friction among some of the officers, as Thomas Cobb mentioned to his wife on 1 April. "You seem troubled at Deloney's conduct to Ritch. I know nothing about it. I allowed each company commander to select his own officer to drill his recruits. Deloney selected Williams. Of course I asked no questions."[14]

Two and a half weeks later, word was getting around Athens about the friction within the legion cavalry. "Yancey sent me your father's letter to him about Rich," Cobb wrote his wife from Dam No. 2. He continued:

> He certainly laboured under a great mistake both as to Rich and the Recruits of the troop artillery. I allowed each Capt. to select his own officer to recruit and also his officer to drill. I never authorized recruits in any company to organize in Georgia. No harm was done Rich therefore, and he made an ass of himself by making such a fuss about the order for Williams to drill. Rich is a poor drill officer. Williams is a good one. I had no hand or part in the assigning of these officers. I only say these things to relieve a false impression under which I see your father is labouring. Rich is perfectly satisfied.[15]

The month of April was a difficult one for Will Delony. Although back from his recent furlough, he was quickly overtaken by sickness. "At Weldon I overtook Deloney quite sick," wrote Cobb to his wife. "I fear he is going to have an attack of fever. I made Dr. White stay with him today and he will move to Goldsboro tomorrow if he is able."[16] A later visit to his friend found Deloney "still confined to his room from sickness, but the Dr. says is daily improving."[17] *The Southern Watchman* ran a notice on 7 May under the banner "On Furlough" that "Capt. W. G. Delony, who has been seriously ill for some time past, reaches his home in this place, on Thursday evening last. We are pleased to learn that his health is improving."[18]

As for the legion cavalry, things were not going along very well with them either. Even though Cobb was busy trying to get his new recruits organized and added to the ranks, he was having difficulty just getting the troops together and present. On 2 May, Col. Young was sent to Goldsboro to take command of the cavalry and to organize the new recruits into companies and squadrons.[19] In the meantime, more trouble was cropping up, as Cobb confided to Marion, "I received notice today

---

[14] Thomas R. R. Cobb to Marion, 1 April 1862, T. R. R. Cobb Papers.
[15] Ibid., 19 April 1862.
[16] Ibid., 24 March 1862.
[17] Ibid., 1 April 1862.
[18] *Southern Watchman* (7 May 1862).
[19] Thomas R. R. Cobb to Marion, 1 May 1862, T. R. R. Cobb Papers.

that my cavalry has been ordered to Fredericksburg or near there and has Petersburg on the way. This is very annoying. The recruits and new companies are just arriving at Goldsboro. So that my legion will be divided into three sections."[20] On 7 May, the legion cavalry were sent to Fredericksburg about 50 miles above Richmond to keep an eye on Union troop movements as McClellan began gathering reinforcements. Maj. Z. A. Rice recorded, "We have had pretty heavy duty to do since we came here in the way of videtting."[21]

Ten days later, Cobb was still trying to sort things out. "I heard that my cavalry were much disorganized and fearing no engagement for a day or two," he wrote Marion from Richmond. He continued:

General Magruder ordered me last evening at 7 o'clock to come immediately to this place to collect them and carry them to join my legion.... Col. Young with my four old companies is at Guinea depot on the Fredericksburg road, forty five miles from this place, while the four new companies are on the road somewhere, without transportation and coming on the hoof. They will be halted at this place and remain here until they are armed and equipped. I shall leave Johnny Rutherford here to arrange for them until Major Yancey arrives.[22]

Cobb established a base camp about 9 miles outside of Richmond on the Trent Farm along the banks of the Chickahominy on 16 May: "We are resting on the river in the midst of fields of wheat and clover...a more beautiful camp I never saw." Cobb named the place Camp Clover[23] and went on to write, "The woods in which our fires burn brightly are beautifully green. A large fine spring is within ten paces of my camp fire. Beautiful white azaleas and beds of violets and daisies cover the entire ground. Every thing is quiet as a Sabbath day and nothing is heard tonight, but the whippoorwill.... If I only had my cavalry now, they would be of great service in reconnoitering our flank."[24] Gilbert Wright wrote his wife, Dorothy, that "this country around our camps abounds in plenty of corn & fodder & clover for our horses."[25]

---

[20] Ibid., 2 May 1862.
[21] Z. A. Rice to his wife, 19 May 1862, in Stephen Davis and William A. Richards, "An Atlantan Goes to War: The Civil War Letters of Maj. Zachariah A. Rice, C.S.A.," *Atlanta History* (Spring 1992) 30.
[22] Thomas R. R. Cobb to Marion, 12 May 1862, T. R. R. Cobb Papers.
[23] Camp Clover was located in Henrico County on the south bank of the Chickahominy River below the Mechanicsville bridge. See Smedlund, *Camp Fires*, 91.
[24] Thomas R. R. Cobb to Marion, 16 May 1862, T. R. R. Cobb Papers.
[25] Gilbert Wright Letters, 16 May 1862, photocopies T. R. R. Cobb House.

While Cobb waited for his newly recruited cavalry companies to come in, the main body of his cavalry encamped at Camp Caroline in Spotsylvania County.[26] Always the organizer, Cobb wrote his wife that "Major Yancey has reached Richmond and is attending to my new cavalry companies. I can get no arms or equipments for them and consequently am very much annoyed at their situation."[27] Meeting his new Cavalry recruits as they came in, Cobb was startled by what he saw. "I find my new cavalry here in a bad fix, but no worse than I expected. Two companies are still on the way and a part of a third. Not a single arm can be obtained for any of those here, and the prospect of getting them is very remote. I am still lacking over 200 saddles."[28] John Brooks of the legion wrote his father on 24 June, "We have drawn our bridles, blankets, spurs, and sabres, but no saddles nor guns. The officers say to fight with pikes if a battle come on before we draw guns or pistols."[29]

"I went round today and saw all the men," wrote Cobb, "and found then in good spirits and behaving well. I propose to go tomorrow or next day to spend a few days with my old cavalry companies on the Rappahannock."[30] Two days later he wrote, "My cavalry Cos. (new) are camped on the opposite side of the City from the Legion.... If I leave the infantry, they become disorganized. When I leave the cavalry the same result follows."[31]

With his legion disorganized as it was, and on top of everything else involved in trying to get the new recruits settled in, Cobb was faced with another disheartening prospect. "Yancey writes me confidentially," he wrote Marion, "that he intends to resign, thus adding another to my many troubles."[32]

The following day, Thomas Cobb had cheerier news for his wife: "The recruits of troup artillery are behaving excellently, so are Deloney's."[33] A couple of days later, Cobb was able to report that "we have moved camp once more and are now about one mile below the Mechanicsville Bridge.... All of my new cavalry troops are here now except Jones and a few stragglers. I have succeeded in getting sabers for all. Two companies are still without saddles. I shall put two of the companies on duty

[26] Camp Caroline, in Spotsylvania County, was a temporary camp established between the Rappahannock River and the headwaters of the Mattaponi River. See Smedlund, *Camp Fires*, 83.

[27] Thomas R. R. Cobb to Marion, 16 May 1862, T. R. R. Cobb Papers.

[28] Ibid., 18 May 1862.

[29] N. J. Brooks to father, 24 May 1862, Kennesaw Mountain National Battlefield Park Archives.

[30] Thomas R. R. Cobb to Marion, 18 May 1862, T. R. R. Cobb Papers.

[31] Ibid., 20 May 1862.

[32] Ibid., 16 May 1862.

[33] Ibid., 23 May 1862.

tomorrow. Anderson's[34] falling back will bring my old companies to me at last and thus I shall have my whole command together once more."[35]

Cobb's elations, however, came crashing back to earth on 26 May when he was forced to report to Marion that not only had Major Yancey indeed resigned, but also that "Capt. Knight is at home sick. Col. Young absent with the old cavalry. The new cavalry here with green officers, and a battle impending."[36] Writing from Camp Randolph the next day, Cobb reported to his wife, "There was some talk of moving us ten miles down the R. R. towards Kinston, and the object of my ride was to examine the locality and look out for a camp. We shall be loth to leave here as we have a beautiful camp.... Capt. Deloney came down last night. I have not yet seen him, as he is in town, in a private house, but Dr. White tells me he is quite sick and very low spirited. I shall visit him in the morning and if he is no better I shall telegraph for his wife."[37] Two days later, Cobb got even more disheartening news when "Capt. Stovall resigned today because I would not have him appointed Major without giving Deloney a hearing before the department."[38]

On 30 May, Cobb confided to his wife, "My four old companies of cavalry are ordered to come to me tomorrow morning. So soon as I get the Battalion together I shall organize it thoroughly.... By Stovall's resignation (who has acted like a dirty dog) Deloney becomes Major. Young will be Lt. Col. Williams and Rich will each be Captains in Deloney's old squadron."[39] Cobb immediately forwarded a recommendation for Delony's promotion to major of cavalry to George W. Randolph, the Confederacy's secretary of war.[40] Gaining approval, Cobb made his decisions public and reorganized the legion cavalry, naming P. M. B. Young lieutenant colonel, William G. Delony major, and W. L. Church as adjutant. At the same time, he promoted Lt. Zachariah Rice as captain of the Fulton Dragoons. Cobb also designated the 1st Squadron composed of Companies B and G of the Fulton Dragoons; 2nd Squadron was composed of Companies A and I (Richmond and Fulton counties) of the Richmond Hussars of Augusta; 3rd Squadron of Companies C and H of the Georgia Troopers of Athens (Clarke, Hall, Jackson, and Lumpkin counties); and 4th Squadron of companies E, Roswell Troopers from Cobb and Gwinnett, and F, Grubb's Hussars of DeKalb.

---

[34] Gen. George Thomas "Tige" Anderson. See Biographical Roster.
[35] Thomas R. R. Cobb to Marion, 25 May 1862, T. R. R. Cobb Papers.
[36] Ibid., 26 May 1862. See Biographical Roster.
[37] Ibid., 26 March 1862.
[38] Ibid., 28 May 1862. See Biographical Roster.
[39] Ibid., 30 May 1862.
[40] Thomas R. R. Cobb to G. W. Randolph, 2 June 1862, "Letters Received," C.S.A.I.G.O., D-459-1862, NARS.

Delony missed all of the turmoil within the legion. He was particularly missed by Thomas Cobb: "I am very sorry Deloney did not come on," he wrote his wife. "I hope he will not fail to leave on Monday next as he promises to do. My mind will be easy comparatively when I get these Battalions organized."[41] The reorganizing of the legion cavalry may have been the primary reason why they were not involved in the fighting during the battle of Seven Pines (Fair Oaks).

* * *

Augusta March 8 1862

My Dear Rosa

We arrived here safely tonight and will remain until morning as we make nothing by going on tonight. Col. Cobb recd another dispatch saying that the Legion and the 16th Ga. Regt. (Col. Howell Cobbs old Regt) and the 2nd Florida Regt. were all ordered from the Peninsula to Suffolk and Genl Howell Cobb will be in command. We have heard nothing more. I have thought of my poor little scrap and our precious children the livelong day and feel homesick and heartsick of being compelled to leave you all so suddenly. I hope most sincerely that it will not be long before we can again meet. Indeed I think we will not have to remain long at Suffolk if the reinforcement is sent to repel Burnsides as I think it is. If sufficient numbers are sent to Suffolk he will make no attack but go somewhere else I think very shortly & I do not yet despair of being again with you by the 15th April. I shall miss you all now more than ever & I hardly know what will become of me without the prattle of my precious little children, all alone in my tent, with my poor little wife too all alone at home. God bless you all Darling & keep you in health and good spirits is my earnest prayer. Dont give up, it will all turn out right I hope and believe. I saw Dick at Union Point looking miserable. He ought not to continue in the service. From his cough & what he tells me I would not be surprised if he already had consumption.[42]

Kiss my little folks for Papa and tell Rosa to write to me and I will answer her letter forthwith. My love to Aunty with a heartful for my precious wife.

Ever yours
W. G. Delony

Camp Hunter March 13 1862

My Dear Rosa

I wrote you yesterday and hope today to hear from you but no letter yet and I do not know how to account for it. I had hoped to be able today leisurely to write

---

[41] Thomas R. R. Cobb to Marion, 30 May 1862, T. R. R. Cobb Papers.
[42] Tuberculosis.

you a good long letter but I had to go with the Col to see the Genl directly after breakfast, have just returned, have eaten for dinner, fried eggs & hard biscuit and am just about starting on a reconnoitering expedition below. Tomorrow I am ordered to go on a scouting expedition which was delayed from today till tomorrow because of the news from Newbern. When we go I presume we will be absent for several days, and as I now think the expedition entirely unnecessary I go very unwillingly. Burnsides will take Newbern and I am very confident we will have nothing to do here, consequently I am sorry to think I ever left Athens, & this feeling makes me so homesick I scarcely know what to do with myself. The truth is I am becoming discouraged at the utter want of capacity evinced by our leaders & I do not know whom to trust, and being here constantly on the move and accomplishing nothing, performing services so useless to the cause of the South makes me feel badly enough. Our horses are so poor that they could make no impression on unarmed regiment & yet we are drilled to death in stately style and so everything goes on from the President down. I am disgusted & disheartened. We want new leaders.

God bless you all Darling. I will write you before leaving in the morning. My horse is awaiting me. Kiss our precious little children for me & accept a warm heartful of love from

Your own
Will

Camp Hunter March 13, 1862

My Dear Rosa,

I hope you recd the little note I wrote you on my way to Pig's Point.[43] I did not write as I promised because I found the distance down there much greater than I supposed and only got back last evening after the mail had left Camp. So dont imagine that I have forgotten you for I think of nobody else and if you could see the discomfort of my life how now you would conclude I could never forget such a home and such a wife as I have left.

We are encamped in the woods, and all the cooking utensils of both officers and privates of my Company were left in a mud hole between this & our old camp. We can buy nothing in Suffolk & can get nothing from the Gen. Quartermaster, so that I am living now upon other people, taking my meals whenever I hear of a good one. Maj. Yancy has very kindly invited me to become his guest until I can get my "Kitchen furniture" & the gentlemen have extended the same courtesies, so that I

---

[43] Pig's Point, known today as Harbour View, near Suffolk, Virginia, sits at the mouth of the Nansemond River and was the site of the 5 June 1861 engagement between the Union gunboat *Harriet Lane* and Confederate defenders.

am not abandoned in my extremity. My bedding & India Rubber Coat & pants[44] are all here & all my other things & in a few days I will doubtless be very comfortable.

I had a fine view of the late battle ground of the Merrimac, saw the masts of the Cumberland, & also saw the famous & formidable ole Ericson, which contended so formidably with the Merrimac. The latter is not seriously injured, will soon be repaired.[45]

I have heard nothing from you yet, hoped to hear this morning but was disappointed and the Camp seems more desolate and uncomfortable & gloomy than ever. You can imagine how I miss the dear little children & how homesick I am. If we do go to Tennessee[46] you will have to go to the upcountry where I can occasionally see you, both on my own account & on account of my poor little Scrap for whom I feel most deeply in her solitude & loneliness. I will write you a long letter in the morning telling you all I know. Maj. Charlie Whitehead has just come to spend the night with me so good bye Darling. Think sweetly of your own

Will

Camp Hunter March 16 1862

My Dear Rosa

I yesterday received your letter of the 9th Apr inst and you cant conceive the pleasure of hearing from home. I was on horseback passing through town on a reconnoitering expedition when it was handed me by the postmaster, and a more welcome gift he could not have made me. I can imagine your loneliness and measure it by my own. I never was so homesick, restless, and down hearted in my life. Here I am away from all I love, sleeping on the wet ground, my horse poor, nothing to do, nobody to see, nothing to eat and an oven & a pot to cook it in. The fact is my discomforts are so great that the ridiculousness of my situation makes even misery farcical. I smoke my pipe and think of home and bear it as best I may. If our leaders would only give us something to do besides drilling our horses to death I and all other soldiers would be better satisfied, and my decided opinion is they would be in better health decidedly. I have one man from Clark, Green Jackson quite sick with fever. He is very comfortable at one of the hotels in town with his brother there to nurse him & will I hope do well but I have a poor fellow in Camp dying hour by hour from a gun shot wound. One of his comrades was examining a new pistol

---

[44] Natural rubber.

[45] The battle took place 9 March.

[46] Federal forces under C. F. Smith began advancing up the Tennessee River 4 March resulting in numerous small engagements through the heart of the state.

which he did not understand. It went off in his hands and four balls entered his shoulder & arm, 3 of the balls cannot be found & the Surgeon thinks he is bleeding internally slowly to death. He is a fine young fellow by the name of Tucker Barrett from Lumpkin Co., a good soldier & a clever man. My own health is fine I am looking and feeling well, & you need not feel uneasy about my blue suit as the grey suit that you sent me arrived day before yesterday. The coat fits well, but is not made as Bloomfield agreed to make it. He is a Yankee however and I suppose it was too good a chance for him. If I could get another suit elsewhere, I would send this one back immediately but I cannot. I ordered and he agreed to make a double breasted coat, the one he made is single breasted. I could have supplied good brass buttons enough from my old coat for a single breasted one, but told him expressly that as the Coat was to be double breasted he would have to use & I would be satisfied with his uniform buttons. I suppose he wanted to save his cloth.

I am glad to learn that Dr King has succeeded so well in making up his company & hope he will be in the Legion. You can say to him if he comes to Athens or get Mr King to write him that if he dont get men enough I think I can supply the number if he will give one of my men a Lieutenancy. I cant say that I see any prospect of my coming to Ga shortly. I certainly will come as soon as I can, but I do not know what I will be able to do or where the Legion will be ordered as I cannot understand the policy of the Confederate Government which converts every fight into a disgrace to our arms. Our Army is scattered over the country in small bands of 8 or 10,000 men and whenever and wherever the enemy advances we "retire" as a retreat is called. We have had about 7,000 effective men to repel Burnsides. If he comes here, he will have from 20 to 40,000 and we will "retire", where to or when this thing will end I can [not] see. I am disgusted. The single state of Georgia has 60 or 70,000 men in the field and it seems impossible for Pres Davis to assemble in one body 50,000 troops upon any battle field from all the Confederate States. I can only hope for the best. There is no present prospect of a fight here however and I am glad of it as the mud of the Peninsula has made sad havoc of my horses.

God bless you all Darling. How I should like you and our precious this gloomy March day. I thank my poor heart good. You must not let the dear little creatures forget me and make little Rosa write to me & tell Tom if I catch a little Yankee I [will] bring him one. Col Cobb is in Richmond. I think I can be elected Col. of the new Regt of Cavalry. Heaven bless you and protect you Darling is my daily prayer.

Ever Your own
Will
P. S. Our camp is named after Mrs Hunter.

Suffolk Mch. 17, 1862

My Dear Rosa,

Yours of the 10th I recd today am glad to hear all are well but feel truly sorry for my poor little Scrap all alone & deserted at home. I hope some one will soon be raised up to stay with you until this abominable war is over. Montague can tell how I miss you and our dear precious little children and how lonely and desolate the camp now seems. I am busy all day long from rising until night and can get thru the day pretty well but when the night closes in I am so lost and homesick I am miserable indeed. I wish the Yankees were near enough to render scouting parties necessary. The excitement then would make camp endurable.

Ritch I expect has his hands full. His orders were to leave for Atlanta on the 11th if there was no prospect of raising a 3rd Company. I agree with you that he will fail now. He has now on hand more than that little head of his can well manage. I was accused in a letter of his to Early, in which he said he was "putting the boys thro' the drills & wished he had Early's head to help him." It would be a brilliant pair of heads tho. I am disgusted with jackasses _____ and _____ them all about me. I _____ yesterday. The postmaster is near about on me. Kiss the little ones & tell Rosa to kiss Mama for

Yr own Will

I sent to yr care today a telegram to A. B. & Son. His son is very ill. I hope you send it immediately on its arrival.

Camp Hunter March 19, 1862

My Dear Rosa

Here I am seated by a camp fire in front of my tent, a cold rain, east winds blowing, & the Camp quite as uncomfortable as you can well conceive. My portfolio is on my knee for such a thing as a table is a luxury unknown. The Quarter masters Department is too poor to furnish plank for tables or horse troughs and my mess desk is lost so that I have nothing to write on. I could afford a barrel if the Commissary Department were not so badly furnished that we were compelled to return all the flour barrels that are sent us. To add to all my troubles my household & kitchen furniture & all the cooking utensils of my company were lost in the move out here owing to the want of a good head for the Legion. Cobb was absent but Yancey was there in all his feathers.

This letter will be handed you by Lieut Williams who is going to Atlanta to take charge of my recruits. Last night Cobb agreed as I understand him, that Williams & Ritch should both remain as I know to be necessary. This morning he says but one can remain. I tried to let him take Church with him but the Col. says he can not get along without Church as he is the most efficient non-commissioned officer in the Legion. Strange that he can spare Maj. Yancey who goes to take charge of the Atlanta Camp[47] Young being recalled at his own request. Stovall told me that Cobb told him that he ordered me on here because he did not want me to have any advantage of the other Captains. Also that Young told him he ought to have been appointed and that he would do anything for him he could do. So thus and thus men work the wires. What think you. Stovall has come up to my fire and wants to "combine."[48]

I am well, hearty, and contented. The men if left alone will elect me but what wire-working will accomplish, none can tell. I am disgusted "intirely." God bless you all Darling, think of me kindly and I am fully satisfied.

I am going below with two companies of Cavalry and some wagons on Friday to be gone 6 or 8 days gathering or rather buying corn for the Gov. before the Yankees come up and get it, so if you hear from me irregularly now for some time you may know the reason. I shall write to you whenever I can get to a post office to mail a letter and you must not be uneasy about me for I shall be prudent & it does seem to me that the rough life of a soldier agrees with me for I never felt better in my life. I have still some sickness in my company. Jackson is very low, but I think slightly better than he was yesterday and I hope will at least live until his father sees him as he is anxious to have him here. Barrett who was shot is still lingering, without pain and uncomplaining, still I have little or no hope of his recovery. We have no other serious cases. Kiss the precious little ones for me and accept for yourself a heart full of love from

Your own Will

Camp Hunter March 19 1862

My Dear Darling little Daughter

Your sweet little letter that you wrote to me came from the post office today and Papa thinks it was a heap sweeter than the little letters Bella used to write to

---

[47] The "Atlanta camp" was a training camp established for the new recruits that Delony and other officers had recently raised for the legion. "Tomorrow I shall send Major Yancey to Atlanta to take charge of the camp there, where I shall continue to collect cavalry companies and recruits." Thomas R. R. Cobb to Marion, 18 March 1862, T. R. R. Cobb Papers.

[48] "Combining" is Delony's reference to forming a "mess," which was the usual term soldiers used for pitching together in camp duties. A mess was generally a group of four to six men— "messmates" —who took turns cooking for the others, ate together, and slept in the same tent. They generally shared everything, i.e., plates, cups, forks, and food. Officers had their own messes and generally a body servant who also cooked. Rarely did officers and the common soldiers mix in messes.

her dear Mama. I love you My little Darling, just as much as you love me. I think I love you more but I dont know which I love the most you or Bubber Tom or dear little Willie. You are all so sweet and good to Papa and you must help Mama take care of little Tom & Willie till Papa comes home again and then we will all be so happy once more, and Papa will read to you and you will say your hymns for me and you & Papa will teach Bubber Tom how to spell & say hymns too. You must give Mama a sweet kiss for Papa right in the mouth, & kiss Tom & Willie too & tell them all how much Papa loves you all, & give my love to Mama too and tell her she must take good care of you all for Papa, but not to take you to the Depot till Papa comes back & write to me again very soon, for I love you so dearly.

Your own dear Papa
My Sabres are all Sharp.

Weldon N.C. Mch 25, 1862

My Dear Rosa,

I am better today but being under the influence of quinine feel very badly. My tongue is clearing off and I hope in a day or two to be up again. Col. Cobb has very kindly left Dr White with me who is as kind as he can be. Our accommodations here however are very poor and as soon as a passenger train leaves for Goldsboro we shall go on there where I can be more comfortable. I would give $1000 for the sight of your dear face this evening. We are going now. So good bye. God bless you all Darling.

Ever Yr own Will

Goldsboro Tuesday 26th Mch [1862]

My Dear Rosa,

As I was writing you yesterday Dr White came up and hurried me off as a train was about leaving for this place & off we started at 6 oclock P.M. & arrived here at half past two this morning. The hotels were all crowded & I spent the balance of the night on a pallet in the barroom. I am now however comfortably located at a private house a large carpeted room and everything around betokening comfort. I feel better already and indeed have little or no fever. The effects of the quinine I am taking are disagreeable but otherwise I feel quite bright today. If I have fever it is imperceptible to me and I hope that in a very little wile I shall be quite well again. I was very much disappointed in not receiving letters from you by Col. Cobb who left Suffolk on Sunday. You ought to write me regularly. Kiss our dear little children for me and excuse short letters until the quinine leaves my head. The Dr. says I have no typhoid symptoms. God bless you all Darling.

Ever Yr own Will

Goldsboro March 27 [1862]

My Dear Rosa,

The Doctor says today that I am a good deal better, free from fever and doing well. If I could only see you I am sure I would very soon be up but I dont think I was ever so home sick in my life notwithstanding the great kindness I am recovering at the hands of those with whom I am staying—Col & Mrs Raiford. It is hard indeed to be sick away from those we love. I felt well enough this morning to be up but the Doctor makes me keep my bed and has been pouring down the quinine in such quantities that I can scarcely see or hear or think. I have written you now every day since I was taken sick & will continue to do so. Will telegraph if I should grow worse.[49] Kiss our precious little children for me and accept for yrself a heartfull of love

from
Yr own Will

Augusta June 3, 1862

My Dear Rosa

I arrived here safely this afternoon with dry feet and feel quite well tonight except that I miss more than I can tell you the sound of your voice and the prattling of our dear little children. Poor little Tom, I know he has missed me this rainy day. I hope we will not be long separated. If successful at Richmond I do not fear a long continuance of the war. There are a thousand rumors about the fight there Saturday and Sunday.[50] Among others is one that the infantry of the Legion were badly cut up and suffered more than any other Georgia Regt. Others say they were not in the fight at all, so that until we certainly know the truth you had better say nothing about it. I met old Mr Stovall tonight who tells me that Capt. Stovall has resigned,

---

[49] That evening, Cobb made good on his promise to check on the health of his friend. Writing his customary daily letter to Marion, Cobb reported, "Capt. Deloney is much better today and speaks of coming to camp in a day or two. You can tell Mrs. D. to rest easy, for I was resolved to telegraph her, if there had been any necessity." Thomas R. R. Cobb to Marion, 27 March 1862, T. R. R. Cobb Collection. A week later Cobb again checked on Delony and found him "better, but looks badly." Thomas R. R. Cobb to Marion, 3 April 1862, T. R. R. Cobb Papers.

[50] The battle of Fair Oaks or Seven Pines.

and the report in this city is that I have been appointed Major, but who is the Let. Col. seems to be unknown. My coat is not yet done, but in the hands of the workmen, price $35.00 cheaper than I expected. I will get Hal Billups to bring it on for me. I bought 5 pounds of Candy for you and the children which Ned Lumpkin will bring up day after tomorrow. Dr Bradley & Nash are both going on so I will be well taken care of, particularly as I intend to be very prudent. Kiss our precious little ones for me and accept a heartful of love for yourself.

Ever yours,
W. G. Delony

P. S. Mrs Hunter treated me very badly at the depot. Tell her I wont forgive her unless she makes the amend honorable when I next return home.

W. G. D.

On 5 June, Cobb again complained to his wife, Marion,

I returned yesterday from my cavalry camp.... I long to see Deloney and Knight arrive. Their absence clogs my whole movements. I hope to see them both tonight and Miller also. You ask me if they do not treat Hampton Legion the same as mine. *They do not*, hence my complaint. *Until the last week* they have never separated his cavalry from him. For more than six months they had attached *Georgia regiments* to his legion and thus given him command of 2500 infantry when his legion is not as large as mine by fifty percent. He has under 200 cavalry. I have over 700. He has 600 infantry, I have as many. But to swell his command Georgians are attached to his legion and *all pass* as the Hampton Legion. While for more than ten weeks I have been reduced to a Major's command. My wife, my blood boils when I think of the treatment I have recd.[51]

Goldsboro June 6, 1862

My Dear Rosa,

I arrived here safely last night after a tedious route via Charlotte & Raleigh. We missed the connection for the Wilmington route at Kingsville and I was obliged to go by the upper route. We were behind time all the way and your lunch came in very well I assure but our new commissary Miller Lumpkin came on with a large basket full all sorts of good things, so that having nothing else to do we amused ourselves all the day before yesterday in eating & it being a very warm day I drank

---

[51] Thomas R. R. Cobb to Marion, 5 June 1862, T. R. R. Cobb Papers.

too much miserably mean water. The consequence of all which was that yesterday morning I had Cholera Morbus[52] on the cars and when I reached here was completely used up, but after a good nights rest and eating only one bicuit [*sic*] yesterday feel quite bright again today. Williams is here looking miserably, has been sick, but I think will be able to go on with me tonight. No one else of my company is here.

My Tom's horse is looking splendidly. You never saw a finer. The black has been sick and looks badly. I am afraid he will never be worth much to me.

I dined today with Col & Mrs Raiford. They are now all well but have been sick as she wrote you. The baby has grown a good deal but still looks small & feeble for its age. I shall call upon Mrs Stephenson this afternoon. She too I am informed has been quite sick.

I met Capt. Stovall here today on his return home. He tells me that Cobb refused to recommend him to the War Department for promotion as the Senior Captain as it would be doing injustice to me holding that I was Senior. The upshot of all which was as I understand that Cobb submitted to the Department a statement of the facts & it was determined that I was entitled to the Majority, but at the same time Stovall insisted that the Statement Cobb submitted did not embrace all the facts so that I presume that I can be the Major if I desire it, but another difficulty arises. Ritch has been elected Captain of the new company, and he insists that my promotion entitles him to the command of my old company. Williams swears he wont serve under him & Cobb wants to make Williams Senior Captain which in my humble opinion he can't do. In addition I learn that Capt. Rice insists upon an election and desires the position & more over the War Department decides that we have the right to elect a Lt Col but by some arrangement Cobb has had Young assigned to the Cavalry & Young is uneasy in his position, so you cant address your letters to me as Capt. until I get to Richmond & determine what to do. God bless you Darling. Kiss the little Darlings for me and don't let them forget Papa.

Ever Yours
W. G. Delony

---

[52] A gastrointestinal infection with abdominal pain, diarrhea, and sometimes vomiting as symptoms.

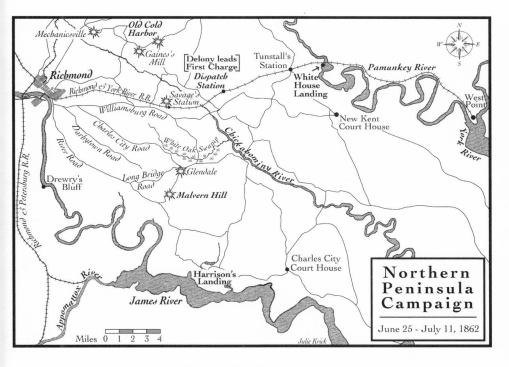

Battles and skirmishes involving
William G. Delony and Cobb's Georgia Legion Cavalry.

Chapter 6

First Blood:
June 1862–August 1862

And every minstrel sound his glee,
And all our trumpets blow;
And, from the platform, spare ye not
To fire a noble salvo-shot:
Lord Marmion waits below!
　　　　　—*Marmion* by Sir Walter Scott

"Miller has not come nor Deloney," wrote Cobb to his wife. "Knight came last night. I shall have him appointed Lt. Colonel today."[1] In the summer of 1862, the legion was heavily involved in vidette duty along the Chickahominy River[2] while at the same time undergoing another reorganization.

　　Robert E. Lee took over command of the Army of Northern Virginia 1 June and quickly began a reorganization. Legions, by then recognized as structurally ineffective, were dismantled. At the time, Wade Hampton was impressively commanding brigades in Thomas J. Jackson's Division. On 28 July, Hampton was transferred to J. E. B. Stuart's cavalry division as Stuart's senior subordinate. He took with him all the cavalry of Cobb's Legion. Predictably, Tom Cobb recoiled. "Today I am informed that my cavalry is placed under Hampton," Cobb wrote home in early August. "In plain English my legion is to be swallowed up and lost in his."[3]

　　Delony's character as a person in private life was already established. Now, as the legion began to settle into more normal military duties, his character also began

---

[1] Thomas R. R. Cobb to Marion, 7 June 1862, T. R. R. Cobb Papers.

[2] The legion settled into their new camp, called Camp Birdie, probably a picket camp named after Cobb's youngest daughter, nicknamed "Birdie." Birdie was less than 2 years old when her father was killed at Fredericksburg. She later married Hoke Smith, who would go on to become governor of Georgia (1907–1909 and partial term in 1911) before being elected senator. From this camp, the legion cavalry "for several weeks did…picket with almost a daily or nightly skirmish, our only way to drill recruits until we were ordered to the Rappahannock to report to Jackson." Athens *Banner* (30 April 1892).

[3] Thomas R. R. Cobb to Marion, 29, 31 July 1862, T. R. R. Cobb Papers.

to arise in those circles as well. Delony quickly was becoming a favorite of those with whom he was serving. "His heart and his purse were ever open to their needs. While on the Peninsula, the first winter of the war, where Hilton, a rugged mountain boy and a fine soldier died of fever, DeLoney sent to Richmond and procured a metalic coffin and sent his body to his father in Hall county, Ga., at his own expense."[4]

Francis Eve, a member of the Richmond Hussars, recounted a story years later in the Athens *Banner* of Delony's character.

> At Massaponax church, on the Fredericksburg Old Plank Road, after a thirty-six hour scout, being a private at the time in the Richmond Hussars, and after making my report went to my company expecting my rations as I had not had anything to eat or my horse either, only to find that there was nothing for us. My language, I am afraid, was neither chaste or elegant and I was hungry enough to fight a circular saw, when Major Deloney's command to "come here sir" made me go to headquarters then under "a black jack" with my wrath pent up for there I knew I had to behave. I stated my cause of grievance both to his, Will Church and Frank Jones' amusement who were lying on the Major's blanket with him. Ordering me down on the blanket between them, the Major with a threat to make me carry a fence rail if I spoke of it, passed that historic flask into my willing hand and my ire and appetite disappeared as John, the Major's body servant, produced the Major's haversack, and I was ordered to eat my fill and make no more disturbance in camp or I would be sent to the guard house, none being nearer than Richmond.[5]

The legion was fairly contented and apparently eating well at the time, as attested to in Thomas Cobb's letter home:

> I weighed just now on Miller's scales, 155 pounds. This is just 41 pounds less than when I came into the service. Miller tells me he has gained twelve pounds since he reached the camp. Deloney has fattened six pounds in one week. The water at this camp has a strong sulphur taste and I would not be surprised if some good effects might not result from it. The men in his battalion are much healthier than the infantry. Close by my tent is an ice-pond and such a croaking of frogs at night you never heard in your life. This morning, while sitting under the shade I saw a large fellow put his head out of the water. I took my rifle and shot him and for the first time in

---

[4] Wiley C. Howard, "Sketch of Cobb Legion Cavalry and Some Incidents and Scenes remembered" (Atlanta: Camp 159, published talk given at U.C.V. meeting) 19 August 1901, 12. 12.

[5] Athens *Banner* (2 May 1893).

my life ate a piece of frog for dinner today. I could not stomach much although it was tender and nice.[6]

On 25 June, Thomas Cobb personally took command of his legion cavalry when Lee launched his strike upon McClellan's Federals east of Richmond. Lee's plan was for the Confederate army to attack those Union forces north of the Chickahominy River at Mechanicsville, Virginia. "Stonewall" Jackson's force was to spearhead the attack with J. E. B. Stuart's Cavalry, including the legion cavalry, covering the advance.[7] The legion cavalry immediately broke camp and moved out to join Jackson's Infantry as it advanced to meet the enemy. The Battle of Mechanicsville the following day was uneventful for the legionaries, as they were involved as a flanking screen, although a few units did skirmish with some of the Union pickets of Fitz John Porter's Union corps comprising McClellan's right flank.

F. W. Walter, a member of the legion, later wrote a friend that the legion left Camp "Meathows [sic] with Stuart's Brigade. At night we came up with Gen. Jackson's command."[8] With Col. Cobb in command, Wiley Howard reported,

We were drawn up in battle array, mounted and expecting for two hours to charge while the enemy's artillery played on our position, the bursting of shells and the occasional whizzing of minie balls about us, the terrific roar of musketry and booming of cannon to our right, the clouds of dust that noted the track of the moving combatants, the occasional sight of the wounded being taken back, and wild cheering of Jackson's men and others as they pressed back the serried ranks of the foe from one line of defense to another, the rapid riding of couriers and staff officers scurrying hither and thither with messages and orders to commanding officers.... The battery which we had expected to charge with the infantry support having been silenced and withdrawn, we moved out and engaged until after nightfall in pursuing and pressing back the retreating foe, skirmishing, taking prisoners, etc. Then we went what seemed a long way down, where the enemy had been, in darkness, passing among the dead and wounded and listening to the heart-rending groans of the wounded as they cried for water and help.[9]

---

[6] Thomas R. R. Cobb to Marion, 19 June 1862, T. R. R. Cobb Papers.

[7] This cavalry force included six regiments of Virginia cavalry and three companies from the 1st North Carolina, plus additional horsemen from Cobb's Legion, the Jeff Davis Legion (of Mississippi), a squadron of Hampton's Legion (South Carolina), as well as Stuart's horse artillery and two guns under Capt. John Pelham. See Stuart's Report, 4 July 1862, OR vol. 11, pt. 2, 513.

[8] F. W. Walter Letters in private possession. Transcripts in file of Keith Bohannon.

[9] Howard, "Sketch of Cobb Legion Cavalry," 5–6.

McClellan ordered Porter to hold his position at all costs so that the Federals could change their base of operations to the James River and the protection of the Union gunboats. Jackson's forces attacked Porter midafternoon. Led by John Bell Hood's Texas Brigade[10] and George Edward Pickett's Virginians, the Confederates were able to break through Porter's defense, forcing him to withdraw across the Chickahominy.

Lee's attack at Mechanicsville and the following day at Gaines Mill, although costly in terms of Confederate casualties (more than 8,000 killed and wounded), achieved its goal. McClellan was forced to retreat down the peninsula. Believing that the Federals would retreat eastward toward White House,[11] Virginia, on the Pamunkey River, Lee sent Stuart and his cavalry toward the town on 28 June to burn the bridges. While on their way, the legion cavalry ran into some enemy cavalry with whom they skirmished before the Federals fell back. Stuart's cavalry, however, did not encounter any Union infantry along the way, an indication that McClellan's main body was not retiring in this direction. By the time the Confederate cavalry reached White House, which had been McClellan's main supply base, they found that the Federals had already safely removed the bulk of the supplies. However, the Federals were not able to carry off everything. "We have captured a great quantity of Stores & supplies &c wagons, Horses camps prisoners &c," wrote Z. A. Rice of the legion cavalry. "We have seen some pretty hard Service bothe man & horse but now we have plenty of Yankees corn & oats for our horses & coffee & sugar for ourselves."[12] Another Confederate trooper also recorded the tremendous haul the cavalry captured from the quickly retreating Federals: "barrels of sugar, lemons by the millions, cases of wine, beer and other liquors of every description, confectionery, canned meats, and fruits and vegetables, and great quantities of ice, all in excellent condition. The eggs were packed in barrels of salt, and where they had been exposed to fire, the salt was fused into a solid cake with the eggs, deli-

---

[10] Hood's Texas Brigade at this time included the 18th Georgia Infantry. This regiment included many personal friends of the members of Cobb's Georgia Legion, and the 18th would be reassigned during Lee's general reorganization in the fall of 1862 to become part of Cobb's Georgia Brigade (Infantry), commanded by Thomas R. R. Cobb.

[11] The White House on the Pamunkey River near West Point, Virginia, was the home of William Henry Fitzhugh (Rooney) Lee. The house was originally owned by Martha Custis, who married George Washington. It was passed down through the family line to Rooney Lee, who inherited the house in 1857. The house was burned to the ground on 28 June 1862 as George B. McClellan retreated following the Seven Days' Battles.

[12] Zachariah A. Rice to his wife, 30 June 1862, Atlanta History Society.

ciously roasted, distributed throughout the mass; it was only necessary to split off a block and then pick out the eggs, like the meat of a nut."[13]

"Sunday we went to White House," wrote F. W. Walter. "There we saw a desolate picture of ruined Federal war materials and sutler stores. At this place our squadron remained for a week to guard the things that were not burned. Here, for that time, we lived high. We had all we could eat. We made bread of all eggs and flour, rather stiff, but we considered it fine."[14]

Lee again attacked McClellan on 29 June at Savage's Station and the following day at White Oak Swamp, hoping that the attacks would propel the Union retreat to the James River to pick up its speed. The legion cavalry, in the meantime, proceeded to Tunstall's Station, where it destroyed track and cars, after which they returned to White House. Wiley Howard, a private in the legion, recorded the unit's actions the following day:

> Early next morning we were to go, striking the railroad leading to the White House on Pamunkey river near West Point. At Dispatch Station we quickly attacked a body of the enemy, Major DeLoney leading, charging them and dispersing them. Our casualties were, Lieut. Early, wounded in the arm, and Bugler Fred Walters, scalp wound with saber, both of Company C, while private Sam Bailey, of the same company, was the first to draw blood with saber from an invader. Having torn up the railroad, we proceeded to the White House, where my company was in charge for two days, when we rejoined the command near bloody Malvern Hill.[15]

Howard was not the only one to acknowledge Delony's efforts in the encounter. Thomas Cobb mentioned Delony specifically in his report of operations from 26 June to 10 July:

Headquarters Georgia Legion

July 17, 1862

> We left our camp on an hour's notice on the evening of June 25, joining General Stuart upon the Brooke turnpike and continuing the march until we met the army of General Jackson near Ashland that night.
> Nothing special occurred with my command on 26th.
> On the 27th, near the close of the battle at Cold Harbor, we were ordered forward into the field. The position in which we were halted exposed my entire line to the fire of one of the enemy's batteries, which lost no time

---

[13] W. W. Blackford, *War Years with Jeb Stuart* (New York: Charles Scribner's Sons, 1945) 71.

[14] F. W. Walter Letters.

[15] Howard, "Sketch of Cobb Legion Cavalry," 6–7.

in opening upon us. Finding my men immediately within the range and the shells striking under their horses and exploding over their heads, I promptly removed them under the cover of the hill; fortunately no casualty occurred.

On Saturday, 28th, one of my squadrons, under command of Major Delony, was in advance, with orders to proceed to Dispatch Station. Finding it defended by cavalry, they were promptly charged and put to flight. On pursuing them beyond the railroad another company of cavalry was found in line, who were as promptly charged and routed.

The only casualties to this squadron was a flesh wound received in the arm by Lieutenant Early; a slight saber cut on the head by a private (Walters), and slight wounds to one or two horses.

Our success enabled us to cut the wires and break the communications between the enemy and his base. While separated from the main column on 28th my command captured three wagons and teams of the enemy and several prisoners that were sent to the rear.

On Sunday, 29th, I was detached and ordered to proceed to Tunstall's Station to destroy the track, cars, &c., at that point, which was done. On that evening I rejoined the command at the White House.

On Monday, 30th, by order, I left one squadron at the White House to complete the work of destruction there, with orders to preserve certain property and send it to Richmond. This squadron did not rejoin me until after the 10th.

I continued with the column until Thursday, July 3, when I was ordered by General Stuart to take position near Shirley, on James River, in the rear of the enemy. This position I occupied until the 10th. I found the rear guard consisted of about 2,000 infantry, one battery of artillery, and about 500 cavalry. These protected a wagon train of 300 or 400 wagons. With the assistance of a few guns and two regiments of infantry I think I could have captured this train and its guard, and I applied accordingly both to General Lee and General Stuart. They were not furnished, doubtlessly for good reasons, until General A. P. Hill arrived on the 6th (I believe), at which time the entire train and guard had crossed the creek and joined the main army.

My scouts brought in numerous prisoners, who were sent to the rear, and my command collected a large number of small-arms and other stores, which were secured.

All of which is respectfully submitted.

Thos. R. R. Cobb
Colonel, Commanding Georgia Legion[16]

---

[16] *OR*, ser. 1, vol. 11, pt. 2, 524–25.

F. W. Walter recorded the following:

> On Saturday, our Squadron received orders to take Dispatch Station on the Railroad.... On account of the rugged and rough country not more than one squadron could be employed. We arrived at the station at about eleven o'clock in the morning.... "Forward Boys!" Commanded Major Deloney, in a loud voice. With sabres drawn we went in a gallop fifty yards down hill and then two hundred yards up the next. The enemy's infantry fire poured out from the woods on both sides. Then we came into the open field where the enemy's cavalry was drawn up. "Charge!" was the command, and with a "Hurrah" that enlivened everything we went in. The Yankees must have disliked this for in a few minutes they were forced to retire. We drove them for about a mile when it became advisable for us to return. I, for my part, received a slight sabre cut on the head and Lieut. Early, a pistol shot through the arm. These were the only wounds received on our side.... We tore up the railroad track for fifty yards and also burned a nearby bridge. Next day we went to Dunston Station where we also ruined the railroad.[17]

On 2 July, Stuart's Cavalry and Cobb's Legion rejoined the Confederate army and went into a new camp dubbed Camp Hardtimes in Henrico County, Virginia, near Richmond.[18] From this camp, Thomas Cobb penned a short letter the following night to Marion.

> In the Woods, near James River Opposite City Point. The battle is about over. The Yankees have retreated and in good order. We are catching stragglers and hope to cut off their wagon train and its escort tomorrow. My whole battalion is on picket tonight watching them. We have possession of the road below them and will have no trouble except from the gunboats, which command the river road on which it is retreating. My battalion has brought in fifty prisoners today and a large number of arms and a quantity of ammunition.... We have had a hard time. Sometimes we have been without a morsel to eat for 36 hours and all the time nothing but what we capture from the enemy. So it has been a feast or a famine, with us all the while. I have eaten raw meat to satisfy hunger. Our horses have fared the same way and with hard riding have suffered much. Charlie is very well. So is Rutherford and Deloney.[19]

---

[17] F. W. Walter Letters.

[18] See William S. Smedlund, *Camp Fires of Georgia Troops, 1861–1865* (Lithonia, GA: Kennesaw Mountain Press, 1994) 145.

[19] Thomas R. R. Cobb to Marion, 3 July 1862, T. R. R. Cobb Papers.

One of the members of the Richmond Hussars, B. H. W., recorded the legion's movements in a letter to his parents that was subsequently published in the local newspaper:

We crossed in the enemy's rear last Wednesday night week, above Mechanicsville, the night before Gen. Longstreet whipped them at that place. We then pushed on their rear down to Cold Harbor, and were in the battle of Friday, the 27th. Our Legion was brought out for charge, but the ground was so bad that we could not. The enemy saw us and shelled us until after dark. As soon as it was dark, they commenced to retreat, and we followed them, then came back to the battle field and slept until daylight. Our squadron was then ordered to scour the field and send all stragglers to their regiments. I never want to go over another battle field. You could see nothing but dead and dying all around you, our men and the enemy lying side by side, the ground covered with clothes of all kinds, knapsacks, and guns, where regiment after regiment had stopped to throw off everything they had so that they would have nothing to impede their fight. We got about thirty pieces of artillery at this fight.

I rigged myself out at this place. I got a sabre, bridle, saddle, overcoat and blanket. I also got a horse, but he was branded U.S., and I had to turn him over to the Government.

About one o'clock we took up our line of march for the railroad; there we burnt a large lot of commissary stores and pulled up the track. We then moved on for the White House, where the enemy had a large lot of stores, amounting to about six millions worth. We captured some two hundred wagons, six hundred mules and horses, twenty-four steam engines, one hundred barrels of whiskey, and about thirty thousand stand of arms. During this time we had lived on the Yankee sutlers' goods—hams, sugar, coffee, cake, cheese, and everything that was good. The only things that suffered were our horses; they had nothing to eat all the time. Two horses gave out under me. We were in our saddles for eight days. I don't think we were out of them 24 hours for the whole time.

We are now within three miles of the James river, below City Point. The enemy are under cover of their boats, and are embarking, it is believed.[20]

On 6 July, Cobb wrote his wife that "the infantry came around us so thick that I have moved back one mile to the rear and am now camped by a mill. Deloney and Johnny Rutherford went up to Richmond this afternoon to get some clean clothes. Deloney has stood the hardship of the campaign wonderfully and fattened all the

---

[20] Written 5 July 1862, published in the *Augusta Daily Morning News* (11 July 1862).

THE LEGION'S FIGHTING BULLDOG

while."[21] This new camp, Carter's Mill, was only a temporary encampment outside of Richmond. From here, Cobb reported that in the recent cavalry engagements,

> Three of my cavalry were wounded at different times, two taken prisoners and several horses killed and wounded. These are the sum of the casualties in the legion. No command, perhaps in the army, has suffered so little. We have not filled the newspapers with dashing exploits, nor have we filled graves with our friends. We have never shrunk from duty or shirked a responsibility. The only two charges made by cavalry during these battles were made by mine. Deloney's, of which I wrote to you and one by Capt. Wright.[22]

While working along the James, the legion carried out a reconnaissance from Harrison's Landing toward White Oak Swamp. Along the way, near Williamston, they took part in an action against several of the Union gunboats. As one of the members of the raiding party later remembered, "The gun boat's terrible firing forced us to believe that it would not do to charge iron clads even on thoroughbreds. We fell back to the vicinity of Malvern Hill."[23] Thomas Cobb also made note of the action: "My Cavalry were only on one of the main battle fields at Coal Harbor and there were subjected to terrible cannonading. I have written to you about the two charges made."[24]

The legion cavalry continued to picket along the James for nearly a week. During that time, the men were in a constant state of readiness, as Cobb reported to his wife on several occasions. On the 14th, he wrote, "The latest news we have from below indicates that McLellan has fallen still lower down the James River, so as to occupy the point made by the junction of the Chickahominy with the James. His gunboats will protect him there on both flanks. The movement shows that he is looking to defensive operations for the present at least. My Cavalry and one other regiment (Jeff Davis' legion I hear) are left below to watch them." Two days later he included, "We hear that McLellan is advancing but understand it to be a camp rumor. My cavalry skirmish with them a little every day or two. No serious casualties. One of my Lieutenants was wounded in his foot and his horse killed." On the 18th he reported, "My cavalry had a pretty considerable skirmish day before yesterday with the enemy and think they killed several. Deloney was in command. We had one horse killed and several wounded, but no casualties to the men."[25]

---

[21] Thomas R. R. Cobb to Marion, 6 July 1862, T. R. R. Cobb Papers.
[22] Ibid., 8 July 1862, T. R. R. Cobb Papers.
[23] Howard, "Sketch of Cobb Legion Cavalry," 7.
[24] Thomas R. R. Cobb to Marion, 11 July 1862, T. R. R. Cobb Papers.
[25] Ibid., 14, 16, 18 July 1862.

With the constant state of alertness, Cobb apparently recognized the possible fraying of his men's nerves and the potential strain on the unit's effectiveness and morale. Like most military men of the time, he sought a remedy. "I applied today for whiskey to distribute to the entire brigade. I believe the men need some stimulant and if I can get it, I shall distribute to them every day for a week or longer."[26] This issuing of whiskey rations is a bit surprising coming from one who was such a strong temperance leader in the prewar years. His attempt to keep his men at ease and ready, however, may have contributed to an unintended consequence. "I am sorry to tell you," he wrote Marion, "that I found Col. Young at the cavalry camp and was told he had been drunk. Keep this profoundly secret. If I can get proof I shall have him cashiered. Deloney is in command of the cavalry below."[27]

The legion cavalry changed their camp once again on 20 July, returning to their old Camp Meadow in Henrico County. They remained here only a couple of days before they were once again on the move.

By the end of July 1862, Thomas Cobb was no longer in direct command of the legion cavalry as they were now operating as a quasi-independent command under Wade Hampton. Cobb continued to receive reports from "his" cavalry but could not issue orders in relation to them. At the end of July, he reported to his wife, "I heard from the cavalry today. They are still at Hanover C. H. and all well." Two days later, he wrote Marion, "Nobody literally, has been to my camp today, except one of my cavalry captains, who told me that the cavalry had passed down to Malvern Hill today to stand picket again before the enemy. He said Maj. Deloney was well, and the health of the cavalry good."[28]

Although no longer in command of the legion cavalry, Cobb notified his wife that he had received very flattering reports from his superiors as to the behavior of his former cavalry, no doubt an attempt to belay any ruffled feathers on the part of Thomas Cobb.

> I wrote this much this morning when I recd. an order to move down to New Market (8 miles lower) at once. It was extremely warm on the march. We are now in the woods and side by side with my cavalry, for the first time in four months. The latter were very glad to see me. Some of them were in a skirmish with the enemy yesterday. By the way, I did not tell you that the Yankees had retaken Malvern Hill, and the object of this expedition seems to be to drive them away. Genl. Lee and Genl. Stuart have both

---

[26] Ibid., 14 July 1862.
[27] Ibid., 15 July 1862.
[28] Ibid., 29, 31 July 1862.

written very complimentary letters about the manner in which my cavalry behaved when on picket here before.[29]

What enmity Cobb held for Jefferson Davis, whom he blamed for the seizure of his cavalry from his command, he did not feel toward Hampton, whom he found "particularly kind and attentive."[30] The numerous cavalry skirmishes of November, as Stuart screened Longstreet's movements through upper Virginia, did little to calm the anxious Cobb. "The Cavalry have seen hard service lately," he wrote Marion, "and it makes me mad to see the Richmond newspapers speaking of the work of my men and saying 'a part of Hampton's Legion' did so and so. I want to get them to Georgia, where we will be responsible for our own acts and get the credit due for our successes."[31]

Encamped near Gordonsville, Virginia, Stuart's command picketed the region between Gordonsville and Orange Court House.[32] Between the 2nd and 8th of August, Stuart's forces, including the legion cavalry, had numerous encounters with Federal forces.[33]

* * *

Athens June 6th 1862

My own dear Will

Our dear little children are all sound asleep. Rosa and Tom having refreshed themselves with a nap this afternoon, have just had quite a romp in their bed but are quiet at last. What a blessed thing it is to be a child in these days of Care and Anxiety. These are my loneliest hours when my vexations and trials and all my own troubles come home to my heart but so long as you are spared to me and in health, I ought to be cheerful in a degree and you too. How I learned that lesson a few weeks since. Darling I do hope that you are comfortable and that things are all arranged to your satisfaction and last and not least that edibles sufficient are comestible to satisfy the cravings of that certain portion of your system with which if Soloman had enjoyed as intimate an acquaintance as I have had the honor to I am inclined to think he would have added to his list of things always crying "Give, Give, Give." I went

---

[29] Ibid., 29, 6 August 1862.

[30] Ibid.

[31] Ibid.

[32] Gilbert Wright Letters, 1, 13, 14 August 1862, T. R. R. Cobb Collection, T. R. R. Cobb House.

[33] Fights ensued against a Federal reconnaissance in force near Harrison's Landing and skirmishes with Federal cavalry at Malvern Hill, Thornburg (Massaponax Church), and White Oak Swamp Bridge.

over to the Hotel this afternoon to see Mrs. Washborne, she has been quite sick and much depressed and cant eat any of the Lampkin messes, so I sent her over some supper and shall repeat the dose as often as my larder will permit. If you could step in some times and see us at dinner you would conclude the pellet system had insinuated itself into other departments besides the nursery. Dr. Penick has entered the Hospital Department of the Army in connection with Mr. Crumley and others, to look after the sick and wounded soldiers from Georgia. Judge Lumpkin gave $1000 of his salary to assist in aiding the penniless wounded to get home. Dr. C Longs youngest child, a Baby, died yesterday. Annie Wares Husband has been very sick, but getting better. So we have evacuated or fallen back from Cornith and Fort Pillow and Memphis abandoned. I cant give up except grudgingly a foot of our soil, but I suppose Beauregard knows what he is about.[34] How much I think about you Darling do you suppose you know? poor old fellow. The Boys of our Army know nothing about this war save in the physical discomforts they have to endure. Sympathy all ought to be for men whose families are at home. Ed Lumpkin brought the Candy. Three little Babies thought Papa was mighty good to think of them and another individual with a capacity for the sweet and the good thought so too. Good night Darling, sweet kisses from us all and the best of every thing that the heart can feel or wish from

Your own
Rosa

Richmond June 9, 1862

My Dear Rosa,

I suppose you are wondering what has become of me and why I haven't written. We only arrived here last night and have had a most unfortunate time in coming, being behind twice in every Rail Road service leaving Goldsboro. I never was so worn out with delays in my life.

I am happy to say that I am quite well however and I do not think you need feel uneasy about me. I have not seen my Company yet nor the Colonel so can tell you nothing about the military except that I am the Major of the Cavalry if I will accept the position. I will write you tonight or in the morning what I shall do.

I wish the abominable war was at an end and I at home again for good with you and our precious little children. I think I could be willing to make peace with mankind and leave the race for honor to others more ambitious. I could be well sat-

---

[34] On this day, Beauregard, who had been on a rather slow, methodical pullback from Corinth, Mississippi, saw Memphis, Tennessee, fall to Union forces after a two-hour naval battle as the town's folk watched with sadness from the bluffs overlooking the action.

isfied to remain quietly at home with my poor little Scrap & practice Law quietly in Athens for the balance of my life, but as it is other wise we must beat the Separation Darling and make the best of it all. I stayed with Bob last night and he tells me that he will send Jennie to Athens the end of this month and that he would have sent her on with us but he lacked the money and could not borrow it. He asked Crawford to wait on him one day longer as he thought he could get it in that time, but Crawford declined doing so. He says he is anxious that Jennie should be with you and that Jennie wants to come, so Darling I think you can hope to have some one "raised up" for you again. I shall not forget to give him your present to the baby. How does poor little Tom get on with out Papa and the buggy. Make George ride you and them out often this Summer. I think it will do you as much good as the children. I hope poor little Willie is well of that Cold. It has worried me a good deal since I left you fearing a return of the croup. Kiss them all for me & think of me sweetly and kindly Darling & write often.

Ever Yrs
Will

Camp near Richmond
June 9, 1862

My Dear Rosa,

I came out to Camp yesterday 3 miles from the city[35] and are now regularly initiated anew into Camp life, feeling quite well and sincerely hoping that I may continue so. How great the contrast is between my present condition & place of sojourn and the pleasant home I have left with all its comforts & its pleasures. None can freely appreciate but those who have had a practical test of what Camp life is. Last night it rained and is still raining today, looking as if it would rain forever, but as I am in a comfortable tent (if any tent is comfortable) and no scouting to do I can at least keep dry. Col. Cobb is here, came over yesterday and has had a great deal to say, quite affable and pleasant & so c.[36]

---

[35] The camp was Camp Meadow located in Henrico County, Virginia, in an oak grove, near Brook Church, about 3 miles north of Richmond. Thomas R. R. Cobb to Marion, 10 June 1862, T. R. R. Cobb Papers; Smedlund, *Camp Fires*, 207.

[36] Thomas Cobb was delighted to have Delony rejoin the legion. Writing to Marion, Cobb reported, "Deloney came into Camp yesterday and slept in my tent last night. This morning it is raining. He told me just now that he had written to his wife how unfavorable his situation this morning compared with his comfort from weeks past. I replied to him that I had just been writing to you how comfortable and quiet I was, sheltered from the rain and away from forced marches. All things are comparative." Thomas R. R. Cobb to Marion, 10 June 1862, T. R. R. Cobb Papers.

Stovall's resignation has beyond all question made me the Major of the Cavalry, Williams is Capt. of my old Company, Ritch of the new. The Lieutenants have not yet been elected, but I may safely say there is no more chance for Church than for the man in the moon. He is entirely lost sight of by everybody & yet all admit that he is the only man fit for the place. I feel rather disgusted with the concern & not a little surprised at the conduct of some of the members of the Company but thus it is the world goes on. Some of Church's bosom friends I learn intend voting for Murphy & dropping Church entirely. I left Athens feeling kindly to everybody, but upon my word as soon as I come again into the world I feel regrets that I have ever seen anything of it, so much meanness and insincerity is met with that we don't know whom to trust and I doubt the sincerity & friendship of all. "Poor human nature," what a compound man is of good & bad, doing good one day & undoing it the next. I believe if it were not for the women Earth would be Hell enough to accommodate the old boy himself. I hear so much and see so much meanness I will have to close my eyes & ears and think only of the good people of Athens in general and my precious little wife & dear children in particular and become a philosopher, live through the war as best I can and look forward to my return home is my only hope for real happiness. You must think kindly of me Dear Darling and not imagine as you are always doing that I dont love you as I ought. If you knew how constantly you and the dear little children were present to my thoughts you would never think such a thought again. Good bye. God bless you. Kiss the Dear little ones for me & write often.

Ever Yours
W. G. Delony

[Camp Meadow]
June 11, 1862

My Dear Rosa,

Yours of the 6th I received yesterday and was delighted to hear from my precious little family at home & that all were well and enjoyed the candy. I am sorry that the pellet system however has been introduced into the dining some and hope that the garden will soon enable you to break up that place if nothing else will. I think this you ought not to be too stingy with yourself and ought to love better. As for me so long as I remain where I am you need not fear for me. We are rather in the rear of this left wing of the Army where there are but few soldiers and surrounded by several farms so that milk, butter milk & butter and vegetables are plentiful. We only have to pay $1.00 per pd for butter when in Richmond it costs $1.50, we pay 30$ per pd for sugar & other things in proportion except strawberries which are the finest I ever saw in my life, the largest & finest flavored and cheap. So you perceive we are not starving at this time, but how soon we may be transported where there is now a large body of men or where they have been I cant tell. I can only say I wish frequently you could see us enjoying the good things. You never saw men with such appetites. Your pickles too are very popular. Young insists they are the finest he ever eat and we all agree with him. I told him you sent him the jar I opened & we would eat his first & mine afterward. The truth is we are living better just at this time than I ever lived in Camp and I have improved astonishingly since I came here and I think I am getting well fast. I am more comfortable too & better suited with my mess arrangements & so don't be anxious and uneasy about me. If I had little Tom to talk with & look after I would be fixed. Hadnt you better send him on. My grand uniform made in Augusta must have been cut for Howell Cobb. You ought to see it. I think the maker must have heard you on the subject of tightly fitting clothing.

God bless you all Darling. Write to me when you can. You seem not to have recd my letter from Augusta. Kiss the little folks for me.

Ever Yours
W. G. Delony

Camp near Richmond
June 14, 1862

My Dear Rosa,

Your letter of the 5th was recd yesterday tho' the one written on the 6th reached me two days before and it was as are all your letters most acceptable, poor little Tom I know he must have missed me & have missed his "ride around" too. I wish it were so that I could see you and the children occasionally & occasionally bring Tom into Camp, here the little fellow would enjoy it. He could look at horses then to his hearts content. I feel right envious of those officers who have their wives out here. Mrs Anderson took tea with us last evening & it was quite a treat to see her. Several of the officers have their ladies here in the neighborhood, tho' we are in such close proximity to the Yankees. The[y] all rode on horseback however and have no children, so they feel tolerably secure. We are doing but little here now in the way of fighting, picket duty however is pretty severe upon the men & our pickets & the enemy are frequently within speaking distance of each other, and at times they hold with each other some very amusing conservations at other times they are in a very dangerous position from the Artillery firing. We have had two horses killed within a week but fortunately the men in both cases escaped. When there will be a general engagement here I cant tell, but of one thing you may rest assured if

122

our General permits McLellan to continue his gradual approaches and wait to be attacked, McLellan will take Richmond. It becomes only a question of time. The only hope I see is in Stonewall Jackson and I am afraid that he is no favorite with Davis & there are rumors of Beauregards going on to supersede him & then that Army too will use the spade instead of the sword at which game the Yankees beat us every time they attempt it, but let's hope for the best. Our troops are in good spirits and if allowed to fight will be hard to whip. I am well, never felt better, an getting strong & have gotten rid of all initiation about my bowels. I never improved so rapidly in my life. Kiss the little Darlings for me & accept for yourself a heartfull of love. Think kindly of me Darling & write often.

Ever Yrs
Will

Athens June 15th 1862

My Own Dearest Will

You cannot imagine how I do want to see and be with you, and how sometimes faith and hope and every thing else nearly dies out of my fearful heart in view of the monstrous fact of our indefinite separation. I went to church this morning and was surprised after service to have a visit from Dr. Smith who got here yesterday, come home for good. His wife don't love him, half as much as I do you Darling and yet I have to do without you, and who enjoys home more than you. I pray every day for strength to bear it, but the strength dont seem to come and I am as restive and impatient as a young unbroken colt and yet I feel how much I have to be grateful for I was truly rejoiced yesterday afternoon to see your dear old handwriting again, and learn of your safe arrival in Richmond for I was afraid you were sick. I am very glad too, to hear that Jennie is coming, but there are generally so many contingencies, and if regulating her movements, that seeing will be believing, I am glad tho that it is her present intention. The Lord works miracles for me I often think, for how could I have even hoped to have had Jennie "raised up for me" if I could forget the doctrine of predestination and that "man is born to trouble as the sparks are to fly upward," and recollect even that "prayer moves the arm, that moves the world," half of the burden of life would be lost to me, but, and but, and but. After I got your letter yesterday, I felt in such a very good humor that I went over to spend the rest of the afternoon with Mrs. Henderson she was ailing and had not made her toilet, so invited me into her room where I found her in her Jacque de nuit.[37] We are getting as thick as hops, she wants to be very sociable she says, and I ditto of course.

---

[37] Bathrobe or receiving robe.

Our Darlings are all well playing just now on the grass. I have fixed a nice play place for them under the broad leafed tree, in the garden where it is shady nearly all day. They are all going after breakfast to morrow to ride in the buggy with George. A great many sick soldiers are arriving here daily. Some it seems, have had to walk from the depot up to the hotel when scarcely able to crawl. Dr. Hoyt made a few very feeling remarks about them being permitted to do so by the citizens, poor old gentleman, he sympathises with the poor soldiers, a subscription is to be taken up to pay Saulter for bringing them over. Good bye my precious Darling, try and be prudent for our sakes and dont let your bowels remain out of fix. Dr. Smith says you wont be able to stand this campaign unless you see that your bowels become healthy. Dont sacrifice yourself if you find they do not improve. God bless you Will is my earnest prayer. All send dear Papa sweet kisses. Your own large share of love from

your own

Rosa

Camp Meadow, near Richmond

June 17 1862

My Dear Rosa

It will be a fortnight tomorrow since I left home and I have heard nothing from you since your letter of the 6th and I feel homesick & lonely when I have no tidings from you and our precious little children. I feel very anxious about dear little Willie, and when I do not hear, I am always fearing that he may be sick. God grant the dear little fellow will get through the summer without any serious illness. You cannot know the regret I feel in being away from you while he is teething. I am happy to say that my own health is perfect. I have not been sick an hour since my arrival in Camp and am improving every day. When I left Athens, I weighed 142 pounds and on last Sunday I weighed 148, so that I think I will soon be myself again. If I could only see you and the little folks occasionally I am sure I would very soon be quite as well as ever. I do not think however you need have any more anxiety about my health. My appetite is a growing one & Col Young and myself are like the locusts of Egypt eating up every green thing that comes in our way. Our Camp is very dull however and no good eating or anything else can compensate for any forced absence from home. Peace would afford me more happiness than all the honors of a successful war, particularly as our position in the Army is so unpleasant. Our Cavalry is in Cobbs Legion & yet we report to Gen. Stuart & the Infantry to Gen. Cobb. The consequence is that we only do the dirty work of the Army and as the peninsula picket duty is all that falls to our lot.

We were not with Gen. Stuart last week in his foray behind the lines of the enemy and I think you may feel well assured that our Cavalry will have nothing to do more honorable than picket duty unless Richmond falls. I think it would be a good idea to let us all go home and draw our pay there. We would do the Confederacy about as much good and then such a place would be so much more agreeable to our wives. I don't think Gen Stuart did right in not taking us with him.

My present position I find to be as I presumed it would be a very easy one, irresponsible and not unpleasant, tho' I must say I would rather be in command of the battalion and second in Command. The officers and men have all received me Cordially and I think are all well satisfied with both Young and myself, but the Captains are all dissatisfied with the rank and position assigned them and are to have a meeting tomorrow and present the whole matter to the War department for decision. All in a friendly spirit thus far and if Cobb is prudent there will be no trouble. Williams is now Captain of my old Company and is a senior officer to Rich and Commands the Squadron—both Companies. My own Company acted very handsomely by him. He declined to take the Captaincy which the Law gave him unless the Company desired it and they sent him a petition signed almost unanimously to accept the Command, so that after all Rich's virulence and animosity, he is in the very position Rich desired him to have. More than that Williams tells me that 18 of the very flower of the new Company have asked to be taken in the old. Church was badly beaten & badly treated by some of his bosom friends. I do not understand their conduct, but that his defeat resulted from the conduct of those he thought were his best friends, indeed his own mess, I have no doubt. Your friend House was triumphantly elected, and Pittard's brother is Ritchs 1st Lieut. Early is 1st Lieut of the old Company, a brilliant set all around. Good night, Darling. Kiss the little folks for Papa and accept a heart full of love from your

Will

Excuse bad writing. I am sitting on the ground and am very uncomfortable having no facilities for writing.

Camp Meadow June 20, 1862

My Dear Rosa,

Last night much to the gratification of a poor unfortunate soldier I received four letters from home. Yours of the 8th, 9th, 11th, & 13th all came to hand by the same mail. I had begun to think that you had quite forgotten me and would have come to that conclusion decidedly had not many of the officers told me that they were in the same predicament, and I am told it is much worse with the letters sent home from Camp. We acct. of the constant movement of troops over the rail roads.

I wish sincerely that the impending battle near Richmond could be fought at once and our fate determined, but of this we can only hope. Our Administration or Commanding General seems to be afraid of attacking McLellan and the latter seems determined to take Richmond by slow approaches and starvation rather that take the hazard of a great and decisive battle. In this game of spade and provisions I cannot but feel that McLellan has greatly the advantage and all I fear is that we may be forced to fight when the advantages are all with the Yankees. Of one thing I am firmly convinced, if our present policy is adhered to much longer, McLellan will be so firmly entrenched in his present position that the fall of Richmond will be only a question of time. But notwithstanding this I as firmly believe that if the troops were allowed to fight now, there is a way to annihilate McLellan's army, but I suppose this won't be done until I am Commander in Chief, or the President's confidential adviser, so if you will come on we will offer our joint services. By the way I had a very interesting lady to tea with me last night. We had hot coffee without milk, toast without butter, cold baker's bread, cold ham and field frogs. Ask Mrs Hunter if you beat that bill of fare when she took tea with you. We are encamped near a frog pond, and frog meat is cheap. All the cost is the killing, and it is the only fresh meat I have eaten in Camp since I have been here, with one exception and I may add that I have tried the frogs but once. As to whether I shall try them in future depends entirely upon my Company.

I am glad to learn that your friends in Athens are still so kind and hope you will continue to be sociable with them. It will do you good and I feel more content-ed in Camp when I know that you are cheerful at home and you cannot be so with-out visiting your friends who I am sure are always glad to see you. Say to Dr. & Mrs Smith that I had no opportunity of delivering the bundle and letter sent him before he left for home. I will deliver it upon his return.

Now about myself, I assure you I never felt better in my life and I think I am better than usual at this season of the year. We have a sulfur spring near us which supplies us with very cool, refreshing water which I drink much to the benefit of the inner man. I have no doubt now that to the use of this mineral water I am indebted for my rapid improvement. In reference to my position as Major I can only say that I am not indebted to Col. Cobb for it, tho' I think he put no obstacles in the way but rather preferred me to Stovall. At any rate Cobb and Stovall both knew this. I would contest the promotion of Stovall and they both had all interview with the Secretary of war and knew what his decision would be and Stovall resigned and I was promoted by seniority of rank acceding to the Act of Congress regulating the matter. Young is Lt. Col. and I would be perfectly satisfied if the Cavalry were an independent organization. Cobb however is too ambitious ever to give up either and the consequence is that we will be always trammelled in our movement. I am perfectly satisfied to serve with Young. He and all the company officers all recd. me in the proper spirit and I am willing to reciprocate their good feeling as manifested. Cobb has been very polite and very kindly and very obliging, but I cannot for my life feel towards him as I would wish. I could be better pleased if he would remain with the Infantry altogether. He is now in town, rode in this morning to oblige me ostensibly, & so expressed himself, but for the life of me I cannot confide in his protestation. Perhaps I misjudge him however, but he is certainly very ambitious. Kiss all the little folks for me. God bless their dear little souls, how I should like to see them. Don't let them forget me. Have you sold your up town lot to Dr. Long? How did your wheat turn out? I hope well. Good bye. God bless you Darling.

Ever Yr own
Will

Camp Meadow June 23, 1862

My Dear Rosa,

I cannot tell why it is I feel so anxious about you and our precious little folks at home, but last night I could not sleep thinking of you and dear little Willie. I have not had a line from you since the receipt the other day of four of your letters at once, though I have no doubt you have written. This looking for letters in Camp and not securing them causes many a restless sleepless night and I think if ever I do get a chance at the blessed Yankees I will make some of them ache for it. But I wont complain, I am well and ought to be thankful for that & I hope you and the little ones are also well. You have no idea how I have fattened since my return to Camp. I weigh more now than I usually do in the summer season and can ride all day if necessary without great fatigue. My horses all look well and so far as Camp life is concerned I have no reason to complain & would not if I could hear regularly from home. It is quite a monotonous life we are leading here however no scouting & no other excitement to vary the unchanging monotony of our daily duties which follow with too unwavering regularity to be interesting, occasionally the Yankees shell our pickets and since my arrival they have killed two horses for us and captured one of the videttes, a member of Dr King's company, but these things happen so much as a mere matter of course that no excitement ensues. Capt. King went out with a small party below our lines, satisfied himself that the man was captured & that we had done all we could to recover him had he been sick on post, duty was done & the momentary excitement is over. And thus it is with all of us. The poor Devil who is killed or captured is soon forgotten & other thoughts than of him soon occupy the minds of those who are left behind. Every day there is more or less firing along the lines generally by the Artillery and one or two, sometimes more killed or wounded on either side and the loss of a man makes but little impression upon the Army. You ladies cant understand this and do not know how apathetic and indifferent men become to human suffering, and it is well you do not, if women were no better than men, this Earth would tempt the Devil himself to leave his mansions below for a more congenial atmosphere.

We are today to have a grand review of the Cavalry battalion by Genl. Stuart and I think he will see as fine a body of men & as well mounted as any in the service. I learn that several ladies from Richmond are coming out to witness it and in honor of my little wife I shall wear the uniform she made for me. How much I would like to have you present and what a welcome I would give you, you can well imagine. Three of our officers have their wives on here and you cant conceive how cheering it is to us to have them occasionally in Camp. Two of them are to dine with Young and Myself today and if you could complete the picture it would be perfect. The fact is I am beginning to think seriously of making some sort of an arrangement by which you can be nearer to me if Richmond is not soon taken, but of this more after the battle. There are a thousand and one rumors afloat about the movements of the enemy & I am very much inclined to think that our leaders are seriously contemplating an early attack, and if the plan proposed be adopted, you may hear of a brilliant victory which God grants may put an end to this war. I sent you a letter yesterday by Lieut Gilmer which I hope you will receive, this goes by James. Write me after. I will preserve your letters some time or other and they are always acceptable no mater how old. I will write regularly to you. Kiss our precious little ones for Papa. I think of them always. God bless you all Darling, think of me kindly and don't be anxious about me. My health is perfect. My best regards to all my friends & my love to Mrs Baxter & Mrs Hunter.

Ever Yours
Will

Tell Willie Church to come on as soon as he is able. A new company is to re-organize of sharp shooters & Wright is to be Captain. Camfield & Church two of the Lieutenants, and the whole Company to be picked men, armed with the arms of Lawton's Company. This is hard, we are trying to organize the Company agreeably to the order of Gen Stuart & we will succeed.

W. G. D.

Tunstall Station
On York River R. R.
June 29, 1862

My Dear Rosa,

I write you from this place 20 miles from Richmond. We have been at work this morning tearing up & destroying the rail road & burning cars &c. We left our Camp on Wednesday last & have been on the move day and night ever since, pursuing the Yankees in this direction and Capturing and destroying their stores &c, & particularly cutting off their communication with Yorktown over the rail road. Old Stonewall Jackson has maintained his reputation in this battle and has achieved a signal victory over the Yankees on their right flank. I am very anxious to learn what Lee has done before Richmond. If he has done half as well there as on the Yankees right wing McLellan is gone, & our independence achieved but I am afraid he will be sheltered on the James River by his gun-boats. What a pity the Merrimac is no more. If we had a navy to engage the enemy on water the victory would be complete.

Col Cobb has telegraphed twice home, yesterday and today and mentioned my name so you know that up to this time I am unhurt. Lieut Early was wounded in the left arm by a pistol ball. It is a flesh wound only and therefore not dangerous. Walters the bugler has a slight saber cut on his head, and a member of the Richmond Hussars (Stovall's old Company) had one man killed which embraces all the casualties in the Legion except the loss of a few horses, tho the only men engaged in actual combat was my old squadron, Williams & Rich's companies led by me. We were the advance guard yesterday and I was ordered by Gen. Stuart to take a certain station (Dispatch Station) on the R. R. and to attack any party that was guarding it. When I reached the place my advance guard (Lieut Early & 10 men) were fired into by the Yankees and I immediately order a charge by the Squadron. We were so placed that I did not know the story of the enemy & I was equally confident they did not know my force. As the Command charged the Troopers gave a yell and came up in gallant style, the enemy poured a volley into us or rather at us at a distance of 50 or 60 yards and then ran. We were after them with a yell & for about half a mile we had the prettiest sort of a race. They left the main road & turned in a narrow road to the right leading to a field where another Company was drawn up in line of battle. When I came in sight I called to my men & there was another skirmish & another race. We overtook their rear, sabred several of them & took one prisoner & lost two horses & one wounded. They fired back at us all the way, and but for a Yankee Regiment of Infantry ahead of us which compelled me to stop the pursuit before we got across the field we would have given them a better taste of Georgia steel. I had about ninety men. We captured 120 of them. Gen Stuart has complimented me upon the conduct of this squadron in the charge. Kiss the little ones for me. I begin to hope I shall soon be able to come home for good if I can survive this battle. God bless you Darling.

Ever Yours
Will
I am quite well.

Near James River 12 Miles below
Richmond July 7, 1862

My Dear Rosa,

I have been too busy to write you since I have been below, hope you have recd my despatches. We have again had busy time with the enemy tho' thus far I have not been in any active engagement, and in but little danger. My old Squadron how-ever day before yesterday were entirely cut off by the enemy and had a desperate fight under Command of Lieut Early. He brought off his command with the loss of only 4 men, two killed McElhannon of Ritch's company & one of Capt Kings men who was with him, and Stovall & Dearing were captured by the enemy. Stovall's bridle was broken & he could not control his horse and Dearing would not leave him. The truth is they had both disobeyed Early's orders or neither of them would have been taken. They will soon be exchanged and will have learned a good lesson. Providence was with Early in his fight. He escaped almost miraculously, behaved with great gallantry as did all my old company and they all deserve great credit. I am ordered off, so must close. Will telegraph to you every chance I get. God bless you all. Kiss the children for me.

Affectionately
Will

Richmond Va.
July 7, 1862

My Dear Rosa,

I am now in Richmond having come up last night to get some clean clothes and some thing to eat. Upon going to Camp I found that John left yesterday morn-ing for the Legion with clothes provisions for me but took a different route from the one I travelled. I however succeeded in getting a change of clothing and feel much more like a gentleman today I assure you. We have had a hard time you may depend upon it. Yesterday morning Young and I got up and found we had nothing to eat but the hardest and stalest of hard biscuit. A negro fellow with a waiter of hot coffee, hot rolls, & boiled & cold ham was in our immediate neighborhood in search of Col. Edwards. Young was soon introduced as the gentleman in question and we fared sumptuously. What think you of the morality of the Army? Our defence is that with Edwards ignorance is bliss, with us knowledge was starvation until we partook of his comfortable breakfast.

I am glad to say that I feel and am very well, having stood the Campaign much better than I anticipated. The poor wounded soldiers however are suffering terribly this hot weather, without ice, and are dying by the hundreds. I cannot think that our loss in this series of battles will fall short of 25,000 men. The Enemy's loss will no doubt amount to 30,000. Gen A. P. Hill told me that out of his division of 15,000 men he had lost 5,000, Jackson's loss was also very severe. It was a glorious victory but dearly bought, and in my opinion will have to be fought over again before long though most persons in this differ from me.[38] I do not think however the Yankees will ever fight as well again. I saw Dr King today for the first time, was glad to see one from home. I would give a mint to see you and the children now. I could then return to the Army feeling better and stronger. I do not know what becomes of your letters. Your last mail was dated the 15th June. Do you write regularly? Kiss my precious little ones for Papa and don't let them forget me. Tell Tom I have a horse for him which he can ride. I sold my black for $400 & bought him for $500. He is a magnificent animal & as gentile as a dog, afraid of nothing. Dick Taylor's here. I have not seen him. Good bye. God bless you Darling. Think kindly & sweetly of your poor

Will

Athens July 13th 1862

My Darling Will

I was much rejoiced yesterday to see your dear old hand-writing once more, as I have had that pleasure only once in three weeks. I have heard of you however thru different people and had a message from Dr. King to the effect that you were looking better than he ever saw you. We are all perfectly well, and jogging along as usual. I am enduring time, existing wont say living the Endurance, a passion virtue and if this war continues I may learn to enjoy my hermits life. May not the reason of my letters not reaching you be? there being sent to the Infantry. I will enclose this to Bob you may get it by that means for if you are as dependent upon my letters as I am upon yours, I am sorry for you when they fail to come. Our good old Dr. was

---

[38] The Seven Days' campaign ended with the Battle of Malvern Hill and McClellan's retreat down the James to Harrison's Landing. The Confederates lost 20,000 casualties, while the Federals lost nearly 16,000. Despite McClellan's vastly superior numbers, he failed to take Richmond.

sick to day and could not preach, but we had young Mr. Axson in his place. It was our Communion Service. Hall Billups'es poor little wife went up solitary and alone and made her profession. Tom Hoyt has lost his oldest daughter with scarlet fever in Ky. We are having tolerable warm weather and very dry. Our vegetable garden perfectly burnt up. We would have had a large crop of fine potatoes but for the drought any quantity of little ones, but the vines are turning yellow and I dont suppose they will grow any more. I have planted some winter beets and made a few ineffective efforts to get some winter cabbage started. The Misses Cunninghams come very frequently to see me, they are among the few who know how to appreciate small courtesys. Geo went out with Mr. Pittard yesterday in the country and got a load of fodder. He has just got thru hoeing the garden tho, and after he has done the same in the flower garden, will commence hauling winter wood. Oh Darling that I could only hope to have you at home this winter poor fellow you must be something like me only enduring. Console yourself with the recollection dear Will that you have somebody at home thinking of you, and pining for you. If you could walk in any evening after eight oclock you would find our Darlings sweetly sleeping in the room, Lilly enjoying her first nap, and in our room, dear little Willie keeping me company, he is stretched out now, in your place, and looking sweet enough to eat. He talks as well as Rosa does. God bless the children. I think our scupper nong vine is dying. I sent for the man to come and see what is the matter with it. Darling do send me a Richmond paper the one most reliable. So you and Col Young have got to stealing, or in more eloquent language appropriating. It is to be hoped before Col Edwards made his appearance he had been other wise provided for for to confront a hungry man is no small undertaking as I know by experience. I had my first ripe tomatoes for dinner to day and thought of you as I always do whenever I have any thing enjoyable. We will have any quantity of okra. I understand Gen. Magruder, H Cobb and Toombs were all drunk the day their commands were engaged. I sincerely hope at least the case of the second mentioned individual it is false. Good night my own darling, think often and sweetly of your own dear Rosa and [be] armed against every appearance of evil, and God bless you my dearest Will is the constant prayer of your own affectionate

Rosa

Landing Tavern near James
River 140 miles below Richmond
July 15, 1862

My Dear Rosa,

I sincerely hope that you have fared better than myself in receiving letters though for the past three weeks you have doubtless written three letters to my one. I recd yours of the 23rd by Church & of the 30th by Dr. King, and two others by mail the latest date being the 19th ult. Besides these I have received no letters from you. What has become of them I cant conceive. I have written to you but seldom because I have had no opportunity. For three weeks we have been moving about constantly both day and night and at times I have been almost worn down with fatigue and hunger. When our Army retired the Cavalry battalion of the Legion were left to cover the retiring columns of the Army and since then we have been doing picket duty in conjunction with two other regiments. Our pickets now stand in sight of the pickets of the enemy and not more than 1 1/2 miles from their camp, and our nearest Infantry support is 6 or 8 miles distant, and last night I think is the first night that we have not had a skirmish with the enemy. Some days the firing has commenced at daylight and continued occasionally all day and half the night. We have had one Lieutenant slightly wounded, 2 men taken prisoners & one horse killed, and one negro captured also, who came into camp last night grinning from ear to ear having escaped from the Yankee sentinels. We have killed one of their men & wounded one of their officers that we know of and think we have done them other damages but know no more certainly. We have stood our ground up to this time and so far as our duty required have concealed from the enemy the movements of our Army for our picket posts are now within 300 yards of the point they were when our entire army was here. I think this is doing pretty well, particularly as they have brought both Infantry & Cavalry against us to drive us in. Gen Stuart gave Young a little mountain howitzer, a very small cannon & eight rounds of ammunition. One day we concealed it behind a fence so they could not discover its size and fired upon them 4 times & you never saw such scattering. We have 4 rounds left in case of an emergency & Young is now in Richmond trying to get more ammunition and another cannon. Cobb is with his Infantry commanding his brothers Brigade.[39] I will take back all I ever said about his being a good officer. We have seen some lately which has tried us all thoroughly and I regret to say I have but little faith in him. It is I find a very different thing to command a regiment in Camp and on the march with an enemy in your immediate front & I rather think Cobb also finds it a

---

[39] At this point in the war, Cobb's Brigade included his brother's Georgia legion, as well as the 16th Georgia Infantry (which Howell originally commanded), the 24th Georgia Infantry, and the 15th North Carolina troops.

very different matter. Young is a good officer. I learn that we are to be relieved from this outpost duty on Saturday next & I hope then that we will have a little rest both for men and horses, some, indeed more of our Cavalry have had no change of clothing for three weeks lying on the ground with a blanket to cover with, exposed to two rain storms & one poor fellow came to me this morning complaining that he was chafed all over from riding so much with his dirty clothing. We have now moved our head quarters four or five miles from our picket posts nearer to Richmond and every day are sending some of the men to our old camp to clean up. The Yankees too are protesting against picket fighting, and as they commenced it, I rather think from this they have got the worst of it & I hope and believe now they will let us alone. It is wonderful to me how well I have stood the campaign and notwithstanding the fatigue & danger there is something very fascinating in it to me, but after all Darling there is nothing like home and my Darling wife and precious little children how I have missed & still long to see you no tongue can tell, and how often in this march I have wondered what you would say if you could have seen me. My bedding has been an india rubber Coat on the ground upon which I slept and covered with my travelling blanket with my saddle for a pillow when it was safe to take it off my horse. Now however we have our quarters in a house and sleep in a straw bed, had mutton chops & fish for breakfast this morning & having no alarm for 24 hours feel quite refreshed this morning. I had looked to have been able to give you a first account of our actings and doings since we left our old Camp but it will take a week of quiet to enable me to do so. I think I shall have to send you a copy of our Adjt's report when made and let that suffice until we meet. Several men have been found wanting in whose courage I had my best faith. I hope you have received all my telegrams. God bless you all Darling. Kiss the little ones for Papa and don't let them forget me. Write to me often. I hope now the mail will be more regular.

Ever Yr own
Will

P. S. July 16, 1862

Since writing these writings I have recd yrs of the 6th by R. Nash & am glad to learn that all are well & also glad to say that we are to be relieved in the morning. We had another quiet night. I think the Yankees are satisfied to play quits. God bless you all Darling.

Camp Meadow near Richmond
July 21st 1862

My Dear Rosa,

We moved here last night between eleven and twelve oclock and leave at 1/2 past one today for Hanover Court house. I shall have to leave my fine horse Tom. He has been going so long without shoes that he cant go no longer at all. My other horses would have been no better had I not stolen the time to have them shod, and unfortunately half of the battalion I find that is in this war it is a great misfortune not to be a Virginian. For nearly two weeks one Battalion has had daily skirmishes with the enemy with a disparity of force of one against from 3 to 5. We too were at least ten miles from any support & the enemy supported by the immediate presence of McClellans entire Army. Our men have been up & in the saddle every day and almost every night all that time and now we are not allowed two days to recruit. Young made the application this morning & was reprimanded for doing so. When I remember that all the Va. Regts. of Stuarts Brigade have for the last ten days had a good time on easy duty or on no duty at all, & that two other Cols were allowed to draw straws for the privilege of going to the White House pleasant recruiting post after recruiting for ten days, I cant but feel what is the truth that in this war the post of honor is to be a Virginian & the post of labor & danger is to be a Georgian. I have had more bullets flying about my head on picket duty in the past two weeks and have been in ten times more danger than I was in both the fights I was in during the battles before Richmond. We were relieved on our post by a Va. Regt. which is in disgrace with Stuart because every officer in it has applied to be transferred to Genl. Robertson's brigade who formerly commanded it & with whom Stuart is at inanity. I'll return the assertion they don't maintain their ground these days as we have for ten. I am willing always to do my duty, but I don't like to do other peoples & get no credit for it. But with it all I ought to be thankful for the dangers I have escaped and the manifest improvement of my health through all the fatigues and privations I have suffered. We have had two bundles of oats for our horses today. My fine horse had no time to eat yesterday as we were fighting with the Yankees all the morning and travelling all the afternoon & evening. Our men have escaped almost providential. One has been killed & but three captured, but we have had several horses killed, & have seen 8 or 10 Yankees carried off the field either killed or wounded. I have just bought another horse since beginning this letter for $275, was obliged to have another and I think have got a very good deal by Jim Lampkin, will write as soon as I can, intended to write you a long letter now, but had no idea Stuart would hurry us off. God bless you all Darling, write to me often. Direct to Richmond for the present to Bob's care, recd the one sent here. Kiss the little folks for me.

Ever Yr own
Will

Athens July 25th 1862

My own precious Will

I am extremely anxious to hear from you of your having been relieved from Picket duty as it is not only dangerous, keeping me all the time uneasy, but it is too hard on you such very warm weather, and I want to know of your having a good rest, and last and in this instance least, I want to see your dear old hand writing a little oftener. Every alternate night finds me at my desk writing to my old fellow, but as nothing ever disturbs the smooth current of events in Athens, I have nothing to tell of, but our little home, our little children, and tho oft told tale of love. Mrs. Hunter and myself went to see Gov Cobb yesterday but did not find him in, so I presume he is getting well again. Then we went to see Addie Jackson. The Judge[40] has been and is still quite sick with gastric fever. Then we went out to Gov Lumpkins, on the way we passed our children. Mrs. Hunter would insist upon taking them along to see Miss Mattie Lumpkin as there was no room for Lilly, said she'd be nurse and Willie kept her pretty busy. She is as kind as a sister to me, and begins to have a pretty big place in my heart. I saw Mr. Moss yesterday he had just returned from Atlanta, orders had been received there to prepare for the immediate transportation of 40,000 troops thru the Corinth army going to be south west Tennessee somewhere. We are going to work in earnest, and if God would only send foreign recognition I think peace would not be far distant. Andrew has had a slow fever for nearly ten days but is beginning to improve. Catherine has a very badly swollen foot. The Dr. has been blistering it but not getting any better, he had ordered it leeched, she will lose the use of it entirely this winter if it does not get better I think. A man called the other day and paid me $27 due you. I gave him a receipt but I cant to save my life recollect who it was, a nice elderly gentleman, looks something like Dr. Hoyt. He collected it he said. Darling I am losing my senses and how, and as it is caused by my constant thought about you keeping me absent minded about every thing else, you must make all due allowances for me, and forgive my harum scarum way of attending to your business. I will have the 500 due in Sep to pay to the Bank if you say so but had I not better buy a years supply of Corn as soon as the new crops coming in makes it cheaper, and flour and salt, all will be terrible if this war continues. Think about what I had best do. Mr. Henry Hull oldest daughter Mary Ella has been attacked with St bitus Dance.[41] It is so sad.

---

[40] Joseph Henry Lumpkin. See Biographical Roster.

[41] Saint Vitus Dance, better known as Sydenham's chorea, is a condition more commonly found in females, characterized by rapid, uncoordinated jerking of the hands, feet, or face. Generally, the patient had a previous bout of acute rheumatic fever.

Dear Will do be as prudent with yourself as you can be. Think very sweetly of me Darling and always know my heart is with you in every thing. A sweet kiss from us all and a heart full of love. God bless you my Darling.

Your own

Rosa

The little flour we made is very inferious, very dark and not suitable for light bread, cant get to rise. I tried it myself. Good night Darling. Its only your share if think you don't belong to yourself but to us.

Your own.

[July 27, 1862]
Camp Discipline Hanover C. H.
Hanover County Virginia

My Dear Rosa,

I wrote to you last Monday just before leaving for this place where we arrived that night. We have been very busy since our arrival here and coming to organize our camp and under the stringent orders of General Stuart institute something like discipline. In the midst of our labors yesterday Col. Young was sent off with two Squadrons of Cavalry and the Artillery under command of Sergt. Church upon a scout toward Fredericksburg. The enemy had driven in our pickets and Stuart has gone up with a small force to look after them. Since they left I have been as busy as a bee, have established our Camp and commenced drilling & disciplining, and the recruits I find need both badly. Our Camp is in an open field and at 4 oclock this hot afternoon you can imagine me feeling any thing but comfortable in my tent with not a shade tree in sight, but as Napoleon said, "I have attacked" & I prefer even this to comforts of picket duty on the James. We have heard since coming here that the Yankees report 3 men & horses killed in our last skirmish with them on Saturday last. I think the 8th Illinois Cavalry and 6th U.S. Regulars will remember the Legion. I have heard nothing from you since I have been here tho' a good many letters have been brought up from Richmond for the Battalion. I will notify Bob to forward all your letters to me and for the present direct to this care as I do not know how long I will remain where I am or where we shall go. I do not think however the Cavalry will long remain idle. I feel very willing to accompany our Army going North as I believe that is the only route of convincing the Yankees that we don't mean to be whipped, and the shortest way to end the war. I am so homesick I am getting as down as I used to be in Richmond. If I could see you and our precious little ones occasionally I would not dislike to be a soldier. As it remains I sometimes get very sick of it. You have never told me how much wheat you made nor how you like your new Cow. You can do as you please about the lots up town. Don't sell if you don't want to as I am perfectly willing to keep them & am very indifferent about selling at all. Kiss the little folks for me & write often. I send this evening to Richmond for paper of which I have been destitute for some time. I have but one blanket with me & but few clothes. I left everything with a friend of _____ when I first left Camp on the 24th and had no chance to make any arrangements for my comfort as I came up. God bless you all Darling is the earnest prayer of

your own
Will

The news from every quarter is encouraging & the achievements of the Arkansas[42] assure us that the Mississippi can be recovered & we can always beat them on land. Don't be gloomy Darling. All will be right in time & I hope the next New Year will find me at home with my precious wife and children and our country free and Independent and at peace with the world. A heartfull of love from

Your Own
Will

Hanover C. H. Hanover Co., Va
July 28, 1862

My Dear Rosa,

I was made happy this morning by the receipt of three letters from you one of the 18th, 20th, & 22nd and am truly glad to hear that you are all well and our precious little children so interesting. I would give worlds to see you all this morning & have a good long talk with you and a romp with the babies, but I am afraid that it will [be] a long, long time before I can come home for good. The immense preparations at the North for our subjection and the determination on our part to achieve our independence at any sacrifice, portend a desperate and fearful struggle, and when or where it will stop none can tell. Europe seems afraid or unwilling to intervene and I think we will have to fight it on alone and in all probability be a long time at it. Lee has however hope for the best and prays that the war will be a short one and that we may soon be reunited at home once more in peace and quietness.

---

[42] The ironclad *CSS Arkansas* attacked Federal naval vessels just north of Vicksburg on 15 July. The *Arkansas* steamed through the midst of David Farragut's Union warships with all guns blazing, badly damaging three of the Federal ships. This attack by the *Arkansas* kept the Mississippi open for the Confederacy for another twenty-three days. On 6 August, the Federal ironclad *Essex* and four other Union ships attacked the *Arkansas*, badly damaging her. In the midst of a raging fire onboard, the *Arkansas*'s crew was forced to abandon and then blow the ship up to keep it out of enemy hands.

I am much surprised to learn that George has only brought you six bushels of wheat that the land made more I am confident and there has been foul play about it. It either was not cut and saved or it was sold afterwards. I think you had better buy some flour, but I am astonished at the continued high price of corn. I learn that the crop all over the South where it is already made is very large and in almost every section of the country it is promising, except in small portions like ours and it seems to me that instead of increasing in price, it ought now to begin to fall a little. How would you like to take a trip on to Richmond and pay me a visit with the children? If we are to remain on picket duty below Richmond for any length of time I think you could very well come on and spend the summer with me or near me in a neighboring farm house.

Kiss my little ones for me and don't let them forget Papa. Tell Tom that his horse is getting on finely and is doing good service and I will try and bring him on when I come for good. Tell little Rosa to write to me & kiss Darling Willie for me, a heartfull of love & more.

Yr own
Will

New Market Church Near James River
12 miles below Richmond Aug 11, 1862

My Dear Rosa,

I yesterday received the letters from you, the latest dated the 31st July and am sorry to learn that dear little Rosa has been unwell. Sometimes I am troubled almost beyond endurance in thinking of our precious little ones, with the fear that some of you may be sick and I away from you. Bless their dear little souls. Papa would give his right arm to be with you all again with the country at peace and our home quiet and happy once more, but when will these things be? I saw Charlie Oliver last night who brings me later intelligence and that all are well. He says he would have called for a letter but did not know he would see me so soon. The Artillery & Infantry have both been down here, and indeed most of our Army expecting to have to take back Malvern Hill, but the exhibition of our force was sufficient & the Yankees left without a fight and most of the Army has again withdrawn. Cobb in command of his brother's brigade still however within a mile of us, and as soon as the General returns will I presume take command of the cavalry again. I wish very much he would either do that or would give us up altogether. I find I have been foolish in feeling that I could not have a separate command and I ought never have come into the war without commanding a regiment. It is a responsible position but I believe I could have filled it. If Cobb comes over I am inclined to think Young will leave us if

THE LEGION'S FIGHTING BULLDOG

he can get another Command and Cobb will either resign or be permitted, at least I
hope these things which would leave me in command of the cavalry and I would ask
no better position. Now I would not desire all this to occur but for my experience of
men and things for the last two months, and I do not know that it will happen, perhaps the wish is father to the thought, so say nothing about it. I would be perfectly
satisfied with my position if my superior officers had my full confidence. Col Young
has been very highly complimented, together with the officers and men of the Cavalry both by Gen Stuart and Gen Lee, in letters written to Col Young officially
through Gen Hampden our immediate commander. Gen Lee's letter was signed by
himself and both were highly complimentary. Well, Col Young is the man who
receives the benefits & honor of these compliments and perhaps you will be surprised to hear that in all our skirmishing & fighting below here Young has never
been under fire except when in retreat and running from shells. Whenever there has
been an alarm at our picket posts he has never gone to them to see for himself but
sends some body else. The consequence is that I am beginning very seriously to
doubt his courage and am unwilling to be led by him. That he is a man of good
judgment as an officer there can be no doubt but what his judgment would [be]
with a storm of bullets flying about his head I cant tell. The result of the whole matter is that I now simply obey orders. I do not expose myself and shall not when he
does not, so it is now a pretty safe business. I was secretly amused two days ago.
Gen Hampden was with us below and our pickets had been driven in. Hampden
wanted to visit our extreme outposts and also wanted to shell off the enemy's pickets
in sight of Malvern Hill. Young very hastily & greedily said he would accompany
the Gen to Malvern Hill with the cannon & shell the enemy and ordered me with a
detachment of sixty men to skirmish the woods and drive off the enemy from the
part that the Gen wanted to visit. I went out and drove off the Yankees with a blast
of the bugle without firing a gun. Young and Hampden on the hill after firing a few
rounds were fired upon by a gun boat which at first was invisible to them and I am
told Young led the retreat in rapid style. The men were laughing at him so one of
the Captains told me yesterday. Now all this is at least extremely unfortunate and I
am sorry for it for I think he is a clever man and in every other sense a fine officer.
Hampden is a splendid fellow, a bold brave man, cool and sensible and a perfect
gentleman. I am highly pleased with him and he has made a fine impression upon
the men. Now all this you must say nothing about. I may be mistaken about Young
& hope I am. Time will show the truth but in the meantime I wish I had more confidence.

   We ought to have been relieved yesterday, but instead of that Gen Stuart has
ordered Gen Hampden to remain here and do all the picket duty with his brigade &
Stuart's favorite Virginians are with him at Hanover with horses all shod & men in

FIRST BLOOD

good condition to fight. You may judge of our condition from the fact that Capt. King & Capt. Jones have just gone out on duty with 35 men out of about 200 in the two companies. Young has no horse fit to ride & my fine horse Tom has a sore back that is awful to look at. My other fine bay (Marmion)[43] is in a bad way too. God bless you all Darling. Kiss the little folks for me & dont let them forget Papa. Write to me often. Our duty down here now is not unpleasant if we could shoe our horses. I think the Yankees are satisfied to let us alone now since they find they cant hold Malvern Hill if they take it so dont be uneasy.

Much love from Yr own
Will

---

[43] Marmion was Delony's greatly beloved horse, named for "Lord Marmion," the main char-acter in Walter Scott's epic poem of the same name, first published in 1808, about the Battle of Flodden.

141

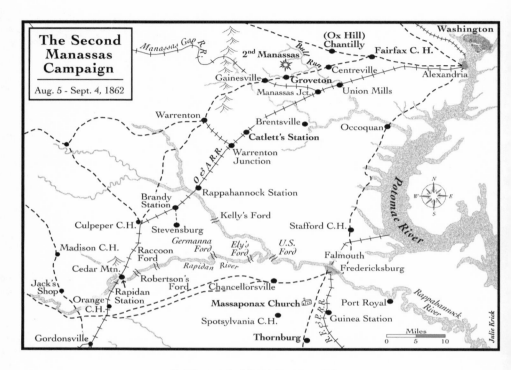

The Second
Manassas
Campaign

Aug. 5 - Sept. 4, 1862

Manassas Gap R.R.

Washington

(Ox Hill)
Chantilly

2nd Manassas

Fairfax C. H.

Bull Run

Gainesville

Groveton

Centreville

Alexandria

Manassas Jct.

Union Mills

Warrenton

Brentsville

Occoquan

Catlett's Station

Warrenton
Junction

O. & A. R.R.

Rappahannock Station

Brandy
Station

Kelly's Ford

Stafford C. H.

Culpeper C.H.

Stevensburg

Madison C.H.

Germanna
Ford

Raccoon
Ford

Ely's
Ford

U.S.
Ford

Falmouth

Cedar Mtn.

Rapidan River

Fredericksburg

Jack's
Shop

Robertson's
Ford

Chancellorsville

Potomac River

Orange
C.H.

Rapidan
Station

Massaponax Church

Port Royal

Guinea Station

Rappahannock River

Spotsylvania C.H.

Gordonsville

R. F. & P. R.R.

Thornburg

Miles

0   5   10

Julie Krick

Battles and skirmishes involving
William G. Delony and Cobb's Georgia Legion Cavalry.

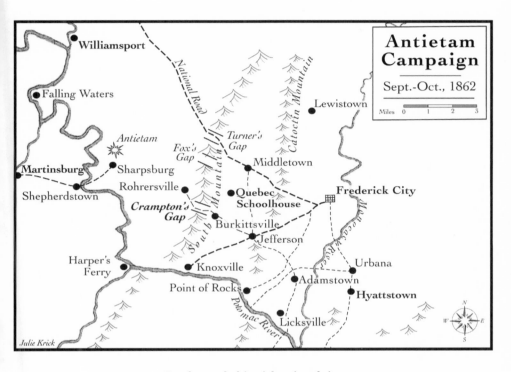

Battles and skirmishes involving
William G. Delony and Cobb's Georgia Legion Cavalry.

Chapter 7

Maryland, My Maryland:
August 1862–October 1862

His broad clear brow in sunlight glowed;
On burnished hooves his war-horse trode;
From underneath his helmet flowed
His coal-black curls as on he rode.
        —*Marmion* by Sir Walter Scott

With Lee's release in mid-August of Special Orders #183, all of the cavalry in the Army of Northern Virginia were to be placed under the command of J. E. B. Stuart as the official commander of all the Confederate cavalry in the Army of Northern Virginia. The 2nd South Carolina Cavalry was created by consolidating Hampton's Legion, the 4th South Carolina Cavalry Battalion, and a couple of independent South Carolina companies.[1] Hampton's Brigade was then comprised of the 2nd South Carolina Cavalry, along with Cobb's Georgia Legion, the Jeff Davis Legion (Mississippi), the 1st North Carolina Cavalry, and the 10th Virginia Cavalry.[2] The Confederate Cavalry under Stuart now numbered 6,400 cavalrymen, divided into three brigades, along with three batteries of horse artillery under John Pelham.

Cobb's Legion continued its routine of picketing in northern Virginia throughout early August. This routine changed on 16 August with notice of enemy movements in the area of Bull Run, north of Fredericksburg. Scouts began returning with information that McClellan was abandoning Harrison's Landing and moving toward the Chickahominy with part of his force landing at Aquia Creek, where they could join up with Gen. John Pope on the Rappahannock River. This advance by two significant Union forces placed the Federals in a position to support each other as they moved on Richmond.

---

[1] Stewart Sifakis, *Compendium of the Confederate Armies: South Carolina and Georgia* (New York: Facts on File, Inc., 1995) 40–41.

[2] The Phillips Legion (Georgia) and the 1st South Carolina Cavalry were added to Hampton's Brigade in November 1862.

Lee determined to counter this movement and try to bag Pope before any re-inforcements could arrive from McClellan. He sent Stuart and the Confederate cavalry on a raid around Pope and into his rear, where they attacked and captured Pope's supply train at Catlett's Station on the Orange and Alexander Railroad.[3] Stuart's cavalry raid marked the beginning of the Second Manassas Campaign.

During the raid, the legion captured Pope's baggage train and all of his personal papers, after which the legion cavalry engaged "in a number of skirmishes and hot little bouts near Thoroughfare Gap," wrote Wiley Howard.

> Our command was in front when Stuart planned to surprise the enemy's wagon train on the road near Hay Market. DeLoney, at head of column, was just entering the thicket to pounce upon the train when it was found to be heavily guarded by strong infantry marching alongside the train with fixed bayonets, and our presence being discovered, we were subjected to a very uncomfortable cannonading by a battery of the enemy overlooking the situation. DeLoney was recalled and we had to about-face, but our leader did so stubbornly and under protest, for he was a game fighter and dared to attempt anything, even though it seemed impossible to others.[4]

This move by the Confederate cavalry forced Pope to turn about, allowing Jackson, now joined by Stuart, to move through the Bull Run Mountains around Pope's right and position themselves in the Union rear just west of the old Bull Run battlefield. By evening, Jackson's troops were at Bristoe Station. Arriving at Manassas, the Confederates captured large amounts of commissary supplies, food, and a few hundred prisoners.

On 29 August, Pope attacked Jackson near Groveton, Virginia. The Federals outnumbered their Confederate counterparts 75,000 to 48,500. Jackson's Confederates were positioned in a railroad cut near Sudley Springs just north of Groveton and the Warrenton Turnpike. But Pope's attack came piecemeal and did little to dislodge the Confederates from their defenses. Renewing his attack on Jackson the following day, Pope met with the same results as the previous battle.

As the 30th dawned, Pope, believing that the Confederates were retreating, decided to attack once more. Hitting Jackson on the Confederate left, the Federals had some initial success, but Longstreet's force plowed into the Union left flank,

---

[3] Pvt. Nathan B. Webb of the 1st Maine Cavalry referred in his journal to Catlett's Station as a "grog shop" and the Rappahannock River as a "muddy brook." Nathan B. Webb Journals, September 1861, William L. Clements Library, University of Michigan.

[4] Wiley C. Howard, "Sketch of Cobb Legion Cavalry and Some Incidents and Scenes remembered" (Atlanta: Camp 159, published talk given at U.C.V. meeting) 19 August 1901, 2–3. 2–3.

taking Bald Hill and Henry House Hill (where fighting had taken place in 1861 during the first battle).

On 31 August, Stuart's cavalry reviewed the Federal position and reported to Lee, who planned to turn the Union right. The following day, Jackson was able to accomplish that movement at Chantilly while Lee kept up pressure on Pope's front. After severe fighting all along the front, the Confederates took control of Chantilly, and Pope pulled his forces back within the Washington defenses, effectively ending the Second Manassas campaign. Union losses were 1,724 killed, 8,372 wounded, and 5,958 missing. The Confederate army lost 1,481 killed, 7,627 wounded, and 89 missing.

Stuart's cavalry harassed the retiring Union army nearly the entire way as they fell back towards Washington in full retreat. On the morning of 1 September, the Confederate cavalry skirmished with infantry and cavalry remnants of Pope's army at Flint Hill, near Fairfax Court House, as part of the Battle of Ox Hill. Here, Hampton reported hitting Pope's rear guard, where he gave the Federals an incentive to keep moving. "The enemy retired," Hampton wrote, "and were followed by my brigade."[5] With Pope's defeat, Lee relieved Richmond and was now ready to take the war to the North.

The first week of September, the Confederate army began crossing the Potomac into Maryland in the Leesburg area. James Munnerlyn of the Jeff Davis Legion wrote his sister that as they crossed, "the water reached our saddles and some small horses had to swim. As Regt after Regt reached the Maryland side, the men cheered and the bands played Maryland My Maryland."[6] The legion cavalry marched to Poolesville, where they drove off some Federal cavalry. On the 6th, the grey horsemen moved to Urbana, capturing a Union signal corps, and encamped for the evening. For the next few days the legion operated in this area, taking part in a number of small skirmishes as they screened the Army of Northern Virginia from the direction of Washington. Hampton's Brigade constituted Stuart's center in the Urbana and Hyattstown area, while Beverly Holcombe Robertson's Brigade under Colonel Thomas T. Munford covered the right between Poolesville and Sugar Loaf Mountain and Fitz Lee's Brigade covered the left between New Market and the Baltimore and Ohio Railroad.

Urbana in 1862 was "a pretty village of neat white houses" located just 40 miles from Washington and a few miles southeast of Frederick, Maryland. From his headquarters in the town, Stuart kept an eye on any Union advances. Here, he also looked to the morale of his men and to the residents of the village by hosting a

---

[5] *OR*, ser. 1, vol. 12, pt. 2, 19.

[6] James K. Munnerlyn to sister, 8 September 1862, Munnerlyn Papers, Southern Historical Collection, University of North Carolina at Chapel Hill.

number of balls. At the local female academy, "they decorated the dance hall with roses; they sent invitations to local young ladies and to selected Confederate officers; and they asked a band from the 18th Mississippi to provide music. Dancing halted only once when a dusty courier dramatically arrived, saying to Stuart in a loud voice that the Federals were attacking. As small arms fire sounded in the distance, the gallant Confederate officers left swooning ladies behind and sped to the fight."[7]

On 11 September, Stuart's forces fell back from Urbana to Frederick as Jackson's forces were converging on Harper's Ferry. Bringing up the rear of Stuart's Cavalry was Hampton and his troopers. The Confederate cavalry was shadowed by Federal cavalry under Col. Alfred Pleasonton as the Confederate cavalry moved to join up with D. H. Hill's command. As Cobb's Legion Cavalry prepared to march through Frederick City on the 12th, they came under fire from a Federal gun with the 30th Ohio Infantry and two companies of cavalry in support. The gun opened fire and the legion cavalry made a saber charge through the streets, scattering the enemy and capturing Colonel Augustus Moor of the 28th Ohio. Undeterred, the legion cavalry continued on through town and encamped near Middletown, with the Jeff Davis Legion picketing the National Road between Middletown and Frederick. The following day, a trooper arrived at Stuart's headquarters with news that a heavy enemy force was advancing along the National Road. Stuart ordered his force to fall back, but to do so slowly so as to impede the Union advance. This advance was actually part of a reconnaissance in force being carried out by the 1st and 2nd Brigades under Colonel Eliakim Scammon and the now captive Col. Moor respectively. Hampton later reported:

> Having two squadrons on picket at the bridge over the Monocacy (on the road from Urbana) and near that point, it was of utmost consequence that I should hold the approaches to the city by the National road until these squadrons could be withdrawn. With this object in view, I took one rifled gun to the assistance of the two guns that were on the pike, and placed a squadron of the Second South Carolina Regiment to support the battery.... The enemy opened fire on the squadron, killing 2 of the men. Finding that my other squadrons were coming in, I withdrew slowly to the city, sending my guns to occupy a position which would command the road from the city to the foot of the mountain.[8]

Following the attack at Crampton's Gap and the rapid pullback of Confederate infantry on the morning of the 13th, Hampton's forces withdrew slowly from Middletown to Burkittsville, where the brigade was to form up with Robertson's

---

[7] Chris J. Hartley, *Stuart's Tarheels: James B. Gordon and His North Carolina Cavalry in the Civil War* (Jefferson, NC: McFarland, 2011) 82.

[8] *OR*, vol. 19, pt. 1, 822.

Brigade. To speed their movements, once in Middletown, Hampton was detached southward along a different route through the Catoctin Valley toward Burkittsville along with the baggage train. Along the way, Union cavalry of the 8th Illinios Cavalry and 3rd Indiana Cavalry shadowed the Confederate troopers. The legion cavalry made brief stands east of Middletown and then west at the Catoctin Creek Bridge against the enemy trying to slow their pursuers down a bit.

Col. John Farnsworth, commanding the 8th Illinois and 3rd Indiana Cavalry, attempted to run down Wade Hampton and the Confederate baggage train. Farnsworth sent Maj. William H. Medill and about 250 men after the fleeing Confederates. Traveling on wet roads due to the recent rains, the Union cavalry had a difficult time locating Hampton's command. Galloping towards Burkittsville from Middletown, the Federals found a fork in the road. Medill decided to take the right fork, Mountain Church Road, while Hampton's force earlier had taken the left fork, Marker Road. Marker Road runs further south before eventually merging back onto Mountain Church Road. Neither of the opposing commanders realized it at the time, but they were set on a collision course.

Viewing the enemy closing along a parallel road, Hampton hurried the baggage train on. Realizing that he had beaten the Federals to this point, Hampton set an ambush for the pursuers at a small country schoolhouse known as the Quebec Schoolhouse. "On the road to this place," reported Hampton, "I discovered, on a road parallel to the one on which we were, a regiment of Yankee cavalry. Taking the Cobb Legion with me, I directed Lieutenant-Colonel Young to charge this regiment."[9] Cobb's Legion, at this point, numbered only about 100 men due to the recent severe campaigning.

As they began to arrive in sight of the Confederate cavalry, Medill's troopers saw the rear of the Confederate baggage train and spurred their horses, not recognizing the concealed grey troopers in the schoolhouse and the nearby trees. "Our pursuit of the wagon train was enthusiastic for a couple of miles," remembered William Pickerill of the 3rd Indiana Cavalry, "until we came in sight of it [the Confederate Cavalry], slowly winding its way up a mountain road leading out of Burkittsville, the next hamlet below Middletown. In the rear of the train were six brass guns and cavalry enough to eat us up."[10]

Once over the ridge and out of view from the Federals, Hampton made his move. He ordered Col. Young and the legion cavalry to wheel about with part of the legion under Young charging straight up the road, while Delony took the rest on a half circle around the woods, shielded from view by the Federals. As Pickerill described,

---

[9] Ibid., 824.

[10] William Pickerill, "Quebec School House," *Valley Register* (8 April 1898).

We halted and formed in a meadow by the wayside and calmly viewed our retreating booty and wisely decided to let it escape.... The major commanding gave the command to about face and we filed off down the rocky ravine road, hemmed in on either side by a very crooked worm fence, on our return to Middletown and our regiments. The rear of our column had just entered this rocky, narrow way when a shot that seemed to come from over behind the schoolhouse whizzed over our heads and left a white spot on the body of a little hickory we were leaving to our right. We could not believe that innocent-looking old schoolhouse concealed our enemies, but two men from the forward end of the column filed out and passing through a pair of bars started up the winding road leading to the schoolhouse door. But they never reached their destination. When halfway up the hill, they, as well as we, heard a yell, and over the little ridge and down upon us leaped a body of Confederate cavalry.[11]

Delony's force hit the Federals slashing with saber and pistol into the rear and left flank of the blue-clad troopers. The Federals broke and fled back in the direction they had come with the legion cavalry pursuing them for nearly a mile, killing or wounding nearly thirty and capturing five. It was a short but vicious fight. The legion lost forty-seven men killed and wounded, including among the wounded, Col. Young, Capt. G. J. Wright,[12] and Lt. Holly Camfield. Among the killed were "1st Lieut. Marshall and Sergt. Barksdale, eighty years of age with grandsons in his company among the killed."[13] Hampton estimated that losses to the Federal cavalry numbered thirty to forty. He wrote in his official report that "[Lieutenant] Colonel Young, who led the charge, received a painful wound in the leg.... I take pleasure in calling attention to the behavior of this command. Colonel Young led with great gallantry, and, after his fall, Major Delony. After driving in his cavalry, I moved on to Burkittsville, where we remained during the night of September 13."[14]

On the 14th, the Union VI Corps under William B. Franklin moved toward South Mountain and Crampton's Gap in an attempt to cut off the increasing pressure on the Harper's Ferry garrison. After severe fighting at South Mountain, Crampton's Gap, Boonsborough, Fox's Gap, and Turner's Gap, the Federal garri-

---

[11] Ibid.

[12] Wiley Howard recalled, "Wright will long be remembered as he lay holding up his bleeding foot and cried to us as we passed, 'give 'em h__l, boys, they've got me down!'" Howard, "Sketch of Cobb Legion Cavalry," 3.

[13] Pickerill, "Quebec School House"; Athens *Banner* (30 April 1892); Edward G. Longacre, *Gentleman and Soldier: The Extraordinary Life of General Wade Hampton* (Nashville, TN: Rutledge Hill Press, 2003).

[14] *OR*, vol. 19, pt. 1, 824.

son at Harper's Ferry capitulated. With the town's surrender, Confederate forces captured 12,000 prisoners.

With the fall of Harper's Ferry, Gen. Robert E. Lee began to gather his forces near Sharpsburg, just west of Antietam Creek. The following day became one of the bloodiest days in American history as Maj. Gen. George McClellan and his 75,000 men of the Army of the Potomac attacked the 40,000 badly outnumbered Confederates. The day's fighting ended with nearly 12,500 Union and 14,000 Confederate casualties. Night fell with the Confederates still holding the battlefield.

Crossing the Potomac on the 17th, the legion continued to Harper's Ferry. Howard reported that "we marched up the river and crossed in deep water near the right end of our firing line in front of Sharpsburg and worked our way to the left, where Stuart, Fitz Lee and others were operating on McClellan's flank and were subjected to some fierce and destructive cannon-ading, not to speak of the zip of the minies."[15] At Sharpsburg, the legion, and the rest of the Confederate cavalry were positioned on the left of Jackson's line on the Hagerstown Pike extending from the infantry to the Potomac River. The legion made a demonstration against McClellan to keep the Federals guessing as to what the Confederate army intended next. "The night after the last day's fight," wrote Howard. "General Hampton lead us across the Potomac between Falling Waters and Sharpsburg, at an old blind ford."[16]

On the 18th, the legion proceeded toward Williamsport, skirmishing along the way at Buckettsville and Pleasant Valley.

Here again did the Cobb Legion drive the Federal Cavalry back on the infantry breastworks, and held them until late in the afternoon when we were driven back fighting step by step and re-crossed into Virginia under the cover of our artillery, whose bursting shells gave us the only light of a cloudy night, the Potomac almost swimming, but whose inferior ammunition "honey combed" as we called it, was almost as dangerous as the Yankee balls that shattered around us.[17]

The legion established a new camp near Sulphur Springs, Virginia, on the Rappahannock River.

At the end of September 1862, both Cobb's Legion Cavalry and the legion's infantry were reunited, however briefly, for the first time in many months. Thomas Cobb wrote his wife from the cavalry encampment at Camp Tom in Frederick County, Virginia.[18]

---

[15] Howard, "Sketch of Cobb Legion Cavalry," 3.

[16] Thought to be a place called "Mason's Ford."

[17] Athens *Banner* (30 April 1892).

[18] The camp was so named for Thomas R. R. Cobb, although Cobb and many others referred to it as Bunker's Hill or Buckletown. The camp was located between Harper's Ferry and

My cavalry are here in the rear of the army doing picket duty. They are reduced to about half their original strength by difficult causes, prominent among which is broken down horses.... Maj. Deloney is very kind and very well.... One of my cavalry, with a squad of thirty men charged a Yankee regiment, arrested the colonel, ran his sword through a captain so he could not pull it out and then got another and killed two or three men. This man was a private and a wagoner. Genl. Stewart told Genl. Lee my cavalry was one of the largest and best regiments he had, and objected to its coming here.[19]

The legion cavalry spent about a week in the Winchester vicinity,[20] skirmishing with Federal cavalry. On 1 October, some elements of Hampton's command skirmished at Shepherdstown, and that same day at Martinsburg. "We assisted in tearing up the Baltimore & Ohio Railroad beyond Martinsburg as far as a little place called Funktown," wrote Howard. "I think, where in a brisk and hot little fight Lieut. Salter, of Company H, was killed, besides other casualties. For some time we camped near Bunker Hill, between Winchester and Harper's Ferry."[21]

* * *

Fredsby. R. R. 30 miles N. of Richmond

Aug 25, 1862

My Dear Rosa,

Your letter of the 18th by H Cobb I have just recd with the letter of Mr Mitchell. I am rejoiced to learn that you are well. We left Hanover as I wrote you & came up this way. Day before yesterday I was quite sick with diarrhea, but was well enough yesterday to leave camp at 6 A.M. & scout all day until 9 1/2 at night when I returned to Camp. We have just recd orders to be ready in an hour & a half with our whole force and three days rations, so you see there is no rest for us. Young is sick at a house 9 miles off and I am in command, and I am happy to say feeling quite well and hearty again.

In reference to the lot, you can say to Mr Mitchell that Dr Lipscombe can have the middle lot or the other at $2500, but say nothing about the price as I will sell to such a neighbor cheaper than to a man I care nothing for. As to the division

---

Winchester, 7 miles west of Winchester. See William S. Smedlund, *Camp Fires of Georgia Troops, 1861–1865* (Lithonia, GA: Kennesaw Mountain Press, 1994) 270.

[19] Thomas R. R. Cobb to Marion, 29 September 1862, T. R. R. Cobb Papers.

[20] Now West Virginia.

[21] Howard, "Sketch of Cobb Legion Cavalry," 4.

of the place, ask Mr Mitchell to have it surveyed for me & divided by stakes according to both my plans and then do your side up and if you don't like the form in which it leaves our lot don't sell at all. Understand that you are to be suited in a lot before any one else and whatever you may do I shall be fully satisfied with. I would write to Mr Mitchell, and a larger letter to you but, everybody is running to me so Goodbye Darling. Exercise your own judgment about the lot. I would as soon have Dr. Lipscombe's note as the money. Kiss the little ones for me and think often & kindly of me.

Ever Yr own
Will

Fairfax Culpepper City Va
Aug 29, 1862

My Dear Rosa,

You perceive I turn up at this place on my way to report to Gen Lee. I am twelve miles in advance of Hampton's Brigade making forced marches and am writing tonight by candle light in the open air with the wind blowing and Sergt. Major Jones holding his hand to keep the candle burning, and such is camp life, and it is astonishing how we accommodated ourselves to circumstances. I am well however and grateful for it and my surest trial and a sure one it is, is that I so seldom hear from you. When I shall hear again Heaven only knows. Young is sick in Richmond & I am in command & some of the officers trying my mettle, but I am perfectly satisfied. I can't see to write so good bye. Will write at the first post office I come to again. God bless you all Darling. Kiss the little ones for Papa & think sweetly & kindly of me.

Ever yours
W. G. Delony
Private

Hampton is treating me elegantly. We are now receiving about the first practical compliment we have ever had. I have been in advance of his brigade two days & in response to a demand from Gen Lee for a Regt., have been ordered forward promptly & handsomely.

W. G. D.

Camp Near Urbanna Md
Sept. 10, 1862

My Dear Rosa

I have recently received your letters of the 18th 20th 22nd & 24th Aug. and you can have no conception of the pleasure afforded me by my singular good fortune. It is a little surprising that for the first time since I left you that on such a march I should have the pleasure of hearing from you through four successive letters. I know you will be terribly anxious about me but Darling you must bear up under our separation with true womanly courage and endeavor as dutifully as may be to endure it with the hope that our present campaign may be the last, and then, peace and independence to the South. Our officers & men are all in fine spirits and all determined to do all that men can do to end the war with a day of thunder. I wish you could [have] witnessed the crossing of the Potomac by our Cavalry. We had been ordered to encamp for the night on the other side and the men were cooking, feeding horses and preparing for a comfortable bivouac, when the order came from Gen Lee that every Confederate dragoon must sleep that night across the Potomac. Beef, bacon & bread were very soon forgotten wagons left behind and our troops in the saddle and on the march. As soon as we came in sight of the Potomac the boys gave one of the loudest, most long protracted & glorious shouts you ever heard. We crossed by moonlight and the whole scene was one of the most inspiring I have ever witnessed. I could but hope that the recrossing might be attended with as much good feeling and cheerfulness. We bivouached that night five miles from the river near Poolesville. I stopped in town bought a Coffee pot, two tin cups, sugar @ 15 1/2 cts, & Coffee @ 30 cts pr pound and with some crackers & meat that we gathered together Young and myself made out a very comfortable supper about 12 at night. Orders were recd to move at 5 in the morning on last Saturday morning the 6th and we arrived here that day. We have a Comfortable Camp & have been able to give our horses a little much needed rest. The Yankee pickets are about two miles below us at Hyattstown. On the afternoon of the 8th the enemy drove in our pickets and came up quite near our Camp. We drove them back that night and reestablished our picket lines which are on a range of high hills just this side the little village & on the opposite hills are the Yankees in full view, with Hyattstown in a little valley between us, debateable ground, into which both sides return at the hazard of being captured by the other. We captured one prisoner yesterday who came on our side [of] the town. One of our men dashed down upon him & took the Yankee & his horse & arms without a fight. He was surprised & too frightened to offer resistance. After the skirmish on the 8th I was ordered by Gen Hampton to remain at the picket post with about sixty men and was up all night with the Yankees just in front, which by the way is not the most agreeable mode of spending ones both day [and] night. The truth is of all the duties which I have been called upon to perform while in the army, I know of none more unpleasant than to watch the movements of an enemy of an unknown force, at night with a command that you know is insufficient to make a respectable fight. I have been interrupted a half dozen times & I have been suddenly called off.

Ever Yrs
WGD

Haynesville, Va Sept. 23, 1862

My Dear Rosa

For the first time since I left Urbana in Maryland I have an opportunity of sending you a note. Our mail has left the Brigade since then but at the time I was on picket and our Cavalry knew nothing of it. A kind of Providence has protected me thus far through the dangers of the series of recent battles and I am happy to say I am safe and well and I hope that for the present the active Campaign has ceased tho' of this I of course know nothing but give only my surmise. Our Generals I think will fall over upon Winchester and I know that it is their opinion that the Yankee Army is too badly cut up to pursue us and risk another fight. Lees late Campaign has been most brilliant. The fight at Manassas was a brilliant victory to our arms then followed the capitulation of 11,300 at Harpers Ferry and last Wednesday the great fight at Sharpsburg, where the enemy attacked us and our army repulsed them & slept on the battle field & held it all the next day, the enemy declining to renew the conflict. That night our Army recrossed the Potomac into Virginia without molestation & on the following day the enemy attempted to cross over seeming to believe that we had skedaddled.[22] Gen A. P. Hill who was in command at that point (Sheppardstown) allowed 3 of their brigades to cross and then attacked them and but few ever got back to the Maryland shore. The river was almost choked up with their dead bodies and it is impossible to estimate their loss, but it was very heavy as it was also at Sharpsburg. Our Army is in fine spirits but very dirty and tired. As some evidence that we ought to be so I will state that the day of the fight we were under arms all day, had one horse killed by a shell and several other shells in a proximity too close for comfort. Early the next day we were engaged all day in hunting up the stragglers and before getting supper were ordered to march not knowing where. Upon my application were allowed an hour to feed horses and cook supper, & then took up the line of March crossed to the Va side of

---

[22] "Skedaddled" was a slang term used by soldiers on both sides to describe the panicked retreat from a battle where soldiers usually discarded their weapons and any other equipment that might slow their progress away from the danger.

the Potomac had one man's leg broken & one badly bruised otherwise by the falling of their horses & several nearly drowned in crossing the rockiest & worst fords I expect on the Potomac. We then stopped in a field two or three hours waiting on the balance of the brigade, then resumed the march about 2 oclock in the morning. After sunrise were ordered to halt to feed horses stopped an hour, moved on & re-crossed the River above Williamsport, then down the river at a trot for several miles & in a gallop into Williamsport about a mile ahead of the Brigade & the Yankees at a gallop out of the other end of town. Then we were ordered to drive them farther off and we charged and they ran for a mile or two. I then posted our pickets & returned to Camp at Williamsport about 9 oclock at night, after being in the saddle for 36 hours and 20 hours of the time continuous marching, with no rest to me. The next day we moved again. I still in the advance and after marching 2 or 3 miles came up with the enemy. We had some skirmishing & then the Artillery was ordered up. We shelled them most of the day. Our regt. being under arms all the time as a support to the battery and expecting every minute a charge. Notwithstanding this I was constantly obliged to send along the lines & wake up the men who from sheer fatigue would slip off their horses and fall asleep. Late in the afternoon a large force of the enemy coming up we had to retreat, continued the skirmish until dark and then recrossed the river at Williamsport under cover of our batteries and a more beautiful sight I never expect to see. I have never yet seen such fireworks at night. The shells flying over our heads from all our own cannons & we feeling safe for the first time during the war with shells in such close proximity. During the retreat I was in the rear, again next the enemy, with rumors & reports that they were in hot pursuit. We went up the river for 3 miles & I was left on picket that night the next day & the next night and yesterday afternoon reached the Brigade Camp & rested last night soundly and at ease. This morning I feel like a new man and have come to the conclusion that Hampton must either have great confidence in me & my men or he thinks we are good food for powder. I certainly feel very gratified for the protection He has afforded me. As Capt. Wright says I received my star without fighting for it, but they have made me work for it since. Young was wounded in the leg on the 13th. It is a flesh wound, painful but not dangerous. Wright was wounded in the right arm, bone not broken but bruised. Camfield had his arm broken. Lt Marshall was killed. Sergt Barksdale also killed. These I think you may remember, others were wounded some very badly, whom you don't know. Several are missing taken prisoners. I have a great deal to tell you that I cant write. We have had a hard time since we went to Maryland. I discovered but little sympathy there for us, & this is the feeling of the army. We don't want her with us & don't want to go there again unless we go as into an enemy's country. I think differently of the Virginians since I have witness their trials and their true manliness in this part of the state, but Darling I want to see you and our precious little ones so badly that I even envy them in their desolated homes. I saw a little child the other day that reminded me of Dear little Willie, a sweet pretty little girl. It makes me homesick to think about you. I feel that I could write you for a week, but the man who takes this is about to leave, so good bye. Think kindly of me. I can only hope that you will get this letter, there is no certainty of it. Kiss my dear little ones for Papa & tell Tom he has the best horse in the country. I ride no other now & he is still in good order.

Yr own
Will

Young has gone to Richmond. I have been in command since he was wounded.

Camp Near Bunker Hill Va.
Oct 1 1862

My Dear Rosa

We are here at this place about Midway between Martinsburg and Winchester the balance of the Brigade being at or near Martinsburg. We were sent here when Jacksons Army moved several days ago upon a requisition from Gen Lee upon Gen Hampton for 200 hundred of his best men. The order came at ten oclock at night. We travelled until nearly day & rested for two hours then travelled all that day until after dusk and arrived here pretty well worn out, both men & horses. The next morning one of Jackson's staff came to our Bivouac and most insultingly summoned me to report at once with my whole command at Gen Jackson's head quarters, charged with the destruction of private property. From his manner I presumed he was at least a General officer & as I did not know Jackson was not sure that it was not old Stonewall himself. He further ordered me to split rails & rebuild all the fences destroyed. You would have thought that that old Harry was to pay & indeed so thought I. Cobb had just come up & offered to go with me to Jackson but I concluded to meet the fight alone. So up I rode, dismounted and asked if Gen Jackson was present. Rather a fine looking man arose & said he was Gen Jackson. I told him I had been summoned before him, I presumed upon a charge of destroying private property. He said no charges had been preferred, but would be if I had done so & I was glad at the time he made the remark for it raised all the old Adam in me and made me feel easy at once. I told him I wanted him to understand that I was not in the habit of taking or destroying other peoples property without remuneration but that as an officer I took corn & burnt rails where it was necessary for my men & horses, that I had done so the night before & orders had been issued by me before I saw him or his and to pay for both. "That's all right Maj" he said "I am much obliged to you" and he treated me with kindness & courtesy, but I left him notwithstanding with the impression that he fully appreciates his importance. Thus it may be that his remark may have been called forth by my manner for I assure you I was in no good humor & I have not been to his Hdqtrs since, tho' as I am now or rather until Cobb assumed Command was acting under his orders have desired to go to him for direction, but finally preferred to take the responsibility and exercise my discretion. I reported at first to Gen Lee who treated me like a gentleman as he is, as did his aids also, and I cant rid my mind of the old adage, "Like master like we all." Gen Lee is one of the most courteous, pleasant & simple in his manner of any of the old Army officers I have met though I will say that generally they have all been clever to me. When I went to Gen Lee's Hdqtrs, & he ordered me to report to Gen Jackson, Gen Stuart was standing by & Lee said he would have to assign me permanently to Jackson's command. Stuart remarked that he could not spare us as we were one of his best & fullest regiments & he treats us as if he thought so. So that so far as our standing with our Superior officers is concerned we have nothing to complain of. Now you will say that this is boasting & Will ought not to feel so, but I think that when men endeavor to do their duty it is not improper to feel gratified that those who are witnesses of their conduct, appreciate it. I have no desire to see my name in the papers & be puffed for so help me Heaven if I know myself I care nothing for this. If I and my friends can feel at the end of the war that I have done my duty fully, faithfully & fearlessly, my ambition is completely satisfied. Cobb assumed command yesterday having moved to our Camp the day before. The men & officers received him handsomely & I think he can have no cause of complaint. He made them a speech & seemed gratified & I was then called on but I cant speak to them. It seems to me I could as well call up you and the children & make a set speech to you. We are all here together know what each man knows & hence what each officer hears & nothing more, so I told them that I must defer my speechmaking until we all get back to Georgia. Cobb is making an effort to be sent to the coast for Winter service & I would not be surprised if he succeeded. I hope so at least tho' at the same time I am not aiding in the effort. I have seen so many cases of disappointment in picking places in the army that I am satisfied & go where I am ordered without asking questions feeling that I will fare about as well. If we remain in Va. there will be but little to do & I can pay you a long visit I hope. If we go to Ga. you will have to come to see me so I don't know which is best for me or for the command, it is best to get to Ga. if we can. You do not know Darling how I want to see you and our precious little children and how homesick and desolate I sometimes feel. As Cobb is here now and I shall have less to do, I am afraid that I shall be growing gloomy & desponding again. I have been so busy and so constantly in presence of the enemy that I have kept up my spirits, but to be in camp with nothing to do is terrible. But we must all hope for the best & bear bravely all that comes, feeling that all that is right. How I do sympathize with poor Dr. Lipscombe. I know of no one who will feel it more deeply & to whom such a loss will be a severe blow. He has won my heart by his goodness & my admiration by his accomplishments & I sympathize with him most deeply. Kiss my little Darlings for Papa & tell little Rosa I shall write to her next time. I am glad dear little Tom is improving. Be careful to let no one laugh at him & he will out grow the hesitancy in his speech. Kiss Cousin Laura for me & tell her I say she must stay with you till the war is over at least & take good care of my poor little wife for me. We look for a mail today & I hope that for a while I will be able to write to you with some thing like regularity, but the Comd have to do so much outpost duty, our facilities for writing are very limited. I am as well & hearty as you ever saw me. You say "don't sleep on the ground." My Darling half the time I have no place else to sleep. I have not learned the accomplishment of sleeping on horseback but I have seen many a poor fellow who has & envied him, but don't you be troubled about my sleeping. I never was in better health & less free from Cold. God bless you all. Kiss the little ones for me.

Ever yours
Will

Camp near Bunker Hill, Va
October 2 1862

My dear Darling little Daughter

Papa wrote a long letter to Mama yesterday and couldnt send it to the Post Office but he can send it today and I must write my little darling a letter because she was so good as to send Papa a dear sweet little letter that Mama wrote for her. Yesterday afternoon the Yankees tried to kill some of our soldiers and took the town of Martinsburg but our soldiers fought the Yankees and took the town back again and run the Yankees off but Papa is a long way off from the Yankees now and they cant shoot at him. God has been good to Papa and hasnt let the Yankees hurt him and my little daughter must pray to God that the Yankees shant hurt him and you must be good to Mama and Bubber Tom and dear little Willie and take good care of them all until Papa comes back again. Papa hopes he will be able to come and see all his dear little children this winter and when he comes he wants little Tom to say some hymns for him. Tell Bubber Tom his horse is a good horse and is fat and pretty and if Papa does come home for good he will bring Tom's horse with him and try to get a play pony for Willie and will be sure to bring something pretty for his dear little daughter. You must take good care of Mama and tell her to take good care of my little darlings. Tell her and George and Tally and Jay all howdy for Papa and kiss Mama and Bubber and Tom and Willie for Papa and write to me again and tell me what you all do every day and be a dear good little girl and God bless you and all at home my precious child is the prayer.

Of your own

Papa[23]

Camp near Bunker hill, Va

Oct 3, 1862

My Dear Rosa,

I wrote you and dear little Rosa yesterday and the day before and as I have the opportunity of sending a note to Richmond to be mailed have avail myself of it with the hope that they may all reach you. I am quite well and for several days have had nothing to do—cause quietly I am enjoying my lazy dignity beyond expression. The few days rest we have had have benefited man & horse & the only drawback is the sense of homesickness always consequent upon such a state. How I wish I could peep in upon you all in Athens for an hour or two this morning & see you & our dear little children in our happy little home. I send my signature upon the other page which you can hand to Mr. Hill. It is to secure my note. I would send you some money but it is impossible. If I risk the mail it is too uncertain so you must make out as well as you can until some opportunity presents itself which I hope will not be long. Kiss our dear little ones for me and don't let them forget Papa and tell little Rosa to answer my letter. Everything is very quiet at present but Lincoln & McClellan are both near recovering & the show will again burst with violence & virulence before long. Our Army is in full spirits & drilling every day with the fullest confidence of success. A heart full of love to my precious wife & little ones from

Will

---

[23] That evening Delony had a visitor in the person of Thomas Cobb. From the cavalry camp, Cobb wrote his wife, "Wish you and Mrs. Deloney could have been and heard Maj. D. and myself last night as we laid on the grass in the dim moonlight, long after all the others were asleep, and talked about home and the dear ones there and the hopes of peace and our plans and wishes for a quiet life by our own firesides. You would have concluded that we were sick of War." Thomas R. R. Cobb to Marion, 3 October 1862, T. R. R. Cobb Papers.

Camp at Bunker Hill
Oct. 6, 1862

My Dear Rosa,

We are still lying quietly in Camp with nothing for the Field Officers to do—particularly the Major, and I am enjoying the rest amazingly. How I wish I could spend these few days of rest at home with you and our precious little children but I fear that the day is far distant when we can go home in peace and quietness & hear of this infamous war no more. But after all the trial of strength between the two sections had to come. The conflict was impressible and I rejoice that it has come in my day and not in that of my children. Bless their little souls I am willing to endure all the horrors of the war to avert them from their heads—with the hope that our boys will have the manliness to dare maintain what I am willing to fight for. Col. Cobb has taken full charge of everything and is very cautious & kindly, says Hampton spoke to him of me in handsome terms & expresses as he did in Athens the waste that I commanded the Cavalry. He is proposing to mount his whole command and make of his Infantry mounted rifle men & horse Artillery of his Artillery & go to the Coast of Georgia. Gens. Hampton & Stuart & McLaws & Longstreet & Lee have all recommended his proposition as well as our move to Georgia, actually some of them in very complimentary terms but with the understanding that we are not to leave until the present Campaign in Virginia is ended. When this will be no one of course knows. Many think it is virtually ended now and that McClellan will hardly risk another Virginia Campaign until his Army is recruited and his new troops better drilled. If so we will have no more fighting to do until we come to Georgia and I think this is not improbable for McClellan had a good many new troops at the Sharpsburg fight and our well drilled regiments mowed them down like sheep. Gen. Lee had less than 40,000 troops in the fight and I am satisfied from all the information I can gather that his loss in killed wounded and missing was not over 6 or 7000. The Yankees I notice are themselves beginning to appreciate the skill and generalship of Gen. Lee and if McClellan come into Virginia now he will risk everything. Our Army has been increased by the poor barefooted fellows curiously called stragglers coming up and being supplied with shoes & clothing. They are in fine spirits—have the most blind unbounded confidence in their Generals you ever saw and are ready to move against the enemy at any hour of the night or day & their willing to do their duty. I hope that we will soon be relieved here and start for home. I think in about six weeks we will do so. I shall endeavor [to] come by railroad in advance of the Legion and wait at Athens with your permission until the rest come up. Capt. Archer who has his wife with him says if Cobb will leave his quarter master & Commissary with him he will take the men & horses through & let the other officers go about to see their families so you perceive we are all busy making our arrangements for a visit home. The idea of going to Georgia has made the men crazy and nothing else is now thought of and indeed the disease is infectious.[1] Before there was a good prospect of misery I was in difficulty but now that I think we will all certainly come to our good old state once more, I am as crazy as the balance of them. Rutherford leaves this morning for Richmond to see the Secretary of War for Col. Cobb and I have no doubt that he will approve the commendation of Gen. Lee & the other Gens. and an order in accordance with it will be promptly issued. Good bye Darling. Kiss our little ones for me and write whenever you can. I have had no letters from home since the 12th Sept. Heard a sermon yesterday for the first time since before the Richmond fights. Col. C. & I went to church & afterward dined with two very pretty girls & it will be well for Mrs. C that the Col. leaves here soon. A heart full of love for my Darling little wife from her ever

Will

---

[1] "I came down yesterday and finding a chance to send a letter to Richmond, I write to you. The object of my visit was to get Genl. Lee's consent to transfer my legion to Georgia this winter, and I am happy to write to you, Darling, that I have succeeded. I have in my pocket the written order to this effect, and I know not when I have had such reason for contentment.... Genls. Hampton, Stewart, Longstreet and McLaws all joined in cordially endorsing and recommending my application and Genl. Lee was exceedingly kind and complimentary. The order is to take effect *as soon as the present campaign* is concluded. Genl. Lee says it cannot possibly extend beyond the 1st of December. So that before 1st January next I am assured I shall have my command re-united and returned to Georgia. Genl. Lee recommends me to mount my infantry battalion, so that my whole force will be cavalry. My men are delighted at the prospect." Thomas R. R. Cobb to Marion, 4 October 1862, T. R. R. Cobb Papers. Still later, "Winchester, Wednesday, Oct. 15th, 1862, *I could not disband my infantry*. More then 500 remained on the rolls. To *mount them* and thus make my command homogeneous was a great point. The command of 2,000 mounted men is a *most desirable* one and with it I ask for no more promotion.... Genl. Lee orders me to take command of Howell's brigade. I do so reluctantly because I preferred being with my cavalry." Thomas R. R. Cobb to Marion, 15 October 1862, T. R. R. Cobb Papers.

Chapter 8

Holding the Line:
October 1862–November 1862

Their horses are swifter than leopards,
more fierce than the evening wolves,
their horsemen press proudly on.
Their horsemen come from afar:
they fly like an eagle swift to devour.
—Habakkuk 1:8

Breaking camp on 7 October, the legionaries moved to Camp Rapidan near Raccoon Ford on the Rapidan River in Virginia, where they remained until December.[1] From his position along the Rapidan, Stuart determined to make another attempt at glory. Cobb received news of Stuart's intended raid while in Winchester serving on a court-martial review panel. Always interested in the whereabouts and condition of his men, he requested that Delony notify him of any movement involving the legion cavalry. "I hear by rumor," he wrote his wife, "that Stewart went off last night with all the cavalry on a raid into Maryland. Major Deloney promised to send a courier for me, if he recd. orders for moving. As no message has come I doubt if my cavalry are in the expedition."[2] The legion did not accompany Stuart on this second encirclement of McClellan and the Union army, a move many today still contend to be controversial.

Due to the recent weeks of near constant movement and skirmishing, the legion cavalry was in dire need of some rest to regain their strength, both physically and numerically. As Stuart and his 1,200 grey-clad troopers rode out, Cobb's Legion Cavalry, or what was left of them, remained in camp. The four-day raid did little for Stuart's acclaim or to improve the image of the cavalry in the eyes of their infantry counterparts. One man was killed during the encirclement, and they obtained little useful intelligence in the process.

---

[1] See William S. Smedlund, *Camp Fires of Georgia Troops, 1861–1865* (Lithonia, GA: Kennesaw Mountain Press, 1994) 235.

[2] Thomas R. R. Cobb to Marion, 4 October 1862, T. R. R. Cobb Papers.

During the fall of 1862, there was much excitement among the men of Cobb's Legion, both infantry and cavalry, about the prospects of the legion being reassigned to Georgia. With the Antietam Campaign at an end and things beginning to settle down for the season, it looked as though there would be a lull in operations for a few months. Thomas Cobb wrote his wife, "To operate on the coast of Georgia is to me a pleasant prospect. My men hail it with joy. We are the envy of all the army in this good luck."[3] A few days later, he was again writing, "Only fifteen are reported sick in the infantry battalion and about twenty in the cavalry, and of these not one is considered at all dangerous. I have sent for Major Deloney to come up and see me today about our movements. The men are all in extasies about our removal to Georgia."[4] On the 20th, Cobb was again updating his wife on their removal to Georgia: "Rutherford succeeded very well in my matters in Richmond, leaving no doubt of our removal to Georgia provided any faith can be 'put in princes.' Any how I am going to work to prepare for such removal."[5]

Other forces, however, soon began to conspire to change the legion's plans for a homecoming. On the 20th, the legion cavalry was in Martinsburg with Jackson destroying track of the Baltimore and Ohio Railroad.[6] That same day, Cobb wrote that the legion infantry "are ordered to move early in the morning. We are to go to Kearneysville on the Balt. and Ohio R. Rd. about ten miles from Harper's Ferry, where we are to report to Genl. Jackson and assist him in destroying the rail road."[7] Four days later, the legion infantry, with Cobb in command, returned to their old camp at Bunker Hill. Cobb reported to his wife on their recent activity:

We returned to our camp last night, after three days of hard marching and work. On Tuesday we marched 18 miles to Kearneysville. On Wednesday we went six miles farther towards Harper's Ferry, below Duffield Station on the Balt. & Ohio Rail Road and tore up and burnt the track in full view of the Yankee camp and returned to Kearneysville that night, and back to camp yesterday. I never saw such perfect ruin to a rail road. Every cross tie was burned and every rail bent for twenty two miles. So that if the Yankees ever attempt to occupy this country again, they will have to rebuild and re- fit the rail road entirely, and this will take considerable time. Genl. Jackson was there in person superintending the work. He is a very plain and simple

---

[3] Ibid., 15 October 1862.

[4] Ibid., 18 October 1862.

[5] Ibid., 20 October 1862.

[6] "Rode down to the cavalry camp.... When I reached the camp, I found they had all moved the night before, with Jackson to Martinsburg. The nature of this expedition I do not know, but *guess* that it is to destroy the track of the Baltimore and Ohio R. Rd." Thomas R. R. Cobb to Marion, 20 October 1862, T. R. R. Cobb Papers.

[7] Ibid..

man having little conversational power, and only two elements of great-ness—implicit self-reliance giving great impartibility of temper and feeling and never-yielding Faith. I like him very much and his conduct to me evinced a mutuality of feeling on his part. The cavalry were camped by me at Kearneysville, so I saw Deloney and Miller. Both are very well.[8]

Although Thomas Cobb and Will Delony were friends prior to the war, Cobb was becoming more and more dependent and convinced of Delony's capabilities with regard to the legion cavalry. Cobb was also beginning to get the idea that he would probably never lead his legion cavalry again. His writings to Marion in October, during the operations in West Virginia, allude to his growing confidence in Delony as a leader of men. "Maj. Deloney came up on Saturday and remained several hours with me," Cobb wrote. "I never saw him looking so well. He is very fat and seems cheerful. He is an excellent officer and I much prefer leaving my men in his command to Col. Young's. I hear that Young is promoted to be a colonel of ordinance. I should not regret it, if it be true."[9]

November brought big changes to Delony and to the legion cavalry. With no further prospects of going to Georgia due to the recent movements of Union forces, the legion and Hampton's Cavalry moved from Martinsburg eastward with the rest of Stuart's Cavalry through the Loudoun Valley[10] of Virginia between the Blue Ridge and Bull Run Mountains on their way to Loudoun, Fauquier, and Rappahannock counties. Stuart's purpose was to slow McClelland's progress as much as possible as he crossed the Potomac and moved southward.

With the promotion of Thomas Cobb from colonel to brigadier general[11] on 1 November, Delony was promoted to lieutenant colonel of Cobb's Georgia Legion Cavalry. Newly promoted to colonel, P. M. B. Young, who had just returned from recuperating from his recent wounding, joined his legionnaires as Hampton headed south, riding into Upperville on 3 November. The following day, Hampton's force rode into Linden Station, where they met Stuart. After conferring, Hampton was instructed to cross the mountains and meet up with additional cavalry under Thomas Rosser at Barbee's Cross Roads.

---

[8] Ibid., 24 October 1862.

[9] Ibid., 20 October 1862.

[10] The Loudoun Valley lies between the Catoctin and the Bull Run mountains to the east and the Blue Ridge Mountains to the west. Covering an area approximately 10 miles wide and 35 miles long, the valley was, and still is, a very rich, fertile area of Virginia.

[11] Cobb officially took command of Cobb's Brigade, earlier commanded by his brother, Howell. For the first time, the brigade became an all-Georgia unit, including the 16th, 18th, and 24th Georgia Infantry, Phillips's Legion Infantry, and Cobb's Legion Infantry. In May 1863, the 1st Georgia Sharpshooters were added to the brigade.

At this same time, Union forces were also seeing a shake-up of their own. Following McClellan's failure to follow and destroy the retreating Confederate army in the aftermath of the Antietam Campaign, Lincoln once more replaced his commanding general. The new commander of the Army of the Potomac was Ambrose Everett Burnside, an Indiana native and West Point graduate. Burnside had twice turned down the offer to lead the Federal Army of the Potomac prior to the campaign. At Sharpsburg, he commanded the left wing of the Army of the Potomac. Now, Lincoln once more turned to Burnside, and despite his own misgivings of his abilities, and with the encouragement of others, Burnside accepted the commander's position.

Determined to be aggressive where his predecessor repeatedly chose undue caution, Burnside planned a fall offensive against the Confederate capital via the town of Fredericksburg. What resulted was one of the most decisive Confederate victories of the war.

Early on the morning of the 5th, Stuart attacked Alfred Pleasonton's Federal cavalry at Barbee's Cross Roads, but when he received word that Union cavalry were assembling in his rear near Warrenton, blocking any sort of withdrawal, Stuart broke off contact and pulled back. Although the report proved false, the Confederate cavalry took up new positions along the upper bank of the Rappahannock.

The pullback accomplished, Hampton set his lines from Gaines' Cross Roads to Sperryville to Amissville in order to guard Stuart's left flank.[12] James B. Gordon, lieutenant colonel of the 1st North Carolina Cavalry, reported on the action that day:

> About 12 o'clock, I was ordered, through courier from General Hampton, to send one squadron to the cross-roads, 1 mile from camp, to act as sharpshooters. In a few minutes afterward I was ordered by General Hampton in person to move the remainder of the command (four squadrons, 275 men) up to support the Cobb Legion, which was near the battery, three-fourths of a mile distant, but to place the regiment in such position as not to be seen by the enemy, and so as to be protected from their artillery.... The Second South Carolina Regiment did not come to my support, as promised. I have learned since that it was blocked in the road by the Cobb Legion. Major Delony, of the Legion, came up with a few men, and he, in connection with Captain Cowles and Lieutenant Siler of my command, made a dash at the enemy, when they ran back.[13]

[12] Edward G. Longacre, *Gentleman and Soldier: The Extraordinary Life of General Wade Hampton* (Nashville, TN: Rutledge Hill Press, 2003) 110.

[13] "Report of Lieut. Col. J. B. Gordon, First North Carolina Cavalry," 22 Nov 1862, *OR*, vol. 19, pt. 2, 146.

Federal cavalry continued to probe all along Hampton's line, including near Gaine's Cross Roads, where the legion cavalry was posted. "Our cavalry kept in constant contact with the enemy," reported Stuart, "not a day passing without a conflict. In one of these, near Gaines' Cross-Roads, a portion of Hampton's command behaved with great gallantry, and routed the enemy. In this engagement Major Delony, of the Cobb Legion, was wounded."[14] To the men of the legion, this action came to be called Little Washington. Wiley Howard recorded the legion's participation in this action:

Another incident and close call in DeLoney's career occurred near what is or was known as Little Washington among the mountains east of the Blue Ridge in Virginia, the exact time of which I cannot recall. The enemy in some force were advancing and we were held in position, rather concealed by a hill along the road, flanked on either side by stone fences, the head of column just showing on brow of the hill. DeLoney being in command had just sent forward some dismounted sharpshooters who deployed and advanced some distance to left of the road, feeling the enemy cautiously and slowly falling back to the command. The Colonel, leaving Major Zack Rice with the command, rode down the hill considerably forward in sight of the sharpshooters, observing, if possible, and estimating the advancing enemy, when suddenly a troup of mounted men came cantering up the road, having cut off our mounted videts further down the road, seeing De-Loney, who had just turned to ride back to the command alone, pushed forward in gallant style, thinking, no doubt, to chase and capture him; but suddenly, at the foot of the hill and in plain view of the head of our column, he wheeled his horse and like a lion at bay prepared to meet the onslaught and alone cope with a party of about ten far in advance of the others. Emptying both his pistols and deliberately drawing his saber, he met them as they dashed around and about him. Major Rice had great difficulty in keeping back the column from dashing down the hill, and only allowed some eight or ten to go. These went like lightening to the rescue of our brave and beloved DeLoney. Among them, I remember was gallant Jim Clanton. DeLoney was fighting like a mad boar with a whole pack of curs about him, having his bridle hand dreadfully hacked, his head gashed and

---

[14] "My cavalry had a pretty heavy skirmish with the enemy yesterday, about twenty miles above this place. They were completely hemmed in by the Infantry and cavalry and had to fight out. One man was killed in Capt. King's Co. Some twenty were wounded, none of them from around Athens that I can hear of and several horses killed. Major Deloney and Miller unhurt. I get this news from two of the wounded who came to me tonight, along with five others who lost horses. I have had their wounds dressed and fed them all. They are now lying around my firs. I shall feel some anxiety to hear more from them." Thomas R. R. Cobb to Marion, 6 November 1862, T. R. R. Cobb Papers; Report of J. E. B. Stuart, 27 February 1864, *OR*, ser. 1, vol. 19, pt. 2, 144.

side thrust, when one athletic fellow, after vainly ordering him to surrender and DeLoney shouting, "I will never surrender!" seized his saber wrist and grappling for the mastery, shouted, "Surrender! By God! I am the best man!" But our valiant knight held fast the hilt of his trusty blade, shouting defiance in his face as the two leaned forward on their horses till their heads nearly touched, when the rescuers fell upon the squad in merciless vengeance. Stalwart Jim Clanton, spurring his horse, knocked others aside and plunged his saber into the contending athlete. DeLoney quickly drew up his blade and with almost superhuman effort cleaved his antagonist's skull as he fell forward. As I remember, four of our men who went to the rescue were wounded and more than that number of the attacking party bit the dust.... Col. DeLoney, next day, while sitting on a log where we camped, with head and hand bandaged, showed me a small metalic flask, which he carried in his inside coat pocket, near the region of the heart and lungs, which showed an entire saber point thrust nearly a quarter of an inch wide clear through the metal, remarking that he had sometimes felt that he would hate for his wife, in case he fell in battle, to know that it was there; but, with a humorous smile said he now thought it a good idea for every man to have one on him at the vulnerable spot when the cold steel struck with such force.[15]

* * *

Camp at Bunker Hill
Oct 11, 1862

My Dear Rosa,

Your letter of the 29th sent by Mr. David was received day before yesterday but much to my regret did not see David as he was within 5 or 6 miles of me I think it would have been as little as he could have done to have come farther or at least have sent me word when he was to return. You may know I was delighted to hear from you as your last letter received by me was dated the 12th Sept. and these long intervals of silence are terrible to those so far away from home. Capt. Archer leaves

---

[15] Wiley C. Howard, "Sketch of Cobb Legion Cavalry and Some Incidents and Scenes remembered" (Atlanta: Camp 159, published talk given at U.C.V. meeting) 19 August 1901, 4. An account of this same encounter was published in the Athens newspaper in 1892. "At Little Washington, charging with that handful of the Richmond Hussars who chanced to be mounted when our camp was surprised by the 5th U.S. Cavalry in order to give the Legion time to saddle up and form. [Delony] Fighting with sabre three regulars at once and with coat slashed by sabre thrusts, his silver flask providing an effective breastplate, as four deep indented cuts on its metal side evidenced. And as he attempted to aid one of our Augusta boys, Jim Clanton, afterward my 1st Lieut. saving his life, cutting down two of them with a right and left cut. The Major soon dispatching the other." Athens *Banner* (30 April 1892).

today and will take this as far as Augusta and I venture to risk the mail thence to Athens with $400 which I hope will make your money matters easy for the present. My poor little financier. I know you are in a peck of troubles. My fear is that the worst hasn't come yet. I don't know what the poor are to do this winter with clothing and provisions so dear and the land so full of extortioners. One of the notes I send you is a Confederate $100 interest bearing note. I am told that the Banks refuse to take them if you find any differently in passing it keep it and let me know. It is perfectly good so you may be independent about it. I would send you different money but our Quartermaster has now no other. We are still quiet—that is the Army is and we are still here with Jackson gathering up Virginia Conscripts and doing some easy picket duty. Gen. Hampton & his Legion are at Martinsburg, tho just at this time Gen Stuart & Hampton have gone on a scout. I think into Maryland. If so you'll hear of it by telegraph before this reaches you. Hampton wrote to me to join him with 100 or 150 men but I could not as all the time we had not that number in Camp so we may miss another of Stuarts brilliant reconnaissances. Col. Cobb soon after his arrival here was detailed on a court martial at Winchester and has been there all this week. I hope he will soon return again as I am very tired of commanding another mans regiment. Our Army are drilling constantly and are in good condition if the further prosecution of the present Campaign is deemed necessary tho I hope there will be little fighting as I am very anxious to leave for Georgia and see you all at home. It is quite chilly this morning and reminds us that winter will not be long delayed here among the mountains. Rutherford is in Richmond and I presume in a day or two we will know certainly when we are to leave if we are to leave at all. How I should like to be with you all this morning & hear little Rosa read & talk and Tom and Dear little Willie chatter to Papa. I am afraid they will be terribly disappointed if I should come home this winter and not bring Toms horse. You will have to give him one of yours. Whether we are ordered to Georgia or not I hope to see you all. I have been with the Regt. in all its fights & skirmishes always on duty and never absent & as soon as Col. Young rejoins us I have no doubt I shall be able to get a furlough for 30 days. Hampton I know will do all he can for me in this matter or anything else. Write me as often as you can. There is now mail and telegraphic communication between Winchester & Richmond & your letters will meet me there for the present tho probably the Army will fall back to Staunton tho of this I know nothing. I only surmise as much. God bless you all Darling. Think of me kindly. Kiss our precious little ones for me.

Ever yours
Will

Camp at Bunker Hill
October 14, 1862

My Dear Rosa,

Yesterday morning I was agreeably surprised by the receipt of your three letters of the 14, 18, and 21st Sept, and tho' they all of an old date they were most welcome messengers of love from home. I am satisfied that if you will direct your letters to me as you used to do, and not to the care of Bob I will receive them sooner. The Postmaster at Richmond forwards the Army mail to the Army and the consequence is that everybody here receives letters from home but me. Mine accumulate in Bob's hands and he never forwards them by mail but waits until he sees some member of the Cavalry in Richmond and sends them up by him. I believe I have never told you that Bunker Hill is on the Turnpike from Martinsburg to Winchester about equidistant from the two places. It is a small village, of only a few families. We have been here now long enough to be weary of the inactivity and want of excitement and variety. Col Cobb has been absent all the time since his return and I have been unable to leave Camp a single time since Sunday week and I am becoming more homesick than tongue can tell. I have been with the Legion 4 months and [a] week now, have never been absent and dont mean to be for a month or two longer, when I think I can make up a good case for leave of absence. Dont you think I am entitled to one. Gen Stuart has returned from his trip into Maryland, has taken a good many prisoners & horses & lost but one man, taken prisoner left behind—too drunk to travel. The Army is very quiet and not a word of news varies the dull monotony of the Camp. I presume McClellan will not make another early advance upon Richmond nor will Lee do much more this fall, tho' my opinion is that we have time yet to strike another blow before the winter sets in with severity, and our Army is in fine spirits and condition. How I wish we could follow up our late victories with effect and conquer an early peace & I could once more come home to my precious wife and children, but such hopes are idle dreams. I can see nothing bright in the future. The North seem to be supporting Lincoln in his mad fanatical purposes & I can see no gleam of sunshine no hope of peace. We will have to fight Lincoln as long as he is in power and I see no probability of his being out for many years to come but my mind is made up. Cost what it may, suffer what I may, I shall fight them while I live until our independence is established. I sent you $400 by Archer which I hope you will get. Do as well as you can. You may rely upon $100 per month from me except when I pay you a visit or have to buy a horse. I hope your pea crop has turned out well & that you will be able to make yourself and the dear little children comfortable for the winter. What you are to do for bacon I can conceive it will be fabulously high. God bless you all Darling. Kiss our dear little ones for me & dont let Rosa study too much. I am very sorry to learn that Cousin Laura will stay no longer with you as you must be very lonely by yourself. Take good care of the little chicks and be of good cheer Darling. Think kindly of me & write often & tell me all about yourself and the little ones.

Ever yr own
Will

Camp near Martinsburg
Oct 31, 1862

My Dear Rosa

It is now almost a month since your last letter was dated and why I never hear from you I cannot imagine. The last letter recd by mail was dated the 21st Sept. I was never so homesick in my life and [last] night I had the most vivid dream of you & the children I ever had—waked up and could not sleep & sat by the camp fire for more than an hour thinking of home and my wife and little ones. Do write to me often. I will then get some of your letters. I may see all of them if you direct to Richmond but not to the care of Bob. We have been doing some service lately. For the last week I have been sleeping within a mile of our extreme outposts & have had but one undisturbed nights rest in that time. We have lost 2 men & six horses and have not hurt the Yankees. We have been all the time in the midst of Union Traitors & have had to keep a sharp look out at every step we took. Gen Hampton allowed me to move my camp to this point near Martinsburg much to my relief. We have been at Hedgesville[16] among the mountains near the Potomac 8 miles from Martinsburg and about 20 miles beyond the nearest Infantry support in the immediate presence of the enemy & yet some say the Cavalry do nothing. I do not know when we shall leave for Georgia but I have no doubt we shall soon be there. I never longed so for anything as I do for the order to move. Col Cobb will not apply for it while there is a prospect of a fight. I wish he was here on outpost duty for a while he would soon lose all scruples upon that point as I am afraid we shall have no time to see our families if we do not get to Ga before the Yankees open their Southern Campaign. Kiss the little folks for me & think often & kindly of me. A heart full of love from

Yr own
Will

---

[16] Now in West Virginia; located about 7 miles north of Martinsburg.

Woodville Nov 12, 1862

My Dear Rosa,

This is the first time I have had an opportunity of writing you for some time back. I have been in the mountains having the hardest time since I have been in the service, lying out without tent or shelter of any kind and fighting Yankees to my heart's content. We are now quiet, doing very light picket duty, but how long a rest we are to have I do not know. We left Martinsburg on Monday week, the 3rd made two days forced marches and Tuesday night came up with the enemy & had to bivouac that night without fires & nothing to eat, and it was bitter cold. The next morning just as I commenced eating breakfast at the house of a true gentleman in the neighborhood, I was ordered off, took a very hasty cup of most excellent coffee & took up my line of march. About 12 oclock the fight commenced & for 3 or 4 hours we were supporting a battery and exposed constantly to shot & shell without being able to do anything. Except Ritch's company & Kings who were thrown out as sharp shooters & my old company. Our men all behaved well. We lost 2 killed and 12 wounded. The next day we had no fight. On Friday The Brigade had a fight but we were not in it, being held in reserve. On Saturday, the enemy drove in on our pickets. My Regt. being next the enemy, I rode to the picket post & ordered a Squadron to follow as soon as formed. About the time I reached the picket they were in full retreat and the enemy in full pursuit. I tried to halt & rally them but it was impossible. They ran by me and almost over me and I was left with the Lieutenant to meet the charge of the enemy. I then began my retreat and on they came. When close upon me and thought they had me, they raised a shout and I turned and shot one of them from his horse, and about then the Richmond Hussars, or a part of them came up. I returned my pistol drew my sabre and ordered them to charge, but a herd of beeves passing and the picket men had so broken their ranks that not more than 10 or 12 came into the fight and we had it then hand to hand. The first one I encountered I cut severely over the head & sent him to the rear. About that time I received a blow over my head but he was too close to me, only cut my hat slightly and bruised my hand. I turned on him & we fought for some time. He was so bloody that I ordered him to surrender. "Never surrender" he replied "let the best man win," & with that he grasped me with his hands. He was a large powerful man and his grasp was like a vice. About this time Young Clanton of Augusta came up and struck him with his sabre. He uttered a groan, [and] relaxed his hold on me. I gave him a final blow & all was over with him. In the meantime, I recd from others of the enemy a sabre thrust on the lower joint of my thumb, a slight cut on the right hand, a thrust just above my heart which would have been serious but for a flask exactly like the one you gave me, belonging to Capt. King, which at that time I had in my side pocket. The gash on that shows the force of the blow. I also had a pistol shot in my pants and a rent or two in my over coat which were probably made by balls. After getting out from among them I looked around to see what my men were doing and saw one man in grey clothing. I was about to speak to him when he drew his pistol & presented it to my heart. The pistol snapped & I left, rallied my men and drove back the enemy, having killed six of them and wounded nine. We had one killed & eight wounded besides myself. Poor Young Clanton just after assisting me was shot in the lung but is doing well. Two of the Thomases of Augusta are severely wounded, the others you do not know. All who went in with me, but one or two, were killed or wounded. My deliverance was providential and I feel most grateful for it. During the whole fight I always felt that we would whip the fight. Day before yesterday we had another fight, but it was at long last and we lost none from our Regt. Cobb has been promoted but says it will not interfere with our going to Georgia. Personally, I would prefer remaining here, as I am, perfectly content to serve under Hampton or Stuart, while in the war. They are both fine officers & Hampton I think, is my friend. He wrote Gen Stuart a very handsome note about me. I am coming home just the very first time I can possibly leave. Some think there will be no more fighting, but that does not seem to me to be our policy tho' I think the Cavalry have done all their hardest work for the winter at least I hope so for we have had a dreadful time. My health continues fine, but I am so homesick, as to be pretty cross sometimes. I hope to get a mail tomorrow for the first time in weeks. God bless you all Darling. Kiss the dear little ones for me & write often. A heartfull of love from

Your
Will

I hope in a day or two to be in communication with Cobb and to be able to say what the future arrangements will be in relations to our command. I am determined to see you soon if spared and I do not mean to remain with the regiment if I am any longer to be subordinate to Col Young.[17]

---

[17] While with his infantry, Thomas Cobb received news about the actions of his cavalry and the wounding of Delony. On the 12th he wrote to Marion, "I received direct information from Miller and Maj. Deloney this afternoon. Both are well. They are about 12 miles from here. My cavalry suffered nothing in the last skirmish. Deloney behaved most gallantly in the first (about which his note was written) and was at one time in considerable peril.... Willie Church I intend to make Adjutant to the cavalry battalion." Thomas R. R. Cobb to Marion, 12 November 1862, T. R. R. Cobb Papers.

Camp Near Dawkins
Nov. 16, 1862

My Dear Rosa,

I have an opportunity of sending in the morning a note to you from the Mountains of Virginia. I have recd three letters from you since my last four indeed, but are of an old old date. The latest was the 5th. I can imagine your anxiety about poor old Tom & the Marble aude auxi[18] rejoiced that no harm ensued. I am now writing you by a Camp fire in Rappahannock County & doing picket duty watching the movements of the enemy. The weather has been fine for the last ten days and as long as it continues good I feel there is no hope of our command going to Ga, unless Hamptons Brigade is ordered South, which I sincerely hope will be the case, and of which there is some talk. In the reorganization of the Cavalry Brigades, we were reassigned to Hamptons on the 10th inst and Gen Lee assures Cobb that he will keep his promise to send us South. This looks a little to me as if the Brigade was gone particularly as the Genl I understand, has made application to go. Nothing could please me more than such an arrangement. Col Young sent me a message by one of our men coming on that he would rejoin us in about 3 weeks, and as the message was delivered about 3 weeks ago I shall look for him just as soon as our hard work here is over for the winter, and then I shall certainly leave for Georgia to see my little Scrap at home and rest awhile. I sometimes am so homesick I can scarcely contain myself and would give my weight in gold to have a good long talk with my little Scrap of a Counsellor. Cobb wrote me a note recd yesterday in which he says that Young's promotion does not follow his. How it will be I do not know, but I think Cobb is mistaken and that Young will be the Col & I the Lt Col of the new Regt. If so I don't think I shall remain any longer subordinate to him but will seek some other position more agreeable to me. Some of the officers & men were about to hand me in a petition to take the Command, but they said it would be unanimous or nearly so, certainly so among the officers but I thought it would result in no good and stopped it. Gen Hampton yesterday expressed to me the hope that I would be in command. I think it confoundedly hard that because I did not graduate at West Point I am still to play second fiddle to a man who does nothing, and what is more I don't mean to do it. Ill pay my own expenses and volunteer aid on somebodys staff first. I wish the matter was decided. God bless you all Darling. Write when you can. A stray carrier brings me your letters occasionally and it is always a treat I assure. We have no fighting except a little picket firing every day when our Scouts go down to find out where the enemy are. Kiss the little folks for Papa and tell Willie his is the best horse in the army.

Ever Yr Own
WGD

---

[18] Reference to Rosa.

Brandy Station
Nov 20, 1862

My Dear Rosa

I have an opportunity this morning of sending a note to you to be mailed at Richmond. I was so fortunate yesterday as to receive your letters of the 8th, 9th, 10th, & 12th inst which you may be assured was no little treat to me after a ride all day & a sleep in the open the night before in the rain without shelter. Last night it also rained but we came up with our wagons and enjoyed the luxury of a tent. We are soon to leave again, the men being ordered to prepare 3 days rations, but where we are going I am unable to say. I hope & believe our destination is towards Richmond & as that brings me nearer home I am ready at a moments notice to leave. A cold N.W. wind is now blowing. I think the rain is over and as the Blue Ridge is seen at a distance we are all disposed to be in a good humor this morning. My health is fine tho' I am pretty well tired out and think I am entitled to a little rest at home. Day before yesterday we travelled until night, lay down in the rain without supper, got up by day & continued our march without breakfast and yet our men are cheerful & in good health. Our horses however are completely worn out and yesterday I could not muster 130 for duty out of over 700 and in a little while longer if we have no rest there will be none left. I send you the Yankee account of our little fight at Washington. It omits a good many things. Among others that Lt. Ash was disoriented & surrendered his arms. Those whom he saw were Virginians. They took 3 of my vendettas, about one dozen only of my men were with me in the fight. The others could not come up in time. Ash's sabre is now in the hands of one of the Richmond Hussars, but nevertheless he is a gallant fellow & made a gallant dash on our picket post. After having extricated myself from the Yankees I passed Ash almost doubled up & crawling to his force. My first impulse was to cut him down but he seemed so badly hurt my better thoughts restrained me which I do not regret. He was then without horse or sabre.

We have had another skirmish since I saw you. Ritch behaved gallantly, as he has done on several occasions. We killed 12 of the rascals, lost one man taken prisoner and one slightly wounded in the thumb. I hope now that our fighting is over for the present. If there is any more of it will be an Infantry fight and a great battle. I think however the Campaign is about ended for the winter in Virginia and that very soon we will be on the way for Old Georgia. Gen Stuart has not yet issued his orders to Gen H. but Hampton thinks we will go toward Richmond. God bless you all Darling. I would write more but did not know until this moment that Lumpkins boy was going to Athens. He will tell you all about us. Kiss the little ones for me and be very particular not to permit any one to laugh at little Tom for stammering. A heart full of love from

Yr own
Will

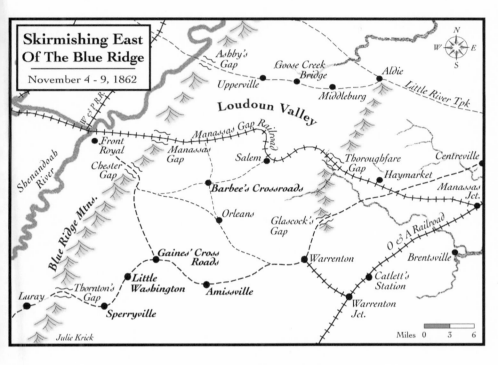

Battles and skirmishes involving
William G. Delony and Cobb's Georgia Legion Cavalry.

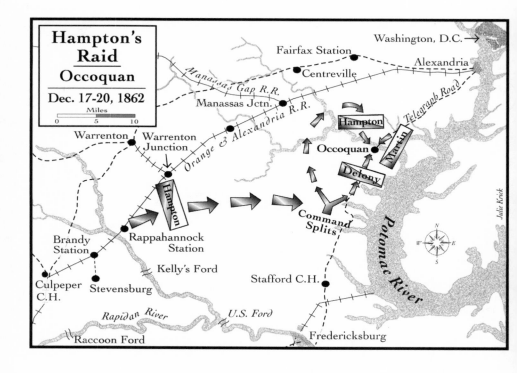

Hampton's Raid
Occoquan
Dec. 17-20, 1862

Miles
0   5   10

Washington, D.C. →

Fairfax Station

Centreville

Alexandria

Manassas Gap R.R.

Manassas Jctn.

Telegraph Road

Warrenton

Warrenton
Junction

Orange & Alexandria R.R.

Hampton

Occoquan

Martin

Delony

Hampton

Brandy
Station

Rappahannock
Station

Command
Splits

Potomac River

Kelly's Ford

Culpeper
C.H.

Stevensburg

Stafford C.H.

N
W   E
S

Rapidan River

U.S. Ford

Raccoon Ford

Fredericksburg

Julie Krick

Chapter 9

Fredericksburg Campaign:
November 1862–December 1862

Do you give the horse its strength
Or clothe its neck with a flowing mane?
Do you make it leap like a locust,
Striking terror with its proud snorting?
—Job 39:19

Burnside was determined not to commit the same mistakes as his predecessors by taking Richmond with a quick thrust south, straight towards the city. To counter Burnside's moves, Lee needed to know what the Federals were up to and assigned Stuart's Cavalry to investigate. In preparation, Stuart established his picket line north of Fredericksburg and the Rappahannock. On 27 November, Hampton selected 174 handpicked men from among his command of the 1st North Carolina, Jeff Davis Legion, Phillips Legion, and Cobb's Legion. With this small force, Hampton began probing the right flank of Burnside's picket line.

Based on the information received from his cavalry probes, Lee anticipated Burnside's offensive and directed the entire Confederate army to consolidate at Fredericksburg. Longstreet's corps arrived by late November and took up position on the high ground of Marye's Heights, just south of the city, overlooking the Rappahannock River. Lafayette McLaws's Division, which included Cobb's Georgia Brigade of Infantry with Thomas Cobb in command, occupied the Sunken Road at the base of the heights.

As Hampton's grey troopers set out on the morning of the 27th from their cavalry camp at Brandy Station on the Orange and Alexandria Railroad, an opposing soldier from Pennsylvania wrote of the ground being "lightly coated with snow made crisp by the previous evening's freezing."[1] Moving rapidly, Hampton crossed at Kelly's Ford on the upper Rappahannock, moving east behind Union lines toward

---

[1] William McCarter, *My Life in the Irish Brigade* (Campbell, CA: Savas Publishing Co., 1996) 110–11.

Morrisville. Hampton's scouts brought him news of a large body of the 3rd Pennsylvania Cavalry located near Hartwood Church, or Yellow Chapel, picketing two separate roads that led north to Warrenton. Having received this information so late in the day, Hampton determined to attack early the following morning. That night his troopers were forced to sleep upon the bare, cold ground without any fires.

The Confederate raiders were up and in their saddles before sunup. Their scouts led the raiders along a narrow trail through the woods that ran between the two roads and two different Union picket camps to a spot that Hampton thought looked good. What he did next went totally against military thinking—attacking simultaneously in opposite directions. Dividing his small force in two, he sent one group striking left and one right into the Union picket camps.

The surprise of grey-clad raiders suddenly bursting out of the woods and charging through their camps threw the startled Federals into complete disarray and they offered no defense to save themselves, surrendering immediately. Hampton and his raiders snagged 92 men, including five officers, 100 horses, two flags, and dozens of carbines and pistols. The triumphant Confederate cavalry returned safely to Lee's lines without sustaining any losses.[2] His bold action won Hampton praise from both Lee and Stuart. For Hampton and the men of Cobb's Georgia Legion, this effort showed that Hampton's force could be a considerable raiding force and that they were very adept at carrying out such escapades. This was the beginning of what became known as Hampton's "raiding season."[3]

Although Delony did not accompany Hampton on this raid, he did take joy in mentioning it to Rosa in his correspondence. Still recovering from his earlier wounding, Delony was very involved in Hampton's next series of forays into enemy territory. With Young on furlough, Delony took command of Cobb's Georgia Legion as they set out from Brandy Station on the 10th with Hampton and 520 "thinly clad and scantily fed" troopers from the 1st North Carolina, 1st and 2nd South Carolina,[4] and Jeff Davis's Legion. The troopers reached the Potomac after two days of hard, cold riding. At a place called Occoquan,

> Hampton divided his command between his most trusted subordinates, Butler and Martin[5].... The brigadier directed Butler to attack the outpost from the north, while Martin supported him by deploying his troopers on all sides of the town.... Butler's ferocious assault at the head of the First North Carolina, the Cobb Legion, and his own regiment resulted in the

---

[2] *OR*, ser. 1, vol. 21, 15–16.

[3] Edward G. Longacre, *Gentleman and Soldier: The Extraordinary Life of General Wade Hampton* (Nashville, TN: Rutledge Hill Press, 2003) 114.

[4] The 1st South Carolina Cavalry was added to Hampton's Brigade in November 1862.

[5] Young was still recovering from his earlier wounding.

quick capture of fifty guards and two dozen sutlers' wagons.... Hampton's force arrived back to his camp with "warm clothing, horse tack, and equipment of all kinds, as well as enough edibles to last more than a week."[6]

Once again, Hampton had achieved a stunning success without losing a man.[7]

Hampton and his force struck again near Dumfries on the 12th, capturing fifty more Federals and seventeen Union supply wagons. Wade Hampton and his force were now gaining a reputation that was beginning to rival that of his superior. With the recent string of successes under his belt, Hampton immediately began planning another raid. The next foray involved just 100 men, as stealth and speed were of the utmost importance. On 17 December, Hampton set out with his small command.

Crossing the river at Rappahannock Bridge upstream of Kelly's Ford, the column rode through the night. As the small Confederate force proceeded, approaching Occoquan from the southwest, they swept up every picket outpost along Neabsco Creek and captured two supply wagons. Just outside of the town, Hampton divided his force, as he was apt to do, into three squadrons. Commanding one himself, he placed one of the other squadrons under the command of Lt. Col. Martin and the other under Delony. Each squadron was to attack the town from a different direction. The Federal garrison was taken completely by surprise. The raiders captured the contents of several local warehouses, twenty pickets, and the personal baggage train of Maj. Gen. Franz Sigel's 11th Army Corps. Hampton returned to camp with twenty supply wagons, 150 prisoners, thirty stands of rifles, and a regimental flag.[8] Hampton's own report tells of the exploit.

I have the honor to lay before you the following report of the operations of a part of my command on the 17th and to the 20th instant: On the day first named, with 100 men from the First South Carolina under Colonel [John L.] Black; 75 from the First North Carolina, under Captains [J. C.] Blair and [W. M.] Addington; the same number from the Second South Carolina, under Captain [T. H.] Clark; 80 from Phillips' Legion, commanded by Major [W. B. C.] Puckett; 75 from Cobb's Legion, under Major [William G.] Delony, and 60 from the Jeff. Davis Legion, under Lieutenant-Colonel Martin, I crossed at the Rappahannock railroad crossing and moved to Cole's store, where we bivouacked that night.

At daylight the next morning [18th], I was at Kanky's store, on the Neabsco Creek, where there was a post of the enemy. Surrounding these and the post above them, the whole party was captured, together with 8 wag-

[6] Longacre, *Gentleman and Soldier*, 114–15; OR, ser. 1, vol. 21, 690–91.

[7] Ibid.

[8] Ibid., 695–96.

ons, only 2 having any stores in them. In approaching this post, Colonel Black, who had command of his regiment, the Phillips and Cobb Legions, advanced down the Telegraph road, while Lieutenant-Colonel Martin came up in command of the rest of the detachments. Dividing my force here, I sent Colonel Martin with his legion, the Second South Carolina, and the First North Carolina, by the river road to Occoquan, Major Delony by the Telegraph road to the same place, while I took Colonel Black and Major Puckett by the Bacon Race road, so as to get above the town. Moving on rapidly, these three columns met near Occoquan, which was entered first by Colonel Martin, who found a train of wagons belonging to Sigel's corps in the act of crossing the river. Dismounting some men, he forced the wagon guard, who were on the other side of the river, to surrender and to come over in the ferry-boat.

In the mean time Major Delony had swept all the picket posts on the Telegraph road, capturing every man who was there (about 20 in number), with 2 wagons, and had joined me near the town. Having heard that 2,500 cavalry were on the march from Alexandria and about to cross at Selectman's Ford, 1 1/2 miles from Occoquan, I hastened to the village and dispatched Captain Clark, with 40 sharpshooters from his regiment and from the Phillips Legion (chiefly from the latter), to hold the ford until I could bring the wagons across the river. To accomplish this there was but one small boat, and the approaches to the river were very bad. While engaged in bringing over the wagons, the enemy appeared in some force coming down to the river. My sharpshooters soon drove them back, and the work of ferrying the wagons over continued. The enemy again attempted to cut off the men engaged in this work, but were again driven back in confusion.

In the mean time the largest force of the enemy were endeavoring to force a passage at Selectman's Ford, which, had they succeeded, would have put them in my rear. Knowing this, I thought it prudent to take off the wagons already brought over and to withdraw. Sending these to the rear with Colonel Black, I ordered Colonel Martin to call in his men and to follow as a rear guard, while Captain Clark was instructed to hold the ford for one hour longer. All these movements were promptly carried out, and Captain Clark held his ground resolutely. As soon as he withdrew the enemy followed him, but he charged them gallantly and drove them back across the river. He then followed me skirmishing with the enemy for 2 miles and holding him in check until the wagons were well on their way. Passing Greenwood Church, I struck out for Cole's store, and encamped that night at Tacket's Ford, on Cedar Run.

The next day's march brought me safely home without the loss of a man. I brought back about 150 prisoners, besides 7 paroled, 20 wagons and valuable stores in them, 30 stand of infantry arms, and 1 stand of colors.... I may mention that I captured every man on the picket line (41 in number) from Kanky's to Occoquan, 8 miles.[9]

Not to be outdone by one of his lieutenants, Stuart set out the day after Christmas 1862 with Hampton, Fitzhugh Lee, and 2,000 men. Along with them, Stuart also brought four artillery pieces under John Pelham. Their object was to raid the Union forces in the Dumfries and Occoquan areas. Crossing at Kelly's Ford on the Rappahannock, Stuart quickly went to work capturing the Union pickets on the opposite shore. The force proceeded northeast to Morrisville, where they turned north and headed to Bristersburg. Stuart divided his force into three parties with each to strike at the Federals along the Occoquan River from three different directions.

Setting out at first light on the 27 December, Hampton moved on a direct line north to Occoquan with 870 men, including "175 First North Carolina, Major [John H.] Whitaker commanding; 150 First South Carolina, under Captain [W. A.] Walker; 150 Second South Carolina, under Colonel Butler; 180 Cobb Legion, Major [William G.] Delony commanding; 130 Phillips' Legion, Lieutenant-Colonel [W. W.] Rich commanding, and 85 Jeff. Davis Legion, under Lieutenant-Colonel Martin—in all 870 men—together with one section of artillery, under the command of Lieutenant [Francis M.] Bamberg."[10] Fitzhugh Lee moved his force toward Chopawamsic Creek to take up a position south of Dumfries where they could guard Stuart's right flank. Stuart, in the meantime, took a more southerly route toward Dumfries.

Hampton discovered a picket camp at Cole's Store about a mile from Occoquan and reported that,

I detached 25 men to get behind them while I drove them in with 20. The guide to the former party unfortunately mistook the road, so that the pickets, when attacked in front, were enabled to retreat toward Dumfries. Of the 15 pickets on this road, my men took 4, and the others, in endeavoring to escape, fell into the hands of a squadron of Lee's brigade, which was on the same road. Having cleared the way, I pushed on toward Occoquan. Colonel Butler, with the main body, approached the town in front, while I took Colonel Martin and Major Delony by the river road, with a view to cut off the retreat of such troops as might be in the town. Colonel Butler drove in the pickets and dashed into the town. There were several hundred cavalry there, but they soon broke, leaving the town. As it was dark, most

---

[9] Report of Brigadier General Wade Hampton, 22 December 1862, *OR*, ser. 1, vol. 21, 695–96.

[10] Ibid., 5 January 1863.

of them escaped, as the attack was made before I reached the point at which to cut them off. Nineteen prisoners and 8 wagons were captured here, while my loss was 1 man wounded.

The next day the division returned toward the Occoquan River, with a view to crossing it. At Greenwood Church, Colonel Butler, with his command, was detached, with orders to proceed to Bacon Race church, where he was told that we would join him. Lee's brigade, which was in front, fell in and routed a party of the enemy soon after we left Greenwood Church, and in a short time firing of artillery and musketry indicated Colonel Butler had engaged the enemy. General Stuart here gave me directions to move across the river, leaving Colonel Butler to follow if he could, or retire to camp if he was not able to join us. I moved my command to Selectman's Ford, over which Lee had already crossed, and, by direction of General Stuart, took two detachments toward Occoquan. We fell in with a small force of the enemy and drove them back at once, but as it was late and we did not follow far.[11]

On their way back to the safety of Brandy Station, Stuart's raiders made use of the captured telegraph wires to ascertain information as to the movements of Union troops in pursuit of the Confederate raiders. "The head of the column reached Burke's Station, on the Orange and Alexandria Railroad, after dark," reported Stuart. "A party was sent noiselessly to the telegraph office, and took possession without the operators having a chance to give the alarm. Having an operator of my own, I was enabled to detect what preparations had been made for my reception, the alarm of my approach having already reached Washington, and dispatches were passing over the wires between General [S. P.] Heintzelman and the commanding officer at Fairfax Station." Stuart then added, "I sent some messages to General [M. C.] Meigs, Quartermaster-[General] U.S. Army, in reference to the bad quality of the mules lately furnished, which interfered seriously with our moving the captured wagons."[12]

Culpepper County Nov. 30, 1862

My Dear Rosa,

We have had no mail for ten days and not a line from home in that time. A few scattering letters came in this afternoon from the Genls Head Qutrs but none from you although I recd one from Clark Co of the 14th inst. We are now near the Rappahannock River about 30 miles above Fredericksburg doing picket duty as high

[11] Ibid., 5 January 1863.
[12] Report of Major General J. E. B. Stuart, 15 February 1863, *OR*, ser. 1, vol. 21, 734.

up as Jefferson and men and horses & officers all pretty well worn out. We have 4 Captains only with us and my duties are by no means easy. John cut my hair today and you would have been astonished as I was at the number of grey hairs mingled with the red. I stay away from you and the little ones much longer doing the work I have done for the past three months you and the little folks will hardly recognize me upon my return home but thanks to a kind Providence my health continues good and so long as that is the case I ought not to complain & shall endeavor not to do so, but if one thing be assured I shall only remain in this Command so long as I am forced to do so. As soon as Col Young makes his appearance I shall apply for leave of absence and return home never to come again to serve under him, if I can obtain any other position. Darling I am sometimes so homesick and low spirits I can scarcely contain myself. I do not know what to do with myself. God bless you all and keep you in good health & spirits until we can be once more reunited in our happy little home. I would give [the] world to be with you all tonight, but can only hope that the time is not far distant when I shall see you again. As for our trip to Georgia I have entirely despaired. Like many other of Cobb's sensation schemes it has entirely exploded. He says we are going, but yesterday our Regt was inspected by the Inspector of Stuart's Cavalry for the arrived purpose of supplying our immediate wants in clothing & of sending our disabled horses off to revive them. This looks to me too significant to imply a move to Georgia. I am bitterly disappointed at the result as is every one else but must submit with as good a grace as possible. I hope Col Young will come on soon and relieved me of the Command and I shall then come home or tender my resignation. I am determined to see you all this winter or be detained in Virginia by a Military arrest. I think I have done duty enough to entitle me to a short leave at least.

Gen Hampton went out a few days ago with a detachment from the several Regts amounting in all to 250 men, came on a party of Yankees on picket numbering 107. He captured 93, only 13 escaped & never lost a man, 85 horses were captured with them pretty good wasn't it.[13] I was not with him. The candle is out so good night. Kiss the little ones for me and much love from

Yr own
Will

---

[13] Known to some as the Dumfries Raid. See Wiley C. Howard, "Sketch of Cobb Legion Cavalry and Some Incidents and Scenes remembered" (Atlanta: Camp 159, published talk given at U.C.V. meeting) 19 August 1901, 4.

Camp on the Rappahannock
Culpepper Co Va
Dec. 6, 1862

My Dear Rosa

Last night I received your letter of the 26th ult, also one of the 18th Oct & 19th Nov. Cousins letter, Laura's letter, one from Plant and your letter to Jennie of the 18th, the day before I recd yours of the 25th so today I feel quite rich, but anxious about dear little Willie. I most sincerely hope that tomorrows mail may bring me another letter saying that he is not seriously sick. I sat up half the night last night thinking & talking of you all and feel so homesick I can scarcely be amiable. We are still in the same place that we were when I last wrote you though since then we have been on a three days scout towards Acquia Creek & were in the rear of the enemy within three miles of their Infantry line. Hampton had out his Brigade and paid me the compliment of sending me with my command & the Jeff Davis Legion (whose commander was the only one I ranked) in the rear of the enemy while he with the rest of the brigade moved down in front. The Yankees had heard of us however through a negro and all escaped but seven—one Lieutenant and six men. We were also deceived as to the position of their main force. We returned to camp tired and hungry, having lain out one night without fire & travelled all the next night until 2 o'clock in the morning. Our guide did not come up as promised and we were disappointed in a grand raid. Hampton keeps the enemy worried and is constantly on the move. The Virginia Brigades are having fine times behind the infantry lines 25 miles from Fredericksburg. We are doing the work and they are reaping the rewards. I was struck with this a few days ago by an article in the Richmond papers complimenting Col now Genl Rosser. Hampton moved with his Brigade towards the enemy. When near Orleans where he expected to find them he ordered me to dash into town, which I did at a gallop. They had left & Hampton pursued them. We overtook them 5 or 6 miles off, attacked them & whipped them. The next day Stuart and Hampton pursued them & Col Rosser dashed into Warrenton & no Yankees were there & he had no fight. Yet upon this a fine article is written and a handsome compliment paid, and Rosser is made a Brig Genl., a young man in Col Youngs class I believe, and I have no doubt a first rate officer and a far better appointment than half that are made. I only state these facts to show how differently Stuarts pets fare from Hampton & his officers. In the very same paper mentioned, no mention is made of Hamptons taking 87 prisoners, which is beyond comparison the most complete little affair of the war on our side. The Yankees beat it when they took Martin J. Crawfords Regiment of Georgia Cavalry. You say Ed Lumpkin told you I was Colonel. It is a great mistake as I am not and not likely to be. Col Young has not come on yet. I have not heard a word from him and do not know what his movements will be. As the Legion has made Cobb a Brigadier for "brave and meritorious conduct" who has never been in a fight, it may for the same reason promote Young to the same position & that would possibly make me Col. I see no other chance. I never go to Gen Stuarts Hd qtrs & have never seen him except on the battle field for the past two months. The truth is that men are just the same in the Army as they are out of it. When Howell Cobb was Secty of the Treasury, I obtained a clerkship for Bob because he was friendly to me, not because Bob was eminent as a clerk, and just so it is in the Army. Stuart is an ambitious man, he wants those about him who are his friends. This is the first consideration, talent is the next and so I find it the world over. A little flattery & a daring spirit will bring promotion, sometimes the former only is necessary. Don't you think I am becoming misanthropic. I do sometimes feel so, but upon the whole I think I am becoming rather a philosopher than a misanthrope, shall do my duty during the war & look for my reward at home, my darling wife and our precious little children. God bless them. What would I not give to see them today. The snow is about four inches deep here, cold & clear today, & the "old fellow" without a dinner. I had to send John out today foraging and as the neighborhood has been eaten out, I have to send him off some distance and go without dinner for a good supper tonight. We have been living on meat & bread, except when John occasionally gets some turnips and makes a dish of delightful soup.

I wrote to Plant the original of the enclosed letter which you must keep for me. His proposition I cannot accept and will not. When you write to Cousin & Laura give them both my love. I also send you a letter recd from a stranger of an older date than the one which Bob, I think recd. I will write to them the next time we catch a prisoner. I think the Georgia trip has played out, and it is impossible to get furloughs now but as the winter has I think now set in & Burnsides hasn't got Richmond yet. I doubt not I shall see you in January, if we are not ordered to Georgia and individually I dont want to go. I would rather serve under Hampton than any one else. He is a fine officer. He likes me & I like him & this is no small consideration. Kiss the little ones for Papa & tell Rosa she must take good care of Mama for me. A heartful of love from your own

Will

December 8, 1862

My Dear Rosa

I was just about retiring for the night when I learned that Jake (Capt Ritch's boy) was to leave for Athens in the morning & cannot omit so good an opportunity of sending you a little love message. I have been more homesick today than tongue can tell & everything is frozen up and I would as I said today rather receive a furlough for 30 days than a commission as Brig Genl. If this cold weather continues much longer, I sincerely hope that furloughs will soon be granted and if so I think I can make out a pretty strong case if Col Young will ever come back to the Regt. so that I can leave it. I wrote you a day or two ago & forgot to enclose my letter to Plant which I now send. I today recd three more letters from you all of them of older dates than those recd before but very welcome and cheering nevertheless. They make me feel terribly homesick however. To see dear little Rosa knitting & hear her and poor Tom & little Willie talk would be a treat indeed, to say nothing of my poor little Scrap whom I want to see more than all the world besides and as the year draws to a close my anxiety to be with you all increases with each passing hour. I am determined to come on in January. I cant stay away any longer. I candidly think I have done enough to merit it. I think now of but little else and am fit for nothing & will not again until I see you all. So long as there was anything to be done & I could feel that I ought to be here I could feel pretty well satisfied, but we are now here doing almost nothing and short as the days really are, they seem very long to me. That Yankee who struck me on the head would have sent me home on furlough if he had struck a little harder. My right temporal artery was bruised & the circulation is still imperfect. A little more would have the Doctors say have produced an aneurism, as it is I am only disturbed by a very unpleasant noise when I lie down on my right side & it does not amount to a furlough wound. Excuse this scrawl as my light is very poor. I write you see on Yankee paper, all we have left & this is the last sheet of even that. Kiss the little folks for me & tell Rosa to send me something—anything. God bless you all Darling, is the prayer of

Yr own
Will

Culpepper Co Va Dec 17 1862

My Dear Rosa

I have only time this morning before leaving Camp again to write you a line. We have been down the River for several days watching the movements of the enemy and guarding the different fords of the river. We are off again this morning with the Genl, but as usual before leaving we do not know where we are going, but certainly to some point to do good in getting reliable information or catching Yankees. We have been living high for a few days on Yankee Sutlers stores having lately captured 22 Sutlers wagons with all sorts of Knick nacks in them. We are all looking here with great anxiety tho' also with great confidence for the great battle before Fredericksburg to come off. We will not probably be in it. Poor Cobb how sad it is

182

to die so far from those he loved so well. I am told he lived four hours after being wounded, said nothing except in reference to his wound and the pain it gave him. He behaved I learn with great gallantry & his Brigade have paid him in his death the compliment of refusing to be relieved from duty on the outpost (where a brigade is placed on picket every three days) but say they intend to make their great fight where their Genl fell.[14]

The box in which my boots were that you sent has just reached me. My boots were gone but Johns were in it. I had to buy a pair for which I paid $55 & can get $75 for asking it. Our men are suffering for the want of boots & shoes. Kiss our precious little ones for me & write often. I have received yrs of the 3rd which I found awaiting me in Camp. I am very glad you have had the children vaccinated but feel for the little things in their suffering from it.[15] God bless you all Dear Darling is the sincere prayer of

Yr own
Will

Athens Dec 24th 1862

My own dear Will

I sat at the window this afternoon watching for the Omnibus, hoping I could not tell why, that by some fortuitous circumstance It would contain my "old fellow" although I knew you were in Virginia. You may be sure I was rejoiced to get your dispatch that you were well for I was feeling anxious and depressed at your long Silence. Ours Darling, are all sound asleep, and just in front of me are three little stockings, hanging up for Santa Clause to fill. Poor little things they are happily unconscious of sorrow, I have three little picture books for Rosa, a trumpet for Wil-

---

[14] Refusing the offer to pull his men back to the high ground of Marye's Heights, Thomas Cobb placed his men behind the stone wall at the base of the heights. Enduring several tremendous thrusts by the Federals under Burnside, Cobb's Georgia Brigade held. During the beginning stages of the famous charge by the Union's famed Irish Brigade, an artillery passed through both walls of the house Cobb was using as his headquarters, exploding in the road behind the wall. Unfortunately, Thomas Cobb was meeting with several officers at that moment in that very spot and a shell fragment cut through his right leg, severing his femoral artery. Falling to the ground, he quickly bled to death. With his death, Col. Robert McMillan, commander of the 24th Georgia Infantry, took overall command of the brigade. An Irishman by birth, McMillan took command just in time for the Georgians to meet the onslaught of the Irish Brigade, just one of the great ironies that sometimes takes place in a war of brother against brother.

[15] Although smallpox vaccinations were prevalent since the time of the Revolutionary War, it was not until the years of the Civil War that doctors began more widespread study of both the disease and the vaccination. Often the vaccinations brought on a lesser form of the disease, although one that still posed a danger to the patient.

lie, and a home made ball for Tom, some apples and candy. We had all hoped to have had you with us Darling and I confess to no small degree of disappointment. Dr. Henderson had a Christmas present of a nice little boy, born this morning and Sarah McAlpine also a boy. I enclose you a note from Mr. Hull in relation to a letter received from Mr. Plant. He came to see me this morning to know what he should do. Mr. Plant did not ask in his letter the amount of interest due, but simply the amount due on the note you hold, so I showed Mr. Hull the copy of the letter you wrote to Plant refusing to take the principal and agreeing to take the interest. We looked at the notes together, one for the amount to be paid Jan 1862 and one for the amount due Jan 1863 also two other notes for the interest all drawn separately. Mr. Hull said that as the note for Jan 1862 had not been paid, there ought to be a years interest on the whole amount due 1863, where as the note only called for half and wanted to know what he was to do, so you had better write him or me explicitly also calculate the amount of interest due you that there may be no mistake. Mr. Hull thought Mr. Plants letter allowed to the whole amount prin and ints, but I rather think not for he expressly says that you had not agreed to take Cotton bonds in payment. I hope I have made the thing intelligible to you, he more over wanted to know if interest was required upon the interest note, I told him I thought not (Mr. Hull I mean). In between us we concluded to wait till you were heard from or might possibly come home. Mr. Plant seemed very desirous of paying by 1st Jan. so if you are not coming home right away, write me at once that I shall tell Mr. Hull. But dear Darling I hope by the time this reaches you Col. Young will have got back, and your on your way home for I cant stand it much longer without you. Do get Charley Harris a furlough if such a thing can be gotten for a private, for his wife is dying by degrees with consumption, contracted since he entered the Army. I hope you wont be modest about asking for a long furlough for if you are to remain in Virginia whats the use of staying there doing nothing. I hope the defeat at Fredericksburg and the realization of Seward will help us some, but after all I have no hope not a particle in any but the Lord. Napoleons theory that Providence was always on the side of the heaviest artillery had been satisfactorily explored. Good night my own dear Will. May God protect and give you to us again, is the heartfelt prayer of your own affectionate

Rosa

Athens Dec 26th 1862

My own dearest Will

Our Darlings have just all gone to bed. I had little Willie rocking him, his little head on my arm and his little thumb in his mouth. I wished poor Papa only could have seen him. Rosa at his age was considered a big girl and had long given her baby place to bubber Tom. Yesterday they were up bright and early and I was awakened by two little cold fingers stuck in my face. Rosa and Tom eager to see the contents of their stockings, a few odds and ends which they thought great things. A big apple took Tom's eye, and he felt aunt Catherine had a beaureau about the size of my hat stand made for Rosa. I dont suppose it cost her a cent less than $500. George's wife brought them a basket of apples, cake and candy (what would the hateful Yankees say to that) and Miss Gillard brought them some candy. Today they all went out with Lilly, and came back with wooden swords and pistols, her presents. Every cent she gets, she spends for them. I spent a solitary Christmas all alone. God grant it may be the last of that sort. Your letter of the 17th I received in the afternoon, it was better than company even tho it was "only a line." I regret to learn of the loss of your boots, for Mr. Barry charged $25.00 for making them. How come Mr. Ritale to leave the box behind him. Did you get the silk hand kerchiefs I sent at the same time, and a long letter he took also. I have heard so seldom from you the last six months that I have not the slightest idea of which letters of mine have reached you. I wrote your name on the sole of each shoe. I hope you destroy my letters. You have never said any thing about your clothes I sent to Bob. Do some time when you are at leisure write me a long letter and keep it for the opportunity. It is right have to wait three or four weeks for a letter and then get a note, probably the best you could do at the time. Mrs. Hunter was to see me this afternoon. I dont know what would become of me without her. I am sure she "weeps with those who weep and rejoices with those who rejoice." Whenever there has been a fight in which she supposes you were in, she comes every afternoon after the opening of the mail to enquire if you have been heard from. I can never forget her affectionate sympathy for me. I never saw any one grieve over the death of one not a relative as she has over Mr. Cobbs. Poor old Dr. Ward went out to walk in the direction of Mr. Whites place, and was taken with a vertigo and did not get home till one oclock at night alarming his family very much and having the neighbors out with torches hunting for him. Mr. Jim Pittard has lost another little child, buried yesterday. Mr. Foster has had another baby, it only lived one week. Mr. Hunter told me to day that old Mr. Moss has [been] very ill in Alabama with pneumonia. I never hear of pneumonia, but I think of you my dear Will, so constantly exposed. Darling always attend to a cold in its very first stages. I have been reading to day Everett's life of Washington. When you go off on hunting expeditions in small squads, do you always take a surgeon. You ought always to. Many lose their lives for lack of immediate attention. I am living in daily hope of hearing that you are coming. Wont they give you a furlough for 60 days? Get as long a one as you can. All your friends enquire kindly about you. I think you have a great many. Little ones send you each a sweet kiss. All want dear Papa to come. Think sweetly of me Will. A large heart full of love from

Your own affectionate

Rosa

Athens Dec 29th [1862]

My Dearest Will

Jonas came to see me yesterday and told me you and Lieut Williams were coming home at the same time, in about a fort-night. I dont like to rejoice till I hear from you to that effect, but I hope it is so. I shall be so delighted to see you. Dick Taylor has just called in to say good bye, going tomorrow. The Coast military seem to have a fine time, nothing to do and a chance to go home pretty often. I had a letter from Hue last night. He is on their plantation a most exposed place I should imagine, only 8 miles from Tybee and an hour or so run from St Catherines. Mr. Walburg who plants on the latter island, has moved off every thing. Hue is the only white soul on his place. He wrote me a great secret but I'll have to tell you. He is engaged to Miss Neal. He has stayed his last with me doubtless and next summer I'll have to try it alone, unless as Jennie says some body is "raised" up for me. Would that I could find something on which to hang a hope, even a faint hope, of having you with me Darling. The New Year dawns very cloudily. I pray that we may all be spared to see it end more brightly.

Our darlings are all well and I discovered another tooth this afternoon for dear little Willie, the cause doubtless of the few days disturbance of his stomach, a jaw tooth. He is going to get his teeth like Rosa, all about. He grows smarter each day and my only regret is that he should get any bigger. We are having beautiful bright weather. I want it to end tho because I know you can obtain no furloughs till it is over. Jonas says you and your two men were the only ones regarded by Gen's order to return. I hope he will grant you a long furlough to atone. Do get longer than you had before because you cant come again in a long time. Try. I bought a bushel of hog's feet yesterday, and will have some nice pickled ones, for you when you come. What a pleasant thought it is seeing my old fellow. Geo is doing better since you went away, but Catherine and Sarah are both so trifling and disobedient, that I am disturbed beyond measure. I shall have to grin and bear it, but if you ever live to get home for good you will have to settle the matter to the satisfaction, who is to be mistress they or me, or else dispose of them and try again. I cant raise my children as I ought or set them a Mothers example wrangling from morning till night, chafing and irritated with ineffectual efforts to enforce obedience and enjoy the comforts of an orderly and well regulated house hold, but excuse me Darling for this digres-

186

sion it is useless to attempt any thing like a reform till you come home for good. Rosa says I must tell you she has learned a whole hymn of four verses since you left and begun another. All of us think often and sweetly of you and you are always present to me Darling. All send sweet kisses to dear Papa and love from Aunty.

Your own large share from
your own
Rosa

Athens Dec 31st 1862

My Dearest Will

Tonight is the last of this month and only two letters I have had from you the entire month one dated 8th and the other 19th the letter mentioned in your dispatch has not come to hand yet, although its ten days since you sent the telegram. I have written you 17 letters, well it is hard to bear. I had a letter from Cousin Laura Huguenin this afternoon. She has heard from her friends at home and received some money and I judge from what else she says it is probable she may not take that place as a governess in Marietta that she was thinking about. I have half a mind to write her to spend the remainder of the winter with me. I have been sitting by the fire thinking it over and wish I had you here to advise with. If I was only sure it would prove a pleasant arrangement. I would be glad to have her on the children's account as well as my own, for poor little things they must feel the gloom that affects me half of the time. She tells me Grandmother is very unwell, broken out all over in little sores, poor old lady this war will finish her I am afraid. Cousin Martha had been quite sick and also Elizas child and Aunty was busy nursing, I thought Aunty had only made up that tale to excuse herself from going down to Sav, but it seems they are really sick. Dick Taylor is really to be married in a few days to Miss McKinley. Mr. John Thomas's Cousin and Cook like her. Don't you know she is no account to marry such a wreck of what was intended to be a man. Lilly told me she saw him last Sunday driving his buggy without any hat on. Dr. Smith told me he heard he had paid $1800 for a diamond ring for her. My corn the Dr. got for me arrived today. 160 bushels at 162 a bu freight and all included which with the 40 bu I bought some time ago at 180 makes out the 200 bu required. Hue had been discharged from service on account of his eye. I suppose the next thing will be to get married. Every thing has passed off very quietly this Christmas among the darkeys Contrary to the expectations of the Lincolnites. I imagined Grandmothers boy Davie started for the hand of freedom and got as far as one of the adjacent Islands to Sav and was captured by some of our pickets and brought back, and is now in jail. I guess he would have had a little more to do there than mind Frisky. This war will end next fall, if not sooner I don't doubt the Democrats will inaugurate peace. If it comes sooner our arms or France or both to gether may be the cause with the blessing of the Lord. Darling I am looking and longing for you and hope you will soon be able to come.

Good night dearest Will. Our Darlings each send dear Papa a sweet kiss. One from me and your large share of love from your own

Affectionate

Rosa

Mr. Hunter was here today. He says "give my love to Will and tell him I hope God has spared him thru so many dangers for some great and good purpose." I shall make up my mind tomorrow about Cousin Laura. I have to do it at once as she will leave for Marietta shortly if she leaves at all, or I would wait for your opinion. A happy New Year to you my dearest is the prayer of my heart.

Chapter 10

Chancellorsville Campaign: January 1863–May 1863

The quiver rattles against its side,
Along with the flashing spear and lance.
In frenzied excitement it eats up the ground;
It can not stand still when the trumpet sounds.
—Job 39:24

As 1863 opened, Cobb's Georgia Legion Cavalry found itself experiencing a shortage of both fighting men and suitable mounts.[1] Following weeks of constant picketing and raiding, the legion found it increasingly difficult to carry out their jobs without the necessary horseflesh. On 5 January, Gen. Wade Hampton reported, "I regret to say that I lost several horses, broken down by the long march, and that very many of them are rendered unfit for service from the same cause."[2]

Compounding the problem of locating enough suitable mounts for his force was the dwindling supply of fighting men. With the constant skirmishing and the ever-growing number of casualties, the legion's companies were finding themselves more and more stretched in fielding the necessary men required to carry out their missions. Both problems began to plague the brigade and continued to do so into the spring. As a result, Hampton's Brigade was sent south below the James River, where they remained for several months, giving them a chance to recuperate and regain some of their former strength.

Due to the lack of replacements, however, the legion was forced to continue their job of watching the front and reacting to whatever transpired, and to do that with whatever they had at hand. For the first six weeks of the new year, the legion was scattered about in a number of different locations: in camp near Raccoon Ford on the Rapidan River on 6 January, near Fredericksburg on 12 January, at Camp Georgia in Culpeper County on 23 January, at Camp Stevensburg in Culpeper

---

[1] As horseflesh started becoming a more and more acute problem, several Southern states made attempts to remedy the situation. For more, see description of "The Horse Infirmary in Georgia," *Southern Watchman* (17 February 1864), excerpted here as Appendix B.

[2] Report of Brig. Gen. Wade Hampton, 5 January 1863, *OR*, ser. 1, vol. 21, 736.

County on 26 January, at Camp Fanny in Culpeper County 31 January, near Grove Church (Kelly's Ford) 6 February, and at Camp Maynard in Culpeper County on 15 February.[3]

Delony reported his position within the legion as "extremely unpleasant."[4] By this time, his leadership was easily recognized by all involved, both in the ranks and among his superiors—but this may very well explain why he was not offered another position. Delony was too valuable a cavalry officer to lose. This may also have prompted his receiving a furlough to recruit.

By February 1863, the need for new horseflesh became so bad that some troopers could no longer be mounted, while those who still had mounts could not push their steeds too far. Near the end of February, Benjamin Watkins of the Richmond Hussars wrote his parents:

> We left Stephensburg on the 16th and thought our destination was Charlottesville. We marched in the snow three days to Cobbham Station, seven miles above Gordonsville, turned round the next day and marched back to Gordonsville, and from there to Madison Court House. We heard then that we were going to Luray on the Shenandoah river. After marching four days in the sleet and snow we find ourselves on the line of Page and Rockingham, waiting orders from Gen. Stuart. We were sent to Page county to recruit our horses, but cannot find forage enough to feed on one day, so we will have to go some where else. Our horses are broken down now; they are not able to carry us over ten miles a day, and in two or three days more we will not be able to move at all. We are in a terrible fix—don't know where our feed is to come from to night. We have fed on wheat alone for the last four days. Our horses have not had a feed of corn for a week. About half our Company are walking, their horses not being able to carry them.
>
> We crossed the Blue Ridge day before yesterday in the snow. We were three feet deep on top of the mountain. We were all day crossing. You could ride along with your feet out of the stirrups and they would drag in the snow. It was sleeting all day yesterday. We travelled thirteen miles. It is a God's mercy that half of us are not dead, for we have to make our bed on

---

[3] Camp near Raccoon Ford of Rapidan River (BSK); camp near Fredericksburg (GJW); Camp Georgia in Culpeper County, Virginia, located 7 miles from Culpeper Court House (BSK); Camp Stevensburg, Culpeper County; Camp Fannie, Culpeper County, located near Culpeper Court House; Camp Maynard, Culpeper County, near Stevensburg. See William S. Smedlund, *Camp Fires of Georgia Troops, 1861–1865* (Lithonia, GA: Kennesaw Mountain Press, 1994).

[4] William G. Delony to Rosa, 22 January 1863, Delony Papers.

the snow of a night. I have not had a night's sleep since we started from Stephensburg.[5]

There are no letters between Rosa and Will between 22 January and 6 May because of Will's return home. "Our highly respected fellow-citizen, Lieut. Col. W. G. Delony," wrote *The Southern Watchman* on 18 February, "returned the other day to spend a short time at his home in this place."[6] During this extended period of time, it is thought Delony recruited additional troopers for the legion after his furlough ended.

Delony wrote to Rosa on 22 January, "I could raise a Regt. out of the detached companies of Ga Cav. on the Coast of South Carolina and Georgia." Since his family originated from the Georgia coast, his knowledge of the coastal area and of the families living there would have been a natural advantage in recruiting, familiarity of which Confederate authorities would naturally have been interested in taking advantage. His recruiting efforts were turning out extremely fruitful during the winter of 1863.

VOLUNTEERS WANTED To fill up the ranks of the several Cavalry Companies of Cobb's Legion. Any unenrolled men desiring to join either of these companies, can do so by application to the undersigned at Athens.
W. G. Delony, Lt. Col. Cav., Cobb's Legion.[7]

Much activity took place in Virginia during Delony's absence from the legion. Between the end of January and the beginning of May, the legion was encamped in the vicinity of Stevensburg in Culpeper County. "I have not written you for several days," wrote Gilbert J. Wright to his wife, Dorothy, on 12 January:

We have been moving our camp about half mile in order to get wood more conveniently, and been quite busy firing up for the winter as the chances are very good for us to remain here for the winter. We have a large tent and a stove and a good bed of straw with plenty of bedding. I have my mattress with me and find it very comfortable. The weather for the last week has been the coldest I have ever seen in Virginia, there is a small snow upon the ground which is frozen into ice the Rappahannock River has been completely frozen over.[8]

---

[5] B. H. W. to parents, 27 February 1863, *Augusta Daily Chronicle & Sentinel* (17 March 1863).

[6] *Southern Watchman* (18 February 1863).

[7] Ibid., 25 February 1863.

[8] Gilbert J. Wright was a lieutenant in the Daugherty Hussars of the legion. G. J. Wright to Dorothy, 12 January 1863, Gilbert J. Wright Letters.

Two weeks after Wright's letter, on 26 January, Joseph Hooker took command of the Army of the Potomac at Fredericksburg with the object of reorganization to support an immediate move on Richmond, or so Lincoln thought. A major snowstorm hit the region in late January, however, confining the two sides to mostly reconnaissance forays and skirmishes. Between 5 and 7 February, there was some skirmishing by units of Hampton's Brigade, with Union cavalry under George Stoneman patrolling the north side of the Rappahannock between Warrenton and the Rappahannock Bridge, especially around Grove Church and Kelly's Ford.[9] Much of the Confederate activity during this time amounted to little more than hit-and-run tactics, earning the wrath of the Federals and the moniker of "bushwhackers" and "guerrillas."

Back in Georgia, things were moving along pretty well for Will Delony's military prospects. By March, so many men had signed up that not only were they successfully filling the open slots in the original companies, but also two additional companies were recruited: Co. K, Richmond Dragoons from Richmond County, and Co. L, Grubb's Hussars from DeKalb County. For the first time in two years, Cobb's Legion Cavalry was up to full regimental strength—at least on paper.

In April, however, things were not going as well for Delony on the home front. We next hear from him on 22 April. Still in Athens, Will was forced to take care of some personal domestic concerns, as mentioned in the local paper:

FIFTY DOLLARS REWARD
RANAWAY from the subscriber, on the 3d inst., his negro man, George. The law will be rigidly enforced against any person harboring him. The above reward will be paid for his apprehension and confinement in any jail.
W. G. Delony. Athens, April 22, 1863.[10]

During this time, the Army was going through yet another reorganization. At the end of March, Army of Northern Virginia Special Order No. 104 was issued to take effect on 1 April. This order officially split the cavalry and infantry battalions of Cobb's Legion and Phillips's Legion with the cavalry battalions being consolidated and permanently assigned to Hampton's Cavalry Brigade of Stuart's Cavalry Division. This "new cavalry regiment," wrote a former member years later, "was given the official designation of the Ninth Georgia Cavalry, but that immortal regiment which would accept no number to be designated by, but held to the name they

---

[9] Third Pennsylvania, 4th Pennsylvania, 16th Pennsylvania, 1st Rhode Island, 1st Virginia, 4th New York, 5th New York, and 1st and 5th United States.

[10] *Southern Watchman* (22 April 1863). George was apparently found, as Delony mentions him 14 May and again in his letter to Rosa 29 May 1863.

adopted when organized. Although a regiment in number of companies ninth Ga. cavalry, as we were ordered to be called by. Yet had we made a reputation as the Cobb Legion, and this esprit de corps was never lost and we could not change our name even to gratify the war department."[11]

Meanwhile, back in Washington, frustration was growing with Hooker's continuing delays. Finally, Lincoln succeeded in prodding his new general into action. Developing a bold plan of attack against Lee, Hooker believed he could bag the Confederate army and end the war. The plan called for a double envelopment of the Confederate army in and around Fredericksburg by attacking Lee from both his front and rear. The battle did not have the desired results that Hooker foresaw. Often referred to as "Lee's greatest victory" and "Lee's perfect battle," Lee outwitted the new Union general with a risky decision to divide his army in the presence of the much larger Federal forces.

The battle was fought from 30 April to 6 May in Spotsylvania County near the village of Chancellorsville. The two sides were not on equal terms. Hooker's army was much better supplied and better rested after several months of inactivity. Hooker also took advantage of improved military intelligence as to the positioning and capabilities of the Confederate army. Opposing the massive Union juggernaut of 70,000 men were Lee's 47,000 poorly provisioned troops scattered all over the state. Some 15,000 men of Longstreet's Corps had previously been detached and stationed near Norfolk while Stonewall Jackson and his 26,000 men were headed toward Fredericksburg from the Shenandoah Valley. The effective Union forces at this time more than doubled Confederate capabilities, creating the greatest imbalance during the war in Virginia up to this point.

With all these advantages, "Fighting Joe Hooker" and his self-proclaimed "finest army on the planet" set out with a simple plan of attack: "Fight!, Fight!, Fight!" But it was not to be for "the finest army on the planet," as Chancellorsville has gone down in history as one of the most lopsided clashes of the war, a Confederate victory, and a battle that earned Lee the reputation as one of the finest generals ever produced in America.

Working his way through Pittsylvania County on 16 April while on forage detail, Pvt. Henry F. Jones of Cobb's Legion wrote home, "I hardly think our Regiment will be fit for duty when the spring campaign opens. The whole brigade is through this country recruiting. Gen. Hampton is at home recruiting his own health."[12]

On 27 April, as the Army of the Potomac began moving from Falmouth to the fords over the Rappahannock, Hooker sent his 10,000 cavalrymen under George

---

[11] Athens *Banner* (30 April 1892).
[12] H. F. Jones, *Soldier Studies*, 16 April 1863 (www.soldierstudies.org).

Stoneman farther upstream to get around Lee's left flank. Crossing the Rappahannock and Rapidan Rivers, Stoneman's orders were to raid deep into the Confederate rear areas, destroying crucial communications and supply depots along the Orange and Alexandria railroad between Richmond to Fredericksburg. Hooker believed this would force Lee to abandon his fortified positions on the Rappahannock and withdraw toward Richmond. At the same time, the Union infantry were to advance to attack the Confederates on Hooker's terms. "My plans are perfect," boasted Hooker, "and when I start to carry them out may God have mercy on General Lee, for I will have none."[13]

Lee, however, had other ideas. Brazenly dividing his greatly outnumbered force in two, an act seen by some to be reckless in the face of a more powerful enemy, Lee kept the Union army in place while the Confederate cavalry kept most of the Union forces screened from spotting Jackson's force as they marched into position to begin their attack. On the afternoon of 2 May, Jackson's Corps launched a full-scale attack on the Federal right flank that overwhelmed and simply rolled up the Federal XI Corps.

Although Stoneman had initial success in securing the crossings over the Rappahannock River with the seizure of Kelly's, Welford's, and Beverly fords, torrential rains on the 14th and 15th stopped the blue-clad troopers in their tracks. Roads became nearly impassable, and after a week of ineffectual raiding in central and southern Virginia, where they failed to secure any of the objectives Hooker established, Stoneman and his cavalry withdrew into Union lines north of the York River on 7 May. This officially brought to an inglorious conclusion the Chancellorsville Campaign.

Following the battle, Wade Hampton established his headquarters at Culpeper Court House while his cavalry continued to patrol between there and the Rappahannock River. The Confederate cavalry's ability to keep Stoneman from achieving any of Hooker's goals was one of the contributing causes for the Union defeat.[14] Lee, by this time, had already determined to make another strike northward into Pennsylvania.

One of the few Union highlights at this time—one with greater consequences later—was that during his initial reorganization, Hooker promoted John Buford to active field command of the Reserve Brigade (cavalry). Buford and his force quickly became a major thorn in the side of Will Delony and Cobb's Legion.

* * *

---

[13] *OR*, Hooker, April 1863. For more on Hooker, see Biographical Roster.
[14] See Stephen Sears, *Chancellorsville* (New York: Houghton Mifflin, 1996).

Athens, Georgia
Jan 2, 1863

My own dearest Will,

The letter I wrote you night before last was a very gloomy one, but I couldn't help it, Darling. I hadn't heard from you for so long a time but your nice long letter of the 24th which I received yesterday cheered me up again. It is a great trial doing without letters, which you know by experience. I read your letter to Rosa when I got to the details of your military movements thinking she would not feel interested, I said to her I'll skip this part. "Oh, no Mama," she said, "read it all. I want to hear all about Papa." They are all making great calculations about the gum drops. I heard Willie tell Lilly tonight when she was undressing him "Mommer, Papa has got a box of candy from the Yankees for me and Tily and Bubber and Mama is going to let me put my hand in and take some." I wish you could have heard them a little while ago. Tom and Rosa in bed, "Come and kiss me Mama" and "me too Ma." Darling, there's no doubt about it little Rosa is wonderfully smart. I gave her a book Christmas day just one week yesterday and she can repeat several things in it which she has learned without any assistance from me. Mrs. Hunter gave her a little Sunday paper a short time since and she has learned several things herself from that. I said to her the other day "which do you love the best, Darling, books or toys?" Books she said and I believe she does. Dear little old Tom loves to eat. He has got to be a great Mama's boy, carries the key basket down stairs for me when we go to meals and waits on me generally. I offered him a bounty of ten cents which stands for Apple or candy if he would learn to blow his nose, but he hasn't got the accomplishment yet. I sympathize with you enough, dear darling, that you must be separated from them but as you say the war must end some of these days and then perhaps we may be happier than we ever were. I am afraid Col Young never will go back. He is in Richmond and I think you would do well to write to him and enquire his arrangements. He left Augusta on the 18th for Richmond. I should certainly let him understand that if he was to be Col. of the Cav Regiment, he would have to command it, but I think the regiment will be yours. Edd Lumpkin certainly told me that Col. Young had told him he had been made Col of Ordinance. I hope it will all soon come right for my poor "old fellow" Mr. Lucas has sold his house for $15000 to Mr. Cook the gun factory man. Maj. Hammond his to Maj. Yancy (The sow will return to her wallowing in the mire) and I learned Dr. Long has sold his also. Did you get the letter in which I told you that Nat Barnard had bought Colts lot up town (by us) and was building. Mrs. Hunter was to see me to-day, anxious about her brother in Braggs Army from which the news of fighting comes. Mr. F. Adams has been in Athens the past week Mrs. Hunter says he took no notice of his child altho he met it several times. She stopped at Mrs. Popes. What a simpleton she was to come here. I went to the Bank yesterday as I told Mr. Adams to post my books to see if my account of what I had drawn agreed with theirs. I paid $95.50 interest on your notes in Bank. You must try and keep cheerful, dearest Will. Think sweetly of me when the gloomy thoughts come. We have had a great many blessings in our day and the Lord sent them, and the ills could not come by chance. I did not write to cousin Laura as I wrote you I thought of doing, sometimes I want to sometimes I dont, can't make up my mind as to what would be best. The truth is it is not company I want its sympathy. Old Mr. Riden came to see me yesterday to say that he had heard from his son and that you were well. He was disposed to be very complimentary for he came to the conclusion that anyone who had such a "lovely wife" as you had he want surprised that you should want to come home, poor old man. Good night, Darling, may God bless and protect you. All send sweet kisses. My large share of love.

Your own affectionate,
Rosa

Athens Jan 4th 1863

My Dearest Will

Your telegram dated 1st I got yesterday and I was rejoiced to learn you had returned safely from the five days scout you wrote me on Christmas you were preparing to take. I had a visit yesterday from a Mr. Jackson who had a son in the Richmond Hussars and who had recently come from where you were. I was very glad to see him as I always am all who have been with my old Fellow. He told me all about the Little Washington affair and spoke of you in the most enthusiastic terms. I regretted to learn from him that Capt Archer had not left Augusta yet, and consequently you still without your clothes that I wrote and asked him to get and take to you as he passed thru Richmond. I begin to despair of Col Young ever getting back to Camp. Mr. Jackson tells me he learnt from him that he had not received any appointment as Col of Ordinance. He thinks Col Young is making an effort to bring you all to Georgia as he sent up to Athens to Edd Lumpkin for Mr. Cobbs papers, that he had obtained from the war department about the transfer. He also tells me reports says Col Young is paying attention to a lady in Augusta. If all that's so it would be well for you and Col Young to understand each other perfectly or you'll have the charge of his regiment all of the time. It may not however be so. If by the removal of Col Cobb he has been made Col why has not a Major been promoted to take your place. If he still is Liet Col why have your regiment not had a Col elected or appointed. I thought those vacancies were always immediately filled. Darling do try and get 60 days furlough, and I would not mail for him to return were I in your place, but force him to do so by leaving yourself. I told Capt Archer when I wrote him about your clothes to tell Col Young that you were waiting for his return to come home, but it don't seem to have hurried him any. All I'm afraid of is that your visit will be put of[f] so long that you either wont be able to come at all or if you do have only a little while to stay. I should certainly let Col Young know I objected to doing every thing. If a man don't let his indignation be felt there's no need in feeling it him self of course I mean if circumstances justify it, and of that in this instance you are the best judge. I'm put out enough with him I know. Don't be modest about asking for a long furlough. Other people stay as long as they please and who is wanted at home like you are. I should certainly write to Col Young to Richmond (where he is) if he is not with you when this reaches you and tell him you have a family at home whose chains you cannot ignore and who need a little looking after and know when you may expect to be relieved. I told William if he was still in Richmond when he passed thru to take your valise to you. If he had gone on to have it, as you would probably soon be coming thru and could get it yourself. If I had not been expecting you I would have sent you a box of something by William as it was I concluded to keep what I had till you came, which I hope will be very soon for hope deferred has made my heart sick. I'm half dead to see you Will, been expecting you so long. Come right off as soon as Col Young gets there or he finds something to keep you there. It seems strange all the Capts. can leave and you cant. Our dear little children are all well. Willie had Croup one night last week, only a slight attack. I vomited him and did not have to send for the Dr. Things look bright for our cause. If France would only step forward and demand an armistice, but I feel safe when A Lincoln dares attribute the fate of battles to "chance." I feel that the vengeance of an insulted God will be visited on them as well as vengeance for our murdered thousands. The enclosed letter I received from Mrs. Johnston. Don't forget to attend to it Darling, either reply to her questions, or write me what I shall say to her. Old Dr. Ward is very sick not expected to live. I believe Dick Taylor expects to bring his wife home this week. I hear they are to be married on Tuesday. All send sweet kisses to dear Papa. My own large amount of love. May God protect you Will, dear Darling, and bring you back to us again and let this be to us indeed and happy New Year is the prayer or your own dear

Rosa

Athens Jan 7th 1863

My Dearest Will

I learned this evening that Dr. Carlton was expected and had a letter for me and as I could not wait I sent George after ten for it, and have just received and read it and am thankful that you are well. I hope you will be able to come soon, for we are all half crazy to see you. Dr. Smith got here last evening and came to see us this morning. I regretted very much to see from his appearance that he has been indulging I should say too freely. I hope I may be mistaken.

Our Darlings are all well and looking forward in eager anticipation for the appearance of their dear Papa. I asked Rosa to night before I came down stairs what I should say to you for her. "Tell him she said when I get to be a big girl Ill send for him." Its too bad you have to be separated from them, and me too Darling. Its too bad you have to be away from your poor little Scrap who can only half live without you. How I do long for peace, and I cant see how the war can last long. I should think the Mason and Slidell affair would teach the Northerners that their rulers will do any thing to accomplish their own wicked purpose. Mrs. Smith sent me some nice Oysters and we had a pie today nice as yours. I thought of you, I always think of you Darling and Aunty says I am always talking about you. Have you got to wait till Lieut. Williams goes back? You must come just as soon as you can for I am afraid something new will air and detain you. I have nothing new to tell you to night. Aunty will probably leave me the last of March. Ellie is going to Marietta to be confined and wants her to meet her there at that time and then Ill have to stand it alone. I hope tho as I have been provided for so far I will be still. If you only keep well and no danger of a fight I can stand any thing.

Good night Darling Will. Think as often and as sweetly of me as I do of you and I hope soon to welcome you home again. All send Papa sweet kisses. Aunty love. Your own Fair share from your own little Scrap.

Rosa

Camp near Culpepper Jany 13 [1863]

My Dear Rosa,

I have received no letters from you in several days and was much disappointed tonight when the mail came in and brought me no letter from home. I have heard nothing yet from Gen Lee and I am afraid to hear. I think if Venable had been successful in getting his favorable endorsement of the order that he would have had it forwarded to me immediately and it will be a week tomorrow since I saw him, but still I hope on. I am too homesick to live and never in my life was I so anxious to see you and our precious little ones. It is a terrible ordeal we are passing through and for the life of me I cannot see when and how the war will end, and we shall all be reunited again and it is hard indeed that after the arduous campaigns since June, when we are now doing comparatively nothing none of us can come home. When I reflect upon all that I have done and suffered since I last saw you and how many sleepless nights I have passed in Virginia thinking of you and our dear little children, my heart sinks within me upon the reflection that our reunion is still indefinite. It is almost impossible for me to write to you Darling, feeling as I do that I cannot say when I shall see you again, (and poor Charley Harris, you would feel for him if you could see him. I shall make one more effort to get him off however and if anything can move Gen Lee I am sure his case will). I try to bear up, but it is hard to do Darling, there are so many things occurring here to dishearten me and then to be debarred the pleasure of unburdening myself to you is sometimes I feel more then I can bear. Col. Young is now in full command, has moved the Regt. to a pine thicket, from which we will have to move as soon as snow falls & the roads become bad, for the men will suffer for fire wood or the horses for corn, so I am not fixing up for the winter yet. We have had no scout since his return and whether or not we will again soon I do not know. I told the Genl. I was utterly demoralized and could do no more fighting until I saw my wife and children. This is just about the way I feel indeed and dont want to see another live Yankee until I see you. You think that the war will end next year. Europe will intervene or the Yankees become convinced of their hopelessness of their cause. For this I fear you are greatly deceived. They outnumber us so greatly, and have disciplined their armies so well that although we beat them when we meet, we exhaust our men in the fight and cannot follow up our victories to meet their fresh reinforcements, which in consequence of their numbers they can always bring up. Vicksburg has not fallen yet, but it is only a question of time if the Yankees display anything like generalship, and then comes the tug of war in the West and God grant that Bragg may be equal to the occasion. His last fight was brilliant but sink or swim live or die, survive or perish if I know my own heart, I am willing to fight on until the end is accomplished. Kiss our precious little ones for me and tell them all how anxious Papa is to see them & tell dear little Rosa that my next letter will be to her. Good night Darling. God bless you all is my prayer.

Ever yr own
Will

Camp Near Culpepper Va
Jany 15, 1863

My Dear Rosa

I have just received and read your letter from Atlanta of the 8th and also one from Athens of the 6th. I regret to learn the serious illness of your father and cordially approve the cause you have pursued & sincerely hope that his illness may not terminate fatally. I have also just heard from my order at Gen Lees Hdqtrs— Venable writes that it still "hangs fire," but I am happy to say that he (the Genl) has commenced granting furloughs and I today made formal application for one with a strong endorsement from Col Young. I have no doubt that it will be granted and in four or five days I think I shall be winding my way homeward. At least I may confidently hope so. My leave however will be only for thirty days, but when I reach home we must together endeavor to get an extension. Young has been home & Wright who will probably be the Major is still there & will be here in a few days so that no field officer will interfere.

The very thought of coming home takes a weight from my heart incalculable & inexpressible, how much I desire to see you and the dear little folks at home no tongue can tell and the prospect of doing so almost makes an old man young again, for indeed I feel that this war is fast making an old man of me in feeling at least. Tho am still doing nothing here. The Yankees have thrown forward such numbers on their picket posts that we have not the force to disturb them, and the Genl in impatiently quiet looking keenly for the first favorable opportunity to make another inroad upon them. The weather is and has been all this month remarkably mild, but little rain no snow, and nearly all the time, bright and sunny as the Indian summer. The wind is blowing tho now as if the winter rains were about to set in and I am sitting in Young's tent in my shirt sleeves by a comfortable fire in his brick chimney as I soon expect to leave I shall defer my winter comforts until I reach Athens. Young is sitting on the opposite side of the table also writing, to whom he will not tell, and not being good at guessing, I cannot tell. I am a little surprised to hear of Dick Taylor's marriage but sincerely hope it may be productive of good to both parties. She is certainly very brave or very loving or both. I hope she may reclaim him but am forced to doubt it. God bless you all Darling. Kiss the little ones for me with the hope that writing a week after this reaches you I will be with you.

Ever yours
Will

Camp near Stevensburg
January 22 1863

My Dear Rosa

Your two letters of the 12th and 13th inst have been recd the latter tonight with much pleasure as only those in camp can fully realize and no tongue can tell. Tattoo has sounded long since the camp is quiet and I alone am apparently restless sleepless and uneasy. This, I presume if the truth were known, I dare say there is many a poor fellow around me feeling as disappointed as myself & with quite as anxious a heart and as ardent desire to visit the loved ones at home. Since I wrote you last, I have been anxiously awaiting the arrival of my order to proceed to Georgia, or the approval of my furlough for which I made application some days ago. Gen Hampton again gave me a warm endorsement but today I received from Hdqtrs our order that all furloughs to both men and officers was suspended for the present.

Gen Lee has received intelligence that the enemy propose to make another move upon our lines and it is consequently necessary that we shall all remain here still longer. One of my scouts returned today from within the enemys lines who reports that all the troops from Baltimore and Washington have been or are being massed before Fredericksburg and another "on to Richmond" move may be soon expected. They are under the impression that Genl Lee has but two divisions at Fredericksburg. If they act upon this idea they will be most terribly beaten, and indeed the hope that they may partially reconciles me to my continued detention in camp. That the enemy have been moving there can be no doubt, but what they propose doing, I have no idea. For the past two days there has fallen rain enough to raise the rivers very considerably and to render the roads most wretched which will impede all military movements. My pickets have now to swim the Hazel River to get to their ports and in such a climate as this in the dead of winter you may conceive what their sufferings are. The Virginia Cavalry are still reposing pleasantly in the rear of the infantry below Fredericksburg.

Col Young is on the Court Martial at Division Hdqtrs and I am in command. I told Gen Hampton yesterday I was very anxious to leave and wished him to get me off, that my position here was extremely unpleasant and if he would do me this favor I would promise not to return again, as it was my intention to obtain if possible some other position which is my fixed determination. I am unwilling to serve under Young and I think my presence here is very disagreeable to him. If I go Wright will also leave, & Young can then promote his West Point friends to our vacant positions. He has less manliness of character than any creature I know of his advantages, and I can only feel for him supreme contempt. He is however as polite and courteous to me as a French dancing master does what I suggest to him but is afraid to do anything without a suggestion. He yet has no Adjutant and will not have until I leave. He is under the impression that I am endeavoring to supplant him and feels uneasy at my presence here. Upon the whole is as a very small man, childish & unmanly & just such a character as I cannot respect as my superior officer. Gen Hampton is extremely anxious for him to command the Infantry, but as that cannot be raised to a Regt he will not do it so I am sure it is best for me to seek some other position, but if I cannot obtain a better one I shall return here and fight it out. I think if I could get off now I could raise a Regt. out of the detached companies of Ga Cav. on the Coast of South Carolina and Georgia of first rate material. I received a letter from Bob tonight. He is now well, has been sick a month, his salary was stopped, and he has lost his position and been assigned to other duty as a special clerk at $4 per day, when he is furnished with work—no work—no pay & up to the time of his writing he had had no work given him. His physicians bill was $300, and all his clothing was burnt up—he is now without money and almost naked. I think it an outrage upon humanity and a disgrace to the Government. I shall write to our Senators about it. Kiss our little Darlings for me and dont let them forget Papa. I still hope that I may soon see you. If the rains will only continue I shall feel confident. In the meantime I shall at least keep on trying. God bless you all Darling.

Ever yr own
Will

Macon Jan 24th 1863

My dear Rosa

I received your letter this morning & was glad to hear from you. Since you left here I have been thinking of what the state of affairs has been for the last 10 years & I now hope it is all settled up for ever, that we are all united in one family your husband included.

Your affectionate father
E D Huguenin

Dear Rosa

The above is written word for word at your Fathers diction. I add a few lines to tell you how he is. When you were here I could not indeed did not think but your Father would get well, although my mother expressed fears to the contrary after waiting patiently by & watching closely I am forced hard as it is to bring myself to the conclusion that he is slowly but surely passing away indeed yesterday his physician assured me such was his opinion, a greater sufferer I am sure you never saw—agony untold he suffers!!—death—would be a happy release. He is patient softness & penitent having united himself to the Episcopal church about ten days ago. I think the hope of prolonged life is strong within him, yet for two days past I feel assured he has many misgivings to day is sad, speaks of never recovering &c. I had him carried out in a chair yesterday over the yard he swept & was much agitated. Rosa his bed of sickness has been a lesson to all if he should be restored he I am sure is a changed man. Should God ordain it other wise. He bows with submission to his maker and to us around bows doubly it assures us of the vanity of all things & God let thy will be done!!

Hoping your husband has returned & well that your little ones are also quite well again and that you have recovered from your sickness.

I remain yours affectionately

Julia E Huguenin

P.S. The children shall keep you advised of how he is. Kiss the little ones and with love to your self and husband from all

Yours &c

J E Huguenin

Richmond May 2nd 1863

My Own Darling Rosa,

I arrived here this morning feeling completely worn out and so homesick that I am sure none but my poor little wife can fully appreciate. I dont think I ever suffered more in my life and I know how my poor Darling misses me, and how sad she is, but you must bear up Dear Darling & think how fortunate we have both been in my being able so long to remain with you this spring. I have arrived here at a stuning time. Hooker has made a bold movement upon Gen. Lee and has taken him, I doubt not somewhat by surprise, but there is every confidence felt in the skill of Lee and the courage of our troops to win success, though taken somewhat at a disadvantage and I presume before this reaches you you will have heard of a terrific battle. We will not be in it. Our Brigade is near Lynchburg. Gen Hampton went there this afternoon. I did not see him, though I walked my self almost down trying to find him. He said he would return here in a few days so I presume the Regt will come here & I will remain probably until it comes. I shall call upon the Secty of War tomorrow & learn from him definitely what to do. Col Young is here arrived this morning is threatened he thinks with typhoid fever—looks badly, but I dont think there is much the matter.

Bob is here and well and Jenny off on Wednesday next. She would have started today but was so sick she could not leave. She is still in Charlotte C. H. and will come to Richmond on Tuesday. The check came due to hand and Bob says he would have started her before but he could not afford to keep her here as board was so high and thought he would wait until Congress adjourned when he could rely upon certainly having her an escort as she was then too unwell. He will start her Thursday and rely upon Providence. I dont think she will have any difficulty in getting on.

I hope you received the fish vegetables &c I sent you by Isaac but I am afraid Dick did not get off the morning I left and that the fish were spoiled. Write to me often Darling & tell my little Darlings to write to Papa. I wish now I could see one of their dear little scrawls. I will write again tomorrow and tell you more definitely where and when I am going. God bless you Darling. Kiss the little ones for me.

Ever yrs

W. G. Delony

Richmond May 6th 1863

My Dear Rosa,

I wrote you last Saturday night and then promised to write again the following day (Sunday) but as it was impossible then to get a letter off I had to content myself with waiting until now. I learn that a train leaves this afternoon & that a friend of mine Lt. Col. Twiggs will leave for home. I shall entrust this to him as the mails are and I presume for a day or two longer will be precious on account of the employment by the Gen. of the railroads for the transportation of troops. Soon after writing you on Saturday the excitement in Richmond began and for two days was up to high heat. Gen Hooker made a bold movement upon Gen Lee, and before crossing the Rappahannock with the main body of his Army sent forward a large Cavalry force to operate in the rear of Gen Lee's Army and interrupt his communications with Richmond and prevent reinforcements reaching him. Consequently quite a considerable force was thrown between Gen Lee's Army and this city and on Sunday last, a thousand rumors were rife to the effect that Richmond was about being attacked and as all the troops here had left to reinforce Gen Lee the Mayor called upon the citizens. The officers of the Army in the city volunteered their services and the citizens came forward very promptly, and Richmond was about being saved by an extempore Army. I had tendered my services thro Col. Young and when about to leave the city for our position, I saw Gen Pettigrews Brigade[15] marching through having just come up from Petersburg and knowing that the Yankees would not have sufficient force to contend against them and that there would be no use for me I beg to be relieved to which Young consented, but as he had command of a battery he could not be, and is still on duty, following up the Yankees & reconnoitering. He received an order from the Secty of War to go with all of the officers and men of Hampton's Brigade to Gordonsville and he has ordered me to remain here until his return from his present reconnaissance, so that I do not think I shall be able to leave here until at least the day after tomorrow and I am paying for John and myself fifteen dollars per day, and in addition to this I am very afraid from all the information I can gather that my fine horse Marmion has been captured by the enemy. If this be

---

[15] Gen. James Pettigrews' Brigade was composed of the 11th, 26th, 47th, and 52nd North Carolina Troops.

so I scarcely know what to do.[16] One thing is certain I shall do no active duty until I can replace him. I will hear positively I hope in a day or two as to whether he has been captured or not. One thousand dollars cannot buy me such another horse and indeed I am told that in Virginia it is impossible to buy them now. But Dear Darling be of good cheer, I can scarcely tell you what my feelings are so mixed as they are with hope & fear impatience & homesickness. I had a long conservation yesterday with a gentleman who has just returned from the North. He is a very intelligent man whom I met in the room of Genl Clark the Senator from Missouri and he tells me that there can be no doubt, but that Lincoln will not be able to enforce his Conscription Act,[17] that in N. York now he has no power, that the Connecticut Election was carried by bringing the Republican soldiers home a few days before the election and refusing furloughs to the democrats, & that Lincoln feels that the North itself is ripe for revolution and his only hope for a continuance of power even during his tenure of service is some military success. He has failed at Charleston,[18] signally failed on the Rappahannock,[19] he will fail in Tennessee,[20] and the only fear I have is that we have a Yankee General (Pemberton) at Vicksburg and I fear yet it will share the fate of N. Orleans.[21] If we can avoid the fall beyond a doubt, with our country free, independent and at peace with the world. Success at Vicksburg is all that we now need to ensure peace and independence and God grant that we may not again be made the victim of another Yankee general through the weakness of our President. It makes me nervous, sleepless, reckless, almost crazy when I reflect that we now have the consummation of all our hopes just within our grasp and all that stands between us and certain success is that Pemberton a Yankee is the sole reliance for the defense of so important a position as Vicksburg. My blood boils when I think of it and I some times wish I could infuse into the Presidents breast the feelings of a man who has before him the prospect of hard service and long continued separation from his family, but my hope is still in Providence and you may still expect to see me at home in the fall, and at home for good, to cure my poor little Scrap of all her neuralgic pains and pet and play with our precious little Darlings.

---

[16] Confederate cavalrymen who remained without a mount for an extended period of time were placed within the ranks of the infantry.

[17] The "Enrollment Act," also known as the "Civil War Military Draft Act," was enacted 3 March 1863. The Act enrolled all male citizens and male immigrants applying for citizenship between the ages of 20 and 45.

[18] This is a reference to the failed naval attack by nine Union ironclads under Flag Officer Samuel Du Pont on 7 April.

[19] A reference to the Chancellorsville Campaign and Joseph Hooker.

[20] A reference to Ulysses S. Grant's operations aimed at taking Vicksburg.

[21] New Orleans fell to Union forces in April 1862.

Jenny will come on just so soon as she can get off—the cars will be too crowded for a few days but you may very soon expect her.

Young has just returned. I presume we will learn in the morning, but as yet, do not know where our Regt. is. Kiss our dear little ones for me. I must close as Young wishes to see me at once. I will write you a note before I leave. God bless you Darling. Think kindly and sweetly of me.

Ever your own
Will

Richmond May 7, 1863

My Dear Rosa,

I have been disappointed in not hearing from you at this place before leaving for the Army, but I presume it is on account of the irregularity of the mails. I shall leave in the morning for Gordonsville which place our Regt. will reach tomorrow also. Col Young will go with me and I am inclined to think we shall at once enter upon a very active Campaign. Gen. Lee's victory grows greater as we learn the facts more fully as is usually the case with him, and our loss very much less than at first reported. The portion of Gen. Longstreets Corps which was at Suffolk passed through Richmond this morning on a forced march and as soon as the[y] reach Gen. Lee, he will I am informed cross the Rappahannock and attack Hookers Army which has suffered very severely so you readily perceive that the Campaign before us is obliged to be energetic and active. God grant us the Victory and an early termination of our difficulties, and to you my dear Darling bear up bravely and trust in Providence for a safe result. My duty calls me to my Regiment and don't be depressed because I am doing my duty. I have confident hopes that Gen. Lee will be successful and that it will be to us the most important Campaign of the war, and with the blessing of God it may bring us peace feeling thus, I shall enter upon it with cheerfulness and hope and be prudent for my little wife's sake, and I know it will all work out right. I have just returned from the Galley where I had my likeness taken for you. I am sorry it will not be ready to send with this letter by Col. Grant. Jenny will bring it on with her. I hope it will please you. Bob will send Jenny on in a few days. Dr. Flournoy was in the city a few days ago and states that she had been very sick. I have drawn upon Athens for four hundred dollars. I shall have to buy another horse. I want you to replace this with that amt. of the interest bearing notes and don't you restrict yourself. There is no necessity for it and you must not do it, and I wish you would ask R. G. Taylor to see the horse of Howard Hays of Lexington and if he likes him buy him for me and send him on by one of our men, who are at home to buy horses. I am told such a horse will cost me here 800 to 1000 dollars and if I get him I can resell though I may buy here. God bless you all Darling. This is the only paper I can get. John is out and Col. Grant leaves soon after dinner which I have left to write this note. I will write from Gordonsville tomorrow night. Kiss the dear little ones for me and accept a large share of love for my precious Darling.

Ever yours
Will

Gordonsville May 12, 1863

My Dear Rosa,

I was bitterly disappointed in Richmond at not hearing from you and most agreeably surprised yesterday upon my arrival here to find your two letters of the 1st and 3rd awaiting me. I called at the post office in Richmond inquiring for letters and myself ordered the mail for Hampton's brigade forwarded to this place and instead of delivering my letters there according to the usual mode of doing business among our Government officials he sent them with the balance of the Brigade mail to this place. I have not yet joined the Regt. It will be here this morning and go on tonight to Orange Courthouse where I will join them to night without a horse to ride. My bay mare is about 100 miles from this place where she had to be left on account of her poorly. It will be I am told 6 weeks or 2 months before she is again fit for duty. Old Marmion did not fall in the hands of the enemy but has been very sick and is altogether unfit for duty, and the horses here are so fabulously high that I scarcely know what to do. If I cannot get one in the Regt. I shall have to pay as much as $1000. Col Young has refused 800 for one that he bought for 350 or 400 just before I went home and so it is every where. I think we will be immediately put to work. Stuart is at Orange, and is collecting a very considerable Cavalry force. Where we will go I do not know, but will write you as soon as I leave.

You need not be alarmed Darling about the threatening attitude of Sibley of Augusta. If he meant to fight he would not have asked an explanation in the way he has, and you may be assured that I have no idea of fighting him. He and Dick Taylor were drunk together in Augusta and the morning I left, they were in the bar room together and Dick was paying him all the money he had. Isaac told me of it and I stepped in took the monies from them and deposited it with the Clerk of the Planters hotel, subject to Dicks orders after his arrival in Athens. They both gave me a cursing to which I submitted very patiently, and Sibley afterwards, being very drunk, cried and blubbered and tried to convince me he was a gentleman and that is all of it, he has no more idea of fighting me than Dick Taylor has. I shall write of course a pleasant letter to Geo. Barnes, particularly as I am inclined to think that he too was tight when he wrote to me.

You don't tell me Darling in either of your letters how you are getting on & how you are feeling now. I sincerely hope and trust that you are not suffering now as much as when I was at home. The warm tems will I hope will entirely cure your neuralgia[22] and your other ailments I trust are better. Write to me all about yourself and our dear precious little children. It was a theme that never grows tiresome and the most agreeable to me of all others. Bless their dear little Souls how I should have liked to have attended their picnic on the Campus.[23] Tell little Rosa I shall expect a letter from her giving me an account of it and all that happened. Jenny will be in Richmond tonight if well enough and will leave for Athens in a day or two, so that you may expect her every day now until she arrives. I shall be delighted to hear of her arrival. The language of your Grand father's will cannot affect it one way or another. I do not think it ever necessary for us to be represented in Macon for the Court has no jurisdiction over the subject matter under the will of your father and cannot bare on us, but it is well enough to be on the safe side. Tell me how your crops is progressing, your wheat corn and potatoes, & what about the deed to the land.

God bless you all Darling. Kiss the little ones for me. Keep a stout heart and think of me kindly and sweetly always

Ever yours
Will

Gordonsville May 14 1863

My Dear Rosa

We are still at this place and will be here probably until day after tomorrow. The Regiment is in command of Maj. Rice and consequently moves slowly, slowly. After our arrival at Orange Court house Stuart will have a grand review[24] and we will then I presume be assigned to our respective positions and duties. For the present I think we will only do picket duty, though I can learn but little of the intended operations of the army, indeed I know nothing and am at a loss to surmise anything. We are very pleasantly

---

[22] Discomfort caused by severe headache.

[23] Campus of Franklin College/Old North Campus, University of Georgia.

[24] J. E. B. Stuart held the first of three viewings of his newly formed cavalry corps on 22 May, 5 June, and 8 June. Complete with mock battles, many of the cavalrymen worried that the reviews would overtax their already suffering mounts, all for Stuart's flamboyant personality. His first "Grand Review" was held on an open plain northeast of Culpeper Court House near a small railroad depot called Brandy Station.

situated here amusing ourselves with sleeping and drinking ice water and having a good time generally. Captains Wright King Archer Ritch and Anderson are all here, and our time has been passing quite pleasantly. Day after tomorrow Darling will complete the ninth year of our married life, since pleasant happy years to me, notwithstanding that nearly two of them have been passed during this terrible war & when I think of the happy hours I passed at home this spring my detestation of the service & my longing for home makes my army life almost insupportable. You need not be surprised to see me at home this summer, with my resignation accepted and a substitute mustered in. In case I come to the conclusion that the last great battle of the war has been fought. I shall certainly adopt this course. Lincoln is now pursuing a course which will either make him the undoubted Dictator of the North or will destroy his Government entirely. If he succeeds, there is no end to the war if he fails as I believe he will peace will soon ensue, and God grant that he may fall. The arrest of Vanlaningham[25] must remove all doubt upon the minds of Northern men of his character and intentions, and I cannot believe they will tamely submit to his longer dictation without some further successes against us. Dear Darling, this very idea of peace and my return home again almost makes me crazy and I only fear that my extreme anxiety may warp my judgment and induce a misconception of the state of affairs at the North, but my hopes of peace are very very strong.

I have received nothing further from home since I wrote day before yesterday. Hope I may hear today. I wrote to Barnes, and you need not be anxious about me, tho' there is I am sure not much danger in Sibley. Be sure and let me know how your crop comes on your wheat corn and potatoes. Write to me all about yourself, how you are feeling and if your suffering are over now. I want to know all about home, what the little folks are doing and saying, & thinking about, how George is doing. If he does not do well, I wish particularly to know it, and at once. And how does your lawsuit and correspondence with George Fort progress, be sure to send me copies of the latter. I am curious to see it.

God bless you all Darling. Think kindly of me and dont let the little ones forget Papa. Kiss them all for me. Give my love to Mrs Hunter and tell her to take good care of you for me. A heartfull of love from

Yr own
Will

---

[25] Clement Vallandigham was an Ohio congressman who served in the House from 1858 to 1863. He was a Democrat and recognized as the leader of the Northern Copperheads (those opposed to the war and in favor of an amicable split with the South). Arrested for making treasonous statements against the Union, he was banished to the Confederacy. Being forcibly removed from Union-held territory and placed across military lines, he was arrested by Davis and taken to Wilmington, North Carolina. He later took passage aboard a blockade-runner and traveled to Canada, from which he later made his way back to Ohio.

Gordonsville May 16, 1863

My Dear Rosa,

Nine years ago tonight you and I were married and today Dear Darling my little wife is far dearer to me than when we were then married, and tho separated today by a cruel war my heart and thoughts are always with you and our precious little children. How I long for this war to end and our little home to be cheerful and happy once more and all of us reunited, your own true heart can tell. I have strong hopes of a peace this fall if one Yankee General Pemberton is only as true as the President considers him and God grant that he may prove so.

Our Regiment arrived here last night. They will be inspected today and we will move on to our old picket line near Culpepper Court house. I rode out to their camp when they came in and they gave me a very warm reception, as hearty cheers as Georgians can give. You cant imagine what a trial it is to me to be compelled to resign the chief command to Col. Young, but I shall do my duty and if we cant agree I shall resign. He is very polite & kind.

I shall be obliged to leave my trunk here. The orders about baggage are very strict and tho some of the officers are going beyond them and taking their trunks I shall keep within the rules as I think the coming Campaign will be severe and we will not have much use for the luxuries of life.

I have not heard from you since I wrote. I suspect our mail has gone up to Culpepper and I hope tomorrow to get several letters from you. Nearly everything Col. Young and myself left in camp I am told is gone, but as we need but little it is a matter of small importance. God bless you all Darling. Write to me often & think kindly and sweetly of me. I shall write to you as frequently as I can. I must now join the Regt. Kiss the dear little ones for me and accept for yourself a heartful of love.

Yours
Will

Camp near Culpepper C. H. Va
May 19, 1863

My Dear Rosa,

We arrived here night before last and yesterday & the night before I read four letters from you. I am truly sorry to hear of your having another attack of neuralgia and of Sarah's death. Dear Darling I feel most deeply for you in the very trying position in which you are now placed, and would to God I could bear your troubles for you, but you must have a stout heart Darling and bear up under your many trials until I can again come home to help you bear them. Dont give up to despondency you have many warm friends in Athens, sweet little children at home and our warm heart in the Army that most affectionately & truly sympathizes with you in all your troubles. Have faith & hope and it will all end happily I trust for us all. I can not cease to hope that the fury of the storm is spent and that many months will not elapse before I can return to Athens with our country free and independent. Let us hope this much at least. I think we have reason, good reason for doing so and we ought to bear our present trials with fortitude and hope and all will yet end well.

We have not yet been assigned to any duty. Gen Stuart will be up today & I presume active operations against the enemy will very soon commence. He is massing quite a large force of Cavalry here and it must be for active service. I presume he will have 10,000 effective men, more Cavalry than we have ever had together in Virginia and all well mounted, cheerful and ready for anything. Our Regt. is in fine condition and have given me a very warm & most flattering reception. Gen Hampton too and the other officers of the Brigade have received me most cordially and I really feel like coming again among old friends. God grant we may all meet again after the war. Col Young is very polite and I think Maj. Rice will resign. I proposed to him a few days ago that we mess together which he declined saying that he had formed his mess—with two privates—so I am still with Young. If Rice resigns & Wright is promoted he & I can mess together very pleasantly, until then I shall remain together. We today will open the first bottle of your catsup & most acceptable it will be for this country is entirely eaten out and we can get nothing from the Commissary. This morning we were notified by the negroes that they had nothing in the larder for our breakfast so we had to send out John who with his usual luck got up some bread & meat & milk & is now out looking up a dinner & thus we are living. What would your housekeepers say to that.

Tell Rosa & Tom that Papa received both their letters and was very glad to hear from them. Old Tom's was particularly characteristic. Bless their dear little Souls, how I should like to be with them this morning and hear their little tongues prattling. I hope from your silence in regard to it that there is no rust in your wheat and that my little farmer will make a notable crop this year. You must write me about it and your potatoes and corn.

I read Dr. Forts two letters one to me and the one to you. He is obliged as he says to pursue the letter of Law, or he will lose money, being personally responsible if he does not which is all quite true and I hope he will therefore appreciate my position, as your trustee. We are precisely in the same relative position, and I am willing that a decree of the Court shall if necessary decide all questions between us. It does not follow that we should quarrel & ought not to do so & for myself I do not desire it.

Willie Church desires to be kindly remembered to you. Remember me kindly to all my friends. God bless you all Darling. Kiss the little folks for me & write when you can.

Love yours
Will

P. S. What has been done about the Kenny lands?

Camp near Culpepper C. H.
May 23, 1863

My Dear Rosa

Several days have elapsed without a letter from home and I feel inexpressibly anxious about you and our precious little children. I sincerely hope that my not hearing may be owing to the miscarriage of the mails and not to any sickness at home. God bless you all Darling and keep you all in health is my daily earnest prayer. I hope that Jenny will be with you when this letter reaches you, or even by this time as Bob sent me word a few days ago that he would start her on to Ga. Everybody is in bed but me and when I dont hear from home I cannot sleep so you must write me often if it is only a line and tell me all about yourself and the dear little folks. I hope you are doing well and that you have supplied yourself with strawberries. You must get what you want and not be low spirited but cheerful for my sake and the little strawberry as well as your own.

We are still quiet here, and up to this time our Regt. has done no duty. We commence picketing tomorrow in the fork of the Rapidan & Rhappahannock some 20 or 25 miles from here. The duty will be comparatively light, requiring only one company at a time, and but for our disasters in the West I am inclined to think the campaign in Virginia would not have been severe. I still hope the news from Mississippi is not so disastrous as the papers of today would indicate.[26]

Gen Stuart yesterday had a grand review of his cavalry here, but there were not more than 4,000 present instead of 10,000. He will however have more but no[t] so many as I expected.[27] Our Regt can only muster about 265 horses for duty. We are

---

[26] On 16 and 17 May, major engagements took place at Champion's Hill and at the Black River Bridge in Mississippi as Grant's forces advanced from Jackson to cut Confederate communications with Vicksburg and prevent Pemberton from joining forces with Johnston. The Siege of Vicksburg began the following day.

[27] On 5 June and 8 June, Stuart held the second and third of his "Grand Reviews" of his newly enlarged force on an open plain northeast of Culpeper Court House near Brandy Station. The following day, Maj. Gen. Joseph Hooker ordered Alfred Pleasonton and the Union cavalry to cross the Rappahannock and attack Stuart in an attempt to locate the main body of the Army of Northern Virginia and discover Lee's plans. Lee began his northward movement on 10 June.

trying to prevail upon the Generals to permit us to send more of the men home but I doubt if they will consent. It is certainly very discouraging to regimental officers to have half of the men always unfit for duty on account of unserviceable horses & I feel sometimes almost like joining the Infantry. And now let me tell you about a grand frolic in which I acted a notable part. Last night I was sitting with Capt King in his tent talking with him about our wives and little ones, & we were just about separating to write home, when in came a messenger from Col. Young asking me to come into town and bring with me 4 or 5 other gentlemen. At once I knew that he and Church and one or two other young men had endeavored to get up a dance for the benefit of the ladies who had come up from Orange Co. to witness the review, and I at once concluded that the ladies would not have partners and that we would go. So King and myself and three others ordered our horses and rode to town. When we walked into the ball room we saw six or seven ladies and the room otherwise crowded with grey uniforms and incipient whiskers, and everybody dancing. I stepped up to Young who at once introduced me to the two Miss Bulls of Orange, talked a little while sat down a while, walked about a little while, and a little while after came out to get my horse and ride home. When lo & behold the servant had brought my horse to camp. I then walked up stairs again and looked up Captains Ritch & Williams of Atlanta and off we started on foot for Camp. We met Col. Youngs boy taking his horse back and rode in. When arriving here we found that King had walked to Camp ahead of us and all thoroughly disgusted with balls and dances at Culpepper Co. H. This was our fate. Church was wise. He paid twenty four dollars for the candles went for a girl who declined to attend and when he reached the ball room discovered that the girls were all engaged so far ahead that he could not find a partner. King thinks the ball was not a pleasant one & I think it will be my last as it was my first. God Bless you all Darling. Write to me often and think kindly and sweetly of me notwithstanding all my faults. Kiss the little ones for me. Good night.

Ever your own
Will

Camp near Culpepper C. H.
May 26, 1863

My Dear Rosa

I received yesterday your letter of the 14th and the day before yours of the 18th and am glad to learn that you are feeling better now and that the dear little ones are all well. I hope Jennie is now with you and that she will comfort you during the summer and that you will keep each other cheerful & hopeful and happy.

I am very glad to hear that you have had so many and such fine strawberries and I hope you have allowed the little folks to enjoy them too. I must believe that good ripe fruit cannot hurt them if eaten moderately. God bless their precious little souls how I should like to see them this morning and hear their little tongues. Tell little Rosa she must write to Papa and tell me all about herself and Tom and Willie and what they do every day & how dear Mama is getting on without me.

We are still very quiet here, Stuart is gradually increasing his force and day by day new regiments are coming in. I am delighted of this increase of force, for last years service was so severe upon us, that the prospect of having help is pleasant indeed. But Darling you ought to spend a week with us to remove all symptoms of depression meat and bread for breakfast, bread and meat for dinner, and meat and bread for supper and when we do add to our bill of fare, we have to do so at a cost which is truly alarming. Fresh meats, chicken &c are away beyond the reach of our money. Butter $2.50 to $3.00 per lb, milk in proportion and vegetables very scarce & high, and with all we can only buy from the commissary 1/4 lb a piece of bacon pr day, whether it be bone or whether it be meat. John says he hasnt had enough to eat since he has been here. It is pretty hard living you may depend, but as we occasionally manage to get up a good dinner as we did yesterday we get on elegantly. Kiss the little folks for me, & give my love to Jennie. Write me often Darling and think sweetly for your poor old fellow.

Will

Camp near Culpepper C. H.
May 29, 1863

My Dear Rosa,

Your letter of the 22nd was recd yesterday and I would have written you last night but the day before I had eaten for dinner some half cooked turnip tops and was not in good writing trim indeed was quite unwell, but today are all right again. John was away with Col. Young who went down to Hanover C. H. to attend Col. Roper's wedding and his boy was sick, so we had to rely upon a negro who certainly does not understand the culinary arts.

I can understand how frightened you must have been at the idea of dear little Tom's being lost, poor little souls it is well they are not aware of the anxiety they are to us. They are very sweet though Darling are they not. Dear little Rosa, and hustling Jacob. Where did she pick up that bright idea. You must write a letter for her to me and tell her to let me know all about herself and her pets and what she and Bubber Tom and Willie are doing. You must be careful not to let her confine herself to her books this summer. There is time enough and she is I think very bright and will rapidly learn as fast as she ought. How I wish Darling I could be with you & enjoy with you their childish days and I still must hope that the time will come ere long when I can return home. All will be well at Vicksburg now since Gen Johnson is out there. I cannot believe that the blunders and losses of Pemberton cannot yet be retrieved by him—at least my hopes are very strong, and if we meet with no disaster then I think we are safe. I see that Vanlaningham has been sent to us I hope the President will prohibit his coming among us. Our foolish people at home will make a lion of him as they did the Roman Raiders in Augusta,[28] and more than this we ought not to suffer Lincoln to make our country his penal colony. My feelings to the whole Yankee race is about the same. I know no difference between Democrats and Republicans. By the way why have you stopped sending me the Athens papers at least send me one of them occasionally. They are always acceptable in Camp, particularly the advertisements, and the accounts of what is going on in and about Athens. What was the result of the public meeting for the defense of our homes and firesides. Who is General in Chief and who compose his staff. Cant I get some position in that army? The position of Surgeon General would be most agreeable to me. I could show my gratitude to the brave defenders of our Country by dressing their wounds and relieving their pains. When the Yankees get to Athens I think I will give up the ship if they get back safely or do any damage to the factories or workshops. It is well enough though to wake up a company and when you have done so, send all the able bodied men to old for Johnson or Gen Lee, and Athens will be safe.

I regret to learn that your garden is suffering for the want of rain. I hope you will have vegetables enough however for yourself & the little folks. How is your up town crop coming on. Let me know all about it. You say nothing about George. I am afraid he is not doing well. You must let me know if he does not and not be afraid to troubling me. Tell him to find out if you can have your wheat threshed in the field. If so by all means have it done and tell him to stack the straw in the fields. The Sledge[29] will show him how to do it. God bless you all Darling. Think sweetly of me and write often. I am very homesick at times and there is nothing like a little from you to cheer me. I am very glad that you are more comfortable now. Give my love to Jennie as I presume she must be with you now. Kiss the little ones for me. A heartful of love from

Will

---

[28] During the spring of 1863, there were several Union raids carried out in northern Georgia, and rumors spread of impending raids on the valuable military installations in and around Augusta.

[29] Augusta newspaper editor.

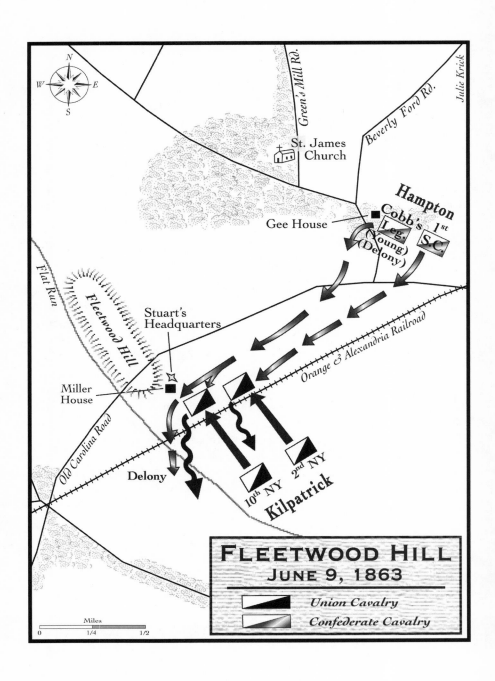

Julie Krick

N
W   E
S

Green's Mill Rd.

Beverly Ford Rd.

St. James
Church

Gee House

Hampton

Cobb's
Leg.
(Young)
(Delony)

1st
S.C.

Flat Run

Fleetwood Hill

Stuart's
Headquarters

Miller
House

Orange & Alexandria Railroad

Old Carolina Road

Delony

10th NY

2nd NY

Kilpatrick

FLEETWOOD HILL
JUNE 9, 1863

Union Cavalry
Confederate Cavalry

Miles
0   1/4   1/2

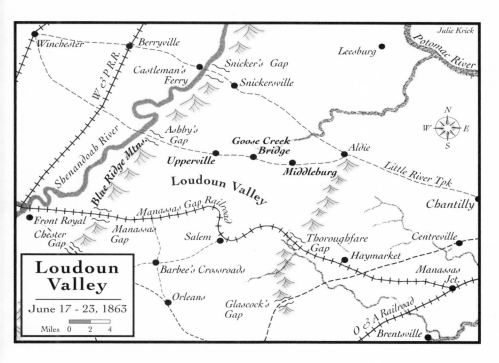

Battles and skirmishes involving
William G. Delony and Cobb's Georgia Legion Cavalry.

Chapter 11

Brandy Station and the Fight for the Loudoun Valley: June 1863

A horseman, darting from the crowd,
Like lightning from a summer cloud,
Spurs on his mettled courser proud,
Before the dark array.
　　　　—*Marmion* by Sir Walter Scott

With the end of the Chancellorsville campaign, Lee was poised to begin his second invasion of the North, carrying the war to the enemy and, hopefully, giving support to the growing peace movement.[1] With Stuart's newly reorganized cavalry force, augmented with new mounts and recruits that officers such as Will Delony were bringing in, Lee began his preparations for striking into the heart of enemy territory. The new plan was to march through the Shenandoah Valley using the Blue Ridge and South Mountain ranges to screen the army as he pushed down the valley into Maryland and Pennsylvania. Stuart's cavalry of about 9,500 men was to add an extra layer of shielding for the Army of Northern Virginia as it tramped northward.

Stuart was still exalting in his ride around the Union army, and he believed the coming campaign afforded him a chance for even more glory. As the Confederate troopers recouped and prepared for what would come next, Stuart determined to show off his horsemen's prowess. "We are having a grand review tomorrow at Brandy Station of all of Stewart's Cavalry," wrote Thomas Marshall of the 12th Virginia Cavalry. "I reckon it will be an imposing sight. We are to have a sham fight and charge artillery loaded with blank cartridges."[2] The review was intended for Gen. Robert E. Lee, but Lee could not attend, as he was too busy planning the army's next moves. A couple of days later, this time with Lee in attendance, Stuart again held a great review on the 8th with his line of cavalry stretching 3 miles long as each

---

[1] See Thomas F. Curran, *Soldiers of Peace: Civil War Pacifism and the Postwar Radical Peace Movement* (New York: Fordham University Press, 2003).
[2] Thomas Marshall, Co. E, 12th Virginia Cavalry, 4 June 1863: www.brandystationfoundation.com/pages/letter1.

of the regiments passed before the reviewing stand. It was a "gallant affair," and Lee admitted that Stuart was in all of his glory that day.[3]

That night Stuart retired to his headquarters on top of nearby Fleetwood Hill, near Culpeper Court House, while his men were encamped and spread out between the Hazel and Rappahannock rivers. The troopers were ordered to get some rest and be prepared to move at first light as the Army of Northern Virginia set its course for Pennsylvania before Union general Joseph Hooker could be alerted as to Confederate movements. Hooker, however, had already received information of a great gathering of all the Confederate cavalry near Culpeper and immediately recognized that something was afoot.

On 9 June, around 4:00 A.M., John Buford's blue-clad columns crossed the Rappahannock River in an effort to disrupt what Hooker thought was an enemy move against his supply lines. Moving down the Beverly's Ford Road, Buford's Division easily pushed aside the 6th and 7th Virginia cavalry. The goal of this attack was J. E. B. Stuart's cavalry encampment at the small railroad station called Brandy Station. This move marked the beginning of the Gettysburg Campaign, and the coming battle was the largest cavalry battle ever fought in North America. In this fight, Cobb's Legion Cavalry distinguished itself by playing a prominent role in forcing the Union cavalry to withdraw back across the Rappahannock River.

Just before dawn on the 9th, hearing heavy firing in the direction of General Stuart's headquarters, Wade Hampton spurred his cavalry toward the sounds. Detailing the 2nd South Carolina to remain in reserve to protect Brandy Station with orders to picket the roads leading to Carrico's Mills and to Kelly's Ford, Hampton moved forward quickly with the 1st South Carolina, 1st North Carolina, Cobb's Legion, and Jeff Davis Legion. Taking up a position along the Beverly Ford Road, on the right of the artillery, which was already engaging the enemy, Hampton threw part of Cobb's Legion forward as skirmishers under Capt. Jeremiah Ritch while Stuart began a two-hour assault to dislodge the enemy from the woods in their front.[4] "I directed Colonel Young, Cobb's Legion," wrote Hampton, "to take a gallop, and to charge the enemy, who were then driving our men in my front. The same orders were extended to Colonel Black, First South Carolina, who followed the Cobb Legion closely. In conjunction with this charge on the enemy in front, I moved with the First North Carolina and the Jeff. Davis Legion so as to turn his right."[5] While Buford's attack was blunted a second union division under David M.

---

[3] Ibid.

[4] Report of Brig. Gen. Wade Hampton, 12 June 1863; Report of P. M. B. Young, Colonel, Cobb's Legion Cavalry, 13 July 1863, *OR*, vol. 27, pt. 2.

[5] Ibid.

Gregg attacked from the southeast, charging up Fleetwood Hill threatening Stuart's headquarters.

About noon, Hampton received information that Stuart's headquarters was in danger of being captured by the enemy and that Yankee cavalry may already be in possession of the camp.[6] Young was immediately ordered to "clear the hill."[7] Without pausing, Cobb's Legion broke off contact with the fight in their front, pivoted, and moved at a gallop in the direction of Stuart's headquarters.

As the Confederate cavalry approached Stuart's headquarters they were met by an impressive sight. As Captain Hart of the horse artillery reported, "There were now Union cavalry on the summit of Fleetwood...the whole plateau east of the hill and beyond the railroad, was covered with federal cavalry."[8] Wiley Howard also remembered that as they topped the hill, "the vast plain was aswarm with bluecoats, mounted and coming at us vigorously."[9]

Howard recalled their approach:

> We were ordered back to save Stuarts headquarters, in front my squadron, the 5th, leading, Col Deloney on my left, Will Church and Jim Clanton on my right in column of squadrons, and as Col. P. M. B. Young gave the order "By squadron front into line Wheel," the Yankees came charging over Fleetwood Hill firing as they came, and with a "Forward Charge" from Young, How we went into them!! Deloney's deep voiced command "Sabres, boys, sabres, no pistols" showing his presence of mind in that whirl and how Willie Church and Jim Clanton defied each other to get the 10th New York Cavalry's flag in generous rivalry—and how they dashed into that huzzaing hatless crazy mob. We had but 129 sabres, and they had the 10th New York, 2nd New York, 1st Maryland, 1st Maine and a squadron of District of Columbia cavalry under their famous Judson Kilpatrick.[10]

With the Georgians of Hampton's Brigade leading the way, the Confederate cavalry thundered up the steep hill from the northeast with Hart's mounted artillery keeping pace alongside. As the Confederates swept up the hill with their typical Rebel yell, Hart's battery veered off to the side, quickly unlimbered, and got off three shots before their cavalry pitched full force into the enemy, stemming their

---

[6] The courier sent from Stuart to warn Hampton was Capt. Chriswell Dabney, 19 years old, a cousin of Stuart's and member of his staff. From conversation with Carl Sell, 31 December 2015.

[7] Fleetwood Hill. Report of Brig. Gen. Wade Hampton, 12 June 1863; report of P. M. B. Young, Colonel, Cobb's Legion Cavalry, 13 July 1863, *OR*, vol. 27, pt. 2.

[8] McClellan, 277; Richard E. Crouch, *Brandy Station: A Battle Like No Other* (Westminister, MD: Willow Bend Books, 2002) 121–22.

[9] Wiley C. Howard, "Sketch of Cobb Legion Cavalry and Some Incidents and Scenes remembered" (Atlanta: Camp 159, published talk given at U.C.V. meeting) 19 August 1901, 16–19.

[10] Ibid.

attack and then breaking the Union advance. The Federals were driven "off in a perfect rout without a pause or a check. Their guns were abandoned and many of their men killed and captured,"[11] wrote Hampton. The Union cavalry began to retreat with Delony, Young, and Hampton chasing after them. In the process, the Confederate cavalry overran one of Gregg's batteries at the foot of the ridge, killing or wounding thirty artillerymen and capturing or disabling all six of its guns.[12] Pierce M. B. Young later recalled, "I swept the hill clear of the enemy, he being scattered and entirely routed."[13] Wiley Howard remembered:

> I saw Major DeLoney, my former Captain, smiting Yankees right and left as he charged along in advance. He sat on his charger grandly, his fine physique and full mahogany beard flowing, he looked a very Titan war god, flushed with the exhuberance and exhilaration of victory. He called to me to rally with others of his old company about him and on he led us pressing the retreating foe right down to a railroad cut, until we had run into the cross fire of the enemy's dismounted men, organized there, I suppose, to stay the stampede of the crowd we had driven back and if possible to arrest our progress. Col. Young, seeing from his position the danger, dashed rapidly down and ordered DeLoney to withdraw, but shaking his head and lion-like beard DeLoney said, "Young, let's charge them," and in two or three minutes five horses fell and a number of our men had been shot. By this time, however, the enemy's whole line in sight were giving way and on we went, those not unhorsed or crippled. So fierce and fast was the fighting, we had no time to accept surrender offered by many Yankees—just rode on and left them behind. Wm. L. Church, youngest child of Dr. Alonzo A. Church, of Franklin College, who went out as 4th corporal in my company, was Adjutant and was unhorsed while contending with two men mounted. He finally succeeded in fatally thrusting one through, who was leaning over and had his hand on him, and as he tumbled off, Church mounted on his adversary's horse and galloped to the front with us. He was indeed a gallant, dashing fighter and though often struck (twenty-five times) by spent balls, escaped serious wounds.[14]

---

[11] Report of Brig. Gen. Wade Hampton, 12 June 1863; Report of P. M. B. Young, Colonel, Cobb's Legion Cavalry, 13 July 1863, *OR*, vol. 27, pt. 2.

[12] Edward G. Longacre, *Gentleman and Soldier: The Extraordinary Life of General Wade Hampton* (Nashville, TN: Rutledge Hill Press, 2003) 136.

[13] Report of P. M. B. Young, Colonel, Cobb's Legion Cavalry, 13 July 1863, *OR*, vol. 27, pt. 2.

[14] Howard, *Sketch of Cobb Legion Cavalry*, 16–19.

The Augusta paper informed its readers of this encounter, gathered from "private letters, as well as official dispatches and newspaper correspondence," which, according to the paper,

> [showed] that our boys did noble service in the recent cavalry engagement at Culpepper [*sic*]. From a letter by Capt. W. B. Young, of the Richmond Hussars, Co. B., we get the same information. We give some passages: Yesterday (9th) was a busy day with our cavalry. The Yankee Cavalry crossed the Rappahannock River at Beverly's Ford early in the morning. Our (Con.) cavalry division moved promptly to meet them. We met them between the ford and Brandy, and had, I think, the largest and hardest cavalry fight of the war. Our caval-cavalry drove the Yankees back at every point. At one time the Yankees, having a much larger force than ours, succeeded in getting in our rear and almost completely surrounding us. Then came some of the most brilliant charges I have ever witnessed. Regiment after regiment of our cavalry charging the Yankees in every part of the field and driving them back in complete rout at every point. Our regiment did its share of fighting, and won for itself a high reputation as a gallant and brave body of men. My company did nobly—fighting a part of the time on foot, in the woods, as skirmishers—in fact, all our cavalry fought gallantly. Serg't. Cobb and M. Harris were wounded, but not seriously.[15]

The battle of Brandy Station involved 21,000 troops on both sides (11,000 union; 9,500 confederate) and produced about 1,400 causalities. After the battle of Fleetwood Hill, P. M. B. Young reported that his force suffered the loss of three officers and forty-one men, killed, wounded, and missing. He added that all of his officers and men

> acted in a gallant and praiseworthy manner. All acted so well that it seems unfair to mention the names of any particular individuals; but I cannot fail to mention the intrepid personal gallantry of my lieutenant-colonel, W. G. Delony. Among others whose distinguished conduct came under my personal observation, was my adjutant, Lieut. W. L. Church; Capt. J. E. Ritch, commanding sharpshooters (who, I regret to say, while dismounted, was captured by a cavalry charge) and Lieutenant [J. L.] Clanton, of Company K. Captain [B. S.] King also deserves praise for the manner in which he commanded his sharpshooters. I desire also to mention the most distinguished gallantry of Privates McCroan and Landrum, who, on foot, refused to surrender when surrounded by the enemy, but cut their way through safely.[16]

---

[15] *Augusta Daily Chronicle & Sentinel* (13 June 1863).

[16] *OR*, vol. 27, pt. 2, 732–33; also quoted in Lynwood M. Holland, *Pierce M. B. Young: The Warwick of the South* (Athens: University of Georgia Press, 1964) 72.

J. E. B. Stuart praised Young and his officers "for a large part of the success" in handling "their commands with skill and judgment, while their conduct was marked by conspicuous gallantry."[17] Total losses for the brigade were officially listed as fifteen killed, fifty-five wounded, and fifty missing. Hampton reported that his command took 216 prisoners

> while the ground over which they fought proved by the dead and wounded on it how faithfully they performed their work.... I cannot close this report without expressing my entire satisfaction at the conduct of the four regiments which were under my immediate command and observation. I have never seen any troops display greater coolness, bravery, and steadiness. The sharpshooters charged and drove back the infantry skirmishers of the enemy, holding them in check perfectly on the extreme right of our line. When the enemy had gained my rear, and it became necessary to dispossess them of the hill they had gained, which commanded the whole position, without the slightest confusion or hesitation (though their critical condition was manifest to all) they moved to the charge, which they executed in the most brilliant manner and with complete success, recovering all the ground which had here been lost by our troops; and the ground which they had so gallantly won they held until the close of the fight. During the entire fight of twelve hours, I did not see, nor do I think there was, one single straggler from my ranks.[18]

Returning to camp, some of the men of Cobb's Legion took the time for their own correspondence as well as some pressing business from back home. "At a meeting of the Richmond Hussars, Co. A, Cobb's Legion, it was resolved as follows: We tender our thanks to little Fannie Bailey, aged four years, a daughter of a private, for the donation of $120 [sic] derived from the sale of her entire stock of toys, which sum is to be used in behalf of the needy of this company."[19] The legion, however, didn't remain in camp for long.

Following the action at Brandy Station, the cavalry were embroiled in a number of fights for control of the Loudoun Valley. Over the course of the next five days, from 17–21 June, Pleasonton's probing Union cavalry were constantly pushing Stuart's five brigades in every corner. This began a second phase of the Gettysburg Campaign. The battles for the Loudoun Valley involved 19,000 troops and resulted in 1,400 causalities, nearly the same figures as at Brandy Station. The fight for the Loudoun Valley was different from Brandy Station, however, in terms of terrain and the fighting experienced by the participants, which was an advantage for the Con-

---

[17] Ibid., 72–73.
[18] Report of Brig. Gen. Wade Hampton, 12 June 1863, *OR*, vol. 27, pt. 2.
[19] *Augusta Daily Chronicle & Sentinel* (19 June 1863).

federates. There were no massed, grand cavalry charges due to the undulating, broken ground. The Loudoun Valley consisted of steep-banked streams, numerous ravines with narrow, high-banked roads, and fields lined off on all sides by stone walls. This prevented extensive troop deployment and maneuvering, as was seen at Brandy Station. Instead, much of the cavalry fighting in the valley was by dismounted cavalry, characterized by "stubborn brawling—the kind of stirrup-to-stirrup mounted cavalry combat with saber and pistol that took a deadly toll of men and mounts."[20]

On 17 June, Judson Kilpatrick's Brigade encountered Thomas Munford's Virginia troopers near the village of Aldie. After several hours of back and forth fighting, Kilpatrick was reinforced and Munford withdrew toward Middleburg, where Stuart had established his headquarters. Col. Alfred N. Duffie and his 1st Rhode Island Cavalry arrived on the edge of Middleburg around 4:00 P.M., disrupting Stuart's evening with the local ladies of the town. Stuart sent Beverly Robertson and his North Carolina Cavalry,[21] which quickly routed the greatly outnumbered Federals. Pleasonton sent more of his force in, and the Confederate cavalry grudgingly gave up the town as Stuart fell back to a new position along Kirk's Branch. Fearing a growing strength among the Confederate cavalry, Pleasonton refused to follow up his successes and ordered his men to rest where they were.

As the fighting at Middleburg ended 19 June, a severe thunderstorm rolled through the Loudoun Valley and continued throughout the following morning.[22] Despite Joseph Hooker's impatience to learn more about Confederate troop movements, Pleasonton remained inactive, using the rainy day to rest and regroup. Lee's invasion of the North was already well underway by this time, although Federal commanders were still in the dark as to the Confederate army's precise movements.

On the morning of the 21st, Stuart established his screening line at the Bittersweet Farm on high ground just south of Ashby's Gap along the turnpike, about 2 miles west of Middleburg. Hampton deployed four of his regiments, numbering about 1,600 men, north and south of the Turnpike, with dismounted sharpshooters pushed forwarded to cover the Kirk's Branch bridge. Hampton's left flank was covered by Beverly Robertson's Cavalry Brigade.

---

[20] "Civil War in Loudoun Valley: The Cavalry Battles of Aldie, Middleburg, and Upperville, June 1863." Report prepared by Cultural Resources GIS of the National Park Service, 2004, 1–2.

[21] Robertson's Brigade was an undersized brigade created primarily for scouting purposes. The brigade was attached to Hampton's Division in the spring of 1863 and consisted of the 4th and 5th North Carolina Cavalry.

[22] Weather played an important role in many of the campaigns during the Civil War. For more, see Robert K. Krick, *Civil War Weather in Virginia* (Tuscaloosa: University of Alabama Press, 2007).

Judson Kilpatrick's Federal cavalry, the 2nd and 4th New York and the 6th Ohio, supported by Strong Vincent's Infantry,[23] made contact with Hampton's forces on the 21st and began pressing the Confederates in an effort to flank or turn Hampton's position. An intense fight developed when the 83rd Pennsylvania burst out of the woods surprising the 1st North Carolina on their right. The result was that Hampton's line began to unravel from south to north.

Hampton conducted a slow withdrawal from the Bittersweet Farm westward to Crummey's Run and Rocky Creek through Rector's Crossroads[24] to the stone bridge across Goose Creek, where the regiments spread out to oppose any further advance. Launching a coordinated attack on both Hampton's front and left flank simultaneously, Pleasonton and Kilpatrick forced Hampton to once again give ground. Stuart began withdrawing toward Upperville, where he set up a new defensive position on Vineyard Hill, astride Ashby's Gap Turnpike. Although forced to retreat, Hampton's Cavalry delayed the Federal advance by more than two hours, allowing Stuart the necessary time to establish his new line along the west side of the creek.

Hampton's regiments were deployed south of the vineyard near the Oakely Farm[25] just outside of the town. Continuing the attack, Kilpatrick's men spurred their horses and pitched into Robertson's North Carolinians. At nearly the same moment, John Buford's Union cavalry attacked the North Carolinians on their left flank, sending the Tarheels skedaddling through Upperville. As Kilpatrick's men chased after the fleeing North Carolinians, Hampton's men let loose with their Confederate yell and plowed into the flank of the pursuing Union cavalry, precipitating an intense and vicious melee with both pistol and saber. Hampton himself was said to have "shot down more than a couple of opponents."[26] The ferocity of the attack brought the Federal movements to an end on the western edge of Upperville. "Our regiment met the enemy with glittering sabers," wrote Wiley Howard, "clearing the field and showing the effect in the large number of the enemy's killed and wounded, while our own loss was moderately heavy."[27]

As the day came to an end, Stuart remained in control of Ashby Gap and Lee's movements remained a mystery to the Federal high command. During the day's fighting, the two Confederate cavalry brigades of Robertson and Hampton, some 3,000 troopers, fended off Union forces consisting of three cavalry and one infantry brigade, numbering about 5,800. Federal forces withdrew to Aldie Gap and

---

[23] 16th Michigan, 44th New York, 20th Maine, and 83rd Pennsylvania.

[24] Present-day Atoka, Virginia.

[25] "Civil War in Loudoun Valley," 29.

[26] Longacre, *Gentleman and Soldier*, 140–41.

[27] Howard, "Sketch of Cobb Legion Cavalry," 7–8.

Stuart moved up as far as Rector's Crossroads. From this position, Stuart decided to embark on an ambitious and highly controversial plan. Submitting his plan to Lee to leave two cavalry brigades to continue guarding the mountain passes, Stuart proposed to take three brigades on a raid around the Army of the Potomac into Maryland. Lee approved of Stuart's plan.

Camp Near Culpepper C. H.

June 1st 1863

My Dear Rosa

Since I wrote you last I have received yours of the 24th and am glad to hear of the well being of yourself and our dear little children. Last evening I recd Bishop Elliotts Sermon, which you sent me with the compliments of Dr. Henderson. I am obliged to you both. I hope the Bishop is mistaken in some points, but I was much pleased with the manly tone and Christian spirit of the sermon.

We are still doing nothing here. Our horses are improving wonderfully and if we can remain quiet a fortnight or three weeks longer our Regt. will be almost as full as it was last summer, but I think we are sadly in need of a good commander. And yet strange to say Col. Young stands I believe higher with the military generally about here than any man I know, talks larger, is more anxious for a fight, visits the girls more, stays less in Camp and has less to do with his Regt. than any body else. He is very polite however, and personally I have nothing to complain of.

I wish the abominable war was over and I at home. The army doesnt suit me, and the truth is, I have a feeling of contempt for men generally. I begin to think they are all alike and they are only redeemed from being devils by the influence exerted over them by the women. If you were not better than we are, what would become of the world. It would be beyond redemption. I have witnessed more contemptible meaness among men since I have been in the army than I ever dreamed of before and as for personal courage, Bishop Elliott is right it is a very common virtue, too much so ever to command respect, for every one has enough of it to enable him to do his duty in the excitement of the battle field, but you will think I am growing misanthropic. It is not so much that I believe Darling as my wish and extreme anxiety to be at home with you and our precious little children and I wouldnt care if I never saw another man until Tom and Willie grow up.

I am quite well again, and hope my poor little Scrap is comfortable and the Jennie is with you. I understand that she [will be] in Richmond on Friday and I presume by the time this reaches you she will certainly be with you. Give my love to her. Kiss the dear little folks for me, & accept for yourself a heart full of love and a thousand kisses from yr own

Will

Camp near Culpepper C. H.
June 5th 1863

My Dear Rosa,

I ought to have written you before but we have been very busy drilling and receiving and getting ready for a move. Gen Hood's division of Infantry is encamped just by us and we had scarcely a moment night or day that we can call our own as there are in the division two Brigades of Georgians.[28]

We have today a grand review of all the Cavalry—5 brigades. Gen Longstreet is here and I learn that his entire Corps will be up here in a day or two and I presume we will very shortly cross the Rhappahannock. The Yankees are certainly under the same impression and are as busy as beavers ditching and digging. I am very glad to learn Darling that you are feeling better and that the dear little folks are all well. They are too sweet. God bless their little souls. You don't know how I miss them and how I long to see you all again. I think the news from the West is cheering and I don't yet give up the idea of seeing you this winter with the war at an end.[29] I recd Mr Kennys letter. He is right about our bargain. I paid him eleven hundred dollars. If there was over 220 acres, I was to pay 5 dollars per acre, up to 240 acres, if over 240, I was only to pay 1200 dol so as there is 232 acres, you must pay him 60 dollars more. Tell Mr Atkinson I have settled his matter with our Quartermaster. He is to pay you $50 and $50 to Ed. Lumpkin for Mrs Cobb.[30] We have to leave here now to attend the review. I will write on my return to Camp. God bless you all Darling. Kiss the little ones for me and write often.

Your own
Will

Camp near Culpepper C. H. Va
June 6, 1863

My Dear Rosa,

We are now under marching orders with three days rations cooked & an additional supply of hard bread to be carried in the Commissary waggons. Gen Long-

---

[28] The two brigades in Hood's Division were Anderson's Brigade, commanded by Gen. George T. Anderson (7th, 8th, 9th, 11th, 59th Georgia troops) and Benning's Brigade, commanded by Gen. Henry L. Benning (2nd, 15th, 17th, and 20th Georgia troops).

[29] Despite intense pressure and a tightening encirclement, Confederate forces continued to hold out against Grant. But the Union force being exerted on the city was increasing as more and more reinforcements arrived.

[30] "Mrs Cobb" is Marion Cobb, wife of T. R. R. Cobb and sister of Ed Lumkin.

street with his entire Corps is here who are also moving. Where we are going, no one knows but presume it will be across the Rhappahannock.

I am quite well and the Regt are in fine health and spirits. I recd yours of the 3rd yesterday afternoon. Am glad to learn that Jennie is at last with you and that you are all well. God bless you all Darling. Write to me often. I will write when I can. We are soon to leave and are all busy as bees getting ready. My love to Jennie & kisses to the little folks.

Yr own
Will

Culpepper C. H. June 10, 1863

My Dear Rosa,

I telegraphed you this morning that I was unhurt and Capt. Ritch was captured. We yesterday had the severest and most extensive Cavalry action of the war. All the Yankee Cavalry crossed the Rappahannock supported by the Infantry and Artillery. The main body crossing at Beverly ford and the adjacent fords opposite Brandy Station on the Orange and Alexandria R. Road, at which point our Legion was encamped. The enemy drove in our pickets at daylight. They were immediately supported by Gen. Jones' Brigade[31] and our Brigade was ordered up & went into action soon after sunrise. Capts Ritch's & King's companies, with companies from other Regts of the Brigade were dismounted and put in as skirmishers and behaved with distinguished gallantry. They charged the Yankees and drove them through the woods for 300 or 400 yards into a point where our men were very much exposed both to the fire of their Infantry and a Cavalry charge. By this time our men had expended nearly all their ammunition and many of them were completely exhausted. Capts King and Ritch then ordered their men to fall back. Ritch telling them that he was too much exhausted to go with them. King led them back & the enemy advanced slowly on them until our ammunition was entirely gone and the enemy captured five of Ritch's men and two of King's were captured, three of Ritch's men were killed, Nick Ware, Carter and young Hardy of Jackson County, M. S. Simmons, Oshields and Harrington were slightly wounded. All concur in saying that Ritch refused to surrender, but fought single handed to the last until every barrel of both pistols was empty and then was taken fortunately unhurt. His gallantry was conspicuous to the entire brigade, as it was done in our sight, but we could not get up in time to relieve them. Young is convinced and I think Hampton will be that sharpshooters ought always be supported promptly by a Cavalry force. Soon after

---

[31] Jones's Brigade was one of Stuart's, commanded by William E. "Grumble" Jones, and included the 8th, 21st, 27th, 34th, 36th, and 37th Virginia Cavalry battalions.

this the report came that we were completely surrounded, another body of the enemy having crossed lower down, and Hampton's Brigade was ordered up to prevent the capture of our Batteries. We moved up at a gallop our Regt in the advance and the enemy ran up two guns on our left flank & we were ordered to charge. I was in the head of the Regt and recd the order Col Young having left us for about 100 yds to communicate with Gen Hampton or rather with one of Stuarts aids. I immediately wheeled the Regt to the left and increased the gait of the horses and the Artillerists did not unlimber their guns. Another courier had by this time come to Young saying that Stuarts Hdqtrs were in possession of the Yankees and our guns at that point would soon be captured. Young then ordered us to the right again and off we went in fine style, Young and myself leading. The Yankees thought we were in full retreat and the 10th N. York and part of the 2nd Maine were sent to charge us in the flank. We had then only about 100 or 120 men at the most. Young led in the first two companies & I the last two in what we call an "En Echelon" movement,[32] the balance of our men being dismounted as sharpshooters in another part of the field. When Young ordered the charge, our men went in with a rousing cheer. I had the old Ga. Troopers and the old Richmond Hussars with me and as Young met the head of their column I struck them on their left flank and the day was ours in less time than I can tell it. We killed their Major, captured their Lt. Col., ten captains and about 40 Lts & privates & strewn the ground with dead & wounded men and horses. Sabers, pistols & carbines were lying around loose. We pursued them until called off & with the Jeff Davis Legion & one squadron of the 1st S. C. Regt we drove off the support of their guns which were taken by the 11th Va. which also did good fighting. Our entire loss during the day is two officers wounded & one captured, 3 men killed & 24 wounded and twenty missing, some of them we know were taken, the others we do not know whether they were killed, captured, wounded or skulking. One horse killed, 15 wounded, 20 missing. We captured a good many of them in return. In the midst of the charge Church's horse was wounded and quicker than thought he was mounted on a Yankee's horse and in the charge again. He behaved very gallantly and came out with a bloody saber. I and old Marmion came out safely once more thanks to a kind Providence, my travelling blanket strapped on my saddle caught a carbine ball, which I now have in my pocket & which but for my blanket would probably have hurt me seriously. Besides what I have related our Regt did a good deal of other service & some of our men did good service, Young Landrum, McCroan & others you do not know distinguished themselves. Young Clanton of Augusta who came up to my relief at little Washington

---

[32] One group attacks first followed by the second and so forth. This type of attack was designed to force the portion of the enemy line first attacked to weaken and thereby call for their reserves, leaving the next sections hit to become more and more compromised.

was struck from his horse and trampled. He is walking about today but in considerable pain not dangerously hurt I hope. He is a man of undaunted courage. Gen Hampton's brother Lt. Col. Frank Hampton of the 2nd S. Carolina was killed. Col. Butler of the same lost a leg, another Regt suffered very seriously.[33] The whole Brigade behaved splendidly. We finally drove the enemy across the Rappahannock just before sunset. We had a large Infantry force at Culpepper 6 miles off but they did not come up to our support until the fight was over. I suspect Stuart did not want divided honors and would not send for them. God bless you all Darling. Kiss our dear little ones for me and think kindly and sweetly of me. Write when you can. We were on horseback until 12 o'clock & the hard work of yesterday makes me feel tired, tho' I was never in better health. Write often. Everything is again quiet

Yr own
Will

Brandy Station, Culpepper Co
June 12th 1863

My Dear Rosa

I have received your letter of the 4th inst since I wrote you last and am sorry to learn that you were indisposed. I hope sincerely that you received my telegram and letter in time to correct the misrepresentations of the Richmond Mess[34] and to relieve your anxiety about our recent fight. Our loss is not so great as we at first supposed. Some of the missing have come in and others are only slightly wounded that we feared were seriously wounded. I do not know the loss of the Division. Our Brigade lost in killed and missing 99 men, our Legion losing 44 of them nearly one half, 16 taken prisoner 6 killed the rest wounded so as to render them for the present unfit for service, others slightly wounded and counted in the above as they are still on duty. Our Regt has been very highly complimented for the part taken in the fight. We were fortunate in retaking Gen. Stuart's Hdqtrs, a very important position at a very critical time when all eyes were turned upon us & our men behaved with gallantry and spirit. I would not be surprised if our charge made Young a Brigadier. It is the first time we have ever met the enemy in an open field in a charge. Heretofore it has been in byways & roads & we succeeded as I have always told you

---

[33] "Lieut Senator Butler lost a leg, Col Frank Hampton was killed of the 2nd S.C. Cavalry, that was badly cut up as was the 4th Virginia Cavalry through whose lines Kilpatrick had broken, in fact, he had driven everything before him until he met the Cobb Legion." Athens *Banner* (30 April 1892).

[34] There was no Richmond *Messenger* newspaper. There was, however, for a very brief period, a *Messenger* published in Petersburg during this time.

we would succeed, with such a set of men to follow. I never have seen, nor do I ever again expect to see a field swept in such splendid style, as was that battle field by Hampton's Brigade assisted by one or two Virginia Regts. But for Hampton I think the day would have been lost. He acted promptly boldly and just in time to turn the tide of battle and every one here is loud in his praise, but as usual I presume he will not get credit for it with Stuart. He is too good an officer & too popular with the Army for that. The highest compliment we have received I think came from Lt. Col. Gordon of the 1st N.C. Regt. He met me soon after our charge with the greeting, "Well Delony, Cobbs Legion have done as usual." The work has worn us all out. I have been half sick ever since the excitement wore off & every one else is in about the same fix. Everything is very quiet though at present and I hope another days rest will bring us all right again. I think we will move forward in a few days tho' I know nothing. Gen Lee may keep us all here for some time yet and certain indications looks that way. He keeps his own counsel. I hope your wheat crop will turn out well. I presume you have cut it by this time. How comes on your corn, potatoes &c. Just think our little chickens are sweeter & better behaved than Jerrys ewe lamb. Of course you do. God bless you all Darling. Kiss the little Darlings for me. Keep up a cheerful spirit & write me often. Tell little Rosa Papa is looking for a letter from her. Tell Tom his horse behaved elegantly in the fight and is beginning to look well again. My love to Jennie & a large handful for yourself.

Ever yr own
Will

Camp near Stevensburg June 15, 1863
My Dear Rosa,

I was much disappointed yesterday in not hearing from you particularly as in your last letter you said you were not well. I have been thinking of my poor little Scrap and I have been worried about you no little my poor Darling. I hope & pray you are well again and that I may hear from you tonight. God bless you Darling when your letters come pleasant cheerfull and telling me of your now well being and that of our precious little children. I am happy and content even in Camp but when I do not hear it is tolerable.

We are now at or near rather our last winters camp and now pleasantly situated than we have been. I hope at least we will not have to pay as we did at Culpepper, $2.00 for a small dish of turnip greens and other things in proportion. Cobbs Legion stands very high with the ladies around here and I hope our dealers will not ask so high. This is a great consideration with gentle men who can get but little else but meat and bread, particularly as the bread and salt meat diet has also produced in this branch of the Army symptoms of Scurvy of which I have a most hotly horror.

I have just received a paper of the 9th. The Constitutionalist which you sent me on the 10th. Your last letter was dated the 4th. Why is this? I am told that Georgia is again excited by a Yankee raid towards Augusta. I hope there is nothing in the rumor and that you are all still safe. I notice that the Richmond papers are very severe upon our Cavalry fight on Tuesday last and I presume the other papers of the South will follow suit in their abuse of the Cavalry. One or two Regts did behave badly, this is the case always in every fight the Infantry have, but we contended successfully against at least double our numbers and drove them successfully across the river. Gen Hampton & Gen William Lee, the old Genl's son[35] done the brunt of the fight. Their brigades fought as well as men ever fought and when I find carping fools at home abusing and villifying us when Yankee bullets and sabers have been rattling in such close proximity to me I feel very much like coming home and becoming a critic myself.[36] Why don't you send me the Athens papers? I am told you have all become very military. How is your crop and garden & how are the little folks all doing? Kiss the dear little souls for me and give my love to Jenny, with a large hurt feel for my poor little Darling for her

Own

Will

In Camp Culpepper County Va

June 16th 1863

My Dear Rosa

About Sunrise this morning we recd orders to move immediately to Brandy Station and tents were struck by such as had them wagons loaded and on empty stomachs we took up the line of march thinking we were again to meet the enemy on the South side of the Rhappahannock. It turned out however that we only sent forward to relieve Gen Jones Brigade and we have again gone into camp, but I suspect it is a temporary one only. It is surmised among the Military that Hooker's purpose is to fall back upon Washington City and send reinforcements out West

---

[35] "The old Genl's son" was William Henry Fitzhugh Lee, second son of Robert E. Lee. At this time. "Rooney" Lee, as he was more often called, was commander of the 3rd Brigade of Stuart's Cavalry Division. Rooney was wounded at Brandy Station and captured two weeks later at Hickory Hill, Virginia, while recuperating. Exchanged 25 February 1864, he surrendered at Appomattox with his father.

[36] Many Confederate soldiers of the period write of these so-called "chimney-corner patriots," who were more than willing to sit at home by their firesides, warm and comfortable, while criticizing every aspect of the war then being fought.

and that Gen Lees object is now to present it which he will certainly do to make the Yankees regret & sue the day they adopted such a policy.

I wrote you yesterday morning and have heard nothing from you yet and I feel very, very anxious about you Darling. I hope my fears may be unfounded but I am thinking of my poor little wife day and night and almost fearing to hear from you. You must not be anxious about me and keep yourself cheerful and take good care of your self for me and posterity. I have not heard from you now since the 4th and you were then not well and how I miss your letters your own heart can tell. I think you Georgia people will imagine so many Yankee raids that the President will be in duty bound to send some troops among to prevent you frightening yourselves and every body else to death and I think I shall apply to come on and establish headquarters in Athens. What do you say to such an arrangement. You can then send off some of them gallant troops recently raised for home defense,[37] Why don't you tell me something of what the chivalry of Athens are doing. I hear it only from others. The ladies I infer do not appreciate the gallantry and self sacrificing spirit of their chivalrous defenders.[38]

How are our dear little children getting on & what are they doing. I am waiting patiently for a letter from dear little Rosa telling me all about the Pigs and Cats & chickens. I hope you have made a supply of wheat and that your garden will be bountiful. I am now in a position to appreciate the value of such home comforts. We were just beginning to live like gentlemen in Stevensburg, had a good dinner every day at the cost of only one dollar apiece which was a luxury we fully appreciated I assure you and I am very sure the old lady who furnished us made nothing by the operation. God bless you all Darling. Kiss the dear little ones for me & give my love to Jenny.

Ever Yr own
Will

---

[37] There was great excitement in North Georgia at the time, and over the course of the next several weeks, a number of "home defense" units were formed in Athens. See *Southern Watchman* (27 May, 3 June, 17 June, 24 June, and 8 July).

[38] Much of Delony's sarcasm here is due to the fact that although Stuart's forces were doing a very efficient job of screening Lee's movements, they were constantly under criticism in the Southern media due to their lack of "victories."

Fauquier Co. Va June 20 1863[39]

My Dear Rosa,

Just as I was leaving Culpepper Co. your letters of the 6th & 11th was handed me telling of dear little Willie's illness and the anxiety I am suffering to hear further from you is torturing to me. I have recd no telegram & hope that he is better but I know telegrams like letters are very uncertain and as I cannot now tell when I shall again get letters from home I can hardly contain myself. I can only hope for the best. Dear little fellow, how it rings my heart to hear of his suffering and my poor little wife without me to help & comfort her. God grant that he is well again. We have been having a hard time since I wrote but I believe men can stand anything. Day before yesterday afternoon we had a skirmish with the enemy at Warrenton[40] in the midst of a terrible thunder storm & of course got thoroughly wet went into camp after night, raining and dark as pitch. After considerable trials genius triumphed & we kindled a fire. John had in the meantime become frightened & run off with provisions, blankets & overcoat & was non est inventus notwithstanding all which I lay down with my feet to the fire slept until 3 1/2 oclock waked up rebuilt the fire, lay down & slept until daylight, troubled all day yesterday, got into camp & my fire was the only one made when it began to pour but John was up & I had a blanket over coat & then it rained I slept feel first rate this morning. John is asleep now, last night was too much for him. Church is all right & we have had a chance to dry up this morning, thus it is still cloudy. We were not in Stuarts fight yesterday. We have captured some of Hooker's dispatches. Lee knows what he is up to but nobody yet knows Lee's programme, except as they can judge from passing camp. We are 30 miles from Winchester near Upperville cooking 3 days rations, where next I do not know, but strongly suspect Lee is after mischief & you will hear from him. God bless you all Darling. I will write when I can. I do not know how I shall send this. Kiss the little ones for me. My love to Jenny & a heart full for yourself.

Yr own
Will

[22 June 1863]

My Dear Rosa, I am thankful to say that I am safe again after a desperate fight yesterday. Our Brigade was driven by a very heavy force of Infantry Cavalry and

---

[39] On the 20th, Stuart moved Hampton's Brigade to "the Bittersweet farm astride the Ashby's Gap Turnpike" outside Middleburg. "Civil War in Loudoun Valley," 23.

[40] The skirmishing referred to was some of the action prior to the Battle of Middleburg. Although not directly involved, some of the legion's companies were involved in the pursuit of the 1st Rhode Island on the 18th.

Artillery for about 8 miles disputing every inch of ground. Our regiment suffered severely and I am afraid that my old company & Ritch's are all captured say nothing of this horror yet. They were in picket & the last we heard of them they were almost surrounded, but as there were five roads meeting at their picket post we hope that Williams may have saved them. My saber scabbard saved old Marmion the ball striking the scabbard first and fortunately only broke his skin. We were put to a terribly severe test yesterday under a terrific and galling fire. I was ordered to drive up with two squadrons to their support, one of our battalions and artillery were in a terribly expanded position. Horses & men were falling at every discharge, but the men behaved like heroes & the Yankees who were sent forward to charge the battery could not be brought up. In the afternoon when the enemy thought it time to use their cavalry they ordered a charge. The 1st N.C. Regt. were retreating when I took the responsibility of ordering up our regiment & in we went, the North Carolinians at once rallied & with the Jeff Davis Legion we swept them from the field, killing wounding and capturing a good many of Buford's Brigade of regulars. Our men behaved splendidly, but we haven't many left. We are being fast used up. A few more such fights & we will need reinforcements from home. God bless you all Darling. Kiss the dear little children for me. God grant you may be all well. I am so anxious to hear from you that at times I know not what to do, so fearful that dear little Willie may not have recovered. Tell Capt. Ritch's friends we have heard from him since his capture through some ladies who saw him. He was well & in fine spirits, unhurt and obstinate to the Yankees as we could expect. They were treating him quite well. We are now at Ashby's gap with Gen Longstreet[41] and I am well. None of our wounded friends are hurt. Church again distinguished himself.[42]

I had to remain in the rear of the retiring column to save my videttes & as they came on to form a rear guard & indeed to retreat is a sorry thing. I was moving my

---

[41] "The enemy advanced his cavalry in full force against General Stuart, and drove him into and nearly through Ashby's Gap. I succeeded in passing part of McLaw's division across the river in time to occupy the Gap before night, and, upon advancing a line of sharpshooters the next morning at daylight the enemy retired.... General Stuart re-established his cavalry." Report of Lt. Gen. James Longstreet, 27 July 1863, *OR*, ser. 1, vol. 27, pt. 2, 357.

[42] "Never shall I forget while rallying the regiment as ordered by Col. Young, Yanks all around us and even our Horse Artillery firing into us, Will Church's look as he came up, brandishing his bloody sabre, his classical handsome face aglow with the glare of battle—'I killed three, Edge, I know, how many did you get!' And then with an impatient imprecation for his momentary boyishness, for he was as proud as he was brave, assisting to rally our men to meet their threatened charge encouraged by the smallness of our force. Never did he refer again to his numerous acts of gallantry, although he rescued our flag at Upperville from a Yankee trooper who had cut down our color bearer and was carrying it into the Federal lines by thrusting his sabre through his body tearing the flag from his hand and bringing it back to the Legion amid a hail storm of bullets." Athens *Banner* (30 April 1892).

new horse & he was as quiet & calm as if no firing was going on, he is invaluable to me. The day was excessively hot & the ride I gave him would have killed half the horses in the legion. You may judge some what of the heat whence I tell you that my bunch of keys next morning were thoroughly rusted in my pantaloons pocket by perspiration. Col. Young was absent at Richmond & has succeeded in getting two more guns, one a 12 lb howitzer & one 3 inch rifled piece. We will now be ready for them when they come again. Their object was cowardly to entice us into the field and open upon us with their artillery. They had six squadrons & I four. Had I attacked them their cavalry would have probably retreated until our ranks were broken by their artillery & their men would have heard of the last of our battalion at Fort Warren or some worse place. It was very good maneuvering on both side & I think nothing I have conducted yet has inspired the officers & men with as much Confidence in me, more than this, it amounts to nothing, except to give me more confidence in my self but Darling I am completely worn out tired to death, and you can have no idea how pleasant the sight is that the flag of truce below gives us a scepter. I learn that we are to be relieved on tomorrow or the next day. (As Dr. Long did not buy the lot when offered to him don't sell the middle lot for less than 3000 dolls. I am very indifferent about selling even at that. The lot next to Willingham sell for 2500 dolls. When I reach Richmond I will write to the magistrate & have it surveyed.) God bless you all Darling. Kiss my precious little ones for Papa and write to me often. Don't be discouraged about the War. McClellan was badly beaten. I am told that 50,000 stands of arms have been taken to Richmond from this battle field & the woods & streams are still filled with them. There are cannon yet to be taken up from the Pamen Key in Chickahominy River thrown there by the enemy _____ _____ echelon of army stores by the enemy.

Fauquier Co. Va, June 23, 1863

My Dear Rosa,

This is the last of my paper. We are now at the position we encamped night before last,[43] not anticipating another fight. The Yankees having fallen back. This day they fought all of Longstreet's Corps. We lost in our Regt 26 men only 3 killed.[44] Capt Williams escaped without losing a man. I can tell you nothing of our army movements, know nothing & except that we have been having a very hard time. John was with me & managed to get us an excellent supper for us last night & breakfast this morning which with a good night rest make me feel quite bright this

---

[43] Camp near Asbury's Gap. *Augusta Daily Chronicle & Sentinel* (1 July 1863).

[44] Total Confederate causalities for the day were estimated at just over 200 killed, wounded, and captured. Federal troops suffered about the same. "Civil War in Loudoun Valley," 34.

morning. I hope Darling you are all well and that dear little Willie has entirely recovered. We are about sending a Courier to Culpepper and hope in 2 or 3 days to
get letters from home. I am thinking of you and our dear little ones all the time.
Write to me often. I will write when I can of that be assured. Whenever I have the
chance to send you a line. God bless you all. Kiss the little folks. My love to Jenny
and a heart full for Yourself

From
Will

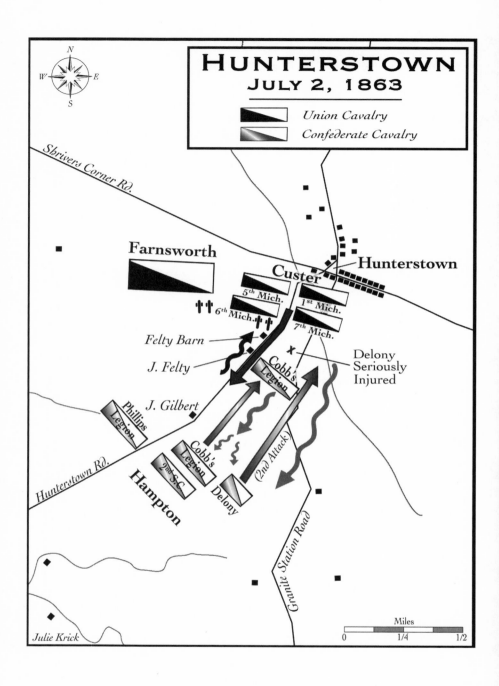

HUNTERSTOWN
JULY 2, 1863

Union Cavalry
Confederate Cavalry

N
W   E
S

Shrivers Corner Rd.

Farnsworth

Custer

Hunterstown

5th Mich.

1st Mich.

6th Mich.

7th Mich.

Felty Barn

J. Felty

Cobb's Legion

Delony Seriously Injured

x

J. Gilbert

Phillips Legion

Cobb's Legion

2nd S.C.

Delony

(2nd Attack)

Hampton

Hunterstown Rd.

Granite Station Road

Julie Krick

Miles
0   1/4   1/2

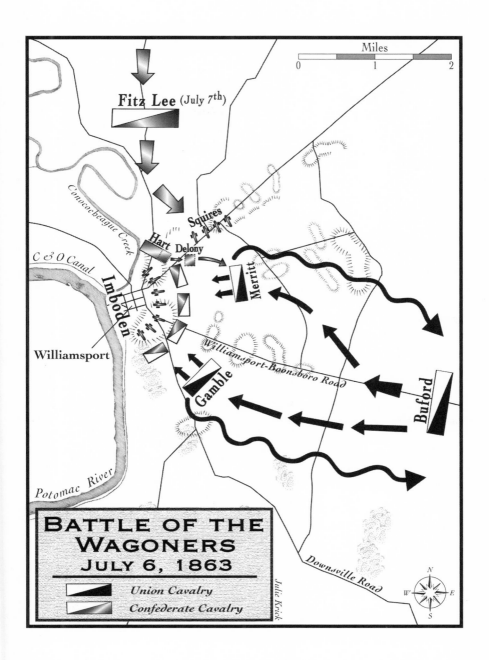

Miles
0   1   2

Fitz Lee (July 7th)

Conococheague Creek

C & O Canal

Imboden

Williamsport

Squires

Hart Delony

Merritt

Williamsport-Boonsboro Road

Gamble

Buford

Potomac River

Downsville Road

BATTLE OF THE WAGONERS
JULY 6, 1863

Union Cavalry
Confederate Cavalry

Julie Krick

N
W   E
S

Chapter 12

Gettysburg:
June 1863–September 1863

In the lost battle,
Borne down by the flying,
Where mingles war's rattle
With groans of the dying.
    —Sir Walter Scott

At 1:00 A.M. on Thursday, 25 June 1863, J. E. B. Stuart and three of his five cavalry brigades, including Hampton's Brigade, set out on what some have termed Stuart's "glory ride." Leaving from Salem Depot, Virginia, Stuart intended to encircle the Union army passing between them and Washington before rejoining Lee north of the Potomac River. It was the beginning of his second encirclement of the Union army, but unlike his first, this one took his cavalry away from the most important stage of the Gettysburg Campaign and its vitally needed assistance to Lee.

There were brief skirmishes at Fairfax Station, Virginia, on the 27th, near Rockville, Maryland, on the 28th, and at Westminster, Maryland, on the 29th. Pierce M. B. Young recorded, "We crossed the Potomac near Dranesville. The army having crossed above...we were at Rockville near Washington, D.C. My regt. was in three miles of Georgetown and in sight of the church spires. We marched on day and night taking prisoners and transportation until we reached Hanover (29th June), Pa.; here we were met by a strong force of cav. under General Kit Patrick; my regt. was again successful and camped by Gen. Hampton."[1]

At Hanover, the Confederate cavalry attacked a Federal cavalry regiment and drove it through the streets of the town. At that same moment, Elon Farnsworth's 5th New York Cavalry arrived on the scene, attacked the Confederates, and nearly captured Stuart. The fighting flowed back and forth until Farnsworth was reinforced with the arrival of George Custer's Michigan Brigade, after which Stuart broke off action and continued north and east in his attempt to get around the Union army, finally arriving at

---

[1] Lynwood M. Holland, *Pierce M. B. Young: The Warwick of the South* (Athens: University of Georgia Press, 1964) 73–74. *OR*, ser. 1, vol. 27, pt. 2, 692.

Gettysburg on 2 July, just prior to Longstreet's attack. Aside from netting some prisoners and supplies, as well as disrupting Federal communications, Stuart's raid did not screen Lee's advance or provide Lee with the much-needed intelligence on the movements of the Federal army.

After their arrival at Gettysburg, Stuart posted Hampton's Brigade astride the Hunterstown Road a few miles northeast of the town. This position was intended to block any movements by a Union force trying to get behind Lee's lines. At the same time, Kilpatrick's cavalry under Custer and Farnsworth began probing for the end of the Confederate left flank. When Custer's 6th Michigan ran into Confederate troopers under Fitz Lee near Cress Ridge, Custer immediately attacked. Lee's 1st Virginia was forced back as Custer's men pursued them. At that moment, two of Hampton's regiments crashed into the flank of Custer's pursuing Michiganders. The suddenness of the Confederate attack caused Custer to immediately begin falling back with Hampton's Brigade in hot pursuit. During the pursuit and counter-pursuit, Custer regrouped his men and launched a countercharge directly toward the incoming Confederate troopers. The two sides collided with immense force resulting in fierce hand-to-hand combat. Young recorded that Cobb's Legion "was attacked in the rear vigorously by a large column of cav.—my regt. being on that day the rear guard was first attacked. We immediately turned and fought desperately till night—most of the time hand to hand with saber."[2]

Near Hunterstown, the Michiganders charged headlong at the Confederate cavalry and Hampton's command dismounted and unleashed a solid wall of shot that unhorsed many of the enemy saddles, including Custer's. "Men and horses went down in a heap before they reached the Legion's position."[3] Custer was able to escape death or capture only by the quick witted heroics of his orderly who rushed in, through a barrage of lead, and took his commander off of the field to safety on the back of his own horse. Within a matter of minutes, most of the men with Custer who were not already dead or badly wounded were fleeing toward the rear.

Instead of regrouping, Hampton ordered Young to counterattack and charge after the fleeing Yankees. Spurring their horses and pursuing the Union cavalry up the road, Young and Cobb's Legion soon found themselves dodging a shower of lead from small arms as well as shells from a rapidly deployed Union battery. At one point during the fight, Pvt. James Parsons of the 6th Michigan engaged in a personal duel with Hampton. According to one story, when Parson's Spencer rifle jammed after firing off several

---

[2] Report of Wade Hampton. *OR*, ser. 1, vol. 27, pt. 2, 679–85, 721–23; also quoted in, Holland, *Pierce M. B. Young*, 73–74.

[3] Longacre, *Custer and His Wolverines: The Michigan Cavalry Brigade, 1861–1865* (Conshohocken, PA: Combined Books, 1997) 148–49.

shots at his adversary, Hampton waited for the trooper to clear his weapon before firing and wounding the private.[4]

The fighting lasted most of the afternoon, ending just after dark when the Union cavalry withdrew to the southeast. During this intense melee, the legion lost five officers and twenty-seven men killed.[5] Hampton reported that "Cobb's Legion, which led in this gallant charge, suffered quite severely, Lieutenant-Colonel [W. G.] Delony and several other officers being wounded, while the regiment lost in killed quite a number of brave officers and men, whose names I regret not being able to give."[6] Howard wrote:

> Our command...while charging a body of cavalry down a lane leading by a barn [Felty Barn] ran into an ambuscade of men posted in the barn who brought death and destruction upon us. Withing five minutes some four or five officers were killed and woulnded and about fifteen men were slain or wounded. Col. Deloney leading the charge on his prancing bay Marion [sic] was unhorsed, his charger being shot, fell on him so that with great difficulty he extricated himself from his prostrate position...three Yankees seeing his almost helpless position and that he was an officer of note dashed upon him to subdue, capture or kill him shooting or cutting him from their horses. But this superior fighter, with his Hugunot [sic] blood boiling, raised himself on one knee and with his desterous and wiry arm fenced and parried their blows...bugler H. E. Jackson...spurred his horse to the fray to Delony's aid, fencing with these daring assailants.[7]

While driving the 6th Michigan Cavalry back, Delony was sabered three times over the right eye, which reportedly came near to cutting it out. Young reported, "I lost in one charge during ten minutes six commissioned officers killed out of my own regt. This was a great mortality for the length of time engaged. My Lt. Col. [Delony] was badly cut with a saber while leading the charge."[8] Delony's wound was much more severe than he alluded to in his letter to Rosa on the 4th.

Of greater consequences at the time was the loss of the brigade's commanding officer. During the fighting, "General Hampton was severely wounded with two saber cuts on the head and was shot in the thigh."[9] While Hampton recuperated from his wounds, Stuart personally led Hampton's Cavalry.

---

[4] Longacre, *Custer and His Wolverines*, 140; Eric J. Wittenberg, *One of Custer's Wolverines: The Civil War Letters of Brevet Brigadier General James H. Kidd, 6th Michigan Cavalry* (Kent: Kent State University Press, 2000) 49.

[5] Athens *Banner* (30 April 1892).

[6] Report of Wade Hampton. *OR*, ser. 1, vol. 27, pt. 2, 724.

[7] Howard, "Sketch of Cobb Legion Cavalry, 9.

[8] "In a charge a week ago near Gettysburg in which Col Delany was wounded with a sabre cut over the head my horse ran away carrying me through almost the entire column of the enemy." Barrington S. King to Bessie. Tammy Harden Galloway, *Dear Old Roswell: The Civil War Letters of the King Family of Roswell, Georgia* (Macon, GA: Mercer University Press, 2003) 28–29.

[9] Will Delony to Rosa Delony, near Gettysburg, Pennsylvania, 4 July 1863, Delony Papers.

With the end of the Battle of Gettysburg, the Confederate army began their retreat back to Virginia. Delony was initially taken to one of the cavalry hospital tents Stuart set up on the Hunterstown Road 4 miles from Gettysburg. The following morning, Delony and the other wounded at the hospital were placed in ambulances in the anticipated retreat. While waiting for the ambulance to move, he was able to write a quick letter to Rosa. Optimistically, Delony assured her his wound was slight and would heal fast. He recapped the Hunterstown fight. praising the legion and the "old Georgia Troopers," and then cut his letter short in order to hear from the courier the plans of their retreat.[10]

Delony and the numerous wounded were loaded into wagons and set out in a 17-mile-long wagon train of nearly 6,000 for the retreat back to Virginia. Adding to the misery of the wounded soldiers was the pouring rain. Lee assigned Gen. John Imboden to safeguard the army's wounded as they retreated to safety. The train was to proceed to Williamsport and then across the Potomac, with Stuart's brigades covering the train's left flank. Some problems arose, however, from the recent rains. Reaching Cashtown, the train turned west toward Hagerstown before reaching Williamsport on 5 July. When Imboden and his Confederate cavalry reached Williamsport at dawn on the 5th, he saw firsthand how the rain had swollen the Potomac River, making it impossible to ford. To make matters worst, Union cavalry had passed through the area earlier, destroying the pontoon bridge over the river just south at Falling Waters, Maryland, causing the train to remain in Williamsport. Before he could commence convalescing, Will Delony was faced with one more battle, as Buford's Cavalry was fast on their rear.

The Federal attack came from Buford's three brigades, 7,000 strong, galloping up the Boonsboro Road. Their orders were to seize the town of Williamsport, destroy the train, and prevent the Confederate army from crossing into Virginia. Knowing that his force of Virginians was not enough to stem the Union advance, Imboden formed a 3-mile, semi-circular defensive line protecting the two approaches to Williamsport along the Hagerstown Turnpike and the Boonsboro Road, setting his defensive line 1 mile east of the town along a ridge, with his right anchored on the Potomac River and his left on a nearby creek.

Recognizing that he was greatly outnumbered, Imboden called upon volunteers from the wounded who could still fight. Hearing the growing boom of cannons, Delony climbed out of his ambulance, mounted his horse and "gathered up the stragglers about the wagons and went to the field with thirteen men," he reported to Rosa, eventually commanding a "heterogeneous crowd" of around 200 that he led in "support [of] Hart's Battery which was formerly attached to our brigade."[11] "With his commanding presence,

---

[10] Ibid.

[11] Capt. James Hart's South Carolina Battery was assigned by Lee to Imboden and joined the wagon train at Cash Town.

bull dog courage and superb generalship," Howard later recalled, "he made a most determined resistance and successfully held them at bay until re-enforcements arrived, thus avoiding a train stampede and a great disaster to Lee's retreat."[12]

The battle raged back and forth for three hours. Trying to relieve the pressure on his right, Imboden ordered Hart to advance on Wesley Merrit's Federal cavalry on his left. Hart attacked by firing his guns into Merritt's right flank and then ordered Delony's motley crew of wagoners, teamsters, and wounded into the fray. Delony wrote to Rosa that his unit "drove the enemy about three fourths of a mile and about dark had completely flanked one of their batteries." Soon afterward, Gen. Fitzhugh Lee's Cavalry Brigade arrived on the scene, striking Merritt's right flank. With the attack of Delony's spirited group and now the arrival of fresh Confederate cavalry, Buford realized his position was untenable and he ordered a full withdrawal. The Confederate wagon train was saved, and Delony dismissed his pieced-together defenders, who then "gave me three cheers and said, if the Yankees came again today they would all come up if I would command them which I promised to do."[13]

For the next several days the wagon train was stuck in Williamsport waiting for the river to subside. By now, Delony was battling a high fever caused by his now-infected wound. Eventually, he was able to find a private home in which to recuperate. Delony informed Rosa on 11 July that he and Captain Barrington King were "comfortably lodged in the house of a Unionist[14] who furnishes everything needed," and their plan was to continue "across the river" where he had "just learned of an opportunity."[15]

The Army of Northern Virginia began the Gettysburg Campaign with 75,000 men and staggered back into Virginia with 23,000 fewer, including losing some of the Army's best officers and men.[16] The three corps, or what was left of them, established camps around Culpeper Court House between the Rappahannock and the Rapidan. As criticism poured in from the Confederate nation over the defeat at Gettysburg, Lee felt the personal pain of a commander's responsibility. Lee's spirits were further dampened by the return of his heart ailment and the accompanying symptoms of angina. He became so despondent that he wrote President Jefferson Davis on 31 July, singularly accepting

---

[12] Howard, "Sketch of Cobb Legion Cavalry," 24–25.

[13] Will Delony to Rosa Delony, Williamsport, 7 July 1863, Delony Papers.

[14] Delony later corrects this statement.

[15] Will Delony to Rosa Delony, Williamsport, 11 July 1863, Delony Papers. The "opportunity" was to go to Staunton, Virginia, with his travelling buddy, King, and stay while recuperating with King's sister, Catherine Evelyn King Baker, whose husband, William E. Baker, was the pastor of the First Presbyterian Church. The home was the birthplace of Woodrow Wilson just seven years earlier. The manse stands today as a national historical landmark.

[16] There were seventeen casualties among the fifty-two Confederate generals engaged at Gettysburg. William D. Henderson, *The Road to Bristol Station: Campaigning with Lee and Meade, August 1–October 2* (Lynchburg, VA: H. E. Howard, Inc., 1987) 51.

blame for the defeat.[17] A few days later, a depressed Lee wrote to Davis again offering his resignation and asking to be replaced with a "younger and abler man than myself."[18] Davis responded quickly, and on 11 August, in a conciliatory letter to Lee, wrote, "Our country could not bear to lose you."[19]

As Delony and Captain King recuperated, Cobb's Legion Cavalry was on the move. On 12 July the legion took up a position at "Hedgersville to cover the Confederate retreat."[20] The recent rains continued to hamper the recrossing of the Potomac until a floating bridge was built near Falling Waters. Both Longstreet's and A. P. Hill's corps crossed on the night of 13 July illuminated by bonfires placed on both sides of the river.[21] "We retreated from Martinsburg," wrote Young, "through Winchester thence up the Staunton Pike and over the mountains to Culpeper Court House taking up our old line on the Rappahannock."[22]

"As I remember," penned Howard, "...a portion of our command together with some scattering detachments of Virginia cavalry, together with three guns of a Maryland battery, under command of Gen. P. M. B. Young, who was just returning to the army after recovering from wounds, played a bold and hazardous game of bluff protecting Lee's army train passing by Culpepper Court House across Hazel Run and on towards Warrenton."[23] As the Federals were gaining ground on Lee's train, Young carried out a bluff that caused the Union army to hesitate, gaining the Confederate army precious time to put more distance between the two forces.

> Two army corps of the enemy had crossed the Rappahannock at Kelly's Ford and were rapidly moving uncomfortably near our wagon train, we having no adequate force of cavalry and no infantry to arrest their progress. Our squadron with the Virginia cavalry, all told not over five hundred men, if so many, were quickly and skillfully disposed by Young so as to conceal our real force and the artillery brought forward and engaged in a protracted duel with that of the enemy. The range was soon ascertained, Young himself personally directing the handling of the guns and sighting the pieces, while our whole command under his orders and, in his peculiar phraseology, kept time to the music of guns and

[17] Emory M. Thomas, *Robert E. Lee: A Biography* (New York: W. W. Norton and Co., 1995) 307, and Clifford Dowley, *Lee* (Boston: Little Brown, 1965) 307.

[18] Douglas Southall Freeman, *R. E. Lee*, vol. 3 (New York: Charles Scribner's Sons, 1935) 156, 157.

[19] Freeman, *R. E. Lee*, 156–58; Thomas, *Robert E. Lee*, 403, 404.

[20] "Hedgersville," as Young wrote of it in his report, is the present town of Hedgesville in Berkley County, West Virginia. Holland, *Pierce M. B. Young*, 73–74.

[21] For more on the retreat from Gettysburg, see Kent Masterson Brown, *Retreat from Gettysburg* (Chapel Hill: University of North Carolina Press, 2005).

[22] *OR*, vol. 27, pt. 2, 679–85, 721–23; also quoted in, Holland, *Pierce M. B. Young*, 73–74.

[23] Howard, "Sketch of Cobb Legion Cavalry," 4–5.

hurtling, bursting shells above us and about our artillery by yelling, as he said, "like hell and damnation." Couriers and others under his orders dashed about, along and in front of what the Yanks supposed to be our concealed line of battle, along the zigzag edge of a wood where had formerly been an army camp strewed with barrels, etc. Our friends, the enemy, stopped apparently dismayed at the audacity of our maneuvering and let their battery pound away at ours and shell the woods promiscuously for more than two hours while the sun was sinking low in the west.... At length nightfall began to come on, our enemy gradually ceased their galling artillery fire and their sharp-shooters stopped whizzing their long range missiles about us, a band, ordered some two hours before from our wagon train, arrived on the scene and was placed by Young in front of our battery and played "Dixie Land," while the boys shouted the rebel yell for all there was in it, and men lighted up bonfires of barrels, brush and what-not along our supposed zigzag line of battle, as if an army after a skirmish held its position and was making the usual campfires, the men playing this farce whooping and hallowing all the while.... The farce was ended, the bold bluff had done its perfect work and our train was safe beyond Hazel Run protected by Marse Robert's infantry.[24]

Stuart's cavalry suffered severely at Gettysburg and were in bad need of rebuilding. Half of the Confederate cavalry was now dismounted and in no condition to react quickly to any offensive threat. When the war started, the proud Confederate cavalry consisted of men who volunteered for service and brought with them their own horses. This gave the cavalry an "aristocratic flavor" that complemented their hard-earned reputation for "independence, dash and bravery."[25] Now with so many horses destroyed, it was difficult to replace the mounts, especially of the quality that once characterized the proud division. On 17 August, with many of the mounts killed or dead of diseases, 120 men arrived in Augusta looking for horses.[26] The troopers who could not find horses were issued rifles and temporarily designated as infantry, unofficially known as "Company Q." Many a proud trooper, however, rejected his reduced status. Their response infuriated Stuart and he abolished Company Q in a circular dated 29 July, denouncing those who had "so long disgraced the cavalry service."[27]

Now safely back in Virginia and settling into their old camp at Camp Stevensburg, in Culpeper County, Virginia, the legion took part in numerous skirmishes over the next

---

[24] Ibid.

[25] Henderson, *Road to Bristol Station*, 8.

[26] *Augusta Daily Chronicle and Sentinel* (8 August 1863).

[27] Ibid., 9.

couple of weeks as Federal forces continued to probe Confederate lines.[28] They remained at Camp Stevensburg until 1 August, when "the enemy's cavalry advanced in large force," reported Young, "and from strange circumstances the only force brought to oppose five brigades of cavalry was Hampton's small brigade which from the heavy inroads of death, wound and disease of the late campaign had been reduced to about eight or nine hundred men in the saddle. We commenced fighting at noon on the same memorable bloody field of Brandy Station on August 1, 1863."[29] In this fighting, the legion once more suffered heavily.[30] Colonel L. S. Baker, commanding Hampton's Brigade while Hampton recovered from his recent wounding, was himself wounded early in the battle, and Young took command of the entire brigade.[31]

On 4 August, Lee shifted his army south behind the Rapidan, around Orange Court House, a better position from which to supply his army.[32] He established his headquarters in a central location a few miles east of the town to better inspect and direct the entrenchment of his army.

Delony informed his wife that he lost his beloved horse, Marmion, at Hunterstown when he was knocked from the saddle and "old Marmion...continued the charge...and went into the enemy line."[33] He still lamented Marmion's loss in his next letter but was somewhat optimistic about replacing his beloved mount "with a fine looking bay" he captured at Williamsport. Several days later, however, his optimism turned to regret as he wrote that the loss of "Marmion was impairable." He sadly acknowledged he would never again have a horse like his "spirited Marmion" and sentimentally confessed his "attachment for the old fella and how I miss him...the whole Regiment deplores his loss."[34]

The injuries to Delony and Hampton, and to many other officers in the Confederate cavalry, were an example of the heavy toll the Gettysburg Campaign took on the Army of Northern Virginia. During the next couple of months, as Delony recuperated, so too did the legion. The loss of seasoned cavalry personnel and front-line horses con-

---

[28] Cobb's Georgia Legion Cavalry remained at Camp Stevensburg until 28 August 1863. See William S. Smedlund, *Camp Fires of Georgia Troops, 1861–1865* (Lithonia, GA: Kennesaw Mountain Press, 1994).

[29] *OR*, vol. 27, pt. 2, 679–85, 721–23; also quoted in, Holland, *Pierce M. B. Young*, 73–74.

[30] "I have not yet learned the loss on our part," wrote W. B. Young, captain of Co. B, Richmond Hussars, of the legion, "although we lost a good many men. S. L. Bashford and J. W. Day of my company are missing, and I am afraid captured. My horse was killed by a shell. A piece of shell passed through my hat, and another piece struck me on the thigh." *Augusta Daily Chronicle & Sentinel* (1 July 1863).

[31] Holland, *Pierce M. B. Young*, 74.

[32] Dowley, *Lee*, 401.

[33] Will Delony to Rosa Delony, near Gettysburg, Pennsylvania, 4 July 1863, Delony Papers.

[34] Ibid., Staunton, 17 July 1863.

siderably reduced the efficiency of the Confederate cavalry. At the same time the Union cavalry was growing in experience, strength, and efficiency.

As part of his plan to rebuild the Confederate cavalry, Stuart asked Lee to reorganize the division into a corps with two divisions. Lee approved and appointed Wade Hampton and Fitzhugh Lee to head the two new divisions and promoted both to major generals. Stuart was hopeful that in the reorganization Lee would promote him to lieutenant general as cavalry corps commander. Lee did promote him as corps commander but kept Stuart's rank as major general. Lee, according to historian Emory Thomas, "used the non-promotion to chasten Stuart without injuring him."[35] The proud cavalry commander was the target of constant criticism by the media and the public after the surprise at Brandy Station and his late arrival at Gettysburg. This public criticism of Stuart's leadership is probably what drove the cavalier leader to reform the cavalry in order to "best meet the increasing strength and efficiency of the enemy's cavalry."[36]

The reorganization was not well received by some of the cavalry leaders. The complaints came mainly from those passed over for promotion. The dissenters included "Grumble" Jones and Thomas L. Rosser, both of whom harbored personal issues with Stuart.[37] Delony may not have been an outwardly vocal dissenter, but he was outspoken in his frustration to Rosa. "The new organization," he wrote, "was neither good for the service nor the country, but only for the special benefit of a favored few."[38] Delony was becoming increasingly disillusioned with military service and the manner in which the war was being conducted. He continually wrote Rosa of his dissatisfaction with officers and the conduct of the war in general. He became so irritated and distraught at one point that he wrote "my services will not be much longer needed by the Confederacy and as soon as affairs begin to look more favorable I shall tender my resignation and I am tired of being ordered about by a set of jackasses and don't mean to submit to it very much longer."[39]

By now, Delony had fought in some fifty engagements since the start of the war, and despite his periodic mood swings, when it came time to engage the enemy his adrenaline flowed to a fever pitch. He later wrote Rosa of his disappointment that an anticipated clash with the enemy never materialized. "Strange as it may appear to one at

---

[35] Emory M. Thomas, *Bold Dragoon: The Life of J. E. B. Stuart* (New York: Harper & Row, 1986) 261.

[36] Henderson, *Road to Bristol Station*, 101.

[37] Ibid., 12.

[38] Will Delony to Rosa Delony, camp near Orange County Court House, (no date) Delony Papers.

[39] Ibid.

home," he wrote, "there is a fascination in danger which allures a solider and perhaps it is well that it is so to those who are soldiers from necessity and sense of duty."[40]

After more than a month recovering from the saber wounds he received at Hunterstown, Delony joined his men at the legion camp near Stevensburg, Virginia, just south of Brandy Station, near the Orange and Alexander Railroad, "very near the last winter encampment."[41] The two saber cuts to his head above his right eye created what he described to Rosa as a "Y"-shaped "honorable scar."[42] The wounds left "quite a sink in my forehead...you can almost lay your finger in."[43]

While Stuart was rebuilding the cavalry, Lee was rebuilding the infantry and artillery of the shattered Army of Northern Virginia. It was necessary for him to use "amnesty, furloughs and executions to fight desertions" in the rebuilding process. By the end of August the army was up to a little over 60,000.[44] Soon after, Davis persuaded Lee to send Longstreet's Corps to aid Pierre G. T. Beauregard and Braxton Bragg in South Carolina and Tennessee. On 8 September, two of Longstreet's brigades were ordered to Charleston to aid Beauregard in meeting the increasing pressure from Union forces on the vital port city. The rest of the corps was sent to Chickamauga to aid Bragg in the upcoming Confederate campaign. The departure of some 14,600 men from Longstreet's Corps left Lee with fewer than 46,000 troops to defend Richmond.[45]

Stuart was able to hold onto the land between the Rapidan and Rappahannock rivers throughout that period until mid-September when Meade made a more concerted push into the area. When Longstreet's departure was confirmed by intelligence on 11 September, Meade prepared a full-scale advance on Richmond beginning in the Culpeper area, where the previous month the opposing cavalry forces had been constantly clashing. Meade sent John Buford's 1st Cavalry Division to spearhead an advance across the Rappahannock. At dawn on 13 September, two divisions of Federal cavalry with infantry and artillery support crossed the Rappahannock driving Stuart all the way back to the Rapidan River below Rapidan Station. Hampton's Brigade, a unit of some 900 veterans, outnumbered almost four to one, fought gallantly but was almost annihilated before it received relief from Stuart and A. P. Hill's Infantry. Stuart's Virginia cavalry lost three artillery pieces and his critics seized the moment to smear him. The Second Battle of Brandy Station was a costly one, although Hampton was not personally engaged, as he was still recovering from his wounds at Gettysburg. Four different commanders led

---

[40] Will Delony to Rosa Delony, camp near Stanton, 5 September 1863, Delony Papers. F. Nash Boney, *A Pictorial History of the University of Georgia* (Athens: University of Georgia Press, 1984) 45.

[41] Will Delony to Rosa Delony, camp near Stevensburg, 17 August 1863, Delony Papers.

[42] Ibid., Staunton, 20 July 1863, 28 July 1863.

[43] Ibid., camp near Stevensburg, 18 August 1863.

[44] Freeman, *R. E. Lee*, 163; Thomas, *Robert E. Lee*, 307.

[45] Thomas, *Robert E. Lee*, 309; Freeman, *R. E. Lee*, 165.

Hampton's Brigade that day; all were wounded and carried off the field including Colonel Young of Cobb's Legion, who was shot in the chest leading the charge. The brigade also lost fifty valuable horses.[46]

Thomas Rosser wrote his wife that this is "the finishing stroke to Stuart's declining reputation."[47] Delony, who long had issues with Stuart, vented to Rosa about Stuart's perceived favoritism to the Virginia regiments. He complained that had the Virginia regiments followed Stuart's order, Hampton's Cavalry would not have been needed to "bail them out." We "saved what was left of them...though outnumbered five to one... we got no credit for this." He vented further that he had "no confidence in Virginia cavalry, they do no fighting and we are damned with them and I think it is all due to Stuart's policy of complimenting his favorites whether they do badly or well.... I shall rejoice when Hampton returns."[48]

In the meantime, Will Delony was forced to continue operating under Stuart's direct command. In his last letter to his beloved Rosa, Delony was certain he would soon be coming home. "I am looking forward," he wrote, "with a good deal of confidence to spending some time with you and the four little ones this winter."[49]

* * *

Near Gettysburg, Pa July 4 [1863]

My Dear Rosa

I have just learned that there is an opportunity afforded me of writing you a short note. I have cause once more for gratitude that I have gone thus far through the late terrific fighting with only a slight wound. A saber cut on the head. I am able to ride about tho' am not on duty. The surgeon says it will heal up very shortly by the first intention and scarcely leave a scar, so don't be uneasy about me as the wound is a slight one. I have lost some warm friends in the late battle. Among others Lt. House was killed instantly in a charge in which I was wounded shot thro the head. Lt. Brooks of Ritch's company, Lt. Pugh and Lt. Cheeseborough of Augusta, and Lt. Smith of Capt. King's company were all killed at the same time day before yesterday or rather Pugh and Cheeseborough are mortally wounded and in a dying condition. Several privates were killed and wounded, none that you know. The charge did not last ten minutes but it was desperate and bloody for the time. Col. Young's horse was killed he was unhurt. Capt. King was badly bruised by a fall from his horse but is still on duty. The legion did its

---

[46] Holland, *Pierce M. B. Young*, 74.

[47] Thomas, *Bold Dragoon*, 263.

[48] Will Delony to Rosa Delony, camp near Orange County Court House, 21 September 1863, Delony Papers.

[49] Ibid. Will and Rosa's fifth child (fourth surviving), Martha, was born in November 1863.

duty as usual with the old Ga Troopers in the lead and we drove the enemy back in splendid style. Yesterday there was another severe Cavalry engagement.[50] Our Regt. was not in it. Gen. Hampton was severely wounded, two saber cuts on the head and shot in the thigh. His wounds are thought to be not dangerous but painful and severe. Col. Baker, of N.C., a good officer, will now command the brigade. I have not had a line from you since I last wrote and still feel most anxious to hear from dear precious Willie. I have no more time to write I am afraid now that I am late for the courier. I am doing well, darling and shall remain with the wagons until I am quite well before going on duty. Young Henry Jackson, House's brother in law, behaved like a hero and after I was cut down, saved my life. Tell his father of it if you see him. I lost old Marmion.[51] After I fell from him, he continued on in the charge and when our men halted he kept on and went into the enemy's line, much to my regret. I have another good one, however. God bless you all, darling. I have just heard that Capt. Carlton is wounded in the shoulder, Sam Alexander in the elbow, Tom Frierson slightly wounded. This is all I know as yet. Yes, Capt. Dean's son Charley and Dickson's son killed. Young Hemphill mortally wounded as I have just heard. Will write you when I can.

Ever yours
W. G. Delony

Williamsport July 7th 1863

My Dear Rosa

Your two notes of the 13th & 14th were received by me yesterday afternoon and the relief they have brought me is inexpressible in words. Dear little Willie has been ever present to my mind & heart and the fear that he was still sick or that worst had happened had become almost insupportable. I wrote to you a few days ago immediately after the severe fighting at Gettysburg, Penn. but I learn that our mail was captured by the enemy & I know that your anxiety for me will be very great but always hope for the best and be assured that I shall always write when I can and when I do not it is because I am out of reach of means to forward letters. On the 2nd I was again wounded in a cavalry charge at Gettysburg with three saber cuts on the head, two of them slight and one of them apparently severe. It was thought at the time it would cause me some trouble but it

---

[50] A detachment of the legion was involved in skirmishing as the Army of Northern Virginia began retiring from Pennsylvania back to Virginia.

[51] Delony was paid $500 for the loss of his horse in the action. His request for reimbursement for the loss of his beloved Marmion was endorsed by P. M. B. Young. "Horse was lost during a charge upon the enemy at the time and date specified, and that Col. Delony was struck from his saddle by a sabre cut and severely wounded & therefore the horse was not lost by any fault or neglect of his but while in the full discharge of his duties. P. M. B. Young, Brig Gen." Delony Papers.

is healing beautifully and I am not suffering from it. I was quite unwell after the wounds but I am satisfied it was from exhaustion and exposure more then the wounds. That night I had a good nights rest for the first time in more than two weeks and today I feel like a new man. We have had some hard fighting lately and our Regt. has on every occasion done its whole duty. In the fight in which I was wounded and Lts. Howze, Brooks of Ritchs company & Smith of Capt. Kings company were killed instantly & Lts Cheesborough & Pugh of the Richmond Hussars were mortally wounded. Col. Young had his horse killed under him & Capt. King was badly bruised by a fall from his horse. Several men were killed and wounded, none that you know or that live in Athens. Henry Jackson, brother in law of Howze, behaved very gallantly and I have no doubt saved my life after I was disabled. I fell from my horse and for a few moments was insensible & he fought desperately over me until he was relieved, his clothes & bugle and saber are all badly cut but he escaped, I am happy to state, entirely unhurt. I hope you will communicate these facts to his father, Andrew B. Jackson, as I appreciate his conduct very highly. Poor Tom's loss has been lamented by every soldier of the Regt, he was as gallant a spirit as ever lived and as true a man, a warm and sincere friend of mine, and his loss I shall always deplore.[52] Had I not been wounded so early in the action I feel confident I could have saved him and Pugh and Brooks. They charged too far after the field was cleared and were killed by Yankee sharpshooters in the woods. I am now with the wagon train but will be able to rejoin the regiment in a day or two. We are at Williamsport on the Maryland side of the Potomac unable to recross the river on account of high water, and yesterday the Yankees thinking they would make a good thing of it, attacked us. I was feeling very miserably but the booming of their cannon aroused me and I gathered up the stragglers about the wagons & went to the field starting with only thirteen men. I looked about and gathered a heterogeneous crowd as I went however to the support of Harts battery which was formerly attached to our brigade. After a while I had over two hundred men, saw one of General Imboden's staff, learned from him the position of our forces and the enemy & sent word to Gen Imboden what I intended doing, if he wanted it otherwise to send me orders. I managed very soon to inspire the men with confidence and led them in. They fought well, drove the enemy about 3/4 of a mile and about dark had completely flanked one of their batteries & if I had had a little more daylight I believe I should have taken it & withal had but one man slightly wounded. I had no idea that the crowd I had would do anything and I presume that was the opinion of the General or we could have accomplished a good deal more. As it was Gen. Lee[53] with his cavalry brigade came up and the Yanks soon left. I called up my crowd and dismissed

---

[52] Thomas Howze was brother-in-law to Henry Jackson, marrying Henry's sister, Lorelia Ann Jackson, called "Lovely" by friends and family. Tom also left behind a recently born son. See Biographical Roster.
[53] Fitzhugh Lee.

them. They gave me three cheers and said if the Yankees came again today they would all come up if I would command them which I promised to do. One of my captains was a chaplain which perhaps accounts for our good fortune. He did his duty very well tho' he would dodge the bullets. You must not be anxious about me Darling, have faith in Providence. He has delivered me in many dangers and I shall still trust in him. I never go into a fight without praying for myself and you and our dear little ones, and it will all be right, Darling, whatever happens—Don't give up. You would not I am sure have me shrink from duty and I shall be always prudent. Poor Gen. Hampton was very severely wounded on the 3rd, two saber cuts on the hand and shot in the thigh. He will recover it is thought, indeed his wounds tho' very painful are not deemed dangerous by the surgeons. My poor Dear Darling you must not forget that I sympathize with you most deeply in all your troubles and remember that I am always thinking of you and our dear precious little children. Tell dear little Tom that the Yankees got his horse Marmion when I fell off, but I have got a beautiful little Pennsylvania pony for him. I am fortunate in having secured another good horse, strong, gentle, and well trained, and among the horses I captured yesterday I got a fine looking bay which I think will do me good service. I shall send this letter by the first opportunity. Capt. Carlton will soon be in Athens & you must go to see him. He will tell you that I am very slightly hurt. God bless You all Darling. Think "sweetly" of me and write when you can. I will get your letters after a while. Do the best you can about George until matters are more quiet here and I will then write you about him. Love to Jenny & kisses to the little folks.

Ever yours
Will

Williamsport July 11, 1863

My Dear Rosa,

You must put up with a short note from me today on account of an almost intolerable pain in my right eye. I have suffered from it very severely. My wound is on my forehead over that eye and I have had a severe cold, the consequence is a neuralgic pain in my eye which at times is insufferable. Since I wrote you last I have also had fever, imitation fever caused by the wound and I did not as I expected to do rejoin my regiment. I am now very comfortably lodged in the house of a Unionist of this place who furnishes everything needed when asked for but never asks after our wants or inquires about our wounds. His wife follows his excellent example and provides two good meals a day. His daughters of whom he has two or three I believe about grown, I never see. Capt King is with me[54] and we are both very philosophic and get on admirably and are both doing

---

[54] Capt. Barrington S. King commanded Co. E, Cobb's Legion Cavalry. Although not wounded in the battle, King was injured: "In a charge a week ago near Gettysburg in which Col.

well and enjoying the excellent ice water, good liquors and (to us) good dinners that we have every day.

I expected yesterday to have crossed the river and gone in the country in Virginia but I am so comfortable here I am inclined to think I shall remain here until my wound heals. It is now doing very well, tho' supporating some. The Surgeons all say there is no danger in it if I am prudent and I am following their prescriptions implicitly, and shall not report for duty until I am entirely well. I am very sorry that I cannot spend this time at home but the surgeons say my wound is not severe enough for that so I must be re-signed. Yours of the 17th & 20th I recd yesterday am delighted to learn that dear little Willie is quite well again and that your garden is so fine and that you are all doing so well. The 20th tho' is an old date and I hope soon to get some more letters from you. Lt. Salter of Capt. Ritch's Company I understand was wounded yesterday, I think, but slightly however as he has not come back to join the Regt. I am going across the river late Va. this afternoon. Just learned of an opportunity King and I both. God bless you all Darling. Kiss the little ones for me, think sweetly of me & write often. My love to Jennie & a kiss for Laura.

Ever Yrs
W. G. D.

Camp near Culpepper C. H.
July 15th 1863

My Dear Darling little Daughter

Papa received your letter when he came back to camp from Staunton and was very glad to know his little daughter was thinking of him so sweetly and loving him as much. Papa wishes very much he could be at home with you and Mama and Bubber Tom and little Willie, and see you and talk with you every day, but he cant come now, but hopes he can come to see you next fall. Papa thinks of you every day and loves to think of you for he loves you all very much. Papa is living out of doors now. When the weather is clear he sleeps under a tree, and when it rains he goes under, what the soldiers call a fly, which is a thick piece of cloth, stretched over a pole. Sometimes it rains very hard and his clothes all get wet. Last night he went to sleep under his fly and it rained very hard and the water was three inches deep

---

Delony was wounded with a sabre cut over the head my horse ran away with me carrying me through almost the entire column of the enemy when running against the fence he fell throwing me heels over head I was considerably bruised but the fall saved my life. My horse jumped up & joined the Yankees with all my arms & accountisements & my saddle bags with many little valuables in them.... I have been feeling badly ever since my fall & yesterday I had to succumb completely worn out with considerable fever." Letter from B. S. King to his wife, Bessie, 10 July 1863, excerpt quoted in Galloway, *Dear Old Roswell*, 29.

where Papa's bed was. He had his boots off and they got full of water and Papa could not sleep any more until daylight & then Papa and Dr. Bradley and Willie Church got some saddles and wet blankets and went to sleep again & when Papa woke up he had to go barefooted until he dried his boots so he could get them on, but it didn't make Papa sick, and when he thinks that he does this so that the Yankees can't hurt his dear little children at home he don't mind it much now, he has got so used to it. You must think of Papa often and take good care of Mama and Bubber Tom and Willie until he comes back to see you. You must make Mama happy and teach Tom and Willie to be good little boys and to mind everything Mama tells them to do.

Papa is glad Mama cut off your curls for he knows you are glad of it, and that you are just as sweet and pretty as ever, and the curls were such a trouble to you and Mama. Tell Mama howdy for Papa. And kiss Tom and Willie and Mama for him and Aunt Jenny and little Laura and be a good little girl and write Papa another letter and tell him all about the pussies & the pigs and Tom & Willie and dear Mama. Goodbye my little darling. God bless you all. A heartfull of love from

Your own dear

Papa

Staunton July 17, 1863

My Dear Rosa,

I wrote you last from Williamsport that I thought I would be able in a day or two to rejoin my regiment but the very day I wrote I was attacked with fever and for 3 or 4 days had fever every day, together with a violent cold and a bloody discharge from my right nostril. My wound too instead of healing at once as I hoped it could began to suppurate freely and to add to my rues fortunes after the fever subsided I was attacked with neuralgia in my right eye from which I have suffered severely and as the erysipelas broke out among the wounded in Williamsport, my Surgeon advised me to leave.[55] I recrossed the Potomac last Saturday and arrived here last night in company with Capt. King who received a severe fall from his horse in the same Charge in which I was wounded. He brought one of his Sister's Mrs Baker at this place, who with her husband Rev. William E. Baker are as kings as they can possibly be, and insist upon my remaining with them until I am quite well again. I had a terrible time getting here but for the last two or three days have been very much better and my wound this morning looks wonderfully improved. The suppuration is

---

[55] A condition associated with an acute infection that causes swelling and pus-filled wounds. Often the result of insect bites or minor skin abrasions, it can produce high fevers, shaking, chills, fatigue, headaches, and vomiting.

lessened and the Surgeon who examined me today thinks it will heal now without further difficult. I was in hope that I would be able to come on to Athens & be cured by you but I cant get off on this wound so must comfort myself by writing to you often with the hope that I will soon hear from you and our dear little ones. My last date from home was the 20th June and I am very very anxious to hear again. As soon as you receive this write to me to this place care of Rev. Wm E. Baker and I will get your letter afterwards direct as usual as I think I shall leave for the Regt. in 8 or 10 days. I am in a terrible condition to be at a gentleman's house. My Uniform was received by the blood from my wound and I haven't a single clean shirt & only one pr. of pants, have had no chance to have washing done since I left Culpepper County until my arrival here and I am generally in a very dilapidated condition. My Campaigning heretofore has been childs play to what I saw and suffered in Maryland & Pennsylvania. I will write you a full account of it in a day or two. John was with me all the time & has been as faithful and efficient as ever, indeed I do not know what I would have done without him. He made a notable capture from a Sutler's store in Company with some Virginians of a bolt of broadcloth, several pieces of fine linen & calicos and other valuables but with his usual sagacity put them in a captured wagon in nobody's care and it was the last seen of them. He was very indignant that he should lose $2000 worth of dry goods, his entire stock in trade and in addition to that every stitch of clothing he had was stolen from him our wagons while he was with the Regt. He came to me this morning for more but I wont have money enough to buy an outfit for myself and told him he must supply himself. I lost that splendid pair of English pistols I had with me at home when I was wounded which I regret more then anything except old Marmion. His loss to me is imparable. I have been trying to replace him and the cheapest horse I have seen that will answer my purpose was offered at $825 so I shall have to scuffle along with my mare and the one I bought in Culpepper, both of them good horses but the latter almost broken down by the severe riding of the last six weeks. I shall not get another such as old Marmion. He was as fresh almost and as spirited the day I made my last charge as when we started on that Campaign. You can have no idea my attachment for the old fellow and how I miss him. The whole Regt. deplore his loss. I hope he will fall with good hands. This is a selfish little Darling, don't imagine it is a gloomy one. I feel fine otherwise and only wish I could see you and laugh over my mishaps for the last month. I feel very thankful I am through as safe as I am and truly feel that we have no thing in my case to feel sad about so dont be gloomy, but cheerful and the day will yet come when we will enjoy together the fruit of our present sufferings. God bless you all Darling kiss the little ones for me and write often. I send you a letter I wrote on the 11th but which I had no opportunity to mail before. I was mistaken however in saying we were at the house of a Unionist. He is Southern in his feelings but in the seizure of tenor now ruling in Maryland was afraid to express himself, and being watched had to be extremely careful in his intercourse with rebels. He wouldn't charge any thing and insisted upon our returning to his house if we meet with any difficulty elsewhere, this is justice to a cline but frightened us all.

Ever Your Own
Will

Staunton July 20, 1863

My Dear Rosa,

It is just one month today since the date of your last letter which I have received and thoughts of home, of you and our dear precious little ones keep me restless, impatient and uneasy. How terrible this war is and how cruel the separations it causes, and what the future will be and how long the war will last, who can tell? An occasional gleam of sunshine comes to us however, like the bow of promise, and hope springs up and dies again in my heart according to the same varying views of the day, but for the fall of Vicksburg, how cheering until the prospect now be for peace, but our Western Generals seem unequal to the task before them. Would to Heaven we had another General Lee. I have lost faith in all others. I believe any one else in his position would lose Richmond in a month but he seems to wrest from his enemies advantages, even under defeat. God grant he may be preserved to us for without him I believe I should almost despair. There is too to my mind a gleam of sunshine in the late news from the North. If Lincoln finds it impossible, as I trust he may to recruit his armies by draft he will be obliged to give up the contest, but Darling I am almost afraid to allow myself to hope for that. I am afraid after all that the late riot in New York and other places, will result in a reaction of feeling, favorable to Lincoln and pyramidal to our bright hopes of peace, and after all we should still have to rely upon our own strengths and stout hearts with a firmer trust in Providence that all will yet be right and in the meantime bear our trials with fortitude and a hopeful confidence in the final result. This at last is always the end of all my musings about the war, sometimes disheartened, heartsick and homesick it seems to me a never ending struggle full of trials and unmitigated suffering but the end to be achieved promises so much of happiness to the survivors and our children that courage & confidence take new root in my heart. If I could only see my dear wife and children a little oftener I could make aware the profession of my life were it necessary to us and our Independence.

My wound is doing well and today would I expect to leave for the army. I expect the wound will leave a bad looking scar on my forehead, an "honorable" scar to which you will doubtless object, but from present appearances I am indulged to think that the scar will be much smaller than the wound, as the only part of it which has caused me any trouble was when the bone was injured just in the center of the wound where the two cuts came together. I am certainly very thankful that it was not worst. Mr and Mrs Baker have both been very kind to me and I have enjoyed my sojourn at their house no little. They have three children, two little girls, one just Rosa's age[56] & the other two years younger, both of them very sweet children with whom I spend a good share of my time. We have become great friends and no one but an absent father can tell how I have enjoyed their prattle. They are well behaved and it is a pleasure to be with them. Mrs Baker is a very sweet woman, sensible, cheerful and I think beautiful. Mr B. is intelligent, pleasant & very happy and I am almost sorry my wound is healing so provokingly fast. I do not know when I have met with a more interesting family, I only know one of which they sometimes remind me and that is in Athens. God bless you and the little ones Darling. Think often and sweetly of me. Kiss all the little folks for me. Give my love to Jenny and accept for yourself a heartful from

Ever Yours
Will

Staunton July 28, 1863

My Dear Rosa,

I have been anxiously hoping to hear from home for the last three or four days thinking that when you received my telegram from this place that you would write and direct to me here but as I have not heard presume the dispatch did not reach you or if it did that it was delayed some time. I have been hoping too that I would be able to come home and spend at least a day or two with you. I must plead as an excuse for not writing you oftener, but all my hopes are blasted and I shall remain here a few days longer and then dont know about my regiment. Capt King's Lady came on a few days ago and since has returned I have been told he declines to do any thing. His dispatch went through promptly and from its wording he informed that he was quite sick and immediately came on and I cant help feeling a little envious of his good fortune, particularly as I could have come home just as well as not if the Surgeons who first attended had only had the required brains to know how long my wounds would take to heal. The Surgeons here say that it will now be well in about a week but they have all been saying that ever since I was first wounded. The bone was evidently injured and I can see but little difference if any in the wound now and what it was a week ago. I received two cuts almost in the same place com-

---

[56] At this writing, Rosa was 6, born in 1857.

ing together like the letter V with a tail to it and it has all healed over except where the two cuts become one and there for about half and inch it is still very sore and suppurating freely and looks much more like the wounds from a pistol ball than a sabre. Since I last wrote you I have suffered little pain from the wound last ten days. I have had some, but a slight stinging sensation there, and I am confused by the Surgeons with the information or opinion rather that I will probably suffer from neuralgia in my right eye the balance of my life on account of the severance of the Aerie above the eye by the blow. This I do not believe at all however as I controlled the neuralgia completely with quinine when I had it and now am totally free from it. Exposure may bring on a return of it, but I do not believe it will. I hope that my wish at most it will enable me to take the field again. Indeed I must leave here. Mr and Mrs Baker are as kind and attentive to me as they can possibly be and I have endeavored to be as little troublesome as possible but really I feel that I am becoming an imposition on them staying here so long without any previous acquaintance with them. They have never treated me as a stranger, and say that they felt that they knew me before they saw me, having heard so much of me through mutual friends, and I really feel myself, as if I had known them all my life. It is one of the most kindest families I ever knew. He is a man of fine talents, a very interesting preacher and devoted to his work, and she is one of the most amenable & lively women I ever saw. Then their two little girls, one the age of Rosa and the other two years younger are very interesting children. They and the "T_____" are the greatest of friends. Their youngest is a boy not old enough yet to be interested in strangers. Mrs Capt King too is a very interesting person reminds me constantly of my little Scrap at home, at times talks exactly like you and thinks there is but one fellow in the world, _____ get him. I cant help _____ him at times at the Capts _____. Altogether I think as I could not get home I am most fortunate in being here, provided I do not _____ a _____ dear Darling. _____ _____ _____ _____ _____ is to use that I have been were able to come home if only for a few days. It is now nearly a month since I was wounded. It will be more than a month from that time before my wound heals sufficiently for me to bear the summer's sun, and I could have gone to Athens just as well as not, but my wound was not half examined, the surgeons were frightened half out their wits when they were dressing it, on account of the enemy's shells, and that the bone was cut (chipped as the surgeon here says). They did not know and they told me it would heal unassisted by the first of month, too short to admit of loss in visit to you. I have been dreaming of nothing, asleep and awake ever since I have been here, but you and the children and I am sometimes afraid that the words will be worn out with my talking about you. They have all fallen quite in love with "Tom" likewise, and he is a splendid little fellow (isnt he). God bless them all. I wonder if they know how anxious Papa is to see their dear little faces once more.

Kiss them for me and tell little Rosa to give Mama a wet kiss for Papa. Give my love to Jenny & a kiss to little Laura with a heart full of love for my poor Darling.

Ever Yours
Will

Athens August 2nd 1863

My own dearest Will

This letter I should have written day before yesterday but was prevented during each day and when night comes I am too tired to write, so you must pardon an occasional irregularity as writing these times is considered of an effort as the position is very tiresome to me. We are all well. The children are just now playing "flag in the middle" and making such a noise I scarcely know what I am thinking about. I heard of you thru Mr. Hemphill, who sent me word by George, he had seen you. Dear darling how far away you do seem from me and I do want to see you so badly. I saw Gen Cobb the other day when I went up to see his wife, fat as ever and sick enough of this war, he came to attend the wedding of his son John to Lucy Barrow. He said I must tell you he hoped your next wound would be a furlough one. I hope not however, bad as I want to see you.

No letters for me again this afternoon and I feel much disappointed, as much as I cannot account for the failure, if you are still at Staunton, unless you are again suffering from your wound. If you have left there I know you have done so too early or rather fear it in any case, feel very anxious. This constant anxiety is tearing out to the spirit. Mr. Sledge sent me a sample of our potatoes up town to look at. They are going to be very fine and if I don't have them stolen will have plenty for all winter. I wish I could hope winter would find you at home for good. This month begins your third year of absence. I hope you will determine it shall be your last whether Lincoln destroys us or not. I really give out at times, especially when the letters get few and far between. You suffer your share on that score I know, poor old fellow. I must try on your account not to be so chicken hearted. The children talk constantly of you, do not feel they will forget. Pa is a big man in this house, nothing new to write about. I don't go out very often. Your friends all enquire kindly after you, but oh dear darling does any one know how I miss you. Do write me as often as you can. All send sweet kisses to dear Papa and lots of love. Jennie unites in much love. Your own large share from your own little Scrap. May God bless you Darling is the constant prayer of

Your own affect.
Rosa

Staunton Aug. 4, 1863

My Dear Rosa,

I have not yet heard from home and it seems strange to me that you have not written to me at this place. It will [be] three weeks day after tomorrow since I arrived here and the day after my arrival I telegraphed you and also wrote, and have been very anxiously hoping to receive letters from you ever since. As I cannot hear and my wound is nearly well, I shall leave in the morning for the regiment with the hope that when I get there I shall find letters awaiting me. Col. Young and Maj. Wright were both wounded last week, which is an additional reason for my returning. Young has a flesh wound in the breast, slight.[57] I am told Wright had his big toe split by a mine ball. I do not know what other casualties occurred. Our brigade is now Commanded by a Lt. Col. the Generals and all the Colonels are wounded.

I am in fine health and have been living so sumptuously at Mr Bakers that it is no little trial for us to come down to beef and bread once more but as duty calls me there so plainly I must think of nothing else. My wound will soon be healed over I think, tho the healing process goes on very slowly, the bone was evidently very badly hurt. I have no pain however and anticipate no further trouble from it. I am very anxious Darling to hear from you and our dear little children. Your last letter was dated the 20th of June and it is now the 4th of August. You cant imagine how great my anxiety is. I have dreamed of being home with you a dozen times, but I soon wake up and the pleasant illusion is dispelled. I console myself with the reflection however that my present sufferings will strengthen my chances for a furlough in the fall when the General returns. I shall write to you as soon as I reach Camp and let you know what we have to do. Don't be unnecessarily anxious. I shall do my duty but shall be prudent and discreet. I am rejoiced I am not Colonel. I would not have the responsibility of the brigade upon me for the world. Kiss the little folks for Papa and give my love to Jenny, with a full share for yourself from

Yr own
Will

Culpepper County Aug. 8, 1863

My Dear Rosa,

I arrived at the Regimental Camp night before last and found awaiting me quite a package of letters from you, the richest treat that I have had for some time

---

[57] In the ensuing fight, Young was shot in the chest and unhorsed. He was carried to Richmond, where he sent a telegram to his parents: "Wound did not enter cavity. Pistol ball passed through flesh and came out. Doing well. Enjoying a novel." Holland, *Pierce M. B. Young*, 74.

past. All your letters came to the Camp. In directing to Staunton you did not follow my instructions and your letter came to the Regiment. You ought not to have directed it to the Legion. We are now encamped between Brandy Station on the Orange and Alexandria R. Road and Stevensburg, almost in sight of our last winters camp and four or five miles from Culpepper C. H. I am now writing from the Wagon Camp about two miles from the latter place. I have not yet taken Command of the Regiment but will probably do so tomorrow. I have just been looking over John's trunk full of Pennsylvania spoils, quite an assortment of dry goods, just such a stock as you would imagine a negro would select. Loose buttons, tape, woolen socks, and large needles to draw them, 8 yards of Calico for the Children a paper of hair pins for Miss, 3 1/2 yards of cassimere for a coat for himself and an indiscriminate assortment of other indescribable articles. He has just called me down to select what I wanted. I got some spool tread for you but only 4 spools of white. He is a curious creature. He came into Camp a few minutes ago with a pair of fine pants, which together with a new uniform coat, he had bought for $100. He thinks he ought to make $50 on the bargain—$150 for the coat and the pants for me. He told Church yesterday, if the "Ferginians" hadn't stolen his goods in Pennsylvania he would have been able to buy him a substitute & could now have been at home eating peaches and watermelons. He is invaluable to me in Camp, but I expect he will be useless to me after the war, if it ever ends.

I understand the people at home are quite discouraged and almost ready to despair, at which I am not much surprised since Jeff. Davis & Gov. Brown are calling out the available men at home. It is not unnatural that they should think our case is desperate when we should call upon them to help us, but we are not whipped yet and don't mean to be. Gen Lee's Army is ready for the enemy whenever and wherever Meade desires to make the attack and you and our friends need have no fears of the result. Gen Lee's mistake at Gettysburg was relying upon the enemy for ammunition. If he had had one days more supply Meade's Army would have been routed, but his mistake was criminal in so great a man, and the result fatal to an early peace. We shall have to struggle on which the Army is perfectly willing to do however much they may regret the necessity. I am feeling very well and my wound is sufficiently healed for me to assume Command. I think I shall do so in the morning. The Regt. were glad to see me back, and will do their duty as they have ever done. Young has quite distinguished himself in the recent fights and I think will be promoted. His wound is not dangerous, the ball ran around his ribs making only a flesh wound. Darling I am very sorry that I cannot be at home with you now during your troubles,[58] but you must keep a stout heart and bear up under them. Providence

[58] At this time Rosa was about to give birth to the couple's fourth child, Martha Roberta Delony. The child, however, would live less than three years, dying in 1866.

has been very kind to us during the war and our trials seem petty when compared with all of those around us. Let us still trust in Him and hope on and endure unto the end. If I survive the present Campaign I have no doubt I shall be able to come on and see you in the fall which will be better than coming now and I will try and arrange matters better for you. I am glad to learn that your garden is so good. You can sell potatoes and buy wheat. Tell Dear little Rosa I have received her letter and will write to her in a day or two. If I do not write regularly don't be anxious. Our post office is now at Orange C. H. more than 20 miles from Camp and we cannot send regularly. I will write when I can. Kiss the dear little folks for me and tell Tom & Willie they must grow fast and take Papa's place & let me come home to Mama and little Sister. My love to Jenny and a kiss to Laura, with a heart full for yourself from

Yr own
Will

Camp near Stevensburg
Aug. 12th 1863

My Dear Rosa,

I received your letter of the 4th inst today and am very glad to learn that you are getting on with your troubles so bravely. I sympathize with you Darling, more than tongue can tell and truly wish that I could be with you until all was over, and the little Stranger made his appearance, but this cannot be and we must both bear up as well as we possibly can. You must not worry about me. I am doing well & am not suffering from my wounds. It gives me really no trouble now and I hope will not again. The Surgeon cauterized it today and I presume it will soon heal up. My general health is fine & upon the light diet, indeed the very light diet of camp I think is likely to continue so. I have been very busy since I assumed command of the Regiment trying to refit it after the severe service of the late Campaign. A good many are barefooted and badly clad and it requires a good deal of trouble to fix them up again and as it usually the case after so severe a Campaign, things move rather irregularly. I am getting things in something like ship-shape again & hope that I will have but little trouble with them. The Yankees are not troubling us much tho we are in close proximity. Day before yesterday they drove in our pickets and I went out to meet them at the head of 64 men—three Companies were on picket & some few others absent, but all in all I do not think we can muster more than 120 men. We are looking for the last Georgia detail in two or three days, which will give us a reinforcement of about 200 men, and we are now sending a good many more home, besides having horses out recruiting, so I hope in some way we will be able to keep up the Legion but I rather suspect we will have [to] impress horses to do it. So look out in Athens. I find so you have a new neighbor. I hope he will prove as good an one as old Mr. Newton, but I am afraid of his negroes, tho he & his family are all amiable & I hope you will find them clever. I read your package of letters over when I do not hear from you and it is a great comfort, I assure you. You say Dick Taylor is going to Columbus. How does he keep out of the service, and how do the other chivalric sons of Athens manage to stay at home. Find out the secret & I will come on and spend my time with you, when you say so. The mail is again coming regularly to Culpepper & I shall be able to write regularly until the advance of the Army. Kiss the dear little ones for me and I will write tomorrow to Little Rosa. I send this by Miller Lumpkin. My love to Jenny and a heartful for yourself

W. G. Delony

Camp near Stevensburg
Aug. 17, 1863

My Dear Rosa

I yesterday received your letter by Henry Dougherty to gether with your daguerreotype and the tobacco bag and knitting of dear little Rosa. The pleasure which they have afforded me is entirely beyond expression. I think the likeness is a very good one indeed, very like you tho' it does not do you justice and I am more than happy at having received it. Tell dear little Rosa that Papa is very proud of her at being so smart and very happy that she is so sweet and a good little girl. The bag is a very nice one and the knitting very well done, and Pa is glad she thought of him.

I have been very very busy in trying to refit the Regiment. Soldiers are like children, lose everything, waste everything, and destroy everything, and one regiment is consequently in need of everything. Another such campaign & I suspect they will come back without their heads. And it is so hard to get anything from our Govt. that the undertaking is a herculean task which is increased by the incapacity of many of our Company Officers, but as we have but little else now to do I hope I may be successful, unless we move very soon.

We are now encamped below Stevensburg very near our last winters encampment, very pleasantly located and with but light picket duty to vary the monotony of our life. Opposite to us the enemy have recrossed the river and since the day before yesterday they have not been in view of our outpost videttes. Their whole army have recently "changed its base" and the wonder with me is that Gen Lee has not made a forward movement. There is but one report from all our scouts and that is that Meade's army is in a terrible condition, and I have been hoping that Gen Lee would be able to make a forward movement. I would not be surprised if he was restrained by the Powers at Richmond tho' I know nothing of it. It seems so evident to me that it is his policy to advance on Meade, I cannot understand the delay. As for the demoralization of our army it is nonsense to talk about it. It is confined to a few croakers. I have never seen the slightest symptom of it, nor have I seen any one who has. One of Ewell's staff officers told me his corps was never in finer spirits or condition, and I dont want you to join in the depression which I learn pervades all classes at home. Yankeedom is quite as bad off as we are and are croaking quite as badly. The truth is both sides have suffered severely, their victories have exhausted them and we have only to present a firm determining front to ensure success. I believe our people have the spirit to struggle on, and believing so, look forward with renewed hope toward ultimate independence, and this at no far distant day. You must keep up your Spirits Darling, it is cruel that we should be so long separated and should suffer so much. I sympathize with you deeply and sincerely in all your troubles and trials and daily wish that I could be with you, but let's do our duty bravely, knowing that if we do our children will be benefitted by our present sufferings. My health is very good. My wound is healing. The pieces of bone which were irritating it I think have all now worked out and I think I shall soon be "all right" again. God bless you all, Darling. Kiss the little folks for me. Give my love to Jenny and a kiss to Laura. Write me often. Much love from

Yr own
Will

Camp near Stevensburg
Aug 18, 1863

My Dear Rosa,

Your two letters of the 8th and 11th inst were received this morning and were most welcome notwithstanding the scolding contained. You must put up with my shortcomings occasionally as I sometimes feel too homesick to write or do anything else. And as to my coming home you must not blame me, but the Medical Fraternity, for I am very sure no man wounded at Gettysburg felt more anxiety to see the loved ones at home more than I did and no one suffered more in consequence of not being allowed to come. I was distinctly told by the Surgeons that my wound was slight and would heal in a week or ten days, showing great carelessness on their part as the wound was never probed and very hurriedly dressed the Doctors "changing base" at every discharge of the enemy's cannon. They were excited and I was the sufferer.

Dr Bradley took out another piece of bone yesterday and there is now but a very small sore, which will heal up in a day or two if the bone is all out which I hope and believe is the case. There will be quite a sink in my forehead and indeed the entire right lobe of my head is "stove in" "dislocated" as Bradley says, and you can almost lay your finger in the suture surrounding it. I have quite given up all hope of justice from anybody during the war & have made up my mind to submit until forbearance ceases to be a virtue & then I shall resign, which you need not be surprised to hear of at any time.

If you could only hear the noise and laughing and singing in Camp, I think you and our friends in Georgia would give up the idea that our Army is demoralized. We are drilling every day and the men are anxious to meet the enemy to get rid of the daily drill. Their noise annoys me some times but I am glad too to hear it. It is a good sign among the volunteers.

I think your idea about saving your raw meat is a good one if you can possibly procure the hogs. I am more than surprised at Mr Halls meat turning out so badly. Who can we trust? I am afraid however that you will find some difficulty in getting the hogs. Tell George I shall expect to find your wood house full and the horses in good order when I come home in the fall. You had better have the Yarborough lot well manured in October and broken up well and sown in wheat. If well manured and well sown it will make wheat enough and if you haven't manured enough it will repay you to buy it, and get Mr Sledge to sow it for you. The other lot has been planted long enough in wheat. I am sorry to say that it will be impossible for me to help you any in the recovery line. It takes every dollar of my pay to support me and John and my horses, and it hardly does that. I had to pay $50 for a pair of pants (very course) when I was in Staunton and $83 for making jacket and vest—$2. a feed for my horses was a frequent bill, and now that I am in Camp I cannot live on bread & beef. I have given it a fair trial and a constant diarrhea was the consequence. I therefore sent John out yesterday and today to buy me some vegetables and I have had the only two good dinners I have seen in Camp since my return, but the Cost is frightful. A citizen brought a very small quarter of lamb to sell me yesterday and asked $7 for it. I couldn't afford to buy but I believe he sold it all to the soldiers. You have no idea of the desolation of this country. God bless you Darling, keep up your spirits, and give me a good scolding every now and then. Write to me often and don't hesitate to use the $1900 of Confederate notes in Bank. I put it there for you in case of need. Be of good cheer. We will come out all right if we prove unworthy of success. Kiss the dear little ones for me and think often and kindly of your

Will

Camp near Stevensburg
Aug 22nd 1863

My Dear Rosa,

I have only time this afternoon to write you a short note saying that I am quite well and in receipt of another letter from home. I would have written you yesterday, but it was our day for Grand Guard duty and we spent the day on picket duty fasting. The 1st S.C. Regt. went down under arms with their Chaplain & we had service in hearing of the Yankee drums, passed a pleasant day tho' a terribly warm one.

My wound is nearly healed over, only a small scab left & this morning I left it uncovered. The scar is a bad looking one and makes quite a sink in my forehead but I am glad to say it is well at last and only hope the Yankees will let my poor head alone here after. I presume from the tenor of the Richmond papers say that Charleston is a doomed city but if it falls don't despair. While brave men live we cant be subdued and a determined spirit will yet achieve our independence. We have not yet reached the point of suffering, endeared for years by our revolutionary sires and we can if we will bear all that they did and still succeed. I have been very busy all day getting off another detail for horses and settling the thousand & one questions which arise as to who shall go, and I am worn out with the heat and annoyance. I will write you again tomorrow.

Kiss the dear little ones for me. I am glad to hear that dear little Tom is improving and is such a manly little fellow. How does he get on with the impediment in his speech. God bless you all Darling, think of me kindly and write me often. My love to Jenny.

Ever Yrs
Will

P.S. John sends you a bundle—the calico is for the children and the rest for Miss. Maj. Dents boy will bring it to you. I send this by Steve Dent, who will tell you how I am getting on.

WGD

Camp near Stevensburg
August 27, 1863

My Dear Rosa

Since I last wrote you I have received two letters from you, one of the 6th and one of the 17th and, dear darling, I sympathize with you more than tongue can tell in your troubles. I was truly sorry that you are so unmanageable and can scarcely walk. I think it portends a boy not a girl as you imagine judging from past experiences they are always more troublesome both before and afterwards but I hope to be with you come what may, boy or girl. I have been very unwell since my last diarrhea. Yesterday and the day before I suffered a good deal but my good friend Col. Twiggs of the 1st S.C. who is encamped near me furnished me with a preparation put up by Dr. Eve of Augusta which has put me all right again and today I feel quite well once more. I am now on duty as one of our examining Board for officers. We meet daily in Stevensburg at 10 o'clock adjourn at two, convene at a private house where we get well cooked vegetables and I suspect this fact has as much to do with my good health again as anything else. Twiggs, Lipscombe, and myself compose the Board and we have quite a pleasant time. This is one grand guard day and you may be assured I am very willing to be relieved from the hot sun. I am glad to learn that your potato crop has turned out so well and hope to share with you and our dear little ones some of the fruits of your industry this fall. I presume your sweet potatoes too will also yield a good crop as you set out yours in such good time for the sake of the little ones, I hope so at least. I hope that dear little Tom is quite well again and that he has had no return of the fever. I can't help feeling anxious about the dear little souls when I hear they are unwell and I am so far away but I hope he is well again. I am sorry, Darling, that the negroes are so troublesome and that Catherine is behaving so badly. By all means hire Mrs. Hardens girl, and when I come home I will try and make such arrangements as well make things more comfortable for you. I fear that Catherine will never be useful to us again and regret to think so for it is so difficult to obtain a reliable negro. About money matters let me say you must not worry yourself. If the interest on your fathers debt is not paid, you will have to draw on the $7900 in Bank. I left it there in that form for the very purpose of relieving you from annoyances. I would as soon have you use that as the interest on your fathers money, indeed, a little matter, so don't worry yourself at all. We are both growing

264

old fast enough and I protest against it. God bless you all, Darling. Kiss the little ones for Papa. My love from

Ever Yr own

Will

I write in pencil as Church is making out his field report and can't relinquish the desk.

Camp Gordon Aug 30, 1863

My Dear Rosa,

I was disappointed today and yesterday in not hearing from you, and I am very afraid that dear little Tom is sick or that you are not doing so well. I shall hope for the best until I hear from you but shall feel very anxious until I do.

This is Sunday, one of the most quiet peaceful and saddest Sabbaths I ever saw and I have been thinking of my little family at home this restless day, and wishing that I could spend at least one day with you. It feels more like Autumn than August as cool as an October day in Georgia and it makes me homesick, and long for the day to come when I shall be able to leave Camp for Georgia.

I shall expect Col Young to return to the Regt. in October and as soon as he comes I will send up my application to pay you and the little folks a visit. You cant imagine Dear Darling how I long to see you and how restless I become at times longing to be with you. One of Stuart's scouts captured a large mail on its way to the Yankee Army and some of the letters are rich affairs and I have thought of you as we have been reading them. Could you see them you would say that all men are alike North & South, but being more charitably inclined myself, I have come to the conclusion that all women are not alike and a scolding from my poor little Scrap of a wife is certainly very different from one that certain Yankee husbands would have received had not a rebel scout arrested the letters and I come to the conclusion that I would like night well to be at home today and receive a good well-deserved scolding from my little wife for my many short comings. When will the day come that I can be at home for good. The Yankee papers that I have been reading today would indicate that the rebellion is to be very speedily suppressed and the rebels all sent home or to country. I cannot very well see the end of it, but I am comforted by a remark just made in my hearing by Capt King to the effect that if he was a betting man he would bet $50,000 that this is our last summer Campaign and the war will end in less than a year, so you must take comfort from that. My great consolation is in the fact that Lincoln cant get the troops, and that Lee's army is still unwhipped and ready for a fight.

In the quiet time we are now having I am amusing myself with Capt King and Lt. Bassett in playing chess to which we have become quite good and out of which I desire much pleasure in beating King who bears it badly. Kiss the little folks for me and tell dear little Rosa to write Papa another letter and tell me everything that is going on at home among the pigs, kittens & c & c. I hope to hear tomorrow from you. God bless you all Darling.

Ever Yr own
Will

Camp near Stanton
Sept 5 1863

My Dear Rosa,

I have dated this note as usual from Camp but more properly it should have been at Hd. qtrs. of the Brigade. I have just had a dark ride from Camp having been summoned here to take Col. Gordons place for a few days in command of the Brigade. I am in consequence the Senior officer of the Brigade and there are only two of the field officers for duty besides myself. We were called out night before last and the entire Brigade turned out less than 600 men. You may infer from these facts the condition of men and horses. We travelled all night until nearly day and if you could have seen me sleeping for a couple of hours, without covering upon the wet grass, I am sure you would have thought I was not prudent as you mean, but no child ever slept more soundly except when a courier or a staff officer, awakened me for a moment to communicate an order. At daylight we were aroused anticipating a hard days fight, but Stuart's guide failed to appear and we marched back again to camp without seeing a Yankee, tired, hungry, and sleepy, and I think I may add somewhat disappointed, for strange as it may appear to one at home, there is a fascination in danger which allures a soldier, and perhaps it is well that it is so to those who are soldiers from necessity and a sense of duty. It serves to render tolerable many of the discomforts and burdens of our life.

Your letter of the 28th I recd by yesterdays mail after returning from the Expedition referred to. I am sorry to hear that you have been suffering. You must be very careful darling with yourself. I feel great anxiety about your situation and I sincerely sympathize with you in your trouble. I hope and expect to be with you however and this hope is a great consolation to me. Gen Hampton & Young will both be here in October and as soon as they come I am sure I shall be able to come home. Gen Hampton I know will let me off as a good many of the wounded officers will then be here. You made a brilliant sale of your gold. I congratulate you upon it. It will never be as high again. All our prospects will now begin to brighten until the end comes, which I hope is not far distant unless we meet with new disasters in the West. There is no danger here. God bless you all Darling. Kiss the dear little people for Papa and think sweetly and kindly of me. My love to Jennie.

Ever Yrs
Will

Camp Near Orange C. H.

My Dear Rosa

I have not heard from you for several days and feel very blue about it and not a little homesick today. We moved here yesterday afternoon after traveling around the country nearly all day feeling tired enough I assure you. It rained all night last night and a gloomy time we had of it. Today too it has been storming very much, but it has at last cleared up and a beautiful cool clear evening we have.

The Brigades are being newly organized but I am happy to say that for the present Col. Gordon of the 1st N.C. Regt. has been retained in command of this Brigade although his Regt. has been transferred to another Brigade. This is very complimentary to him as well as agreeable to the brigade since it would have left us in the hands of Col. Lipscombe[59] of the 2nd S.C. who in my humble opinion is entirely incompetent to command a Regt. much less a brigade. I spoke to Gordon very freely about and I presume the other Field officers did the same thing. The new arrangement about the organization of the cavalry is neither for the good of the service nor the country but only for the special benefit of a favored few. I am strongly inclined to think that my services will not be much longer needed by the Confederacy and as soon as affairs begin to look more favorable I shall tender my resignation and this will be early in the winter. I am very tired of being ordered about by a set of Jackasses and don't mean to submit to it very much longer. We are only now doing picket duty one regiment as a time. I presume our Regt. will be on duty in the morning.

I don't think Dear Darling the day is far distant when the war will be at an end, if Bragg's army is kept in the field.[60] He is pursuing the proper course. Don't despair, everything is working favorably for us, and all will come out right. God

---

[59] Col. Lipscombe was Thomas Jefferson Lipscomb of South Carolina. See Biographical Roster.

[60] Braxton Bragg, commanding three divisions of the Army of Tennessee, fought the battle of Chickamauga on 19 and 20 September. After numerous assaults on George Thomas's Federal forces, Bragg broke off the engagement. For his involvement, Thomas earned the moniker "Rock of Chickamauga." See Biographical Roster.

bless you all Darling think sweetly of me and write often. Kiss the dear little ones for Papa. I will write as often as I can.

Ever Yours
W. G. D.

Camp near Orange C. H.
Sept. 21st 1863

My Dear Rosa,

Your letter of the 11th inst. came to hand night before last while the regiment was on picket on the Robinson Road on the extreme left of our army. We went down on the morning of the 19th and during the day orders came to me from Brigade Hdqtrs enclosing a letter from Gen R. E. Lee, to be on the alert that the enemy were proposing a flank movement on the left and that they would probably cross in my front. That afternoon about half past five oclock three new regiments appeared in our front and their line of pickets were inspected by one of their Genls and his escort about 300 yards from our pickets. We were out more then 500 yds from their Camps, so of course you may know I had an anxious time, having only about 200 men in all. I had breastworks thrown up at the principal ford, made the necessary dispositions for an attack from the enemy yesterday morning and had a restless sleep in the cold with horses saddled and arms at our heads. At 12 oclock and at 3, I got up and all was quiet. At 8 1/2 at night the Yankee dressed beat tattoo all around us, but in the morning only one sounded reveille, much to my gratification I assure. The Yankees had decamped silently during the night for some reason unknown to us, and those that were Left, seemed very uneasy when I visited my videttes in the morning. I was left there with only my regiment notwithstanding the confidence of Genl Lee that the enemy would attack me, and I relieved 2 regiments and was relieved by 2 others and thus it is. There are five regiments in the brigade. We go on picket alone every third day and the others go two at a time. The confidence that is placed in the regt is very gratifying certainly but the duty that their confidence entails, is at times very burdensome, unpleasant and to my mind extremely unfair, particularly when in published orders our distinction is made between this & other Cav., at the fight the other day at Culpepper C. H. It was entirely unnecessary for our Brigade to have been engaged if Stuarts orders had been implicitly obeyed, by God we saw that the Virginians had been badly whipped, having lost 3 pieces of artillery and nearly 3 or more captured and he moved us up and took the fight off their hands, retreated down a difficult road and saved what was left of them. Yet we got no credit for this. All are classes alike. All that we lost were killed and wounded, no prisoners were taken and no artillery lost, tho' outnumbered at least 5 to 1.

Col. Young is in Richmond endeavoring to form a brigade on the Coast of Ga. and move us down. God grant he may succeed. I am tired of this work in Virginia. I have no confidence in Virginia Cavalry, they do no fighting and we are damned with them, and I think it is all due to Stuarts policy of complimenting his favorites whether they do badly or well. Merrit has nothing to do with his favoritism. I shall rejoice when Hampton returns. I am very much of the opinion that Meade does not intend to cross the river certainly there is no movement now indicative of such a result. I think he is making a show of strength which he has not in reality.

The cold winds that we are now having make me feel dear Darling very much like coming home and just as soon as I can possibly get off I am certain to come. I want to leave about the first of Nov. and I think then that I can have my leave extended for at least a couple of months. Gen Hampton will then be here. He and Butler my Brigadier are both my friends and will I know grant me any reasonable indulgence. Young too I think will be inclined to let me stay, so that I am looking forward with a good deal of confidence to spending some time with you and the 4 little ones this winter. Kiss the dear little folks for me and write when you can. We are all doing well here now, plenty to eat and enough for our horses. My love to Jennie and a heartfull for yourself.

Ever Yr own
Will

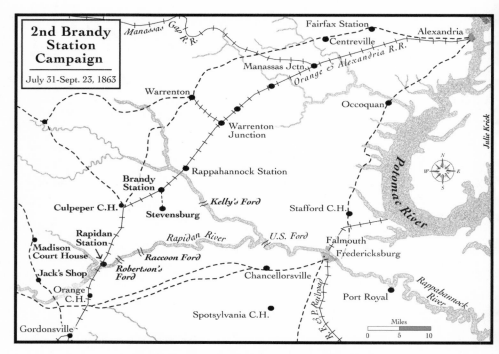

2nd Brandy Station Campaign

July 31–Sept. 23, 1863

Manassas Gap R.R.

Fairfax Station

Alexandria

Centreville

Manassas Jctn.

Orange & Alexandria R.R.

Warrenton

Occoquan

Warrenton Junction

Potomac River

Rappahannock Station

Brandy Station

Kelly's Ford

Stafford C.H.

Culpeper C.H.

Stevensburg

Rapidan River

U.S. Ford

Falmouth

Rapidan Station

Madison Court House

Raccoon Ford

Fredericksburg

Jack's Shop

Robertson's Ford

Chancellorsville

Rappahannock River

Orange C.H.

Port Royal

Gordonsville

Spotsylvania C.H.

R.F. & P. Railroad

Miles

0   5   10

Caption under map: Battles and skirmishes involving
William G. Delony and Cobb's Georgia Legion Cavalry.

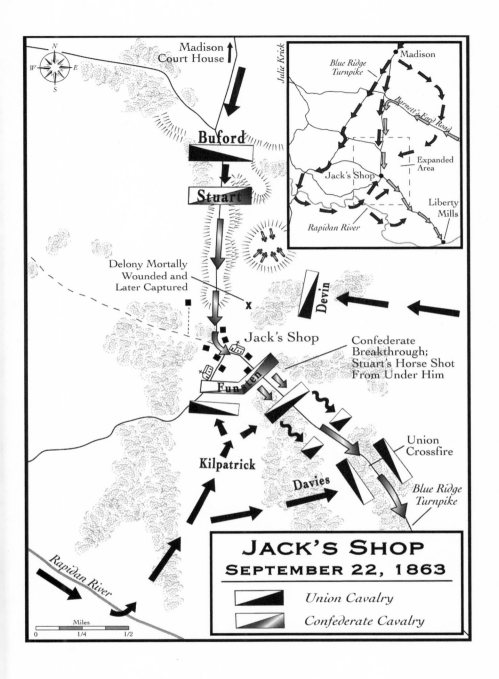

Madison
Court House

Julie Krick

Buford

Stuart

Blue Ridge Turnpike

Madison

Barnett's Ford Road

Expanded Area

Jack's Shop

Liberty Mills

Rapidan River

Delony Mortally
Wounded and
Later Captured

X

Devin

Jack's Shop

Confederate
Breakthrough;
Stuart's Horse Shot
From Under Him

Funsten

Union
Crossfire

Kilpatrick

Davies

*Blue Ridge
Turnpike*

Rapidan River

JACK'S SHOP
SEPTEMBER 22, 1863

Union Cavalry

Confederate Cavalry

Miles

0   1/4   1/2

Chapter 13

Delony's Last Battle:
September 1863

With that, straight up the hill there rode
Two horsemen drenched with gore,
And in their arms, a helpless lord,
A wounded knight they bore.
——Sir Walter Scott

When Stuart was driven out of Culpeper, he set up his headquarters at Brampton, the home of his longtime friend Dr. Andrew Grinnan. Brampton was a quarter mile from Peyton's Ford on the Rapidan. It was from here that Stuart directed the operations of his three brigades during the middle of September 1863. Stuart personally commanded Hampton's Division while the South Carolina major general continued recovering from wounds received at Gettysburg. Hampton's Division, under the 9 September cavalry reorganization, was comprised of three brigades: Butler's Brigade (formerly Wade Hampton's), commanded by Matthew C. Butler, presently being commanded by Col. Pierce M. B. Young while Butler also recovered from his earlier wounds; Jones's ("Grumble") Brigade commanded by Col. O. R. Funsten, which included the 7th, 11th, and 12th Virginia cavalry; and Baker's Brigade commanded by Brig. Gen. Lafayette S. Baker, including the 1st, 2nd, 4th, and 5th North Carolina Cavalry.[1] Butler's Brigade consisted of five regiments including Cobb's, Phillips's (commanded by Delony), and Jeff Davis's legions and the 1st and 2nd South Carolina Regiments. The division also had a battery of the horse artillery commanded by Capt. W. M. McGregor (Virginia) consisting of six guns. Hampton's Division guarding Lee's left totaled approximately 2,500 effectives and were outnumbered nearly 3-to-1 by the two Union divisions opposing them.[2]

---

[1] William D. Henderson, *The Road to Bristol Station: Campaigning with Lee and Meade, August 1–October 2* (Lynchburg, VA: H. E. Howard, Inc., 1987) 47–48.

[2] The force of Stuart's Division was reported as low as 2,000 (Harold R. Woodward Jr., *For Home and Honor: The Story of Madison County, Virginia, during the War between the States, 1861–1865*, privately printed, nd, 71) and as high as 3,000 (David Maurer, "Yesteryears: Madison County's Battle of Jack's Shop Even Stumps Civil War Experts," dailyprogress.com/lifestyles/yesteryears

Reacting to threats became routine for Hampton's Division as they marched and fought almost daily following Meade's crossing of the Rappahannock with two of his divisions of cavalry and infantry on Sunday 13 September. From the 14th through the 19th, the Confederate cavalry saw action at Rapidan Station, Robertson's Ford, and twice at Raccoon Ford.[3] After Meade drove Stuart back to the Rapidan, the Union general planned to continue the offensive push.

Intelligence from Buford's reconnaissance, however, reported the Confederate army was well entrenched around the Rapidan, leading many excited high-ranking Union officers to believe Meade would immediately strike Lee's left. That possibility ended when the news of the Chickamauga disaster (20th September) reached Washington. A nervous Washington administration withdrew two corps from Meade's Army, forcing the commander to forgo his plans.[4]

Since the right flank of Lee's Corps was well secured by Fitzhugh Lee's cavalry division, Meade eyed Lee's left flank with anticipation of striking a blow there. He sent two divisions of Alfred Pleasanton's Cavalry Corps, John Buford of the First Division and Judson Kilpatrick of the Third Division, around the Robinson and Rapidan rivers "to assess the roads in Madison County and the bridges and fords of those rivers."[5]

Lee, anticipating a movement to his left from Meade, sent a letter to Butler on the 19th to be alert. Cobb's regiment was on picket when Lee's letter arrived and Delony wrote to Rosa that "they would probably cross my front." Delony was "anxious with only 200 men in all" facing a potential attack from Meade's army.[6] On the morning of 21 September, Buford and Kilpatrick's divisions, totaling over 7,000 troops, joined forces and crossed the Robinson River at Russell's Ford. Just before sundown they entered the town of Madison County Court House and drove out a small Confederate outpost of fifteen men. The Union divisions camped in the town for the night.[7] The outpost alerted Stuart at Brampton around midnight and he immediately notified his division to be in the saddle at first light.

On Tuesday morning, Buford's and Kilpatrick's divisions split, with Kilpatrick moving out of Madison County Court House with two brigades: Henry Davies, with the First Brigade, and Col. Peter Stagg of the 1st Michigan with the Second

---

_column/yesteryears-madison-county-s-battle-of-jack-s-shop-even/article_5798c608-1c09-11e5-0019bb30f31a.html).

[3] Harriet Bey Mesic, *Cobb's Legion Cavalry: A History and Roster of the Ninth Georgia Volunteers in the Civil War* (Jefferson, NC: McFarland, 2009) 91.

[4] Henderson, *Road to Bristol Station*, 62, 63, 68.

[5] Mesic, *Cobb's Legion Calvary*, 51.

[6] Will Delony to Rosa Delony, camp near Orange County Court House, 21 September 1863, Delony Papers.

[7] Woodward, *For Home and Honor*.

Brigade. Stagg commanded Custer's Brigade while Custer recovered from his earlier wounds. The division moved 8 miles southwest and crossed the Rapidan near Burtonsville.[8] After making the other side, Kilpatrick turned southeast, patrolling the south side of the river, headed in the direction of Liberty Mills.

Meanwhile, Buford split his division sending Thomas Devin's Brigade (less the 6th New York Cavalry) east toward Barnett's Ford on the Rapidan. Buford accompanied Col. George Chapman's 6th New York Brigade, headed almost due south of Madison along the Blue Ridge Turnpike.[9] Stuart, meanwhile, was heading toward Madison County Court House when he received intelligence of the superior strength of the Union cavalry. He contacted Jubal Early, who was entrenched at Liberty Mills guarding Lee's left flank, asking for infantry help. Early declined, saying his "men were tired and needed to rest." Perhaps Early's known dislike of the cavalry was a factor in the profane and grouchy general not honoring Stuart's request.[10]

Stuart had no intention of bringing on a battle with the two Union divisions that outnumbered him more than 3-to-1. His mission was to see what the Union cavalry was up to and report the information to Lee at his headquarters in nearby Orange County. Stuart arrived with his division a few miles north of Jack's Shop at O'Neal's Crossing. Leaving a rear guard at the crossing, Stuart took the remainder of his troops into Jack's Shop. The small hamlet consisted of no more than a few houses and two churches at an intersection where a post office was installed in March 1854. The postal service named the village Rochelle, but it was still called Jack's Shop because of Jack's Blacksmith Shop, which was located there.[11]

When Stuart entered Jack's Shop, he decided to pause and let the troops have their meal and take advantage of the blacksmith's shop to tend to some of the horses.[12] While most of Stuart's Division was resting, a Federal patrol from Chapman's 6th New York ran into Stuart's rear guard at O'Neal's Crossing. After an exchange of gunfire, Stuart ordered parts of Young's and Baker's brigades to dismount and form a skirmish line perpendicular to the turnpike. The rest of the brigade, still mounted, charged the blue-clad troopers. Chapman's men, however, were armed with rapid-firing breechloaders and soon broke the charge. Stuart ordered his men

---

[8] Henderson, *Road to Bristol Station*, 53.

[9] Ibid., 63; Woodward, *For Home and Honor*, 71.

[10] Woodward, *For Home and Honor*, 72; Gary W. Gallagher contends Early, whom Robert E. Lee called "my bad old man," disliked the cavalry, calling them "Buttermilk Rangers" and accusing them of not fighting and of stealing from civilians. "Robert E. Lee and His High Command," *The Great Courses* (Chantilly, VA: The Teaching Company, 2004).

[11] Harold R. Woodward Jr., telephone interview, 28 March 2014. Madison, Virginia.

[12] Woodward telephone interview, 28 March 2014.

to dismount and form skirmish lines. Buford immediately sent a courier to Kilpatrick ordering him to recross the Rapidan and hit Stuart in the rear.[13]

The men of Cobb's Legion were relaxing on the ground in a hollow next to the Jack's Shop, smoking their pipes, the reins of their horses tied to their ankles, "a favorite way with old cavalrymen," while the horses grazed. Suddenly, all hell broke loose as shots rang out from just over the hill and "bullets were whistling around."[14] Young immediately took some of Cobb's Legion with him to the action, leaving Delony, still mounted, in charge of the rest of the legion. Capt. Francis Eve, commanding the Richmond Dragoons, described the scene years later in a Memorial Day speech. Eve vividly recalled he was there with "my two best friends, W. G. Delony and W. L. Church...smoking our pipes.... Little did we think, that in a few moments we would never meet again."[15]

After the Confederates formed their skirmish lines near the crossroads, they advanced steadily through the effective use of their sharpshooters. However, as more Union troops arrived on the scene, the fighting escalated and the tide began to turn in favor of the blue coats as they were able to bring their artillery to bear. Stuart responded with his six-gun battery that countered the Union advance.

It wasn't long before a portion of Kilpatrick's Division came upon the rear of Stuart's position. The 2nd New York of Davies' Brigade was far ahead of the rest of Kilpatrick's Division as they began to funnel in piecemeal. In order to meet the new threat, a shocked Stuart dispatched Funsten's Brigade and part of Young's (from the front line) to engage Davies. Stuart also shifted half of McGregor's six-gun battery on the hill, which had been firing north, to start firing south.[16]

A squadron of the 11th Virginia was the first of Funsten's Brigade to arrive, according to Lt. John Blue. The day was foggy and mixed with the smoke of battle and visibility was extremely poor as the regiment charged downhill, "firing in the air and yelling like savages." The regiment suddenly found themselves in the midst of "a raging sea of blue coats" limiting the use of their revolvers. "It was cut, thrust and parry; parry, thrust, and cut." Cutting their way back to a perceived safety at the top of the ridge they were suddenly met by a volley from an undetected Union regiment that emptied nearly every saddle, with the result being that every member of the

---

[13] Henderson, *Road to Bristol Station*, 56.

[14] Athens *Banner* (30 April 1892).

[15] Capt. Francis Edgeworth Eve, "Address on Confederate Memorial Day, April 26, 1893, to the Ladies of the Memorial Association, Athens, Georgia," Athens *Banner* (30 April, 2 May 1893).

[16] Henderson, *Road to Bristol Station*, 57.

squadron was either killed or captured. Seriously wounded and captured, Blue spent the remainder of the war in the Old Capitol Prison in Washington, DC.[17]

When Buford heard the exchange of the fire south of Jack's Shop, he pressed Chapman to apply more force to break the Confederate line. The line started to sway and give ground. Delony, worried that the line would break, gave Eve permission to mount and advance as skirmishers to give the front line time to regain their horses and mount.

Just when it appeared it could not get any worse for Stuart—it did! Thomas Devin's Brigade, responding to the sound of gunfire, started attacking the Confederates from a third direction. McGregor's six-gun battery was divided again, with two guns firing north, two firing south, and two firing southeast!

As noted in the Athens *Banner*, the regiment was ordered to fall back and form a defensive line

> in front of and beyond the shop, and we fighting back from the rear of the shop. Deloney had waited for us, ordering Church, our adjutant, to form the regiment. The enemy making a forward movement, we had to show a bold front to keep him from charging. Here I was re-inforced by Lieut. D. A. Dougherty, (who was almost immediately shot) with the Atlanta squadron, and who has since the war become known as the merchant prince, and to whom I turned over the command.[18]

Meanwhile, Captain Eve was in the thick of it helping to relieve the pressure on the front line. Eve and Delony led a charge "down a lane leading by a barn, [where we] ran into a ambuscade of men posted in the barn who dealt death and destruction upon us."[19] Eve was soon shot in the chest and at that same moment turned to see Delony's "horse make a lunge, falling with the Colonel against a clapboard fence around a garden in the rear of Jack's shop." Eve said the horse hurled "the fence to the ground in his death struggle."[20] Delony's "baymare" was shot first in the flank and almost immediately Delony was shot in the left thigh with a shotgun blast, "the same shot killing his horse instantly."[21] As Wiley Howard recorded,

[17] Don Oates, *Hanging Rock Rebel: Lt. John Blue's War in West Virginia and the Shenandoah Valley* (Shippensburg, PA: White Mane Publishing, 1993) 267.

[18] Athens *Banner* (30 April 1892).

[19] Wiley C. Howard, "Sketch of Cobb Legion Cavalry and Some Incidents and Scenes remembered" (Atlanta: Camp 159, published talk given at U.C.V. meeting) 19 August 1901, 23–24.

[20] Eve, "Address on Confederate Memorial Day, April 26, 1893."

[21] Barrington S. King, from a Camp Near Orange Court House, to his father, Barrington King, in Roswell Georgia, 26 September 1863, Tammy Harden Galloway, *Dear Old Roswell: The Civil War Letters of the King Family of Roswell, Georgia* (Macon, GA: Mercer University Press, 2003) 37–41.

Three Yankees seeing his almost helpless position and that he was an officer of note dashed upon him to subdue, capture him or kill him, shooting and cutting him from their horses. But this superb fighter, with his Hugunot blood boiling, raised himself on one knee and with his dexterous and wiry arm fenced and parried their blows, Charley Harris who was helping him, being wounded, until Bugler H. E. Jackson of Company C, Cobb Legion, who was coming up from the rear, spurred his horse to the fray and to DeLoney's aid, fencing with these daring assailants, at last by a dexterous movement successfully thrust one man through the side, the others escaping with saber wounds from DeLoney's shimmering blade as he rose to his feet.[22]

Quickly recognizing their situation, Delony ordered "Church, our adjutant, to form the regiment...in lines of battle in front of and beyond the shop."[23] In a span of less than five minutes, "some four or five officers were killed and wounded and about fifteen men were slain or wounded."[24] The action prevented Chapman's force from charging with a possible knockout blow. Barrington King wrote his father a couple of days later with his account of the battle.

We have had another terrible cavalry fight & I passed through all safe. I will tell you about our last fight. We were in saddle at 4 AM Tuesday to meet the enemy who had forced a crossing at Russels ford across the Roberson river (which is our dividing line now to where it empties into the Rapidan there the Rapidan down to the Potomac) on the pike leading from Culpeper C. H. to Madison C. H. We took blind roads leading through the woods until we struck the pike leading from Madison C. H. to Gordonsville about 4 miles from the former place. Shortly after striking the Pike we met the enemy's advance Guard & the fight began. Our force was only Hampton's Division consisting of Bakers, Butlers, & Genes Brigades (Butlers is Hamptons old Brigade in which our Regt. is) in all numbering about 2000 men (the summers campaign has cut us down terribly) Genes Brigade was on the left, ours centre, and Bakers right.

Our fighting began as all our Cavalry fights begin by dismounting & skirmishing. The fight soon became pretty warm & for some hours we held our ground although the enemys skirmishes were 4 times more than ours. About two oclock our right flank fell back or was forced back then the left-flank retreated in almost a panic. Our center remained firm till almost surrounded they fell back in good order to their horses which the mounted men of our Regt & the 2nd S.C. held the ground until every

---

[22] Howard, "Sketch of Cobb's Legion Cavalry," 23–24.
[23] Eve, "Address on Confederate Memorial Day, April 26, 1893."
[24] Howard, "Sketch of Cobb's Legion Cavalry," 23–24.

Regt had retreated down the Pike. The sharp shooters of the enemy were within a hundred yds of us pouring in the bullets our Loss was heavy. Col Delinys horse was shot first in the flank & almost immediately after he himself shot through the leg the same shot killing his horse instantly.... Our loss was 17 wounded (privates) 3 officers, Killed 3 privates. To our great regret Col Deleny, our Surgeon and 4 of our wounded while going to the rear were captured. He is a great loss to our Regt & our whole cavalry division for all the cavalry force know that Cobb Legion with Col Deleny leading them can never be run by Yankees.... We can only mount 140 men for duty now.[25]

Captain Eve was beginning to feel "clammy" with his chest wound and started looking for medical help. He joined the line of wounded that was ordered to move on the turnpike south toward Liberty Mills on the Rapidan. Stuart began to reform his division to cut its way out of the trap and was lining up the wounded when the break occurred. As Eve moved with the line, he "overtook Colonel Delony mounted on another horse although his leg was bleeding." Sighting Eve, Delony assured him, "No bones are broken, but that the horse, in falling, had hurt him more than the shots." Delony asked Eve to "ride forward and tell Dr. Bradley to hurry up with the ambulance and he felt fainty." They exchanged remarks about Eve's wounds and Delony told him he was going to see that he got a promotion and ended by telling Eve to "go hurry up and get Bradley." Eve painfully recalled, "We parted never to meet again."[26]

When Stuart saw that he was being hit from three sides by a numerically superior force that was growing in strength, he knew the situation was critical. He shouted to his troop, "Boys, it's a fight to captivity, death or victory!" It took "inspirational leadership, high morale, and good training and experience" for the division to get out of the trap.[27] Stuart and his men needed all of those assets to meet the crisis. He boldly decided to shift some of his troops from the front line, north of Jack's Shop, to support Funsten who had been attempting to break through Davies's Brigade and open the road to Liberty Mills. Doing so was not an easy task, as more of Kilpatrick's forces were moving to the battle. Stuart, who was directing traffic in the thick of the fight, had a horse shot from under him, a not uncommon happening for the flamboyant cavalry leader. The gamble of shifting troops from the front line to aid Funsten began to pay off. One of Funsten's regiments was able to tear

---

[25] Galloway, *Dear Old Roswell*, 37–40.
[26] Eve, "Address on Confederate Memorial Day, April 26, 1893."
[27] Henderson, *Road to Bristol Station*, 58.

down a rail fence that was shielding some of Davies's troops, which cleared a gap through which the Confederates could pass.[28]

Davies, a crafty commander, continued to make it difficult for Stuart to cut through the trap. In an area further south on the turnpike where the woods came close to the road, he stationed sharpshooters who fired on the retreating Confederates as they galloped by. The Confederates had to endure this crossfire for a half mile before they had a clearing to the bridge spanning the Rapidan at Liberty Mills. Many did not make it. There were running fights all the way with Buford and Davies's men in hot pursuit throughout the 5-mile chase.

With Delony injured, Maj. Barrington S. King was put in charge of the regiment. The unit was immediately placed in the rear as the shield for the retreating division. King positioned a small band of "mounted sharpshooters fifty yards in our rear to keep the enemy's sharpshooters from crowding us too close." The regiment slowly retreated down the pike as the Union combatants were within "one to four hundred yards...that kept up a galling fire all the time." The Union sharpshooters were armed with long-range rifles and were inflicting heavy damage on the regiment.[29]

The Union sharpshooters soon pressed the Confederates so closely that Stuart ordered "the rear squadron to charge them." The regiment took off down the road, causing many of the blue coats to drop their guns and run into the woods.[30] After the successful charge the regiment retreated safely and crossed the Rapidan.

Buford's troops, ever tenacious, followed Stuart's retreating divisions across the Rapidan but soon ran into reinforcements from A. P. Hill's Corps, along with two cavalry brigades from Fitz Lee. The arrival of these fresh troops caused Buford to retire back across the Rapidan, his men worn out after eight hours of combat.[31] The next day Buford left Madison County as more Confederate troops moved to the scene.

"The enemy attacked our left flank with superior numbers," wrote F. W. Walker. "They evidently wished to pay Gordonsville and Charlottesville a visit. However, they were held back until Fitz Lee's Division came up. When they smelled this they withdrew in the night. The fights were quite desperate. The Yankees almost surrounded Hampton's Division. Here we lost Col. Deloney danger-

---

[28] Woodward, *For Home and Honor*, 76.

[29] Galloway, *Dear Old Roswell*, 40.

[30] King reported to his father that the regiment lost seventeen wounded in the battle, including three officers and three privates killed: "We can only mount 140 for duty now [and the regiment] lost nearly 100 quality horses in the last two fights." Galloway, *Dear Old Roswell*, 40.

[31] Henderson, *Road to Bristol Station*, 60.

ously wounded and captured. It is a hard blow for the regiment. Capt. King took command."[32]

To Stuart's credit, he was able to get most of his command, including his horse artillery, out of the trap. However, he was unable to take his wounded with him. Kilpatrick swarmed down and captured the wounded Confederates, including Will Delony and his close friends Dr. Henry S. Bradley and Cpl. Reuben L. Nash. Both men were members of Delony's old Company C and both chose to stay with their beloved friend. Delony was first taken to the Union hospital in Culpeper, where Dr. Bradley administered to him. The next day they were separated, and Delony gave his watch to Dr. Bradley to keep.[33] Delony was carried to Stanton U.S.A. General Hospital in Washington, DC, on 25 September.[34]

Both Buford and Stuart reported the engagement a success, and based on the perceived mission of both sides, the reported successes were probably accurate. The numerical superiority of the Federal cavalry and their ability to develop a double envelopment of Stuart's force should have resulted in the latter's total destruction. At the very least, Buford could rightfully boast of having bested Stuart on this day. At the same time, it was something of a miracle that Stuart was able to extricate himself and his greatly outnumbered body out of the trap, escape, and remain intact. If Kilpatrick's force had not arrived on the scene as haphazardly as they did, Stuart would not have had the time to react and fight his way out as he was able to.

The Battle of Jack's Shop, in which approximately 10,000 troops were engaged, was a costly one, especially for Stuart's Division. William Von Raab, former United Stated Customs Commissioner under President Ronald Reagan (1981–1984), chaired and spearheaded the sesquicentennial commemoration of the battle. According to Von Raab, "twelve to fifteen percent of the troops engaged (almost 1500) were wounded or killed, with the Confederates sustaining the most causalities."[35] During the planning of the 150th commemoration of the Battle of Jack's Shop, the Charlottesville *Daily Progress*, in bold headlines, called Jack's Shop "THE

---

[32] F. W. Walter Letters, in private collection.

[33] Dr. Bradley eventually got the watch to Rosa Delony several months after Col. Delony's passing. Henry S. Bradley to Rosa Delony, Jackson County, Georgia, 29 February 1864, Delony Papers.

[34] Stanton General Military Hospital, named after Secretary of War Edwin M. Stanton, was one of numerous Civil War hospitals in the Washington, DC, area during the course of the war.

[35] Courtney Griffin, "MC to Commemorate Civil War Battle," dailyprogress.com/madisonnews/news/local/mc-to-commemorate-civil-war-battle/article_3f67a896-0ff8-11e3-b24b-001a4bcf6878.html.

BIGGEST CAVALRY BATTLE YOU NEVER HEARD OF."[36] The quote was later attributed to Madison County historian Harold Woodward Jr.[37]

---

[36] *Daily Progress*, 12 July 2010. http://www.dailyprogress.com/lifestyles/learn-about-battle-of-jack-s-shop/article_d357c58a-d06c-5b1a-8efa-7b64edc59fe5.html.

[37] Woodward interview, 28 March 2014.

Chapter 14

Aftermath

> Her long descended lord is gone,
> And left us by the stream alone.
> And much I miss those sportive boys,
> Companions of my mountain joys.
> —Sir Walter Scott

Maj. Delony Wounded again!
We regret to learn that our esteemed fellow-citizen, Maj. W. G. Delony, was wounded in the late skirmish at Madison C. H., Va., and taken prisoner by the Yankees. Surgeon Bradley, of Danielsville, we are sorry to learn, was also captured.[1]

Rosa knew nothing of the fate of her husband for a week until she read in *The Southern Watchman* that her beloved Will had been wounded in the latest fighting and taken prisoner. The announcement was a depressing blow to Rosa, but that bad news paled in comparison to the devastating news that soon followed.

Will Delony lingered for a week in a Washington hospital before dying on 2 October 1863. On 6 October, his close friend, Willie Church, telegraphed Mrs. Pleasant Stovall, the Delony's dear friend in Athens, that an extract had appeared in the *Washington Chronicle* (Federal) on the 5th stating that "W. G. Delony, Lt. Col. of Cobb's Legion joined the Rebel Service in Athens, Georgia died on Friday afternoon from the effects of gunshot wounds he received on the left leg. His funeral took place on Saturday after evening about four o'clock at Stanton Hospital where he died.—W. L. Church."[2] Church added that Mrs. Stovall should "break the news to Mrs. Delony as best you can...on account of her condition."[3] At the time, Rosa was pregnant with the couple's fifth child.

---

[1] *Southern Watchman* (30 September 1863).

[2] Delony Papers, Hargrett Rare Book & Manuscript Library, University of Georgia.

[3] "Her condition" was that Rosa was ten months pregnant with the couple's fifth child. See Angela Esco Elder, "A Community of Condolences: The Civil War Experience of Rosa Delony" (unpublished paper, History Department, University of Georgia, 2012) 6.

The morning after Delony's death, a "magnificent metallic coffin" was left on the hospital steps with a card attached "for the remains of Colonel Delony." Rosa tried in vain for years to find out who secretly furnished the coffin for her husband.[4] One theory among some Civil War enthusiasts is that Union general George Custer left the coffin upon the request of his old West Point friend and Civil War rival, Confederate general Pierce M. B. Young. There is no proof to substantiate the theory, but it makes for an intriguing story.[5]

The same day she received the official news of her husband's death, Rosa received his personal effects from Dr. P. B. Shields, a Confederate surgeon, also prisoner, who aided the Union surgeon at the Stanton Hospital. The effects included a telescope and sunglasses.[6] A few months later, she received her husband's watch that Delony had given to his good friend Dr. Bradley, who had elected to stay behind to care for Delony and was also captured. According to Bradley, after their capture, the two were quickly separated, and as he relayed to Rosa some five months later in a personal letter, he was still angered, as his captors had assured him that he "would be allowed to remain with his best friend."[7]

The tragedy of Will Delony's passing, like thousands of others played out over the three preceding years, had a deep impact on everyone involved with the family. "One can only imagine," writes historian Angela Elder, "the tragedy of the situation as Mrs. Stovall reluctantly knocked on Rosa's door...to break the news."

In addition to her sorrow, Rosa had to deal with the reality of providing for her children and running the house. Rosa's mother-in-law, Maria Delony, expected her daughter-in-law to follow her example of addressing the needs of the children over her own suffering.[8] However, she was gentle in making her point while writing to Rosa from Milwaukee, where she was staying with her widowed daughter Martha. She assured Rosa that "God will help you thru your troubles." She continued by cautioning her "not to give up to your feelings...but think of those precious ones whose sole dependence is upon you, strive to cheer up."[9]

---

[4] Harold R. Woodward Jr., *For Home and Honor: The Story of Madison County, Virginia, during the War between the States, 1861–1865*, privately printed, nd, 76.

[5] Personal interview with historian and Brandy Station preservationist Clark "Bud" Hall, 25 July 2013.

[6] Also included among the personal effects was one promissory note for $49.25, one note for $275, and $5.55 in Confederate money. W. H. Channing to Rosa Delony, 28 November 1863, Delony Papers.

[7] Henry S. Bradley to Rosa Delony, 29 February 1864, Delony Papers.

[8] Elder, "A Community of Condolence," 12.

[9] Marie Delony to Rosa Delony, 11 August 1864, Delony Papers. Will's mother arrived in Washington after he died and was given Will's gold pen case as a memento.

In the winter of 1864, Rosa filed two claims: one for Will's back pay and one for his horse that was lost at Jack's Shop. General Young supported the claim for the horse with the notation, "Horse was lost during a charge upon the enemy at the time and date specified, and Col. Delony was struck from his saddle by a sabre cut and severely wounded & therefore the horse was not lost by fault or neglect of his but while in the full discharge of his duties."[10] Rosa received payment of $800 for the loss of the horse as well as $199.82 for the period from 31 August through 2 October 1863 for her husband's back pay. On 12 April 1864, she received an additional $500 for the loss of her husband's beloved Marmion.

Meanwhile, Rosa, like so many wives who were made widows by the Civil War, had to deal with her personal grief and loneliness. Fortunately, she was surrounded by relatives and friends in a community who reached out to provide sympathy and support. Marion Cobb, the widow of Thomas R. R Cobb, who had lost her husband less than a year earlier, was one who could truly understand and feel Rosa's pain. She visited with her often, offering understanding and condolences. Rosa's cousin, Martha D. Duncan, of Savannah, was one of her most constant and comforting letter writers, as was her mother-in-law. On several occasions, Martha wrote to Rosa about Will's brother Robert, who, along with his wife, Virginia, moved from Madison, Georgia, to Athens to stay with Rosa during her time of grieving. Rosa's burden was exacerbated by her last stage of pregnancy.[11] Having her brother-in-law and sister-in-law living with her during this terrifying time was a blessing and a source of great comfort.[12]

Word of Delony's death spread throughout the city of Athens. On 14 October 1863, *The Southern Watchman* headlined, "ANOTHER GALLANT SPIRIT GONE!" and continued: "Among the vast army of martyrs who have yielded up their lives in defense of human liberty, death has stilled no braver or warmer heart than that of our late gallant townsman, Lieut. Col. Wm. G. Delony, who we regret

---

[10] Garry Adelman and Sam Smith, Civil War Trust Historians and Educations Specialists, unpublished paper on William G. Delony, Washington, DC, 17 April 2013.

[11] Rosa gave birth to Martha Roberta on 8 November 1863, a little over a month after Will's death. Charlotte Marshall, *Oconee Hill Cemetery of Athens Georgia* (Athens, GA: Athens Historical Society, 2009) 285. The elusive Robert apparently left his position in Richmond with the home guard between June and September of 1863 to come home to his family. He later showed up as a prisoner of war, according to a report of December 1864 by Gen. Young after the Battle of Waynesboro, Georgia, on 4 December. *Southern Watchman* (28 December 1864). That is the last appearance of Robert Delony found to date.

[12] Martha D. Duncan to Rosa Delony, 13 October, 6 November, 25 November 1863, Delony Papers.

to learn, has died of the wound received at the late engagement at Madison C. H. Va. Peace to his ashes!"[13]

A year after the end of the war, Rosa was presented with the Cobb's Legion battle flag. In his letter to Rosa, F. H. Ivey, one of the veterans of Cobb's Legion, explained that when Delony fell at Jack's Shop he (Delony) gave the flag to his adjutant Frank Jones with the "dying request that it be forwarded to you." Jones was later killed and the flag was then sent to Jones's mother in Thomasville, who passed it on to Ivey for delivery. Ivey wrote that despite the "painful...memory of your great loss...the banner would be to you an invaluable treasure."[14]

Many mourned the loss of Will Delony. Barrington S. King wrote to his father, stating simply that "I feel his loss very very much and am exceedingly sorry to say I take my recent promotion as Lt Col by his death."[15] Although many eulogized the loss of the beloved Delony, it was the men who served with him in combat who had the unique perspective to praise him both as a warrior and as a knight. General P. M. B. Young, in announcing Delony's death to the regiment, wrote "of the gallant, the heroic, the chivalric Colonel Delony. In the camp he was generous and just; on the field of battle he was the bravest of the brave. His name is engraved on the hearts of all who knew him...let us endeavor to emulate his example."[16]

The Athens *Banner* reported, "To his men, who worshipped him, there was no finer soldier in the army than Will Delony. A first-honor graduate of Franklin College, he had practiced law in Athens, where his popularity was such that he was the first Democrat ever to be sent to the state legislature from the Whig-dominated town."[17]

Several weeks later, Rosa received a very respectful letter from Dr. Chaplin Channing, a Union chaplain at Stanton Hospital in Washington, DC, in response to "a number of questions she presented concerning the circumstances surrounding her husband's care, death, and subsequent place of burial in Washington."[18] A few days after receiving the letter from Chaplain Channing, Rosa received a letter of condolence from the chaplain's office at the Stanton Hospital. This letter was well received and kept with her personal belongings for the rest of her life before being

---

[13] *Southern Watchman* (14 October 1863).

[14] F. H. Ivey to Rosa Delony, 18 May 1866, Delony Papers.

[15] Tammy Harden Galloway, *Dear Old Roswell: The Civil War Letters of the King Family of Roswell, Georgia* (Macon, GA: Mercer University Press, 2003) 46.

[16] James T. Voccelle, *History of Camden County, Georgia* (Kingsland, GA: Southeastern Georgian, 1914, reprinted 1967) 106–107.

[17] Athens *Banner* (14 October 1863).

[18] W. H. Channing to Rosa Delony, 28 November 1863, Delony Papers.

passed along with the other correspondence.[19] The information provided in these letters enabled Rosa to locate her husband's remains after the war.

Following her husband's removal from the cemetery in Washington, DC, a year after the war's end, Will's body was shipped back to Athens, arriving on 24 September 1866, almost three years to the date of his last fight at Jack's Shop. He was buried the next day at Oconee Hill Cemetery beside the campus of the University of Georgia. "A grateful loving people," wrote *The Southern Watchman*, "will enshrine his memory in their hearts, and bequeath the story of his deeds and many virtues as a rich legacy to their children."[20]

Rosa kept alive the memories and the treasures of her husband to their children, especially daughter Rosa Eugenia. On one occasion, while young Rosa was visiting a friend in Augusta, a committee representing the Richmond Hussars, who had served under her father, presented her with "an elegant certificate of honorary membership of that troupe."[21] The Hussars paid their highest respect for their late chief by having a picture of the "gallant and lamented Colonel Delony" placed on their banner.[22]

As glowing as the eulogies were from Will Delony's family, friends, and even superior officers, the praise was even more powerful from one of those who fought under him, Wiley C. Howard, who wrote of his former commander:

> [He was] golden-hearted, brave, brainy Delony how his men loved him and how he stood by them...the Henry of Navarre of our cavalry, a real hero above the most extravagant descriptive powers of the gifted novelist writing fiction. He deserved a Brigadier General's Commission, but never sought notoriety or promotion. I admired his character so much that I gave up a first Lieutenancy in an infantry company at Americus and begged a private's place in his company. He took me, though the ranks of his company were already full, and I am proud to have been considered worthy to ride and fight with him.... He died in prison from a gun shot wound in the leg, received in battle at Jack's Shop on the Robinson river, refusing to allow amputation, even though gangrene had set in. If in this sketch I may seem to give him undue prominence, it is because I know he deserved it and on account of my great admiration of his character and the fact that he was my original Captain, and I saw and knew more of him and of his deeds of daring and devotion than of others. His illustrious career gave the command more fame and reputation than any other field company officer or

---

[19] Boeck to Rosa Delony, 3 December 1863, Delony Papers.

[20] *Southern Watchman* (26 September 1866).

[21] Augusta *Chronicle* (26 April 1877).

[22] Ibid., 20 June 1877. The picture is most likely the painting of Delony on horseback.

man in the regiment. The world never produced a better, braver soldier, truer patriot or grander hero than William G. Delony.[23]

In 1892, in a memorial article on Cobb's Legion for the Athens *Banner*, Howard wrote,

> William G. Deloney, Captain-Major, Lieutenant Colonel, idol of the Cobb Legion, our chevelier Bayard, where was your peer? Cut down in the midst of a most brilliant career, marked by bullet and sabre cut, whose gallantry had been recognized by all the commanding officers under whom he had served, adored by his men who dreaded his displeasure even more than they did Yankee bullets. I can picture his martial form even now, with red lined cape thrown back to give full play to his sword arm, his sole brown eyes changed to a fiery scintillating black, his face aglow with the glare of the battle dashing in front of us, one glance down the line and with a "Follow me Cobb Legion" more inspiring than a bugle blast, and how we would go for them.[24]

Even after Rosa died in 1897, young Rosa continued to search for any information concerning her father. She preserved all of the letters exchanged between her parents during the war. She especially treasured the ones her father wrote her when she was only five or six years old. Her persistence paid off in 1904 when she received a letter in response to one she had written to John A. Wright, who she discovered had been a patient in the same Washington hospital with her father. Wright explained to young Rosa that at the time, he was a boy of 18 when Delony was admitted to the hospital. Wright was wounded at Chancellorsville while serving with the 140th Pennsylvania Volunteer Infantry. To Rosa, he reported, "Our surgeons were very attentive to him being favorably impressed by his fine personal appearance and gentlemanly bearing!!" He added that when it was apparent her father's condition turned critical, "your father beckoned to me to come...to read to me from the Bible...particularly the 14th chapter of John." Wright did as asked, and after reading several verses said that Delony burst into tears and said, "Oh, I could die in peace. I could die in peace if I was only home with my wife and children; but it is so hard to die here far from home and among strangers.... I prayed with him and he joined in the prayers." Wright concluded by revealing that after the war he became a Methodist Episcopal preacher and served for 33 years in east Ohio. He concluded, "When I meet your father in Heaven I expect to talk about that death

---

[23] Wiley C. Howard, "Sketch of Cobb Legion Cavalry and Some Incidents and Scenes remembered" (Atlanta: Camp 159, published talk given at U.C.V. meeting) 19 August 1901, 26.

[24] Athens *Banner* (30 April 1892).

bed scene in Stanton Hospital which during all these years has been one of precious memory to me."[25]

Young Rosa married John H. Hull in 1883, and the couple had four children. Hull was one of the most prominent family names in the history of Athens and the University of Georgia. They moved into a "high-style Victorian home" built by the elder Rosa for her daughter to raise her family.[26] Rosa Hull passed on to her four children all of the memories, the recorded history, and oral traditions that were passed on to her by her mother. Rosa and John Hull's fourth child, Leila May, who married Maj. Hunter Harris in 1923, became the guardian of many of the Delony and Huguenin papers before passing them on to the Hargrett Rare Book & Manuscript Library in the Richard B. Russell Special Collections Library at the University of Georgia. Leila May's sister Rosa Delony, the oldest of the four children, who married Gordon Cubbedge Carson, also possessed many of the Delony-Huguenin papers and documents.[27]

Before Leila May was married, she spearheaded the placement of a monument to her grandfather that was unveiled on Confederate Memorial Day, 26 April 1915.[28] Most of the commemoration exercises that day took place at the chapel on the university campus. Among the many speakers were (Maj.) Wiley Howard who over a decade earlier wrote his sketch of Cobb's Legion and his reminiscences of his beloved Lt. Col. William Delony. Among the many incidences he recalled that day of his commander was the "care and thoughtfulness of Colonel Delony for his men and of the tenderness in the relation between him and his followers." He further told the gathering of two remarkable examples of Delony's personal bravery in battle. Howard was "chocked with emotion on a couple of occasions as he recalled the memories of his friend and hero leading a charge or fighting single-handed from six to ten of the enemy." After the chapel ceremony, about sixty Confederate veterans and members of the Daughters of the Confederacy, who were in attendance, proceeded in "carriages and automobiles to the cemetery for the unveiling of the monument to Delony."[29]

---

[25] John A. Wright to Mrs. J. H. Hull (Rosa), 18 January 1904, Delony Papers.

[26] The house located at 323 Hill Street in the Cobbham District was sold by the children in 1946, and after several owners, it is now in the possession of Tony and Elizabeth DeMarco, who in 2000 performed extensive renovations.

[27] The Carsons lived in Savannah, and Gordon Carson did extensive research on the genealogy of the two families. Some of the research findings are already in the Hargrett Library at the University of Georgia, while the remainder are presently in possession of Emily C. Carnes of Richmond Hill, Georgia.

[28] In the twentieth century, before Memorial Day was federalized to a weekend holiday in late May, the South was more diligent in honoring those who died in the Civil War.

[29] Athens *Banner* (27 April 1915).

The main speaker at the gravesite prior to the unveiling was Dr. Edward D. Newton, a student of Delony's before the war, when the latter was a teacher at the university. Newton became the driving force in the founding of the Athens Garden Club, the first women's garden club in America. He began his eulogy by saying, "Today we honor southern knighthood." He spoke of his "love and admiration for my teacher and my gallant comrade of Lee's army."[30] After Newton's eulogy, taps was played over the grave by the university cadets as Leila May unveiled the monument that stands today in Oconee Hill Cemetery.[31]

Macon Daily Telegraph

[dateline Athens April 25]

Memorial Day was marked in the unveiling of a monument in Oconee Cemetery to the memory of Col. William Deloney. The unveiling, with taps sounded over the grave by the university cadets, was by Miss Leila May Hull, a granddaughter of the late Colonel Deloney, and the remarks, touching and eloquent, at the grave were delivered by Dr. E. D. Newton of Athens, a pupil of Colonel Deloney when he was a teacher before the war in Franklin College. The State Normal, the Lucy Cobb girls, the Georgia students and high school children were in attendance. The crosses of honor were delivered for the chapter of Daughters by Mrs. S. J. Tribble, and the awards were made of prizes in the essay contests directed by the U.D.C. A great dinner was served to the veterans by the women of the Rutherford chapter of Daughters of the Confederacy.

The Delony legacy is carried on still today by the ancestors of Will and Rosa: the Carsons, the Carnes, the Hulls, the Maiers, the Steeles, and many others. The legacy is carried on in the town that Will and Rosa loved so well. Today they rest, side by side, in the shadow of where many thousands gather on Saturdays every fall, as is most fitting, to cheer on modern-day warriors in a different type of war. After all, William G. Delony was the first Bull Dog of Georgia.

* * *

Marietta 2d Oct 1863

My dear dear Rosa

The Athens paper of this morning gives us the sad news of our beloved Will's wound & his being also a prisoner. Most truly, do we feel for him & sympathize with you, for I can well understand the heart agony you are enduring. But my dear

---

[30] Ibid., 27 April 1915. During the war, Newton served both in Cobb's legion and later in Robert E. Lee's Army of Northern Virginia as a surgeon during the Overland Campaign.
[31] Marshall, *Oconee Hill Cemetery*, 285.

Rosa thank God that his precious life is spared & let us pray & hope for the best. He shall of course with you feel most anxious & when you do have tidings of express him, do let us know. For his sake, for your own sake, & that of your dear children try to be calm & composed, & may a merciful God restore your beloved husband to you. I have seen so much suffering lately, that it has unnerved me. Our poor wounded from above daily are being brought down. Marietta is one vast hospital & almost every private house has some of the sick & wounded also. Arthur Whitney is with us, sick in bed, Chronic Dysentery. He looks miserably. Two young Lieuts from Tenn are sick & are wounded in right hand. I also have the care of. The latter will never again have the use of his right arm, & yet seems cheerful. May God bless our noble men, & be with them in this their hour of need. I also see the death of Edwin Baxter & must write a few lines to my afflicted friend. Oh! Rosa, I can feel with those who suffer. Lucie is quite well & hearty. Hugh been suffering all summer from teething. We have tried to get a house for the winter at Macon, Americus, & other places, but have failed. I dread to carry the family to Savh to be in a state of excitement all winter. I have tried also for board for Aunty & Nellie & cant get it. The latter expects to go to Montgomery. I remain as long as it is safe with Mrs Brown. Aunty I suppose will have to go to Savh. She sends much love & sympathy to you, as do Ma D & Nellie. Bob is at Bath, goes from there to see Lula. With love for Virginia. Kisses for the children & a large share for yourself, believe me in truth.

Your aff & sympathizing cousin
MDD

Oct. 13, 1863

Rosa,

My poor suffering sister, how my heart bleeds for you and how I weep with you. I cannot comfort you my own heart is too bitterly grieving. I can but put my arm around you and weep with you for one we so tenderly truly loved. I know that he was the idol of your heart and I know that God alone can sustain you while passing thru' these deep, deep waters. Little over a year since my beloved son Tom was ushered instantly into eternity my Angel child, that I so loved and now one that I honored while I loved him with a sisters holy tender love. To you my darling I can but pray and weep I can fully understand each heart throb. The yearning for the loved, the agony that we never shall see them more. But oh! Rosa, look upward our circle above is larger than the one below. Many gone before are there to welcome us but a little while and we shall see them face to face, no more to part. And now, my darling sister, let me urge you as a christian for Wills sake (yes he may be near you watching over and caring for you) for the sake of the little ones depending upon you to be calm and trustful. Look to our Father God in this your approachable hour of bitter trial. Lean you head upon the bosom of your sympathizing Savior's and feel that you are not alone. Our chapter in family worship this morning was the death of Lazarus. Martha's grief for her Mother was such that Jesus wept. Yes, my Rosa, that same heart now feels with us and He would not send a pang that He could spare us. Our trials are his but his beloved must suffer here. OH! may He comfort you may He speak peace to your bleeding heart and may you be spared to train up these little ones for God. Our precious William, I trust, is now with God, Free from sorrow and anguish a noble martyr to a noble cause. You knew him better than any one else and you knew what noble, pure spirit his was. Tom Cobb and himself loved each other in life and I think of them now enjoying the blessed rest of the people of God. Dear Marion, she will feel with you and understand your bitter grief. God help you and your dear ones. Sarah help you your dear ones. Sarah Hunters kind letter reached us this morning at the breakfast table. It was a terrible shock and I can only pray for the resignation for you and for myself. I did so love him. I was so proud of him and only a day or two since was telling him of our poor wounded soldiers, about my brother, as I tenderly called him. We feel much indebted to dear Sarah for so kindly and affectionately writing us and I feel that we have her heartfelt sympathy. A whole community, Dear Rosa, feel for you for none knew him but to respect and how many hearts tenderly loved. Robert is in Madison but will grieve to hear this sad news. Aunty feels sincerely and truly for you and says she wishes that she could go to you and nurse you and comfort you but her own heart is suffering for she truly loved our noble Will. Kiss his darling children for me and for their sakes be calm and trust in a merciful God who while he afflicts feels for us. May he bless you my darling and comfort and sustain you is my earnest prayer. Mr. Duncan, Nellie, and Batard (who is here for a few days) send tender sympathy and earnest wishes for your welfare and that of your dear little ones. Aunty warm love and I—oh my dear sister, my heart goes out to you with weeping tenderness and prayers and for our little ones. Love to Virginia and Sarah Hunter and believe me most tenderly your Sister

Martha D. D.

Macon, Ga.
Oct 15, 1863

Dear Sister Rosa,

We have just heard of the calamity which has befallen you and your little ones. We all feel for you and wish that we could see you in some way. Mother is so very ill that we are afraid to tell her, and if she knew all she could not write. She was a little better yesterday but to-day is a great deal worse. She suffers a great deal. Some one sits up with her every night. The Dr. says that under the most favorable circumstances it will be a long time before she can leave her room. I know dear Sister, that you feel very desolate but our heavenly Father who has cared for you all your life long will still watch over you. I am thankful that Grandmother is with you now. Grandmother Fort and Miss Taylor write with me in kindest love and sympathy. Lila and Buddy will write in a day or two, if they do not send their letters by the mail.

Your affectionate Sister
Neallie Huguenin

Marietta Oct 16th 1863

My poor bereaved & broken hearted Child,

I should have written to you sooner, to express my deep sympathy for you, but I was so very unwell & the sad news put me in bed. Oh my poor Child I cannot express my own grief. I know I have lost a dear friend, but my sorrow is nothing compared to yours, for I know what a devoted wife you always have been, & how you idolized your noble & affectionate Husband & I know his great anxiety about you when taken prisoner, how you would grieve & how miserable he felt to be wounded, & separated from you. When he most needed your tender care, precious dear William, I am sure he is gone to rest, for I saw he was a changed man the last time I was with you & lived out the Christian Character, then now that had made a public profession, & my Child you knew his best & ought to be thankful that he has given you the evidence that he was a Christian, & with those hopes you ought to try to feel more resign to the will of God, & not give in to grief & think of your own situation, & then those darlings he has left you to take care & bring up. Oh my poor Rosa, I know you do feel deeply & many a bitter tear will you shed for years to come, look at your children & try to live for them. I know the world will be sad wilderness to you, but try for the sake of your children to be resigned, no one can take the place of a mother, hunt & be resigned to the will of our heavenly Father, & he will be the father of the widow & the Fatherless, he never will forsake those who put there trust in him. I cannot express to you half I feel for you. I wish it was in my powers to go & help nurse you & take care of my dear little pets, but I am so situated. Having the entire care of my darling Lucy, 7 I cannot take her with me, that I am compelled to give up very often what my heart desires, & her Grand Mother has not the health to take the least charge of her at night, & she is so much attached to me, that she would not be satisfied with any one else at night. This is really a trial to me my dearest Rosa, for at this time, I known I could assist you in some way. This is the most terrible bereavement that ever falls to the lot of woman but of Rosa remember God does not willingly afflict just trust him, and be still. He will carry your chrushed and bleeding heart to him, & you have a sincere friend our poor affected friend Mrs Basher that I know, if well enough will be with you in your trial of anguish, how I have felt for her give her my best love, & tell her she knows how I loved & thought so highly of her dear Tom. I hope your Grand Mother may be enduced to remain longer with you. I know Virginia will do all in her power to sooth & comfort you for who is a good Christian & my love to Sarah Fluater, she is another fine friend to you & yours. Nellie sends her tendered love and sympathy to you. She knows full well how to feel for you, do get Virginia to write to me as soon as you are confined for I assure you, I shall be anxious until I hear you are safely through, our love to her, your cousin wrote you Tuesday. She & Mr Duncan sends affectionate love to you. God bless & comfort your heart dearest Rosa prays

Your affectionate
Aunty

Dear dear Rosa,

I think of & pray for you day & night. God knows how tenderly my heart goes out to you & his dear little ones. Take care of yourself & trust in our Father God, who has promised never to forsake us. Oh! My sister, what can I say to comfort you from aching heart I know too well, how vain is the help of man & how the heart cries out with agony & only God can say "Peace be still." Kiss your little darlings for me. If I had health & strength I would go to you my child, but my hands are now full & my health far from good. Hoping to hear from you, I am with best love your own aft cousin & sister.

MDD

Love to Virginia & Sarah H, also dear Mrs Baxter when you see her.

Savannah, Georgia
Nov. 6, 1863

My dear, dear Rosa,

Altho' we only reached here yesterday I feel very tired. I am so anxious to hear from you that I write to beg that Virginia or Sarah Hunter will be kind enough to let me know how you are. My poor child, how I do feel for you and how I pray that a merciful God would sustain you in the hour of trial and be More to you even than the noble husband God has taken. Oh! Rosa, when bowed down with sorrow, what could support us how could we live but for the feeling that our Father reigns and in mercy remembers us. Try, my dear sister cousin to realize a Father's hand in this afflictive dispensation and take care of yourself for your dear children. Who can fill a Mothers place? We stopped a few hours in Macon and Mr. Bloom kindly drove me up to see how Mrs. Huguenin was. I saw Mrs. Fort and she told me that her condition was a very critical one altho' they had strong hopes that she might recover. She does her suffering with great fortitude. They had not told her of your heavy blow as nothing that would agitate or excite her could be mentioned. Mrs. Fort spoke of you most feelingly and of "your noble husband." She is a dear old lady and I pray that this cup may pass away. I heard Mrs. Dr. Wayne who came down the night we did told Mr. Duncan about you and she also mentioned that Robert Delony was in Athens. Did he bring you any more particulars of our sad, sad loss? Give our love to Virginia and himself and let me hear of you, my dear Rosa, if you are not able to write. Kiss those precious little ones that he so loved and may God enable you to train them up for eternal happiness. My tender love always to Marion Cobb and her dear children. I intend writing her. Mr. Duncan sends kind remembrance and Aunty much warm love and with my large share and earnest prayers, I am

> Your attached cousin,
> M. D. D.

> The 2nd Battln Cav Brigd
> Nov 19th 1863

My Dear Madam

It has been my intention for some time to thus address you but I have been prevented by the fear that even my sympathy would appear too formal and cold for such a grief as yours. No one it is true can fully realize your bereavement but I am sure that no one can realize it to a more full extent than myself. The long an[d] internal acquaintance I had with your noble husband, had as you well know resulted in a deep and lasting friendship and I now know and feel that I have lost my most dear and cherished friend, one who I could always look to as an example for nobleness generosity and purity, and who's advice would have been invaluable in after life.

This loss so sudden and unexpected, not only cast a shadow of gloom over his own command but the entire Division, who like all others that knew him had learned to love him. In his loss the government has lost one of its ablest and most devoted defenders and our community one [of] its most high toned and brightest citizens. Often have I wondered why we should have been robbed of Gen Cobb & Col D. men capable of doing so much good in this world while so many who could me thinks are spared. The dispensation of providence is truly mysterious and inexplicable, and how specifically so in this instance.

Of his last moments I am of course unable to give you any information as I was not present but from what I had noticed (and others also) I think you can very quietly hope that he was prepared for that last great hour.

For more than a month Col King and myself had noticed that he seemed more thoughful [*sic*] and had insisted on having divine services and prayer meetings in camps, which he always attended, frequently also he would request us to sing hymns for him which he had not previously been accustomed to do, his greatest favorite being that hymn known as "I launch my bark upon the sea this land is not the land for me." These and other indications showed plainly that some great change of religious feeling was evidently going on with him, which all trust and believe rendered him ready and prepared to die.

Useless indeed would it be for me to express my feelings as I have already said it would appear too cold, gladly would I draw near and unite my tears with yours over his loss, a loss so terribly great to you, so incomparable to me. I can only hope that "he who knows all things" may sustain you in this your great visitation and as the God of the widow and orphan may watch over protect and bless you and your dear little ones.

And in conclusion allow me to add that as I was his friend true & faithful and that as such I must be yours, if at any time by my sacrifice you will allow me by serving you to prove that friendship by assisting you in any way you will greatly oblige one who always has been and ever will be the friend of you and yours. Nothing that I can ever do can repay him for his great and continued kindness to me. Sympathizing and praying for you in this your dark hour of trouble. I remain dear Madam your friend always

W L Church

Savannah, Georgia
November 25, 1863

My very dear Rosa,

I wrote you twice before leaving Marietta and then upon my arrival here am thankful to hear of the birth of your dear little girl and your doing well. May God be with you, my darling, comfort and sustain your heart and give you strength to train up your dear little ones. You have a great work, Rosa. Four immortal spirits to train for life eternal. May you be permitted to raise them for God. I did not receive Sarahs letter written on the 9th until this morning altho' I had heard thro' your Grandmother of the birth of the little girl. We were all glad to hear that it was a girl. Aunty went to see and saw your Grandmother. I went afterwards but she was engaged that morning and had begged to be excused. Since then I have not felt

293

strong enough to walk that far the weather being damp and warm and our horses are in early. When able I shall go again. I am glad to hear that Mrs. Huguenin is better and trust that she may be spared to her family. Remember me kindly to Robert and his wife. How much longer will they be with you? Aunty often speaks of you with much affection. If it had not been for dear little Lucie, she would have gone to you immediately and remained until after your confinement, but I am not strong and aunty has the entire charge of Lucie at night and the little thing is devoted to her and thinks that there is nobody like her. It was a trial to aunty not to go to you and she often speaks of you with much affection and regrets not being able to see you and those dear little ones. She begged me to send much love to you. Kisses for the children and love also for Virginia and Robert, to them give mine also. When you feel able, my darling Rosa, write me and tell me about yourself and dear little ones and our God be all in all to you now in the dark home and comfort your heart as only He can. Kiss my darlings and accept all the love and tenderness of a sisters heart. Mr. Duncan desires to be affectionately remembered. God bless you prays daily

Yours most affectionate,
M. D. D.

Stanton Hospital
Washington, D.C.
Nov 28th 1863

Mrs Rosa E. Delony
Athens, Georgia
Madam,

Your letter, dated Oct 27 making enquiries in regard to the death of your husband Lieut Col. W. G. Delony has this day reached me and I reply as follows,

1q. The Chaplain who was with your husband has lately died. But I learn from others that Col. Delony was glad to receive the Chaplains visits, read much from the Scriptures and seemed resigned to the Will of God. His close was peaceful.

2q. Your husband's wound was a severe one in the thigh. Surgeon Bradley of his own regiment who first attended him hoped to save his limb as no bones were broken. And Surgeon P. B. Shields made prisoner with him attended him to the last and aided the Surgeons of the Hospital. Everything possible was done to save him. But he had lost too much blood, and was too weak to rally. At length the wound mortified and he breathed his last on Oct 2nd a week after his arrival.

3q. Your husband's body was buried in the Cemetery of the Soldier's Home, on the hills to the north of Washington. The number of his Grave is 20; in Range 1; & lock 1. A Head Board marks it.

4q. Col. Delony's mother was written to, and arrived from Michigan, soon after his death and burial. She received, as a memento of her son the gold pencil case which he brought with him to the hospital.

5q. All the effects of your husband were entrusted to Surgeon P. B. Shields, to bring on to send to you, whenever he is exchanged. The most valuable of them were two Promisory Notes, one for $275, the other for $49.25. There were also $5.55 in Southern Currency & a Telescope & Sun Glass. But he brought no watch to the hospital.

6q. I may add, that Lieut Hinds of Cobb's Legion saw more of your husband than any other person while he was here and he will be able satisfactorily to answer your questions. Dan'l A. Connor also of Cobbs Legion was brought in the same ambulance and saw something of Col. Delony. He says that he was cheerful and hoping to recover there.

And no Madam while assuring you that your husband received the best surgical care and affection, I can only bid you in faith and hope to look forward to that world where God shall wipe away all tears from all eyes and there shall be no more death.

With respect & sympathy in your bereavement.
W. H. Channing
Chaplain of Stanton Hospital

Washington D.C. Dec 3d/63

Mrs. W. G. Delony,

Dear Madam,

It is with feelings of the deepest sympathy and regret that I am compelled to announce the death of your husband, who expired at this Hospital last evening at about 9 o clock from the effect of a wound in the leg.

He was admitted into this Hospital Sept 25th 1863. His death was very easy and his only anxiety seemed to be for his family, and perhaps it may be a consolation for you to know that he was attended by the Chaplain and placed his faith in Heaven where I feel he has gone. Everything was done that could be done, but he was too low to have his leg amputated.

Any further information concerning his death will be most freely given.

His burial will take [place] this afternoon at 4 o clock under military honor, and a record of his burial place will be kept at this Hospital.

I am most resply
Your Obt. Ser.
E. F. Boeck
Chaplain's Clerk
Stanton Military Gen. S. Corps

TRIBUTE OF RESPECT

Georgia—Clarke county. Superior Court, February Term, 1864.

His Honor N. L. Hutchins, having announced...the death of Lieut. Wm. G. Delony, the undersigned committee, appointed to prepare a proper tribute of respect to his memory, submit the following:

Among the many sacrifices the Bar of Georgia has made for Southern liberty and independence, no nobler, purer or braver spirit has been offered up than that of Lt. Col. Wm. G. Delony, of Cobb's Ga. Cavalry. A native of Georgia; born in St. Mary's, on the Atlantic coast; descended from highly respected ancestry; originally settled in Virginia; he was educated at the University of the State, where he graduated with the highest honors of his class.... [H]e studied law under William L. Mitchell, Esq., and soon after entered upon the duties of his chosen profession, at Athens, with great promise and success. Of most eloquent manners and handsome person... noble bearing, he was soon called by his fellow-citizens to a seat in the General Assembly of the State, where he at once became prominent and influential.... [H]e retired from the Halls of Legislation to enter upon the sterner and more arduous duties of the soldier, and soon raised and organized one of the first companies that enlisted for the war, and went forth as its Captain.

He rose rapidly to the rank of Lieut. Col. of Cavalry, and so strong was the hold he had taken upon the affections of his company, that Dr. H. S. Bradley and Corp. Reuben Nash, who had served with him from the beginning, preferred to share with him the horrors and solitude of Yankee imprisonment, rather than leave him alone in the hands of the enemy, upon the field on which he received his last fatal wound.

Accordingly, they remained with him to minister to his wants, and were taken prisoners. But the heartless enemy soon deprived him of these faithful friends by separating them from him.

Although he died far from home and friends, it is pleasant to know he became a man of prayer months before his decease....

He was a good lawyer—a cultivated gentleman—a brave and accomplished officer—a true patriot....

It was in one of the most desperate and bloody contests of the war that he fell, wounded through the calf of the leg. Falling into the hands of the enemy, his earnest and lofty soul chafed itself away, under the misfortune thus befallen him and his country. Beloved and deeply mourned by all who knew him; none of our brothers more richly deserve a record upon the minutes of this court than our high-minded Brother Deloney.

Colonel Deloney was a most strikingly handsome man with the most elegant manners, but his magnificent appearance seemed insignificant compared with the beautiful virtues and graces of his character....

He was a symmetrically built man, of commanding mien in any company of commanding characters; his full brown or mahogany beard and high massive forehead, intellectual face and eagle eyes, marked him a leader among men. The world never produced a better, braver soldier, truer patriot or grander hero than Colonel Deloney.

Peace to his ashes and all praise to his heroic name and imperishable fame, linked as it is with the hallowed memories of our Southland and its glorious history.

Resolved, That the Bench and Bar of Clarke Superior Court deeply lament the death of one of their most cherished brethren, Wm. G. Delony, Esq., and sincerely sympathize with his family in the irreparable loss they have sustained....

Asa M Jackson, T. M. Daniel, E. P. Lumpkin, Wm. L. Mitchell

A true extract from minutes of said Court, Fed. 4th, 1864. John Calvin Johnson, Clerk.[32]

At Home
Jackson Co Geo
Feb 29th 1864

Mrs Delony
Dear Madam

I send you by my Brother in Law Mr. Jackson, Col Delony's watch. He gave it to me to keep for him while in the Yankee Hospital at Culpeper C. H. Vir. I never saw him after ward. I was assured by the Enemy that I would be allowed to remain with him, but the wretches separated us. Oh, how deeply do I sympathize with you. He was the surest and best friend I ever had, but he was willing to die let us rejoice in the hope that he is at rest.

With feelings of the deepest sorrow I am yours &c
Henry S. Bradley
Asst Surgeon
Cobb Legion

---

[32] *Southern Watchman* (17 February 1864). Voccelle, *History of Camden County*, 107–108.

Milwaukee August 11th 1864

My precious child your letter written on the 23rd of April Martha received a day or two since & we were thankful to see your hand writing, & know that you & my little darlings were well. You must not give up to your feelings my dear child, but think of those precious ones whose sole dependence is upon you, strive to cheer up. God will help you thro' your troubles. I have been on the Farm since May, & we went once there about 10 days since, & insisted on my coming here, for a change, but I would rather be there alone, than here surrounded by people whom I cant respect. I have written to a lady friend who sent me word she thought she could get me a permit but I have little hope of getting to you before winter. May then be able to get permission. I heard of you & my little darlings thro' Mrs H. Sarah Jane sent me 3 letters from the family to read, the last was written on the 16 July. I fear Judge H. has died on this, for he must have been very ill from what she said. Oh, how I long to hear from some of you again, & know when, & how my darling son, God spare him, is my constant prayer & R Lewis poor boy he was always a great pet of mine. I hope his wound is not a dangerous one. I dread to read the list of killed & wounded, & yet I cannot rest until I do. Oh how I wish I could get to you now without waiting. I am sick at heart I regretted to hear about Dick. I think if they know how anxious I have been to get home, that they would have spared me at least, but if any thing can be used for them I shall only be too thankful. M and & Dave in Michigan on the Farm, whether they will go to live there or remain here I cant say, but if she would take my advice she would go there until this war is over, but the girls dislike living there, & I fear they will influence her. All send love to R, Jennie, & a kiss to each of our precious little ones. Do write often for we seldom receive more than 1 out of 10.

Maria Delony

Athens, May 18, '66

Mrs. Delony,

Dear Madam:

While on a visit recently to Thomasville, Geo., the accompanying flag was committed to my care by Mrs. Jones, to be delivered to yourself, with the following statement:

It was the "battlefield" of your late, lamented husband's command; he fell while fighting under it; and afterwards, he gave it to his Adjutant, Mr. Frank Jones, with the dying request that it be forwarded to you. Mr. Jones was himself soon after killed; but his trunk, containing the flag, was sent by a friend to his mother in Thomas county, together with the above history.

You will see that the flag is rent and torn in various places by balls and shells; testifying to the gallantry of those who fought and died where it waved above the storm of battle. It was presented to the command, I think, by ladies of Virginia. Traces of some of their names remain on its marred, battle-blackened stars.

It is painful to me thus to renew the memory of your great loss. But feeling that this banner would be to you an invaluable treasure, I was glad to be the bearer of it. It was the proud ensign of a heroic struggle: it will yet be honored in the eyes of the nations.

Trusting that He, whom you have found a sure Support, will still be your Stay. I am very

Respectfully,
Yours, &c,
F. H. Ivey

Bridgeport, Ohio
January 18th 1904

Mrs. J H Hull
Dear Madam,

Your letter of last Tuesday is before me: stating that you are a daughter of Col. Delany [sic]: and would be pleased to receive any information in regard to him that I have to convey.

I was a Soldier in the Union army during the war of 1861–1865. I was a member of the 140th Penn Vol Infantry, was wounded in my right leg at the battle of Chancellorsville Va; and was taken to Stanton Hospital, Washington City.

On the night of Sept 24th 1863 Your father and several other wounded Confederates were brought into our hospital, and placed in our ward, No. 7. If I remember correctly he was wounded in one of his thighs by a Minnie ball which had penetrated it. His horse had been shot, and had fallen on his wounded limb, severely bruising it. My bed in the ward was near to that of your father. I was able to walk about with a Cane; and was there about one week after he was brought there. I talked with him as with the other Confederates in a friendly way, several times.

I did not know that he was considered in a dangerous condition until about the day before I left. Our Surgeons were very attentive to him, and every one in the ward was very favorably impressed by his fine personal appearance and Gentlemanly bearing. As I learned from one of the nurses, his limb was beginning to mortify; and a consultation of Surgeons was held; and it was decided to amputate his limb as the only possible chance of saving his life. He was told that amputation was necessary; and that even then the chances were against him. The doctors said that he was too weak to bear the operation; and that they would have to stimulate him first. Your father then beckoned to me to come over to him. I did so. He said "The doctors tell me that the chances are against me." I replied "I am very sorry Colonel but you have a chance." He shook his head and said "The chances are against me and I have called you over to read to me from the Bible." I got my Bible. He said "Read to me from the 14th Chapter of John." I began to read "Let not Your Heart be troubled &c" and had read (I think) about ten verses when he burst into tears and said "Oh I could die in peace I could die in peace if I was only home with my wife and children: but it is so hard to die here far from home and among strangers." Naturally his thoughts went to his home and family: and it was hard to die among strangers & etc.: but I am assured his trust in his Saviour enabled him to be resigned to the hard circumstances of cruel war. I have often thought of trying to get into communication with his family, and conveying to you these facts which I know will give you comfort. I was taken away to another hospital that same day and never heard any further particulars in regard to his closing hours. The Ward-Master wrote to me soon afterwards, and told me that Col. Delany [sic] had died. I suppose that his limb was amputated & etc. I forgot to say that I prayed with him and he joined in the prayer. I would be pleased to hear from you, for I was very much interested in your noble father. Did you get any particulars in regard to him while he was in this hospital?

One of the wounded Confederates was a Lieutenant from North Carolina. I have forgotten his name. If he is living I would like to communicate with him. Another wounded prisoner was Otis Bethune of the 63. N.C. I wrote a letter for him to a brother who was a doctor. I failed to note his address in my diary. He was very badly wounded by a piece of a shell which had lodged near the kidneys. If this brother is living I would like to communicate with him.

I am a Methodist Episcopal preacher; and have been in the regular work for 33 years in East Ohio Conference. I was a boy between 18 & 19 when I was in Stanton Hospital.

Is your Mother living? When I meet your father in Heaven I expect to talk about that death bed scene in Stanton Hospital which during all these years has been one of precious memory to me.

If you find it convenient I would be much pleased to learn more concerning your father & family.

Fraternally Yours,

(Rev.) John A. Wright,

Bridgeport, Ohio

Poem of Tribute

For his Wife
Friendship's Offering
To The Memory
of Col. William G. Delony,
who died in Washington City
from wounds received in battle
Sept 22 1863

It is a fearful thing to love
What Death may touch!"
Who would not drop a tear,
    Over his bier,
The kind, the good, the brave?
    For him asleep,
Though in the heroes grave?
Who would not breathe a sigh,
    That *he* should die,
So fit for happier life?
Who does not grieve to think
    Its golden link,
Snapped in unholy strife?
Who knew, could eer forget?
    All must regret
That Death should ever come,
To snatch him in his prime,
    Before his time,
From his own joyous home?
Who would not freely give,
    That he might live,
Treasures of price untold,
To see again that smile,
    And yet awhile,
His noble form behold?
Who does not yearn to hear,
    That voice so dear,

Speaking those words of love,
Affection in its tone
    (Like *his* alone!)
Which could each care remove?
Alas! They come no more!
    We but deplore,
No more that eye we meet,
of gladness full—so bright
    a pleasant sight.
So soft, so kind, so sweet!
Alas! his country's weal,
    Hath made him kneel!
A victim of her shrine!
The costly sacrifice,
    Who does not prize
Above the golden _____
    _____ loved one at his bed,
    Upheld his head,
Or pressed the Dying eye;
That *such a life* should close,
    Mid deadly foes,
Makes grief an *agony*!
None will uphold his arm,
    With tears that burn
But in those hearts there lives,
    What *memory* gives.
Sorrow that ne'er departs.

Brother beloved, farewell!
  Oh who can tell,
How we can part with thee?
Or all through coming years
  Marked by ours today,
How dark life's hours _____

_____

Yet in the days may shine,
  A light divine,
Would Faith uplift her eye;
For in celestial spheres,
  There now appears,
An Angel in the Sky!

M. T. G.
15 Oct 1863

Appendix A

Cobb/Delony Case

Camp Marion Dec. 30, 1861

Col. T. R. R. Cobb
Sir,

I wish respectfully to enter my protest against the appointment of Majors Yancey and Lamar to fill the vacancies recently occasioned in the Legion by the promotion of Lt. Col. Garnett and the death of Maj. Bagley, and I will add in the outset that my objections are not so much personal against the gentlemen promoted as to the principle of their promotion. I desire the question settled by the War Department as to the rule which must govern promotions in the Legion. In the organization of the Legion, I am informed (and for this information I am indebted to Maj. Yancey) that the distinct understanding between Gov. Brown and yourself and through you with the President was that the election of the Field Officers was reserved to the officers and men of the Legion and that Gov. Brown refused to furnish arms unless this right was guaranteed to them by the President.

This right was exercised by the Legion in your own election and all the original Field Officers since then vacancies having occurred Capt (now Brig Genl) Garnett was appointed Lt. Col. And Lieut. (now Lt. Col.) Young was appointed Major, and all parties being satisfied & acquiesced in these appointments I apprehend however that we have not lost the right of election by having once exercised that right, nor by subsequent acquiescence in appointments to which no one objected. The legion having at one time certainly possessed that right and I now insist that I as an officer of your Legion objecting, Majors Yancey and Lamar cannot exercise the functions and authority of Majors of the Legion until their appointments are confirmed by an election.

It is perhaps known to you that up to evening before you last left for Richmond I was anxious to have an early settlement of the question of the vacancies and that although in the vote taken before the officers of the cavalry battalion I was the first to receive within one of an election and that I was informed that there was some doubt as to whether I had not been elected I agreed if Capt Stovall would to withdraw my name entirely. It is further known to you that I did finally withdraw my name from you entirely as it was embarrassing to you in making up your final decision made manifest to me by your conversation with me the morning before you left for Richmond solicited by yourself.

I therefore wish simply to remark, that I make these objections and enter this protest because the reasons you have assigned for the promotion of one of the above named officers, ought not in my opinion to have anything to do with military promotions. I desire to have the principle of promotion in the Legion settled and the adoption of any equitable rule, impartially adhered to will be satisfactory to me whether it by rank, merit or election.

Very Respectfully
W. G. Delony
Capt. Co. C, Ga Legion[1]

Hd Qrs "Ga Legion"
Camp Marion
Jany 1st 1862

Genl. S. Cooper
Adjt Genl C.S.A.

I enclose to you as requested by Capt Deloney, his protest against the appointment of Majors Yancey and Lamar in my Legion.

This protest makes only one point. Viz. The power of the President to appoint the Field Officers in this Corps. Before giving a history of its organization, I must deny the accuracy of the information of Capt Deloney as to the understanding between the President and Gov Brown, through myself. There was no such understanding. I will add that the latter clause of Capt Ds letter complains of the reasons assigned by me of the appointment of Major Yancey. At the request of Capt D, I annex copies of the notes to which he refers in this clause I tendered the Legion to President Davis, upon the express condition that he was to appoint the Field Officers and on that condition alone it was accepted. The express understanding between us, was that they were to be Army men. That understanding and condition were made known to the officers and men of every company accepted into the Legion, and was fully understood, and agreed to by Capt Deloney as he is free to acknowledge.

When I applied to Gov Brown to arm the companies he objected to doing so, without the form of organization under Georgia Laws. I told him my agreement with the President, but promised with the Presdts consent to have an election at the time of organization. The Presidents consent was given, and in compliance with my

---

[1] W. G. Delony to T. R. R. Cobb, 30 December 1861, "Letters Received," C. S. Sec. of War, M437, Roll 24, NARS.

promise to Governor Brown, I had the election, explaining to my officers and men at the same time, the reason for the formality. Subsequently vacancies occurred, and were filled by the President without objection from any quarter. When the two vacancies of Lt. Colonel, and Major occurred I collected together my officers and told them, that under the original agreement, I had the right to nominate Army men, without consulting them, but that the list had been so exhausted that I should be compelled to select from 2d Lieutenants & very young men, that the experience of my officers had been sufficient to enable me to recommend two of them to fill the vacant majorities (proposing to promote Major Young to the Lt Colonelcy) provided they could agree among themselves upon the officers to be recommended by me. This proposition met with unanimous approbation. (Captain Deloney being present). The infantry officers unanimously recommended Capt Lamar (who held the oldest commission) as Major of Infantry and upon my recommendation he was accordingly appointed. The cavalry officers failed to make a choice, there being a tie upon the last ballot, between Captain Yancey and Captain Lawton. All of the Lieutenants, however presented me with a written petition, a copy of which is annexed, that I would select for myself one of the four Captains, for Major of Cavalry. Captains Stovall and Deloney both generally united in the same request to me. Capt Lawton was absent. Capt Yancey said nothing. In this state of affairs I called the Captains together, and said to them that I was inclined to abandon filling this vacancy as I disliked to decide between them. That night at 2 A.M. I was to start for Richmond, about (12) (midnight) I received from Capt Deloney the formal withdrawal of his name, and an earnest request that I would have a Major appointed or elected. On reaching Richmond I recommended the name of Capt Yancey, and he was appointed. This is the history of the whole transaction. Captain Delony objects to the reasons assigned by me for the promotion of Capt Yancey. I remember assigning reasons only in a friendly letter to Capt D. & these were "Capt Yancey's age, position, and attainments." I might have added the tie between himself and Captain Lawton, but must confess that this fact would not have controlled me, had my judgement and sense of justice, pointed out another, as more worthy. I will add that my only objection to an election by the Troops, was the demoralization which I feared would result from it. For a few days I spoke of such a mode of nomination and was warned by the evil consequences quickly manifest. This letter has been read to Capt Deloney.

Respectfully submitted
Thos. R. R. Cobb
Col. "Ga. Legion"[2]

---

[2] T. R. R. Cobb to S. Cooper, 1 January 1862, "Letters Received," C. S. Sec. of War, M437, Roll 24, NARS.

Appendix B

"The Horse Infirmary of Georgia"

Excerpted from *The Southern Watchman*, 17 February 1864
Magnolia Hill, Johnson County, Ga.
January 25th, 1864

Having ever felt a deep interest in that noble animal...a visit I have just made to the infirmary, established in Laurens county...for the treatment and care of diseased, wounded and disabled animals belonging to the government.

The Infirmary is located in Laurens county, near the line between that county and Johnson, on the lands of Dr. Thomas A. Parsons, and about twelve miles from Oconee station on the Central Railroad, and one mile from the Oconee river. The locality is healthy, the land rolling and productive, the water facilities excellent, and the pasturage very good in spring and Summer. The government rented 3,000 acres of land from Dr. P. last Summer and immediately began the work of erecting stables, lots, corn and fodder houses and other necessary buildings. There is considerable cane on the tract, and over 200 acres of luxuriant Bermuda grass, both of which afford fine pasturage for the horse.

Horses that have become diseased, or been worn down, or otherwise disabled in public service, in South Carolina, Georgia and Tennessee, are sent here for treatment. Large comfortable stables, and high dry lofts, have been provided for them. If they are suffering from glanders or other contagious disease, as farcy or distemper, they are assigned to a hospital for that particular disorder, which is located at a safe distance from the other stables and lots. If they have been wounded or crippled, or have a bad case of fistula, or scratches, each one is put in a comfortable stable to himself; and so if they have been disabled by hard usage, they are placed in roomy stalls at night and turned out to graze and exercise during the day. Each animal is curried and rubbed daily, his legs and feet washed, and his particular malady or hurt carefully attended to. Indeed all the diseases to which the horse is subject, are here thoroughly treated by experienced and practical veterinary surgeons and farriers, whose zeal is highly commendable, and whose success has been remarkable. The establishment is systematically arranged and managed, hostlers conversant with their duties are assigned to the care of the animals, under the superintending care and direction of the farriers. In certain diseases, as in glanders and farcy, gentle exercise is prescribed, and the horses are led or ridden for short distances.

The general opinion is that glanders is a fatal disease, but I am assured that over thirty cases of it have been cured at this establishment. Of the whole number of diseases and disabled animals thus far sent to the Infirmary, nearly eighty-five per cent have been saved. Many of them after being cured and recruited, have been returned to the army. Others are improving rapidly, and will soon be in a condition for service. The rule adopted by the commandant of the post is not to send back an animal until it has been thoroughly recruited and rendered fit for duty. Such as can never be made available for active service, especially mares, are advertised and sold at public outcry to farmers. Some of the animals were received in the lowest condition, but under the close attention and skillful treatment given them, they are now doing remarkably well. A number of cases of lameness sent to the Infirmary arose from non attention to the hoofs and feet.

The commandant of the post is Capt. J. G. McKee, of Columbus, Georgia, an officer of rare zeal and fidelity who has been disabled in the service. He is devoted to his business and is one of the most energetic men I have met with the public service. He has in his employ fifty negroes and eight white men. He is now preparing accommodations for 2,000 more horses, which are expected to arrive soon, and this will render it necessary to employ additional help. No white man is employed except disabled soldiers and persons unfit for service by reason of age or other infirmity. The farriers and veterinary surgeons attached to the Infirmary are Messra. W. P. Davis and J. Disbrow, both of whom are devoted to the horse and exceedingly skillful in the treatment of the diseases to which he is subject. Indeed all the employees at the post, white and black, manifest a zeal and an earnestness that is truly refreshing in these days of shuffling and affected patriotism. The horse receives here the same care and attention as the sick or disabled soldier does at the hospitals.

....Previous to the establishment of this Infirmary horses worn out or disabled in the service, were turned out to perish around the camps or left behind on the march; whilst all animals having the glanders, heretofore considered incurable, were taken out, and shot.... The drain thus kept up upon the stock of horses of the country has been enormous, the prevailing idea seeming to be that the supply was inexhaustible....

P. W. A.

Biographical Roster

But oh! My country's wintry state
What second spring shall renovate?
What powerful call shall bid arise
The buried warlike and the wise:
　　　　　　　—Sir Walter Scott

Adams: One possibility for "Mr. Adams...fresh from Legislative halls" is F. M. Adams, a member of Georgia's Secession Convention from Camden County.

Adams, F.: Probably Flournoy Woodbridge Adams, who was "intendant" (mayor) of Athens in 1860 and later died in New York City of smallpox. He married Emily "Emma" Eliza Barnett.

Addie: "Little Addie" is probably a Delony slave.

Addington, W. M.: William M. Addington was from Macon County, North Carolina, and enlisted in May 1861 in the 1st North Carolina Cavalry; promoted to first lieutenant in October 1861 and then to captain in August 1862.

Alek: Alek was a Delony slave.

Alexander, Sam: Samuel L. Alexander was the first lieutenant and adjutant in Co. K, Athens Guards, 3rd Georgia Volunteer Infantry. He was wounded in the elbow in the fighting near Gettysburg in July 1863.

Allen, E. J.: Better known as Allen Pinkerton, Allen was born in Scotland and emigrated to the US in 1842. In 1849, he was appointed as the first police detective in Chicago, and the following year formed the North-Western Police Academy, later known as Pinkerton & Co. and then the Pinkerton National Detective Agency. Pinkerton served as head of the Union Intelligence Service during the war using the alias Major E. J. Allen.

Anderson: Gen. George Thomas "Tige" Anderson (1824–1901) was born in Covington, Georgia. He served as a lieutenant of the Georgia Cavalry during the Mexican War. When the Civil War began, he was elected colonel of the 11th Georgia Infantry and fought during the Seven Days' Battles, at Second Manassas, and at Sharpsburg. After promotion to brigadier general, he fought at Fredericksburg and at Gettysburg, where he was severely wounded. After recovering from his wounds, Anderson returned to the army and took part in the battles of Chickamauga and

Knoxville, after which he returned to Virginia, where he continued to fight until Appomattox. After the war, he became the chief of police for the city of Athens.

Anderson: "Mrs Anderson" was Sarah Terence Owens, the wife of Young J. Anderson.

Anderson: "Capt Anderson" was Young J. Anderson, a Savannah lawyer who married Sarah Terence Owens of Augusta, Georgia, in February 1861. When the war broke out, he joined Co. A, Richmond Hussars, Cobb's Georgia Legion Cavalry, as a private, was promoted to captain and served as the battalion's assistant quartermaster. He resigned from the service for unknown reasons while the legion was encamped at Culpeper Court House in May 1863.

Andrew: Believed to be a Delony slave.

Ansley, J. A.: Jesse A. Ansley was from Augusta, Georgia, and became a newspaper editor there in 1861. He later partnered with Charles Rigdon in the production of the Rigdon-Ansley revolvers for the Confederacy, produced from 1864 to 1865 in Augusta.

Archer: "Capt Archer" was Thomas B. Archer, a livery worker in Augusta prior to the war. He enlisted as a lieutenant in Co. A, Richmond Hussars, Cobb's Georgia Legion Cavalry, 17 August 1861 in Augusta. He was promoted to captain 26 May 1862 after the resignation of Thomas P. Stovall. Wounded by a gunshot to the left thigh, Archer was admitted to the hospital in July 1864. He was paroled 27 May 1865 in Augusta. After the war, he married and owned a livery business in Fulton County.

Atkinson: "Mr Atkinson" was Simon A. Atkinson, born in New Hampshire. A newspaper editor in Madison, Georgia, in 1850, Atkinson later became the editor of the Augusta *Evening Dispatch* until the paper closed during the war. He died in Brooklyn, New York, after the war.

Aunt Eliza: Will's aunt Eliza Bolling Deloney.

Aunt Mell: "Aunt Mell" is probably either Emma Holmes Mell or Sarah Elizabeth Mell, sisters of Patrick Hues Mell. Both were from Liberty, Georgia.

Aunty: Rosa's "Aunty" is probably Eugenia Huguenin of Savannah, who married Hugh Rose, also of Savannah, in 1828.

Axson: "Mr Axson" was Presbyterian minister Rev. Samuel Edward Axson (1836–1884), who served several churches in South Carolina and Georgia. During the war, he served as the chaplain of the 1st Georgia Infantry. During the last year of his life, he was confined to the State Hospital in Milledgeville, where he died. Samuel Axson was the father-in-law of Woodrow Wilson (from his first marriage).

Bagley, E. F.: Edward F. Bagley, from Alabama, was serving as first lieutenant of the 4th US Artillery when the war broke out. He resigned his commission in "the old army" and offered his services to the Confederacy. He was appointed major in Cobb's Georgia Legion Infantry in 1861 and was listed as "killed" 20 November 1861 in his service records. He was accidentally killed by his own men.

Bailey, Sam: Samuel W. Bailey was a student from Clarke County who enlisted as a private in Co. C, Cobb's Georgia Legion Cavalry, on 1 August 1861 and surrendered on 1 May 1865 in North Carolina. After the war, he married and became a dairyman in Clarke County.

Baker: Lawrence Simmons Baker (1830–1907) was a West Point graduate ('51) and had already served for ten years in the Regiment of Mounted Rifles before resigning to join the Confederacy in May 1861. Baker was elected lieutenant colonel of the 1st North Carolina Cavalry and then promoted to colonel of the 1st in March 1862 when the 1st North Carolina Cavalry became a part of Hampton's Brigade. He took command of the brigade when Hampton was wounded in the fighting near Gettysburg in July 1863. In August, Baker was wounded and promoted to brigadier general after returning from recuperation. He commanded some of the reserves at the Battle of Bentonville in 1865. Following the war, he farmed and was employed by a railroad company in North Carolina.

Baker, William E.: Rev. William Elliott Baker (1830–1906), minister of the Presbyterian Church in Staunton, Virginia, was married to Catherine Evelyn "Eva" King, sister of Barrington S. King of Roswell, Georgia. Rev. Baker was minister at the Presbyterian Church in Staunton, Virginia for twenty-seven years (1857–1884). He and his wife eventually returned to Georgia and Roswell, Cobb County, where the King family lived.

Barksdale: Green B. Barksdale, from Dougherty County, enlisted as a corporal in Co. D, Mell Volunteers of Cobb's Georgia Legion Cavalry, on 10 August 1861 in Albany, Georgia. Promoted to sergeant in May 1862, he was killed in action 13 September 1862 at Quebec Schoolhouse in Middletown, Maryland.

Barnard, Nat: Nathaniel Law Barnard (1835–1910) was a farmer from Athens. He was a member of Moore's Battery, Georgia Artillery. After his first wife died in 1886, he remarried in 1888 and moved to Savannah.

Barnes, George: George Thomas Barnes (1833–1901) was a lawyer from Augusta. During the Civil War, he served as a second lieutenant in the Washington Light Artillery and as a member of the Georgia State House of Representatives from 1860 to 1865.

Barrett, Tucker: Walton or Walter Tucker Barrett, from Lumpkin County, Georgia, was a student when he enlisted as a private in Co. C of Cobb's Georgia Legion Cavalry, on 1 August 1862 in Athens. He died 22 April 1863 in Suffolk, Virginia.

Barrow: "Mr. Barrow" is David Crenshaw Barrow (1815–1899). He was a state senator from Athens before the war, became a member of the Secession Convention in 1860, and served on the board of trustees of the University of Georgia. He was the father of Lucy Pope Barrow.

Barrow, Lucy: Lucy Pope Barrow of Athens married John Addison Cobb, son of Howell and Mary Ann Cobb. She was the daughter of David Crenshaw Barrow.

Baxter, Edwin: Edwin Gilmer Baxter was born in Athens, Georgia, and graduated from the University of Georgia in 1855. He died in 1863 in Texas.

Baxter: "Mrs Baxter" was probably Mary Wiley Baxter, wife of Thomas Wiley Baxter, who died in Milledgeville, Georgia, in 1844.

Bell: Two possibilities exist for Bell: 1) Madison M. Bell enlisted as a private in Company C, Cobb's Georgia Legion Cavalry, on 1 August 1861 in Athens. Following the war he became the state comptroller general, living in Fulton County. Married after the war, Madison Bell died in 1896 in Atlanta. 2) Marlin (Mahlon) M. Bell of Lumpkin County enlisted as a private in Co. C, Cobb's Georgia Legion Cavalry, on 15 August 1861 in Athens. Married before the war and for a second time following the war, Marlin Bell died in Forsyth County, Georgia, in February 1905.

Bella: "Bella" is probably a Delony family member but is otherwise unidentified.

Bill: There are six possibilities for "Bill" within Delony's Company: William E. Anderson, William H. Early, William J. Helton, William R. Lord, William H. Reid, and the most likely candidate, William D. Simmons. All enlisted in Delony's Company as privates in 1861 except William Simmons, who enlisted as a corporal at that same time.

Billups: "Miss Billups" was probably Anna Yates Billups, youngest daughter of Col. and Mrs. John Billups of Athens.

Billups, Hall: Henry "Hal" Carleton Billups (1830–1884) was a graduate of the University of Georgia and attended Jefferson Medical College. At the beginning of the war, he was elected captain of Co. K, Athens Guards, 3rd Georgia Infantry. He was later promoted to colonel of the regiment.

Billups: Colonel John Billups (1802–1872) and his wife, Ann Matilda Weed Abbot. Colonel Billups was a member of Mitchell's Thunderbolts, a militia unit of octogenarians formed to protect Athens in 1864, which was disbanded after only a few months due to lack of Confederate control over the unit. The colonel was appointed to oversee the erection of earthworks around Athens in 1864.

Bishop: Thomas Bishop (1803–1866) moved to Athens from Vermont in 1839. The merchant and strong Presbyterian was well liked about town despite his public Unionist sentiments. He was a member of Mitchell's Thunderbolts, a militia unit of octogenarians formed to protect Athens in 1864, which was disbanded after only a few months due to lack of Confederate control over the unit.

Black, John L.: John Logan Black (1830–1902) from Cherokee County, South Carolina, was elected lieutenant colonel of the 1st South Carolina Cavalry in October 1861. He was promoted to colonel of the unit in June 1862.

Blair, J. C.: John C. Blair was from Watauga County, North Carolina. He enlisted in May 1861 in Co. D, 1st North Carolina Cavalry, as a second lieutenant. In May 1862, he was promoted to captain of Co. D. He was captured at Beaver Dam Station, Virginia, in 1864 and spent most of the remainder of the war being moved from one prison camp to another. Blair took the Union loyalty oath and was released in June 1865. His prisoner records listed him as being 5' 10" tall, with a dark complexion, dark hair, and blue eyes.

Bloomfield: Robert Lee Bloomfield (1827–1916) moved to Athens in 1848 and became a major merchant, industrialist, and philanthropist in the city. Although sometimes frowned upon by some in town for his Yankee background, he was well thought of. Bloomfield became a member of Mitchell's Thunderbolts, a militia unit of octogenarians formed to protect Athens in 1864, which was disbanded after only a few months due to lack of Confederate control over the unit.

Blue, John: From Hampshire County, West Virginia, John Blue served as first lieutenant in Co. D, 11th Virginia. The account of his wartime experiences are published in *Hanging Rock Rebel*, edited by Dan Oates (Shippensburg, PA: White Mane Publishing Co., 1994).

Bob: See Robert Delony.

Bobby: Other than being identified as having married a cousin of Rosa's, "Bobby" is otherwise unidentified.

Bradley: Dr. Henry Stiles Bradley was a physician from Madison County, Georgia, who enlisted as a private in Co. C, Cobb's Georgia Legion Cavalry, on 1 August 1861 in Athens. In June 1862, he was appointed the assistant surgeon for the legion. Bradley was captured, along with Reuben Long Nash, in September 1863 at Jack's Shop while attending to the wounded Will Delony and was subsequently imprisoned at City Point, Maryland. Following the war, Bradley worked as a physician in Tadmore, Hall County. Later in life he became a minister in Gainesville in Hall County, Georgia. He was married prior to the war and died in Wilkes County, Georgia, in 1895.

Bragg: Braxton Bragg (1817–1876) was a West Point graduate ('37) who served against the Seminoles and in the Mexican War. He was a Louisiana planter at the start of the Civil War. Bragg was a favorite of Confederate president Jefferson Davis and was one of only eight Confederate officers to reach the rank of full general. He commanded the Army of Tennessee until November 1864. Bragg was constantly at odds with his own subordinates, which hamstrung the effectiveness of his command. For this he was finally removed from command after the disaster of Chattanooga and replaced by Joseph E. Johnston.

Broiles: "Broiles" was a member of the Georgia House of Representatives in 1860. He was possibly George Edwin Broiles from Macon, Bibb County.

Brooks: Cicero C. Brooks enlisted in the spring of 1862 as first sergeant of Ritch's Company, Co. B, Georgia Troopers, Cobb's Georgia Legion Cavalry. Promoted a few months later to lieutenant, he was killed near Gettysburg in July 1863.

Brooks, John: John N. Brooks enlisted as a corporal in Co. E, Cobb's Georgia Legion Cavalry, on 15 March 1862 at Roswell. He was captured at Beverly's Ford, Virginia, on 9 June 1863 and exchanged 4 August 1863. He was in Georgia trying to obtain a horse when the war ended. Afterward, he became a schoolteacher in Coweta County, Georgia, married, and died in October 1899 in Pike County, Georgia.

Brown: Joseph Emerson Brown (1821–1894) attended Yale Law School. After graduation, he became a practicing lawyer until 1849 when he entered politics. Brown won a seat in the state legislature, where he served one term, followed by two years as a judge. He then ran for and was elected governor of Georgia and served four two-year terms. He was Georgia's populist Civil War governor.

Buford: John Buford (1826–1863) was a West Point graduate ('48) who saw service on the frontier and against the Mormons in Utah (1857–1858) prior to the Civil War. When war broke out, Buford was captain of the US 2nd Cavalry. In November 1861, he was promoted to major, then made a brigadier general in June 1862 under Pope. He was wounded at 2nd Manassas, where he commanded the Reserve Brigade. Buford took part in Stoneman's Raid during the Chancellorsville Campaign and directed a cavalry division at Brandy Station, Aldie, Middleburg, and Upperville. Buford's Brigade initiated the fighting at Gettysburg. He died later that year of typhoid fever.

Bull: The "two Miss Bulls of Orange [County, Virginia]" are otherwise unidentified.

Burnside: Ambrose Everett Burnside (1824–1881) was a West Point graduate ('47) who served six years in the US Artillery prior to the Civil War. He also did garrison duty in Mexico and was wounded in 1849 fighting Apaches in New Mexico territory. He resigned from the army and settled in Rhode Island in 1853 to develop and manufacture his breech-loading carbine. Burnside was a brigadier general in 1861 and commanded the North Carolina Expeditionary Corps in its invasion of the eastern part of the state. He commanded Union forces at Second Manassas, South Mountain, and Antietam. Burnside was finally convinced (after earlier declining the appointment) to take charge of all Union forces prior to the Fredericksburg Campaign. Following the Union disaster at Fredericksburg, Burnside was reassigned by Lincoln to head the Department of the Ohio, where he dealt with Confederate raiders. Burnside commanded with some distinction at the Battle of Knoxville in late 1863. Following the war, he served as governor of Rhode Island for three years and then as a senator.

Butler: Matthew Calbraith (1836–1909) was elected captain in Hampton's Legion in early 1861, became major in July 1862, colonel of the 2nd South Carolina Cavalry in August 1862, and brigadier general in September 1863, commanding a brigade in Hampton's Division under J. E. B. Stuart. Butler was wounded in the foot in early 1863, forcing the amputation of his lower leg. While recuperating, P. M. B. Young was placed in command of the brigade. Following the war, Butler was a lawyer and state legislator in South Carolina. When the war with Spain broke out, Butler offered his services and was appointed major general of volunteers. After the war, he became an officer with the Southern Historical Association.

Camack/Camak: "Mrs Camack" [sic] is Helen Smith Finley Camak, wife of James Camak. She was the daughter of Presbyterian minister and president of the University of Georgia, Rev. Dr. Robert Finley. Her son, Thomas Camak, joined the Mell Rifles of Cobb's Georgia Legion Infantry in 1861. Elected captain, Thomas Camak was later killed at Gettysburg.

Camfield, Holly: Caleb Halstead "Holly" Camfield transferred as a private to Co. D, Cobb's Georgia Legion Cavalry, on 10 August 1861 in Albany. He was promoted to sergeant in mid-1861 and then to lieutenant on 31 December 1861. In late 1863, he was again promoted to captain. In April 1864, he was promoted to major in an infantry regiment and paroled at Albany in May 1865. Camfield worked as a bookkeeper before and after the war. He was married to his first wife prior to the war and married a second time after the war. He died in 1904 in Dougherty County.

Carlton, Capt.: Henry Hull Carlton (1834–1905) enlisted as first lieutenant in the troup artillery, eventually rising to the rank of colonel. After the war, he became a newspaper editor twice, a lawyer, and Georgia congressman (1886–1890). Henry's brother, Benjamin, was killed at Sharpsburg in 1862. Henry Carlton was instrumental in organizing Confederate veterans in the 1880s and 1890s. He served during the Spanish-American War in Puerto Rico as a major.

Carlton, Mr.: John Richardson Carlton (1795–1888) fought in the War of 1812. A strong Methodist and father of Henry Hull Carlton, John was a master builder and the source of many of the fine homes in Athens.

Carlton, Dr.: Joseph Barnett Carlton (1822–1881) was a surgeon in Robert Toombs' Brigade (1st, 2nd, 15th, 17th, & 20th Georgia Infantry). He later served in both the Georgia House of Representatives and Georgia Senate.

Carter: Bennett H. Carter enlisted as a private in Co. H, Cobb's Georgia Legion Cavalry. He was killed in June 1863 in the fighting at Brandy Station.

Catherine: Two Catherines are referenced: 1) Rosa's aunt was Catherine Baker and 2) one of the Delony slave's cooks was named Catherine.

Chandler: Green W. Chandler was an overseer from Jackson County, Georgia, who enlisted as a private in Co. C, Cobb's Georgia Legion Cavalry, on 4 March 1862 in Jefferson. Following the war, he farmed in Jackson County and then Gwinnett County, Georgia. He married after the war and died in 1901 in Gwinnett County. Buried in Barrow County.

Charlie: There are three possibilities for "Charlie." See Charley Dean, Charlie Harris, and Charlie Oliver.

Cheeseborough: John W. Cheeseborough was a lieutenant from Augusta. He enlisted as a member of Co. A, Richmond Hussars, Cobb's Georgia Legion Cavalry and was killed near Gettysburg in July 1863.

Church, Alonzo: Dr. Alonzo A. Church (1793–1862) was the sixth president of the University of Georgia. Born in Vermont, Church became a member of the faculty as professor of mathematics in 1819 and then selected as president in 1829. He served as president for thirty years, retiring in 1859. He was the father of Willie L. Church and "Mrs. Craig."

Church, Ester: "Mrs. Ester Church" may be Ester S. Church from Clarkesville, Habersham County, Georgia.

Church, Willie L.: William Lee Church, better known as "Willie," enlisted as an 18-year-old on 1 August 1861, in Athens. From Clarke County, he enlisted as fourth corporal in Co. C, Cobb's Georgia Legion Cavalry. He was promoted to sergeant in late 1861. By mid-1862, he was promoted to lieutenant and then to captain on 4 December 1862. Church was said to have led a charmed life in the legion. Although courageous and sometimes rash, he was noted for his quick thinking under fire and was struck twenty-five times by spent balls but escaped serious injury. He lived for a time in Florida after the war and died 31 March 1871 in Madison County, Georgia.

Clanton, Jim: James Luke Clanton (also referred to as "Young" Clanton) was a student from Augusta who enlisted as a private in Co. A, Cobb's Georgia Legion Cavalry, on 17 August 1861, in Augusta. Noted for his courage and aggression under fire, particularly at Brandy Station, Clanton was promoted to lieutenant of Co. K, Cobb's Legion, on 10 February 1862. Wounded several times, he was convalescing when the war ended, although one witness stated that he was present when the legion surrendered. He married following the war and died in 1892 in Harlem, Columbia County, Georgia.

Clark: "Genl Clark" was John Bullock Clark Sr. (1802–1885), a Confederate senator from Missouri. Clark fought in the Black Hawk War and the Missouri Mormon War prior to becoming a US senator from Missouri.

Clark, T. H.: Tillman H. Clark of Edgefield District, South Carolina, enlisted in Co. I, Edgefield Hussars of the 2nd South Carolina Cavalry, in June 1861. The following year he was promoted to captain.

Cobb, Howell: Older brother of Thomas R. R. Cobb, Howell Cobb (1815–1868) one of the most prominent men of Athens during the nineteenth century. Howell was a member of the "Cobb Faction." He was a lawyer, state legislator, solicitor general, speaker of the US House of Representatives, Georgia governor, and secretary of the treasury in the James Buchanan administration. After Georgia seceded, and during the formation of the Confederacy, Howell was named the presiding president of the Provisional Confederate Congress. Named as a possible candidate for president of the Confederacy, he had his named withdrawn from consideration so that Jefferson Davis might be elected unanimously. Howell Cobb began the Civil War as colonel of the 16th Georgia Infantry, soon after promoted to brigadier general, commanding Cobb's Brigade, and fought at Yorktown, Seven Days', and South Mountain. He was then appointed major general and sent to southern Georgia/northern Florida to take command of the defenses in that region. Howell Cobb commanded at the battle of Columbus, Georgia, late in the war. Following the end of hostilities, he returned to his law profession and suffered a massive heart attack in 1868 while in New York City on a shopping trip with his wife.

Cobb, John: John Addison Cobb was a son of Howell and Mary Ann Cobb. He served on his father's staff during the early part of the war.

Cobb, Marion: Marion McHenry Lumpkin Cobb was the wife of Thomas R. R. Cobb and daughter of Joseph Henry Lumpkin, Georgia's first chief justice of the state Supreme Court. She was a friend of Rosa Delony's.

Cobb, Mary Ann: Mary Ann Lamar Cobb was the wife of Howell Cobb and daughter of Zachariah Lamar of Macon, Georgia. She was a friend of Rosa Delony's.

Cobb, T. R. R.: Thomas Reade Rootes Cobb (1823–1862) was the younger brother of Howell Cobb. A prominent Georgia lawyer from Athens and a leading figure within the "Cobb Faction," T. R. R. advocated for Georgia's secession as early as 1858. In the fall of 1860, T. R. R. was one of the most vocal members of Georgia's secession debates. He became a member of the Provisional Confederate Congress and chairman of the judiciary committee tasked with creating the new Confederate Constitution. He formed his own military unit, Cobb's Georgia Legion, and offered its services to the Confederacy. Elected colonel, he led the legion (infantry and cavalry) during the Peninsula Campaign. He commanded his infantry at Seven Pines. Promoted in November 1862 to command Cobb's All-Georgia Brigade (infantry), he commanded the defense of the stone wall at Fredericksburg. T. R. R. Cobb was mortally wounded by shrapnel late in the action and died soon after from loss of blood. He was a friend and legal associate of William G. Delony's, and his wife, Marion, was one of Rosa Delony's friends.

Colquitt: Alfred Holt Colquitt (1824–1894) was a lawyer from Monroe, Georgia. He served as a major in the Mexican War and then as a member of the US House of Representatives from 1853 to 1855. A delegate to Georgia's Secession Convention, Colquitt was elected colonel of the 6th Georgia Infantry and fought in the Peninsula Campaign and during the Seven Days' Battles. Promoted to brigadier general in 1862, he commanded at South Mountain, during the Antietam Campaign, Fredericksburg, and Chancellorsville. Following the war, he served as governor of Georgia from 1876 to 1882 and then was elected to the US Senate from 1883 to 1894.

Cook: "Mr Cook" was Ferdinand Frances Cook, one half of the famous "Cook Brothers" gun factory that moved from New Orleans to Athens in August 1862 when New Orleans fell to Union forces. This factory was a target for a portion of Stoneman's unsuccessful raid south from Atlanta in 1864.

Cousin: "Cousin" is Martha Deloney Duncan of Savannah. She was a daughter of Lucy Ann Barnes of Athens.

Cowles: William Henry Harrison Cowles (1840–1901) was from Yadkin County, North Carolina. His service records indicate that he was elected as first lieutenant of the 1st North Carolina Cavalry in 1861 and promoted to major of the regiment in 1863. Sometime during 1862, Cowles was apparently acting captain within the 1st, as mentioned by Delony in the correspondence, although his service records never mention a promotion to captain.

Cunninghams: Possible Mary J. and Sarah H. Cunningham from Oglethorpe County, daughters of James and Martha Cunningham. The two would have been around 20 and 17 years old at the time.

Craig, Mrs.: Elizabeth Church Craig was the daughter of Alonzo Church, a prominent member of the Presbyterian Church, and friend of Rosa Delony, Marion Cobb, and Mary Ann Cobb.

Crawford: Dr. Crawford Long (1815–1878) was a surgeon and pharmacist. He moved from Madison County, Georgia, to Jefferson, Jackson County, Georgia, and then to Athens prior to the Civil War. He is most famous for his discovery of ether as an anesthetic in medicine, and his office in Jefferson, Georgia, is now a museum. He was a cousin of Doc Holliday's.

Crawford, Martin J.: Martin Jenkins Crawford (1820–1883) was a lawyer and judge prior to the Civil War. He served as a member of the US House of Representatives from Georgia from 1855 to 1861. In May 1862, he organized and commanded the 3rd Georgia Cavalry as part of the Army of Tennessee. Following the end of the war, he served again as a judge and was selected as a member of the Georgia State Supreme Court from 1880 to 1883.

Crumley: William Macon Crumley was 18 when he enlisted as a private in Co. I of Cobb's Georgia Legion Cavalry in March 1862. He was from Augusta, Georgia. Following the war, he returned to the merchant trade, working at a hardware store in Fulton County, Georgia. In 1821, he received a Confederate pension in Fulton County.

David: John White David was a laborer from Jackson County, Georgia. He enlisted in 1861 in Athens as a private in Co. C of Cobb's Georgia Legion Cavalry. After losing his horse during the Gettysburg fighting, he was sent to a recruiting camp. Captured in May 1864, he was sent to Elmira Prison Camp in New York. He died there of typhoid fever and was buried at the camp (Woodlawn Cemetery).

Davie: Slave of Grandmother Eliza Vallard Huguenin's in Savannah.

Davis, Jefferson: Jefferson Davis (1808–1889) was a West Point graduate ('28) who fought in the Mexican War as colonel of the 1st Mississippi Rifles. He was wounded at Buena Vista. Following the Mexican War, he served in the House of Representatives from 1845 to 1847, followed by service in the US Senate, and then as secretary of war in the Franklin Pierce administration, before heading back to the Senate. Davis was a supporter of Mississippi's secession. With the formation of the Confederacy, he was elected president in February 1861. Throughout the Civil War, Davis made attempts to manage the war from his office, something that constantly hampered the Confederacy's ability to fight effectively. He fled south after the fall of Richmond in April 1865 and was captured near Irwinville, Georgia, on 10 May 1865. Sent to prison at Fort Monroe on charges of treason, he was never tried and finally released after two years. His citizenship was finally restored in the 1970s despite his never requesting it.

Dean, Charley: Charles N. (or W.) Dean was a private in Co. K, Athens Guards, 3rd Georgia Infantry. He does not show up in the service records. He was killed in the fighting at Gettysburg on 2 July 1863.

Dean: Captain Dean is unidentified.

Dearing: William P. Dearing was an 18-year-old from Richmond County who enlisted as a private in Co. C, Cobb's Georgia Legion Cavalry, on 3 May 1862 in Athens. He transferred to the troup artillery in November 1862. Following the war he married and worked as a coal dealer and then as manager of the Neely Institute in Fulton County, Georgia.

Delony, Martha: Martha Delony, William Delony's sister, married Capt. John Williams Gunnison, a West Point graduate. In 1853, Gunnison undertook the Gunnison-Beckwith Expedition through Utah in search of a route for a Pacific railroad. On 26 October 1853, Ute Indians attacked Capt. Gunnison and his party of eleven, and he and seven of his party were tragically murdered. The attack took place during what has been termed the "Walker War" between the Utes and Mormons in Utah. Martha maintained for the rest of her life that her husband's death was orchestrated not by the Utes, but rather by Mormons dressed as Indians. The event became known as the "Gunnison Massacre."

Delony, Robert: Also known as "Bob." Will's brother Robert Jr.'s history is difficult to trace. He married Virginia "Jenny/Jennie" R. Delony and they had one child, Laura Virginia, who was born 22 October 1860. Robert and Jennie were living in Athens in 1861, as the letters attest. On 15 May 1861, Robert wrote Howell Cobb trying to secure employment "in Montgomery...to support my family" (Coleman, *Athens, 1861–1865*). Robert became a clerk in the Confederate government in Richmond. On 20 June 1863, he enrolled as a private in Capt. Albert Ellery's company D, 3rd Battalion, Local Defense Volunteers, in Richmond Virginia, a unit organized of "clerks of the 2d Auditor's, Comptroller's, Produce Loan, and War Tax offices, Treasury Department." In October 1863, Robert and his wife stayed with Rosa, helping her with the four children during her grieving of Will's death. Later, in December 1864, Robert enlisted in a local militia unit and was captured following the battle of Waynesboro, Georgia (*Southern Watchman*, 28 December 1864). Although still on the muster roll, Robert was recorded as "killed in 1863 in the Civil War." His daughter, Laura Virginia, was baptized in the Emanuel Episcopal Church in Athens on 25 January 1864 (Emanuel Episcopal Church birth records), but Robert was not present for the baptism. Parish birth records of the Emanuel Episcopal Church found in the Carson Family Papers revealed the following: "Laura Virginia Deloney, (Born on Oct. 22, 1860) Daughter of Robert J Delony and Virginia R. Deloney [note the spelling contrast with the 'e'] was Baptised on Jan. 25, 1864." Because Robert was not at the baptism, it aroused suspicion that he had been killed, as alleged incorrectly in the Carson Family Papers.

Dent, Steve: Stephen P. Dent enlisted as a private in Co. B, Georgia Troopers of Cobb's Georgia Legion Cavalry, in 1861. His service records do not mention any promotion to major.

Devin, Thomas: Thomas Casimer Devin (1822–1878) was one of the best Union cavalry officers of the war. As colonel of the 6th New York Cavalry, he became one of John Buford's favorite officers, earning him the name "Buford's Hard Hitter." He led a brigade at Brandy Station and was instrumental in the attack on Stuart's forces at Jack's Shop in 1863. Following the war, Thomas Devin was stationed in Arizona as lieutenant colonel of the 3rd US Cavalry.

Dick: Believed to be a slave of William Delony's mother.

Dickson: Capers Dickson enlisted in Co. B, Richmond Hussars, Cobb's Georgia Legion Cavalry, under Captain Young in 1862. He transferred to Co. I in early 1863. Although Delony mentions that he was killed in the fighting near Gettysburg in July 1863, he was apparently wounded, as he was back with the unit later. Dickson was again captured in May 1864 and imprisoned at Fort Delaware. In May

1865, he was in a hospital in Richmond recovering either from his earlier wounding or from his time of imprisonment.

Dorsey: Andrew Benson Clarke Dorsey (1837–1902) was a successful Athens businessman prior to the war. He enlisted as captain of Co. I, Glade Guards (Hall County), 24th Georgia Infantry. He transferred to the troup artillery in February 1863.

Dougherty, Henry: Henry R. Dougherty enlisted as a private in 1861 in Co. B, Georgia Troopers, Cobb's Georgia Legion Cavalry. In 1862, he transferred to Co. B, Fulton Dragoons, Georgia Legion Cavalry.

Duncan: Mrs. Duncan was Martha Deloney Duncan of Savannah. She was a daughter of Lucy Ann Barnes of Athens.

Early: William H. Early enlisted in Dahlonega in Co. C, Cobb's Georgia Legion Cavalry, on 1 August 1861 along with his four brothers: Alfred, Joseph, Lamuel, and Williamson. He was promoted to first lieutenant in May 1862 and was wounded in the arm at Dispatch Station on 28 June 1862. He was paroled at Greensboro, North Carolina, on 1 May 1865. Following the war he married and settled in Lumpkin County, Georgia.

Edwards: Oliver Evans Edwards (1819–1863) was a South Carolina legislator who raised a regiment for the Confederacy at the beginning of the war. In September 1861, he was elected Colonel of the 13th South Carolina Volunteers (Infantry). He died in 1863 from wounds received at Chancellorsville.

Ellie: "Ellie" is unidentified.

Eliza: "Eliza" was Will's and Rosa's first child, born in 1855. Tragically, the child lived less than a year, dying in 1856 in Athens (29 June 1855–20 June 1856).

Eve, Francis: Francis Edgeworth Eve enlisted as a private in Co. A, Richmond Hussars, Georgia Legion Cavalry. He was elected captain of Co. K, Richmond Dragoons, Georgia Legion Cavalry, in February 1862. Eve was from Augusta.

Ewell, Richard : Richard Stoddert Ewell (1817–1872) was a West Point graduate ('40) who served in the southwest and fought in the Mexican War. He was commissioned a brigadier general in June 1861 and then major general in January 1862. He was appointed lieutenant general in May 1863 to succeed Stonewall Jackson. Ewell fought with distinction at First Manassas and in the Valley Campaign as well as the Seven Days' Battles and Second Manassas, where he lost a leg. He commanded the 2nd Corps at Gettysburg. Following Spotsylvania, Ewell's declining health compelled him to retire from active duty, whereupon he took charge of the Richmond defenses. Nicknamed "Old Baldy," he farmed in Tennessee following the war.

Fannin: Isham S. Fannin served in the Georgia House of Representatives from Madison, Morgan County, in 1860. After the war, he joined the Internal Revenue Service in Augusta, Georgia.

Ferry: There are two Lucius Ferrys listed for Danbury, Connecticut: Lucius L. and Lucius G. are listed in the 1850 census as being born in 1834 and 1836, respectively. Neither were married at the time.

Flournoy: It is believed that "Dr. Flournoy" was Robert Watkins Flournoy (1811–1894).

Floyd, J. C.: John C. Floyd was elected sergeant major of Co. A, Lamar Infantry of Cobb's Georgia Legion Infantry, in 1861. He was promoted to second lieutenant of Co. A in 1862.

Fort, George: George Washington Fort (1828–1866) was born in Washington, DC, and was a practicing physician in Milledgeville, Georgia.

Frierson, Tom: Thomas H. Frierson of Athens enlisted as a private in 1861 in Co. K, Athens Guards, 3rd Georgia Infantry. He was slightly wounded during the fighting near Gettysburg in July 1863.

Funsten, O. R.: Oliver Ridgeway Funsten (1811–1871) was a lieutenant colonel in the 11th Virginia Cavalry. He was promoted to colonel of the regiment in February 1863.

Gamble, William: From Duross, Lisnarick, County Fermanagh, Ireland, William Gamble (1818–1866) first served as a dragoon in the British army who emigrated to the US in 1838. Gamble fought in the Second Seminole War and then worked as a civil engineer in Chicago. During the Civil War, he served first as the lieutenant colonel of the 8th Illinois Cavalry and fought with them during the Peninsula Campaign, where he was wounded. He commanded the 8th Illinois until just prior to the Gettysburg Campaign, when he was assigned to command one of the two brigades in Gen. John Buford's Union Division of Cavalry. His unit was the first to come into contact with the Confederate army, which kicked off the Battle of Gettysburg. Gamble died of cholera in Nicaragua while en route to California in 1866.

Garnett: Richard Brooke "Rich" Garnett (1817–1863) was selected by Thomas R. R. Cobb in August 1861 as lieutenant colonel of Cobb's Georgia Legion Infantry. Soon after, he was promoted in November 1861 to brigadier general and fought under Stonewall Jackson. Stonewall had Garnett court martialed after the battle of

Kernstown, but the verdict was suspended. Garnett fought with some credibly at Sharpsburg during the Antietam Campaign and at Fredericksburg. He served as one of Stonewall's pallbearers at his funeral. Garnett was killed at Gettysburg during Pickett's Charge.

George : One of William Delony's slaves and his personal body servant.

Gilmer: Albert C. Gilmer (Gilmore) enlisted as a private in Co. H, Cobb's Georgia Legion Cavalry, on 28 February 1862, in Athens. He was elected lieutenant the end of May 1862 and resigned due to poor health just a few weeks later, in June 1862. From Hall County, Georgia, he was a farmer with a wife and three children.

Girardey: The only possibility found is John N. Girardey, a clerk in 1860 in New Orleans.

Glenn: Luther J. Glenn of Athens raised Glenn's Company of Infantry. Elected as captain in 1861, the company became known as Co. C, Stephens Rifles, Cobb's Georgia Legion Infantry. In 1862, Glenn was promoted to major and in late 1862 to lieutenant colonel of Cobb's Georgia Legion Infantry. He retired from the service in January 1865.

Goodman: Probably Nathan Goodman, a private in Co. B, Cobb's Georgia Legion Cavalry, who served most of the war as courier for Gen. Howell Cobb.

Gordon: James Byron Gordon (1822–1864) was in the mercantile business and did some farming prior to the Civil War. He enlisted as first lieutenant of the Wilkes Valley (North Carolina) Guards, and later was appointed major, then lieutenant colonel, then colonel of the 1st North Carolina Cavalry. He fought extremely well at Bethesda Church, Dumfries, and Buckland Mills. Gordon was mortally wounded at Meadow Bridge in May 1864 during Sheridan's raid on Richmond. He was well respected by his men. The 1st NC Cavalry was added to Hampton's Brigade in July 1862.

Grandmother: Rosa's grandmother was Eliza Vallard Huguenin, a large property owner of Savannah and in the rest of the state.

Grant: "Colonel Grant" was Lemuel Pratt Grant (1817–1893), an engineer and railroad magnate in Georgia before the war. He was chief engineer with the state militia and credited with bringing the railroad to Atlanta. Grant Park in Atlanta is named for him and is located on his former property. L. P. Grant is often referred to as the "Father of Atlanta." He was the younger brother of John Thomas Grant of Athens, also an engineer, and Lemuel's partner in the railroad business.

Grinnan, Andrew: Dr. Andrew Grinnan was the owner of "Brampton" on the Rapidan River near Culpeper Court House, Virginia.

Hal: See Henry Carleton Billups.

Hall: "Mr. Hall" of Athens is not known, although he was probably the same "Mr. Hall" who seems to have been an overseer working on some of the Cobb family properties.

Hammond: James Henry "Harry" Hammond Jr. (1832–1916) was the son of his more famous father, James Henry Hammond, former governor of South Carolina. The son grew up at Silver Bluff Plantation in Barwell District in South Carolina on the Savannah River near Augusta, Georgia. He became a professor of natural history at the University of Georgia prior to the Civil War. Obtaining the rank of major, he served as a quartermaster in the Confederate army.

Hampton, Frank: Frank Hampton (1829–1863) of Richland County, South Carolina, was the younger brother of Wade Hampton. Frank was elected captain of Co. B, 4th Battalion (also known as the Richland Cavalry), within Hampton's Legion of Cavalry. He was promoted to lieutenant colonel of the 2nd South Carolina Cavalry in 1862 and was killed in the fighting at Brandy Station in August 1863.

Hampton, Wade: Wade Hampton (1818–1902) was the first man to attain brigade command under Stuart without any prior military training. He served in both houses of the South Carolina legislature prior to the Civil War and was reportedly the largest landholder in the South. When war broke out, he organized Hampton's Legion and became the unit's first colonel. Taking the legion to Virginia, he participated in First Manassas, where he was wounded. He was appointed brigadier general of cavalry in May 1862. In July 1862, he was placed under J. E. B. Stuart and participated in most of Stuart's operations for the next two years of war. Severely wounded during the Gettysburg Campaign, he was afterwards promoted to major general and succeeded Stuart after the latter's death at Yellow Tavern. Hampton performed admirably in the defense of Richmond until January 1865, when he was ordered to join Joseph Johnston in the Carolinas. After the war, he served two terms as governor of South Carolina followed by twelve years in the US Senate. Wade Hampton was one of only three civilians to attain the rank of lieutenant general in Confederate service who had no previous military training.

Hannah: A slave child of the Delony's.

Hardy: Augustus F. Hardy enlisted as a private in Co. H, Cobb's Georgia Legion Cavalry. From Jackson County, he was killed in June 1863 during the fighting at Brandy Station.

Hart: James Franklin Hart (1837–1905) of Union District, South Carolina, enlisted as captain of the Washington Artillery Volunteers at the beginning of the war. The company was known as "Hart's Company" of the South Carolina Horse Artillery and later went by the name "Hampton's Legion Artillery" and then "Stuart's Horse Artillery." Hart and the Horse Artillery served with distinction throughout the war in Virginia. Hart lost his left leg during the war.

Harrington: Charles Harrington was a private in Co. H, Cobb's Georgia Legion Cavalry. He was slightly wounded during the fighting at Brandy Station in June 1863.

Harris, Charlie : Charles R. A. Harris enlisted as a private in Co. C, Cobb's Georgia Legion Cavalry, on 1 August 1861, in Athens. He served as both a courier and a scout. Harris was captured in Fauquier County, Virginia, on 15 March 1864, imprisoned at Fort Delaware, and paroled in February. He was on furlough when war ended. Following the war, Harris married and lived in Fulton County, Georgia.

Hatton, Joseph: Dr. Joseph Hatton was an Englishman living in Richmond County, Georgia, when he became assistant surgeon in Cobb's Legion Infantry at the beginning of the war. Following the war, he chartered the town of Grovetown in Columbia County, Georgia.

Hays, Howard: Howard Alexander Hays (1830–1898) was a farmer in Lexington, Oglethorpe County, Georgia.

Hemphill: "Young Hemphill" was William Arnold Hemphill (1842–1902), the son of William Stevens Hemphill. He joined the troup artillery as a private from Athens when the war broke out. While thought to have been mortally wounded in fighting near Gettysburg on 2 July 1863, instead he was captured and sent to a hospital on David's Island, New York. He was exchanged 8 September 1863. After his recuperation, Hemphill served as a lieutenant in Moore's Artillery from Athens. Following the war, he moved to Atlanta, established the *Atlanta Constitution* newspaper in 1868, and served as mayor of Atlanta from 1891 to 1892.

Hemphill: "Mr. Hemphill" was William Stevens Hemphill (1817–1874), born in York District, South Carolina. He moved to Athens prior to the war and served in the troup artillery for thirty days after his son, W. A. Hemphill, was wounded at Gettysburg.

Henderson: "Dr. and Mrs. Henderson" were Dr. Matthew Henry Henderson and his wife, Ada Screven Henderson. Dr. Henderson was the rector of Emmanuel Episcopal Church in Athens, Georgia.

Heth, Henry: Henry Heth (1825–1899) was a West Point graduate ('47) who finished last in his class. He was supposedly the only officer in the Confederate army that Lee addressed by his first name. Heth served on the frontier prior to the Civil War. Resigning from the US Army, Heth was elected colonel of the 45th Virginia Infantry. After service in western Virginia, he was promoted to brigadier general in January 1862. He led his brigade under A. P. Hill at Chancellorsville. Heth's Brigade initiated the fighting with John Buford's Union cavalry that sparked the Battle of Gettysburg. Promoted to major general in February 1864, he surrendered at Appomattox. Following the war, he engaged in insurance in Richmond.

Hill, A. P.: Ambrose Powell Hill (1825–1865) was a West Point graduate ('47) and served in the Mexican War and against the Seminoles in Florida. He was well known in the Confederate high command for his signature red battle shirt. When the Civil War began, Hill resigned from the US Army and enlisted in March 1861 as colonel of the 13th Virginia Infantry. In February 1862, he was promoted to brigadier general. After rendering excellent service during the Peninsula Campaign, he was promoted to major general. Hill served during the Seven Days' Battles, at Cedar Mountain, and at Sharpsburg, where his "Light Division" reinforced Lee in time to repel the Union attack. Wounded at Chancellorsville, Hill was promoted to lieutenant general in May 1863 and led the 3rd Corps at Gettysburg. He was killed near Petersburg on 2 April 1865 by a Federal straggler, just one week before the surrender of the army. Hill was one of Lee's favorite officers.

Hill, D. H.: Daniel Harvey Hill (1821–1889) was a West Point graduate ('42) from York District, South Carolina, who fought in the Mexican War. Hill was superintendent of the North Carolina Military Institute when the Civil War broke out. Resigning, he was elected colonel of the 1st North Carolina Troops in May 1861. Promoted to brigadier general in July 1861 and then to major general in March 1862, he fought on the Peninsula and during the Seven Days', at Second Manassas, during the Antietam Campaign at South Mountain and Sharpsburg, and at Fredericksburg. Hill commanded the defenses of Richmond when Lee began moving north, kicking off the Gettysburg Campaign. In July 1863, he was promoted to lieutenant general and sent west under Bragg. An outspoken critic of Bragg's, he caused problems not just with the commanding general, but also with President Davis. Hill fought briefly at Petersburg in 1864, but aside from that saw no further action until the closing days, serving under Johnston at Bentonville. Following the war, he served as the president of the University of Arkansas. He was a brother-in-law to Stonewall Jackson.

Hilton: William J. (T.) Helton was a farmer who enlisted on 1 August 1861 in Athens as a private in Co. C, Cobb's Georgia Legion Cavalry. He was from Jackson County and not Lumpkin County. He died 17 January 1862.

Hodgson: "Mr. Hodgson" is believed to be either Edward R. Hodgson or William V. P. Hodgson, both of Athens.

Holt: Hines Holt from Columbus, Georgia, represented Muscogee County in the Georgia Senate in 1860.

Hood: John Bell Hood (1831–1879) was a West Point graduate ('53) who served in California and Texas prior to the Civil War. Hood is an example of what happens when an officer is raised in rank beyond his capabilities. A success as a brigade and division commander, he was an unmitigated failure as head of the Army of Tennessee. Hood began his Confederate service in October 1861 as colonel of the 4th Texas Infantry. Promoted to brigadier general in March 1862, he commanded Hood's Texas Brigade, which included the 1st, 4th, and 5th Texas Infantry, along with the 18th Georgia Infantry, which included two companies raised in Athens. Hood was appointed major general in October 1862. He lost an arm in the fighting at Gettysburg and a leg in the fighting at Chickamauga in 1863. He then served under Joseph Johnston until superseding him during the Atlanta Campaign. Following Atlanta, he marched the army into Tennessee, where it was shattered at Nashville. Hood was relieved at his own request and command was restored to Joseph Johnston. He resided in New Orleans after the war.

Hooker : Joseph Hooker (1814–1879) was a West Point graduate ('37) who fought in the Mexican War. He was a farmer in California when the Civil War began. Starting out as a brigadier general in August 1861, Hooker was promoted to major general in May 1862. He was wounded in the fighting at Sharpsburg and then commanded the Union Army of the Potomac following Burnside's sacking after Fredericksburg. Hooker was defeated at Chancellorsville, where he apparently lost his nerve following a shell explosion on the porch of his headquarters. He was finally relieved of command during the early stages of the Gettysburg Campaign. Hooker was a quarrelsome officer with both subordinates and superiors, although well liked by the rank and file. He was nicknamed "Fighting Joe," which he did not like. His use of female camp followers to boost the morale of his men created the term "Hooker's Girls," which was simply shortened to "hookers."

House, Thomas: Thomas House was 32 years old when he enlisted as farrier in Delony's Company, Cobb's Georgia Legion Cavalry, in 1861. In March 1862, he transferred to Co. C, Georgia Troopers, as the veterinary surgeon. In June 1862, he was elected as second lieutenant of the same company and was killed during the

Gettysburg Campaign in July 1863. He was a brother-in-law to Henry and Green Jackson.

Howard, Wiley: Wiley Chandler Howard was a 22-year-old law student at the University of Georgia when he enlisted as a private in Co. C, Cobb's Georgia Legion Cavalry. From Oglethorpe County, he was promoted in late 1863 to sergeant and elected lieutenant in August 1864. He was paroled at Greensboro, North Carolina, on 1 May 1865. Following the war, he became a lawyer in Jefferson, Jackson County, and then continued in law after a move to Fulton County. He was also a bill collector in Fulton County. Howard married after the war and died in 1930. He recorded the only complete record of Cobb's Legion in 1901 as *Sketch of Cobb Legion Cavalry and Some Incidents and Scenes Remembered* (Clearwater, SC: Eastern Digital Resources, 2007).

Howze, Thomas: See Thomas House.

Hoyt: "Dr. Hoyt" was Nathan Hoyt from New Hampshire, Presbyterian minister at Athens Presbyterian Church. He served the church for thirty-six years. He was the Delonys' minister.

Hoyt, Tom: Thomas A. Hoyt (1828–1903) was from Athens, the son of Rev. Nathan Hoyt and brother of William Dearing Hoyt. He was born in South Carolina and was a student at the University of Georgia from 1844 to 1846. In 1860, he was a minister in Abbeville District, South Carolina.

Hoyt, William: William Dearing Hoyt (1831–1903) was the son of Rev. Nathan Hoyt and brother of Thomas A. Hoyt. He served as a private in Massenburg's Battery, Georgia Light Artillery (Jackson Artillery).

Hues: See Patrick Hues Mell.

Hull, Henry: Dr. Henry Hull (1798–1881) was too old to serve in the military when the Civil War broke out. He later joined the Home Guard in Athens as a member of the controversial "Mitchell's Thunderbolts," a militia unit of octogenarians formed to protect Athens in 1864, which was disbanded after only a few months due to lack of Confederate control over the unit.

Hull, Hope: William Hope Hull (1820–1877) was the son of Asbury Hull, nephew of Henry Hull, and cousin of John Hope Hull.

Hull, John H.: John Hope Hull (1856–1913) married Will and Rosa's daughter Rosa. He was the son of Henry and Mary Ann Nisbet Hull. The two separated and John moved to St. Louis, where he died.

Hull: "Mrs. Henry Hull" was Mary Ann Nisbet Hull (1817–1885) from Athens, the wife of Henry Hull.

Hull, Mary Ella: Mary Ella Hull was Henry Hull's oldest daughter.

Hull: "Mr. Hull" was William Hope Hull (see "Hull, Hope").

Hunter, B. T.: Benjamin Terry Hunter (1835–1917) was born in Abbeville, South Carolina. He was a professor in Atlanta, living in DeKalb County in 1860. He served as first sergeant in the 10th Battalion of the Georgia Cavalry (State Guards), although there are no service records for him as having served in the unit. By 1870, he was living in Athens, where he operated the Athens High School briefly in 1873. By 1880, he was living in Macon. He received a Confederate pension in 1915 as an "Indigent Veteran."

Hunter: "Mrs. Hunter" was Indiana H. Moore Hunter, wife of Benjamin T. Hunter.

Imboden: John Daniel Imboden (1823–1895) was a schoolteacher and then lawyer in Staunton, Virginia, prior to the Civil War. He entered Confederate service as captain of the Staunton Artillery. After service at First Manassas, he organized the 1st Virginia Partisan Rangers and took part in the battles of Cross Keys and Port Republic under Stonewall Jackson. Promoted to brigadier general in January 1863, he later took part in the action at Gettysburg and commanded the escort for the ambulances during the retreat, where he was instrumental in saving the army wounded at Williamsport. Imboden was incapacitated by typhoid in the fall of 1864. He finished the war out guarding prisoners in Aiken, South Carolina. He returned to the law and to business following the end of the war.

Isaac: Slave and body servant to Richard D. B. Taylor.

J. A. W.: See Wimpy.

Jackson, Addie: Believed to be Lovely Ann Jackson, daughter of Robert Bradford and Elizabeth Ann Thomas Jackson of High Shoals, Clarke County, Georgia.

Jackson, Andrew B.: Andrew Bradford Jackson (1819–1892) was a farmer from High Shoals, Clarke County, Georgia. He was the father of both Henry and Green Jackson.

Jackson, Green: Green Barksdale Jackson (1843–1862) was Henry E. Jackson's brother and a 17-year-old student from Clarke County when he enlisted as a private in Co. C, Cobb's Georgia Legion Cavalry, on 1 August 1861. He was a member of the legion's band and died at Suffolk, Virginia, in March 1862. He was a brother-in-law to Thomas House.

Jackson, Henry: Henry E. Jackson (1838–1905) was Green B. Jackson's brother and a student from Clarke County. He enlisted as a private in Co. C, Cobb's Georgia Legion Cavalry, on 1 August 1861. Like his brother, he served as a member of the legion band and was the legion's bugler. He was paroled at Greensboro, North Carolina, on 1 May 1865. After the war, he married and farmed in Oconee County. He was a brother-in-law of Thomas House.

Jackson, Stonewall: Thomas Jonathan Jackson (1824–1863) was a West Point graduate ('46) who fought in the Mexican War. He resigned his commission in 1852 to become an instructor at the Virginia Military Institute (VMI). He was known as an eccentric professor while at VMI, earning the nicknames of "Tom Fool Jackson," "Old Jack," and "Old Blue Light." At the beginning of the Civil War, Jackson became a colonel of the Virginia Volunteers. In June 1861, he became brigadier general and saw service at First Bull Run, where he earned his most famous nickname of "Stonewall." Promoted to major general in October 1861, he quickly became a military celebrity, known by men on both sides of the conflict. Sent to the Shenandoah Valley in November 1861, he waged a brilliant campaign in 1862 against three separate Federal armies simultaneously, defeating each one of them. At Second Manassas, he captured Pope's supply base and followed that with the capture of Harper's Ferry and its 12,000-man garrison during the early stages of the Antietam Campaign. Following Sharpsburg, Jackson was promoted to lieutenant general and commanded Lee's 2nd Corps. He again achieved victory at Fredericksburg, commanding the army's right wing. His fame reached a new high at the Battle of Chancellorsville in May 1863, where his aggressive assault on the Federal right nearly destroyed the Union army. That night, while conducting a personal reconnaissance with his staff, he was mistakenly shot by his own troops. Next to Lee, Stonewall Jackson is the most revered of all Southern generals.

Jackson, Thomas E.: Thomas E. Jackson enlisted as a private in Co. H, Cobb's Georgia Legion Cavalry, on 6 March 1862, in Athens. He was the company bugler. In July 1863, while fighting at Hagerstown, he was thrown from his horse and trampled by the artillery as they were making a charge. Although seriously injured, he recovered and returned to active duty with the legion. Jackson was paroled at Greensboro, North Carolina, on 1 May 1865. Following the war, he lived in Bishop, Oconee County, Georgia.

Jackson, Thomas E.: Captain (1861) from South Carolina.

Jackson: There were two Jacksons in Cobb's Georgia Legion Cavalry in Co. A, Richmond Hussars: William H. Jackson, private, and John F. Jackson, private. Nothing more is known to determine the identity of their fathers.

Jacob: Unidentified.

Jay: Believed to be a Delony slave.

Jennie: Virginia, also listed as "Jenny." William Delony's sister-in-law, married to Delony's brother Robert (Bob). See Robert Delony.

Jesse: Jesse was Thomas R. R. Cobb's carriage driver prior to the war and served as his primary body servant during the war. Jesse continued to live in Athens following the war, working as the Church sextant at the Athens Presbyterian Church. He took the name Jesse Harvey.

John: William Delony's slave and one of his body servants.

Johnston: Joseph Eggleston Johnston (1807–1891) was a West Point graduate ('29) and the highest-ranking US army officer to resign and join the Confederacy. Johnston fought with distinction in the Mexican War, being wounded both at Cerro Gordo and at Chapultepec. He also fought against the Seminoles in Florida. Johnston offered his services to the Confederacy in April 1861 and was named a major general of the Virginia Volunteers. He became the brigadier general commanding the Confederate army at First Bull Run and on the Peninsula. He was wounded at Seven Pines in May 1862 and while recuperating was replaced by Robert E. Lee. Johnston returned and took command of the Army of Tennessee in December 1862. Failing to relieve Vicksburg in 1863, he opposed William Sherman's advance into Georgia in 1864. He was relieved of his command during the Atlanta Campaign, but due to John B. Hood's near destruction of the army at Atlanta, was reinstated in command once more. He continued to oppose Sherman as he marched through Georgia and South Carolina into North Carolina. Johnston surrendered at Bentonville, North Carolina, to Sherman on 26 April 1865. He represented Virginia in the US House of Representatives from 1879 to 1881 and as the US commissioner of railroads from 1885 to 1891. His death in 1891 was supposedly the result of a cold that he contracted while walking bareheaded in the funeral procession of William Sherman.

Johnston: "Mrs. Johnston" is possibly Mary Frances "Fanny" Mansfield Johnston, wife of Richard Malone Johnston of Hancock County, Georgia.

Jonas: Unidentified.

Jones: Malcolm Daniel Jones enlisted as captain of Co. F, Cobb's Georgia Legion Cavalry, on 25 March 1862 in Burke County. He died in 1869.

Jones: Henry Francis (Frank) Jones enlisted as a private in Co. C, Cobb's Georgia Legion Cavalry, on 1 August 1861 in Athens. He was sent to Athens as a recruiter in February 1862. Jones was appointed sergeant on 15 June 1862 and later promoted to lieutenant on 15 April 1864. He was killed in the fighting at Trevilian Station on 12 June 1864.

Jones, "Grumble": William Edmondson "Grumble" Jones (1824–1864) was a West Point graduate ('48) who served out West fighting Indians in the mid-1850s. He resigned in 1857 and took up farming in Virginia. When the Civil War broke out, he joined the 1st Virginia Cavalry as a captain. In May 1861 he was promoted to major, then colonel in July following First Manassas. In September 1861, he took over command of the 7th Virginia Cavalry. He took part in Stuart's raid around McClellan and was promoted to brigadier general in September 1862, commanding Stuart's 4th Brigade. He fought at Brandy Station where he performed well. Stuart and Jones did not get along, and Stuart eventually court martialed Jones for insulting him. Lee intervened and Jones was transferred to the Trans-Allegheny department in West Virginia, where he worked with James Longstreet in eastern Tennessee. He was shot in the head and died at the Battle of Piedmont on 5 June 1864.

Kenny: Joseph Kenney was a member of Co. C, Georgia Troopers, Cobb's Georgia Legion Cavalry.

King: "Dr. King" was Barrington Simeral King. There is a Barrington S. King listed in the 1860 census for Columbia, Richland County, South Carolina.

King: "Mr. King" was Barrington King, father of Barrington Simeral King.

King: Barrington Simeral King enlisted as a private in Co. C, Cobb's Georgia Legion Cavalry, on 1 August 1861 in Athens. He was elected captain of Co. E, Roswell Troopers, in March 1862 during the cavalry's reorganization and upon the death of Will Delony, King became the new lieutenant colonel of the legion. Although born in Liberty County, King and his family moved to Roswell in Fulton County before the war, where his father started a vast mill industry. King was killed near Averasboro, North Carolina, on 10 March 1865.

Knight: Gazaway B. Knight was 36 years old in August 1861 when he enlisted in Cobb's Georgia Legion Infantry. He was elected captain of Knight's Company of Cobb's Legion Infantry, promoted to lieutenant colonel in June 1862, and resigned in July 1862 on account of disability, although a notation on his discharge states, "Ordered home by Col. Cobb." His service records again have him as lieutenant colonel of the regiment in 1865.

Lamar: "J. Lamar" and "Major Lamar" are John B. Lamar. Lamar was from Macon, Georgia, and brother-in-law to Howell Cobb (brother of Thomas R. R. Cobb). He served as adjutant to Howell during the first part of the war. He was mortally wounded during the fighting at Crampton Gap, Maryland, on 14 September 1862 during the Antietam Campaign.

Lampkin, Jim: James T. (G.) (P.) Lampkin was a carpenter from Gwinnett County, Georgia, when he enlisted 14 August 1861 in Atlanta as a private in Co. B, Cobb's Georgia Legion Cavalry. He was promoted to corporal in March 1863. After the war, he became a merchant and married twice. He died in Turner County, Georgia.

Lampkin, T. M.: Thomas M. Lampkin enlisted in Cobb's Georgia Legion Infantry in 1861 and was assigned as commissary for the regiment. He resigned his position in September 1862 on account of disability. He requested and was assigned the position of post commissary in Athens, endorsed by Gen. Howell Cobb, in July 1864.

Landrum: Two possibilities exist: Benjamin Landrum and Monroe M. Landrum were both privates in Co. H, Cobb's Georgia Legion Cavalry.

Laura: Rosa's cousin, Laura Huguenin.

Lawton: Winburn J. Lawton was a planter from Dougherty County, Georgia, when he enlisted as a captain in Co. D, Dougherty Hussars, Cobb's Georgia Legion Cavalry, on 10 August 1861. He was promoted to colonel in May 1862 of the 2nd Georgia Cavalry.

Lee, Fitzhugh: William Henry Fitzhugh Lee (1837–1891) was the eldest and most famous of Robert E. Lee's sons. Nicknamed "Rooney," he joined a Virginia cavalry unit in May 1861 as a captain. By January 1862, he was lieutenant colonel of the 9th Virginia Cavalry and a few months later (April) he was appointed colonel of the regiment. In September 1862, he was appointed brigadier general of cavalry and took part in J. E. B. Stuart's first ride around McClellan. He fought in all the cavalry actions up to Brandy Station in 1863, where he was wounded. While recuperating at home, he was captured and confined. Lee was not released until March 1864, at which time he returned home only to find his wife had died in the meantime. He rejoined the fight and surrendered at Appomattox. After the war, he farmed and served in the state senate and the US Congress. His home on the Pamunkey River, known as White House, was burned by Union forces under George B. McClellan in June 1862.

Lee, R. E.: Robert Edward Lee (1807–1870) was a West Point graduate ('29) who fought in the Mexican War. He later became the superintendent of the Military Academy ('52) and led the US government forces against John Brown during the latter's raid of Harper's Ferry. Offered command of all Union forces by Abraham Lincoln at the outset of the war, Lee turned him down to fight for his native state of Virginia. Since the Confederacy already had an overall military commander, Joseph E. Johnston, President Jefferson Davis placed Lee on his personal staff. One of Lee's first assignments was to strengthen the coastal defenses of South Carolina, Georgia, and Florida. He fought with little success in western Virginia before taking over what would become the Army of Northern Virginia following the wounding of Johnston at Seven Pines in May 1862. As he took over from Johnston, his nickname among his troops was "Granny Lee," but soon they were referring to him as "Uncle Robert" and "Marse Robert." Lee still ranks among many as the greatest generals ever produced in the United States. Following the war, he became president of Washington College (now Washington and Lee University). His application for the restoration of his citizenship was "mislaid" and not found until 1970 in the government archives. It was only then that his citizenship was granted.

Lester: George N. Lester was a large property owner in Marietta, Cobb County, Georgia, who served in the State House of Representatives in 1860.

Levy: Col. William Mallory Levy (1827–1882) served in the Mexican War, after which he practiced law in Natchitoches, Louisiana. He served in the Louisiana legislature from 1859 to 1861. At the outbreak of the Civil War, he enlisted in Co. A, 2nd Louisiana Infantry where he was elected captain. In July 1861, he was elected the colonel of the 2nd Louisiana Infantry.

Lewis: Miles Walker Lewis was a member of the Georgia House of Representatives in 1860. He served from Greene County. He was a farmer and lawyer.

Libby: Possibly one of Will and Rosa Delony's slaves.

Lilly: Believed to be one of the slave children on the Delony property.

Linton: See Stephens, Linton.

Lipscomb: Dr. Lipscomb was Andrew Adgate Lipscomb (1816–1890), who served as chancellor of the University of Georgia during its most turbulent period from 1860 until 1874. He was a moderate who labored to keep the university open during the Civil War and labored to reopen it after the war.

Lipscomb: Thomas Jefferson Lipscomb was major, then lieutenant colonel, then colonel of the 2nd South Carolina Cavalry. The 2nd South Carolina Cavalry was added to Hampton's Brigade in July 1862. Following the war he served as a mayor of Columbia, South Carolina.

Lisson: Unidentifiable other than she married "Mr. Adams."

Longstreet: James Longstreet (1821–1904) was a West Point graduate ('42) and one of the longest living of the Confederate generals. Longstreet fought in the Mexican War and was wounded at Chapultepec. He resigned in June 1861 to join the Confederacy. By October 1861, he was a major general commanding the First Corps under R. E. Lee. As Lee's trusted "Old War Horse," Longstreet fought in nearly every major battle of the Eastern Theater. Lee's trust in Longstreet's skill and competency were well placed, especially at South Mountain, Sharpsburg, and Fredericksburg. As the senior lieutenant general, he opposed Lee in the latter's decision of a frontal attack at Gettysburg, preferring to maneuver Meade out of his position about the city. After the war, he befriended U. S. Grant and became a Republican, which did not sit well with most Southerners. He was appointed US minister to Turkey and lived out his final days in Gainesville, Georgia, where he ran the Piedmont Hotel.

Lucas: "Mr Lucas" was Frederick William Lucas (1823–1905), who was a prominent merchant and businessman in Athens as well as serving as a judge.

Lumpkin, Ed: Edward "Ned" Payson Lumpkin was the son of State Supreme Court Justice Joseph Henry Lumpkin and a law partner with his brother-in-law, Thomas R. R. Cobb. He served in Cobb's Georgia Legion as a member of the troup artillery and later commanded Captain Lumpkin's Battery of Artillery.

Lumpkin, Judge: "Judge Lumpkin" was Joseph Henry Lumpkin (1799–1867), brother of former governor Wilson Lumpkin and Georgia's first state supreme court justice. Lumpkin was cofounder of the Lumpkin Law School, forerunner of the University of Georgia School of Law, and mentor to his son-in-law, Thomas R. R. Cobb.

Lumpkin, Mattie: Martha W. Lumpkin was a daughter of Wilson Lumpkin, former governor of Georgia, and cousin of Ed, Miller, and Marion Cobb (wife of Thomas R. R. Cobb).

Lumpkin, Miller: Miller Grieve Lumpkin was a brother-in-law of Thomas R. R. Cobb. A merchant from Athens, he enlisted as a private in the 3rd Georgia Infantry and transferred to Co. C, Cobb's Georgia Legion Cavalry, on 1 August 1861 and appointed assistant commissary. He was appointed major and commissary sergeant of the brigade of Gen. P. B. M. Young in January 1865.

Lumpkin, Ned: See "Ed" above.

Lumpkin: Wilson Lumpkin (1783–1870) was brother of Joseph Henry Lumpkin. Wilson Lumpkin served as a member of the Georgia House of Representatives from 1804 to 1812, the US House of Representatives 1815–1817, and then as a US senator from 1827 to 1831. Elected governor of Georgia in 1831, he served four years and was then elected as senator once more, which he held until 1841. During his time as governor, he oversaw the removal of the Cherokee from northern Georgia. Lumpkin County, Georgia, is named for him.

Lyle, James B.   : This is a misprint in the *Southern Banner*. The name is James Ray Lyle (1833–1899). Lyle was an attorney from Athens who enlisted as a lieutenant in Co. C, Cobb's Georgia Legion Cavalry, on 14 August 1861 in Athens. After the war, he married, became a lawyer, mayor of Athens, state senator, and later a judge. He died in 1899 in Athens. Nothing more is known of his military service in Cobb's Georgia Legion Cavalry. Although his obituary mentions him having obtained the rank of major, no evidence exists in his Civil War service records.

Magruder: John Bankhead Magruder (1807–1871) was a West Point graduate ('30) who fought in the Mexican War, where he was wounded at Chipultepec. He then fought against the Seminoles in Florida and next served on the Western frontier. He resigned in April 1861 at the outbreak of the Civil War and the following month was appointed colonel of the Virginia Volunteers. Promoted to brigadier general, he commanded the Confederate forces on the Peninsula and participated in the Seven Days' Battles. Afterward, he was sent to the Trans-Mississippi department and remained there for the rest of the war. Known to those who knew him as "Prince John" for his rather flamboyant manner and dress, he fled to Mexico following the end of the war and established a colony of Southern exiles at Cordoba. He returned to the US in 1867 and died in poverty.

Marion : Marion McHenry Lumpkin Cobb (1822–1897) was the oldest daughter of Judge Joseph Henry Lumpkin, Georgia state supreme court justice, and wife of Thomas Reade Rootes Cobb. Marion was a friend of Rosa's.

Marshall: James F. Marshall enlisted as a sergeant in Co. D, Cobb's Georgia Legion Cavalry, on 10 August 1861 in Albany. He was elected lieutenant the end of December 1861 and killed during the vicious fighting at Quebec Schoolhouse in Middletown, Maryland, on 13 September 1862.

Marshall, Thomas: Private in Co. E, 12th Virginia Cavalry. He was captured in June 1863 at Beverly Ford, Virginia, and imprisoned at the Old Capitol Prison in Washington, DC (where the Supreme Court building now stands).

Martha: See Delony, Martha.

Martin: William "Will" T. Martin was an attorney and Unionist prior to the war. When the Civil War broke out, he organized the "Adams Troop" from Mississippi and became the unit's lieutenant colonel. The unit was taken into Confederate service as Co. A, Jeff Davis Legion Cavalry.

McClellan: George Brinton McClellan (1826–1885) was a West Point graduate ('46). He was a very capable organizer and excellent military commander during peacetime, although as a military commander during wartime he has often been criticized as too cautious and slow to react. McClellan developed the "McClellan Saddle," which was used by the military for as long as the US Army continued a mounted branch. He resigned from the service in 1857 to work for the Illinois Central Railroad and later became vice president of the Ohio and Mississippi Railroad. When war broke out, McClellan was appointed major general in May 1861, becoming commander in chief of the Army of the Potomac in November of that year. McClellan was greatly admired and liked by his troops, who referred to him as "the Young Napoleon." Following the Antietam Campaign and J. E. B. Stuart's second ride around the Union army, McClellan was sacked, earning the nickname "Mac the Unready." He retired to his home in New Jersey and ran as the Democratic presidential candidate against Abraham Lincoln in the 1864 election, which he barely lost. Defeated, he was elected New Jersey governor and served his state in the late 1870s and early 1880s.

McCroan: There are three possibilities for McCroan: Augustus McCroan, Henry McCroan, and John J. McCroan. All three hailed from Jefferson County, Georgia, and were members of Cobb's Georgia Legion Cavalry.

McElhannon: George W. McElhanon was a farmer from Jackson County, Georgia. He enlisted as a private in Co. H, Cobb's Georgia Legion Cavalry, on 4 March 1862 at Athens. He was sergeant in June 1862 and captured at Malvern Hill, Virginia, in August 1862. Exchanged, he died in a hospital in Raleigh, North Carolina, on 11 August 1864. He married prior to the war.

McGregor, W. M.: McGregor's Battery, or Stuart's 2nd Horse Light Artillery, was created by dividing John Pelham's Artillery into two batteries. The 2nd fought throughout the war, primarily in the Richmond area, while the 1st often fought in the Shenandoah Valley. The 2nd battery was commanded by Captain William Morrell McGregor. The unit finally surrendered at Appomattox in 1865 with just two men.

McKinley, Miss: Catherine McKinley was the second wife of Richard Delony Bolling Taylor, of Athens, called "Dick" by his friends. (R. D. B. Taylor was also a cousin of William Delony's.) The couple were married in 1863.

McLaws: A native of Georgia, Lafayette McLaws (1821–1897) was a West Point graduate ('42) who served as a captain of infantry for nearly ten years prior to the outbreak of the Civil War. He resigned and offered his services to the Confederacy in May 1861, at which time he was appointed colonel of the 10th Georgia Infantry.

In September 1861, he was promoted to brigadier general, commanding a division under John Magruder on the Peninsula. In May 1862, he was appointed major general. He fought in most of the major battles in the Eastern Theater. Following the war, McLaws became a postmaster, tax collector, and sold insurance.

McLaws, Mary: Probably Mary Ann McLaws (1832–1872) of Augusta, Georgia.

Mell: "Aunt Mell" was Lurene Howard Cooper, wife of Patrick Hues Mell, and an aunt to Rosa Delony.

Mell: "Dr Mell" was Patrick Hues Mell (1814–1888) of Athens. He was a professor at the University of Georgia (mathematics) and a Baptist minister, serving for twenty-eight years at Antioch Baptist Church in Oglethorpe County, Georgia. He later served as Chancellor of the University of Georgia, 1878–1888.His first wife died in 1861 in childbirth, leaving him to raise seven children. A son was killed at Crampton's Gap.

Merritt: Wesley Merritt (1834–1910) was a West Point graduate ('60) serving in Utah when the Civil War broke out. He served as an aide to Philip St. George Cooke during the Peninsula Campaign. Merritt rose from lieutenant to captain to colonel under Gen. John Buford. Merritt's cavalrymen were often opponents of Wade Hampton's forces. Merritt served in the Spanish-American War as a major general.

Mitchell: "Mr. Mitchell" was William Letcher Mitchell (1805–1882), a prominent lawyer in Athens, cofounder of the Lumpkin Law School (forerunner of University of Georgia School of Law), superintendent of the state railroad, member of the Board of Trustees of the University of Georgia, elder of the Athens Presbyterian Church, and member, along with Will Delony, of the "Cobb Faction" in Georgia's secession politics.

Moore, Addie: "Addie Moore" was Adelaide Van Dyke Moore (1834–1865), daughter of Richard D. and Elizabeth S. Moore. Her "intended" was Thomas F. Screven from Savannah, whom she married 26 November 1860 at Emmanuel Episcopal Church in Athens.

Munnerlyn, James: James K. Munnerlyn enlisted as a private in Co. F, Georgia Hussars, Jeff Davis Legion, in 1861. He was promoted to corporal in February 1863 and wounded in July 1863 at Hagerstown (also known as the Battle of Williamsport and Falling Waters). He disappears from the record after February 1864.

Murphy: Several Murphys/Murpheys were members of Cobb's Georgia Legion, although the best candidate seems to be Thomas J. Murphy (Murphey) who, as a 19-year-old, enlisted in Co. I, 1st Georgia Infantry, in March 1861 and transferred to Co. I, Cobb's Georgia Legion Cavalry, as a sergeant on 17 August 1861. Being one of those sent to Georgia to obtain horses in September 1864, he was not subsequently heard from.

Nash, R.: Ruben Long Nash was a farmer from Jackson County who, along with his two brothers, Charles T. and John J., enlisted in Co. C, Cobb's Georgia Legion Cavalry, on 1 August 1861. By the end of 1861, R. L. Nash was a corporal in the company, later promoted to sergeant. He was captured 22 September 1863 at Jack's Shop, Virginia, when he voluntarily remained behind with Dr. H. S. Bradley to care for the badly wounded Will Delony. Imprisoned at Point Lookout, he was exchanged in November 1864, rejoined the legion, and paroled at Greensboro, North Carolina, on 1 May 1865. He was married following the war.

Neal, Miss: Miss Neal is unidentified.

Nellie: "Little Nellie" may be a child of the Duncans. See Duncan.

Newton's widow: Joseph Elizur Holt Newton's wife is unknown other than that she was a Williamson from Jackson County, Georgia. Newton was a farmer in Jackson County who died 22 December 1859 in Jefferson.

O'Connor, Dan: Daniel O'Connor was 27 when he enlisted as a private in Co. C, Cobb's Georgia Legion Cavalry, on 1 August 1861 in Athens. He was from Hall County, Georgia. He was severely wounded at Jack's Shop, Virginia, on 22 September 1863 when a minie ball shattered his left leg. Having his leg amputated, he was sent to Elmira Prison in New York and paroled on 19 February 1865. Following the war, he moved to Montgomery County, Illinois, where he farmed until his death in the 1880s.

Oliver, Charlie: James Charles Oliver was a farmer from Jackson County, Georgia, who enlisted as a private in Co. C, Cobb's Georgia Legion Cavalry, on 22 April 1862. He was captured at Spotsylvania Court House, Virginia, on 29 February 1864 and imprisoned at Elmira Prison in New York. He was released on 17 July 1865. He married prior to the war and returned to Jackson County and his family following, where he continued to farm until his death in the 1880s.

Oshields: John B. Oshields was a private in Co. H, Cobb's Georgia Legion Cavalry. He was wounded slightly during the fighting at Brandy Station in June 1863.

Penick: "Dr. Penick" is unidentified, but he could be Jefferson P. Penick of Morgan County, Georgia, or perhaps related to him.

Parsons, James: James M. Parsons was a private in Co. C, 6th Michigan Cavalry.

Pelham , John: Pelham (1838–1863), born in Alabama, was a cadet at West Point when the Civil War began. He resigned when Virginia joined the Confederacy and signed on as an artilleryman. He was made captain and given command of J. E. B. Stuart's Horse Artillery in 1862. Promoted to major and then lieutenant colonel in April 1863, he showed great skill and courage on the battlefield. At Fredericksburg, he held up the advance of an entire Union division with just two cannon, and despite orders to retire, he continued to fire until his ammunition ran out. Pelham was killed in March 1863 while fighting with the cavalry at Kelly's Ford, Virginia.

Pemberton: John Clifford Pemberton (1814–1881) was a West Point graduate ('37) born in Pennsylvania. He fought in the Mexican War against the Seminoles in Florida and the Mormons in Utah. At the beginning of the Civil War, he was living in Virginia and joined the Confederacy. Promoted to lieutenant general, Pemberton was sent to Mississippi to take command of Confederate forces guarding Vicksburg and Port Hudson. After his surrender of the city of Vicksburg to Grant, most Southerners suspected Pemberton of latent Northern feelings and blamed him for the fall of the city. Unable to procure another command, Jefferson Davis commissioned him as a lieutenant colonel of artillery and placed him in command of the artillery in the defenses of Richmond. He farmed in Virginia after the war and later moved back to Pennsylvania, where he died five years later.

Pettigrew: James Johnston Pettigrew (1828–1863) was an author, lawyer, and diplomat prior to the Civil War. He was a prominent linguist of his time, having traveled widely in Europe prior to practicing law in Charleston. He was aide to South Carolina governor Pickens during the early stages of the state's secession and subsequent dealings with Fort Sumter. When the war broke out, he joined Hampton's Legion as colonel of the 1st South Carolina Rifles (infantry). Pettigrew later traveled to North Carolina in 1862 to take command of the 12th North Carolina Troops (later redesignated the 22nd NCT). He was promoted (against his wishes) to brigadier general in February 1862. He was severely wounded at Seven Pines, where he was left for dead and captured by Union troops. Exchanged and finally recovered from his wounds, he returned to duty. He was back in command of his North Carolina Brigade (11th, 26th, 47th, and 52nd NCT) during the Gettysburg Campaign. Pettigrew and his North Carolinians were positioned on the left of Pickett's Virginians during the famous "Pickett's Charge," where he was again seriously wounded. Helping cover the retreating Confederate forces following Gettysburg, on 14 July 1863, he was shot in the stomach by a Michigan cavalryman. He died three days later.

Phillips: Jefferson C. Phillips was major of the 3rd Virginia Cavalry in 1862.

Pickett: George Edward Pickett (1825–1875) was a West Point graduate ('46) who finished at the bottom of his class. After graduating, he was sent West, where he fought against Mexicans and Indians before resigning in the summer of 1861 to join the Confederacy. By February 1862, he was a brigadier general of Virginia Infantry and fought at Williamsburg, Seven Pines, and Gaines' Mill, where he was wounded. Following the Antietam Campaign, he was promoted to major general and led the famous charge at Gettysburg that bears his name.

Pittard, Bob: John Robert Pittard from Oglethorpe County, Georgia. Brother of I. H. and "Jim" Pittard.

Pittard: Isham Humphrey Pittard was from Clarke County and enlisted as a lieutenant in Co. H, Cobb's Georgia Legion Cavalry, on 3 March 1862. He served as the acting commanding officer of Captain Ritch's company following the capture of Ritch in June 1863. Pittard was captured in February 1864 at Ely's Ford, Virginia, and sent to Fort Delaware. He was released on 16 June 1865. He was twice married following the war and died in Clarke County, Georgia, in 1914. He was the brother of "Jim" and "Bob" Pittard.

Pittard: "Mr Pittard" is probably John Samuel Pittard from the Winterville area of Clarke County, Georgia.

Pittard, Jim: James Marvin (Melvin) Pittard from Oglethorpe County, Georgia. Brother of I. H. and "Bob" Pittard.

Plant: Unidentified.

Pleasonton: Alfred Pleasonton was a West Point graduate ('44) who fought in the Mexican War and against the Seminoles in Florida. As brigadier general he commanded cavalry during the Antietam Campaign, where he earned the nickname "Knight of Romance" due to his notoriously unreliable reports to his superiors of enemy activity. Pleasonton's cavalry force failed miserably to catch J. E. B. Stuart's raiding force during the second ride around the Union army.

Pope: John Pope (1822–1892) was a West Point graduate ('42). He fought in the Mexican War. Pope escorted Abraham Lincoln to the inaugural ceremonies and took command of Union forces in northern Virginia in July 1862. Fighting at Cedar Mountain, Second Bull Run, and elsewhere in the Shenandoah Valley, he was primarily unsuccessful in his encounters with Confederate forces under Thomas J. "Stonewall" Jackson. Pope was relieved of command in September 1862 and spent the rest of the war out West dealing with the Sioux.

Porter, Fitz John: Fitz John Porter (1822–1901) was a West Point graduate ('45) who fought in the Mexican War, being wounded at Chapultepec. He also served in the latter 1850s in Utah against the Mormons. In August 1861, he commanded the Army of the Potomac, then commanded a division under McClellan and later a corps. He was promoted to major general in July 1862 but relieved of command in November 1862 for disloyalty and disobedience of orders. Scapegoated by John Pope following Second Manassas, Porter was exonerated twenty-five years later.

Porter, R. K.: Rev. Richard K. Porter was a Presbyterian minister, originally from South Carolina. He served as chaplain in Cobb's Georgia Legion Infantry. Given the rank of captain, Rev. Porter accompanied the body of Brigadier General Thomas R. R. Cobb to Athens following his death during the battle of Fredericksburg.

Printup: Daniel S. Printup of Rome, Georgia, represented Floyd County in the Georgia Senate in 1860. Following the war, he owned and operated a drug company in Augusta.

Puckett, W. B. C.: William B. C. Puckett enlisted in Cherokee County, Georgia, as captain of Co. C, Cherokee Dragoons, Phillips's Georgia Legion Cavalry, 11 June 1861. He was promoted to major in September 1862.

Pugh: Nathan S. Pugh was 24 years old when he enlisted in March 1861 in Co. I, 1st Georgia Infantry. In April 1862, he was enticed to enlist again, this time as a private in Co. B, Richmond Hussars of Cobb's Georgia Legion Cavalry. He was promoted to lieutenant in September 1862. The last entry for him is at the end of April 1863, although there is a notation of his death at Hunterstown on 2 July 1863.

Raiford: Col. & Mrs. Raiford are unidentified other than living in Goldsboro, North Carolina.

Reese: Dr. Charles Milton Reese (1788–1862) was a native of South Carolina who served the first half of his career in the US Navy. He came to Athens in the 1830s and built a house on Prince Avenue, a few blocks from the Delonys.

Rice, Zachariah A.: Zachariah A. Rice was a merchandiser, slave dealer, and part owner of the *Southern Miscellany* newspaper in Atlanta when he enlisted as a lieutenant in Co. B, Fulton Dragoons, Cobb's Georgia Legion Cavalry, on 14 August 1861. He was elected captain in December 1861 when Benjamin Yancey was promoted to major. He resigned in June 1863 to take care of business and family matters. Following the war, he farmed in Campbell County, Georgia, after which he returned to business, became a judge, and then later served as a city councilman in Atlanta, Fulton County. Rice married prior to the war and died in 1890 in Atlanta.

Rich: See Ritch.

Ritch: Jeremiah E. Ritch was a merchant in Athens when the war broke out. He enlisted as a lieutenant in Co. C, Cobb's Georgia Legion Cavalry, on 1 August 1861. He was elected captain of Co. H, Cobb's Legion, on 26 May 1862. Captured at Beverly's Ford, Virginia, on 9 June 1863 while leading his company as dismounted sharpshooters, he was imprisoned on Johnson's Island, Ohio, in August. Ritch was exchanged on 24 February 1865. After the war, he was a dealer in ready-made clothing. Married, he died in the 1870s in Clarke County.

Robertson, Beverly: Beverly Robertson (1826–1910) was a West Point graduate ('49). He became colonel of the 4th Virginia Cavalry with the outbreak of the war. From June 1862 until May 1863, he commanded cavalry under J. E. B. Stuart during the battles of Cedar Mountain and Second Bull Run. With the reorganization of Confederate cavalry in 1863, Robertson was dispatched to North Carolina to organize new cavalry regiments. In May 1863, he rejoined Stuart and commanded a cavalry brigade under Wade Hampton. He took part in Stuart's famous ride around McClellan. Following the war, he moved to Washington, DC, and involved himself in the insurance business.

Roper: "Colonel Roper" was Joel Cole Roper from Cass County. His service records do not show a promotion to colonel. He enlisted in Co. F, Davis Guards, 18th Georgia Infantry, in 1861, and elected captain of the company soon thereafter. He resigned his position in November 1863 after being elected to the Georgia state legislature. He applied for a Confederate pension in 1895 in Bartow County, Georgia, due to "infirmity & poverty."

Rosa: "Little Rosa" was Rosa Eugenia Delony (9 September 1857–18 September 1937), the daughter and second oldest child of Will and Rosa. She would do much to preserve the memory of her parents, including their correspondence.

Rosser, Thomas L.: Thomas Lafayette Rosser (1836–1910) resigned from West Point just two weeks prior to his graduation in order to join the Washington Artillery of New Orleans as an instructor. He was made colonel of the 5th Virginia Cavalry in 1862 and promoted to brigadier general in September 1863, succeeding Beverly Robertson in command of the Laurel Brigade. After the war, he became the chief engineer of the Northern Pacific and Canadian Pacific railroads.

Rutherford, John: John Cobb Rutherford, also mentioned as Johnny Rutherford, was a 19-year-old student at the University of Georgia when he enlisted as a sergeant in Co. C, Cobb's Georgia Legion Cavalry, on 1 August 1861 in Athens. He was a nephew of Thomas R. R. Cobb and served on Cobb's staff as a volunteer aide-de-camp. He later served on Howell Cobb's staff as assistant adjutant and inspector general. He was paroled 18 May 1865 in Florida and became a lawyer in

Decatur County following the war, and later in Macon, Bibb County. He was married and died 10 March 1891 in Florida.

Sam: Probably a Delony slave.

Sarah: Sarah was a slave and the assistant cook in the Delony household.

Saulter: Thomas W. Salter was a tinner from Athens who enlisted as a private in Co. H, Cobb's Georgia Legion Cavalry, on 5 March 1862. By June he was a sergeant and elected lieutenant on 25 March 1863. He was killed in the fighting near Martinsburg, Virginia, on 19 July 1863 during a raid on the Baltimore and Ohio Railroad. He was survived by a wife.

Seward : William Henry Seward (1801–1872) was a New York lawyer and opponent to Abraham Lincoln. When Lincoln was elected president, he appointed Seward secretary of state, a position in which Seward would serve quite competently. Seward served as the administration's foreign minister to Great Britain and was very successful in handling the extremely explosive Trent Affair. The night of Lincoln's assassination, Lewis Paine, another of the Lincoln's conspirators, stabbed Seward numerous times at his home in an unsuccessful attempt to eliminate several members of Lincoln's cabinet. Recovered, Seward supported Andrew Johnson and continued to serve in the State Department until the election of Ulysses S. Grant. During his time there, he became quite famous for "Seward's Folly," the purchase of land from Russia that would eventually become Alaska.

Shields, P. B.: There is a P. B. Shields listed as being from Morgan County, Georgia, but aside from this, there is very little known about him.

Sibley: Henry Josiah Sibley (1833–1864) was from Augusta. He enlisted in the 5th Georgia Infantry and died during the Battles for Atlanta in 1864.

Sigel, Franz: Franz Sigel (1824–1902) was a native of the Grand Duchy of Baden, one of the German states, who took part in the 1848 revolutions and was forced to flee to Switzerland because of it. He later immigrated to New York and served in the New York Militia. When the Civil War broke out, he became the colonel of the 3rd Missouri. By November 1861, he was brigadier general commanding the 4th Brigade in the Army of Southwest Missouri. In March 1862, he was major general, commanding a division in the Department of the Shenandoah. Sigel took part in several campaigns, including the Maryland and Fredericksburg campaigns, but he had a relatively lackluster career. He served as a pension agent after the war.

Siler: Jesse W. Siler, from Macon County, North Carolina, enlisted as a second lieutenant in 1861 in the 1st North Carolina Cavalry. The unit became a part of Hampton's Brigade in July 1862. Siler was killed in battle at Gaines Crossroads,

Virginia, in November 1862. "His men wept at the sight of his body in the snow" (Hartley, *Stuart's Tarheels*, 363.)

Simmons, M. S.: Moses S. Simmons was a private in Co. H, Cobb's Georgia Legion Cavalry. He was wounded and captured at Beverly Ford on the Rappahannock River during the early stages of the fighting at Brandy Station in June 1863. He was later released from Old Capitol Prison on 30 June.

Sledge, James A.: James Asbury Sledge was the long-serving editor of the Athens newspaper *Southern Banner.*

Smith, D. E.: David E. Smith enlisted as a sergeant in Co. C, Georgia Troopers, of Cobb's Georgia Legion Cavalry, in 1861. In late 1863, for some unknown reason, he is listed for the remainder of the war as a private.

Smith, George: George T. Smith enlisted in Covington, Newton County, Georgia, as a private in Co. A, Lamar Infantry, Cobb's Georgia Legion Infantry. He was wounded and captured at South Mountain during the Maryland Campaign in 1862. Exchanged, he returned to the unit after his recuperation and served the remainder of the war, being wounded and captured again at Sailor's Creek in Virginia in 1865.

Smith: Dr. and Mrs. Smith are probably Robert Mark Smith and his wife, Rosanna "Rosa" Jane Pringle. Dr. Smith was a physician and surgeon who also operated a drugstore with his practice. During the Civil War, he served as the surgeon of the 16th Georgia Infantry. Dr. Smith also served the city of Athens as its first intendant (mayor), and along with the Delonys, he and his wife were members of the Athens Presbyterian Church.

Smith: "Lt. Smith of King's Co." is Thomas H. Smith, who enlisted as a lieutenant in King's Company, Cobb's Georgia Legion Cavalry, in 1861. He was supposedly killed near Gettysburg in July 1863, although his service record states, "Died March 15, 1863."

Smith: "Major Smith" was probably Thomas H. Smith (above).

Stanley: Marcellus Stanley (1823–1890) was a banker, director of the Southern Mutual Insurance, and trustee of the First Methodist Church in Athens. He commanded the Troup Artillery from Athens.

Stephens, Alexander: Alexander Hamilton Stephens (1812–1883) was affectionately called "Little Aleck" by those that knew him. A Georgia lawyer and state legislator, Alexander served in the US House of Representatives from 1843 to 1859. A noted Unionist, he opposed immediate secession upon Abraham Lincoln's election and led the "Stephens Faction" in Georgia politics. As a member of the Provisional

Confederate Congress, he sought to become president of the Confederacy, settling for the vice presidency. Constantly snubbed and outmaneuvered by Jefferson Davis, Stephens became a strong proponent of a negotiated peace during the last two years of the war. Following the end of the war, he was imprisoned in Boston Harbor for five months. In 1873, he was again elected to the US House of Representatives and served in that body until 1882, after which he was elected governor of Georgia. He died just a few months after taking office.

Stephens, Linton: Linton Stephens (1823–1872) was born in Taliaferro County, Georgia. The half-brother of Confederate vice president Alexander Stephens, he served in the state legislature from 1849 to 1855 and was appointed to the state supreme court in 1859, serving two years. He served along with his brother Alexander as a delegate to the Georgia Secession Convention, and, with several of their supporters, formed what was termed the "Stephens Faction" in Georgia politics. The Stephens Faction advocated a wait-and-see attitude toward the recent election of Abraham Lincoln and the possibility of the state's immediate secession that was being proposed by the "Cobb Faction," of which William Delony was a member. At the outbreak of the war, Linton became the lieutenant colonel of the 15th Georgia Infantry, but he resigned in December 1861 due to ill health. He then reentered the state legislature and served there for the rest of the war. He constantly opposed the policies of Jefferson Davis. Following the war, Linton resumed his law profession.

Stephenson: Unidentifiable other than living in Goldsboro, North Carolina, in June 1862.

Stoneman, George: George Stoneman (1822–1894) was a West Point graduate ('46) who served in California during the Mexican War and later on the Indian frontier. Commissioned a captain in the 2nd Cavalry in the 1850s, he was promoted to major of the 4th Cavalry at the beginning of the war. He was promoted to brigadier general in August 1861 and given command of Stoneman's Cavalry until May 1863. Stoneman was considered vain and eager for popularity and promotion. In 1864, during the Atlanta Campaign, Stoneman, in command of all the cavalry under W. T. Sherman, set out south with orders to wreck the railroads running through the region. Determining to make a splash with the Northern public, he chose to release the prisoners being held at Camp Sumter (Andersonville). In this attempt, though, Stoneman himself was captured near Macon and imprisoned at Camp Oglethorpe near Andersonville. How he expected to get the released prisoners back to Sherman's lines still remains a mystery. Later exchanged, he led another raid in southwestern Virginia and western North Carolina during the last weeks of the war. Following the end of the war, he served for a period in the Southwest, and in 1877, he settled in California, where he involved himself in railroads and served the state as a governor.

Stovall: "Mrs. Stovall" was probably Mattie Wilson Stovall (1836–1906), born in Kuruman, South Africa, and wife of Bolling Anthony Stovall.

Stovall, Thomas P.: Thomas P. Stovall was a miller from Augusta who enlisted as captain of Co. A, Richmond Hussars, Cobb's Georgia Legion Cavalry, on 17 August 1861, in Augusta. He resigned from the service on 30 May 1862 and was succeeded by Lieutenant Thomas B. Archer as captain of the company.

Stovall: Could be one of two Stovalls: 1) Bolling Anthony Stovall enlisted as sergeant in 1861 in Augusta, a member of Co. A, Richmond Hussars, Cobb's Georgia Legion Cavalry. In February 1862, he was assigned a member of General Lafayette McLaws's Engineer Corps. He was discharged in May 1862 in order to accept an appointment to the Ordinance Department. 2) Francis (Frank) Marion Stovall was a 19-year-old student when he enlisted in the 8th Georgia Infantry. He transferred to Co. C, Cobb Georgia Legion Cavalry, on 15 August 1861, in Athens. He was captured at Malvern Hill, Virginia, on 5 August 1862 and exchanged on the 26th. He transferred once again on 13 November 1862 to the Troup Artillery and was wounded at Fredericksburg just a month later. Following the war he was a coal merchant bookkeeper in Augusta. He died in 1905.

Stovall: "Old Stovall" was probably Pleasant Stovall, who moved from Virginia to Hancock County, Georgia. He was the father of Bolling Anthony Stovall and Francis Marion Stovall.

Stovall: "Mrs. Pleasant Stovall" is thought to be Volumnia Stovall, wife of Thomas P. Stovall and a close frined of both Rosa and Will. She broke the news of Will's death to Rosa.

Stuart, J. E. B.: James Ewell Brown "Jeb" Stuart (1833–1864) was a West Point graduate ('54) who served most of his time before the outbreak of the Civil War as a lieutenant with the 1st Cavalry on the Kansas frontier. In 1859 he was aide to R. E. Lee during his capture of John Brown at Harper's Ferry. Stuart resigned when war broke out and entered Confederate service as colonel of the 1st Virginia Cavalry. He was promoted in September 1861 to brigadier general. Stuart led his troopers in a daring ride around George B. McClellan's Union forces just before the Seven Days' Battles, furnishing a great deal of useful information to R. E. Lee. He was considered aggressive, flamboyant, and egotistical, yet Robert E. Lee placed a lot of faith in the information that he was able to supply the army with—at least until the Gettysburg Campaign. He was known to favor Virginia troops, even to the point of being known as a Virginia elitist.

Tally: Believed to be a Delony family slave.

Taylor, Dick: Richard Delony Bolling Taylor (1830–1864), often called "Dick" by his friends, was a cousin of William G. Delony. He married Sarah Jane Billups of Athens in 1853. Following her death, he next married Catherine McKinley in 1863.

Taylor, Mrs. J.: Jane Henrietta Burke Taylor, second wife of James Jones Taylor (son of General Robert G. Taylor).

Taylor, Robert: Robert G. Taylor (1787–1859), uncle of William G. Delony, was born in Ireland and arrived in Savannah in the 1790s. He was commissioned a brigadier general of the Georgia Militia during the antebellum period in Georgia and he was one of the richest men in Georgia during this same period. He built the house (Taylor-Grady) in which Will lived while he attended Franklin College (University of Georgia).

Thomas, John: Jonathan Pinckney Thomas was a planter from Augusta who enlisted as a private in Co. A, Cobb's Georgia Legion Cavalry, on 1 May 1862, in Augusta. He was wounded in the arm and left chest in November 1862 near Hamlet, Little Washington, Virginia. Due to the ball being left in his chest, Thomas was deemed unfit for active duty and became clerk for General Young. He was in Georgia at the end of the war on duty to procure horses for the legion. Following the war, Thomas worked as a farmer in Waynesboro, Burke County, Georgia. He eventually died of his wounds in June 1888.

Thomas: "Judge Thomas" was Thomas W. Thomas (1809–1915) of Elberton, Georgia. He was a friend of Robert Toombs.

Tom: Tom Cobb Delony (3 March 1859–24 May 1912), Will's and Rosa's third child. He was also known also as Tommy and "Bubber Tom."

Tommy: The "Tommy" who furnished information to Rosa about the legion is unknown.

Toombs, Robert: Robert Augustus Toombs (1810–1885) was a Georgia lawyer and politician, serving in both houses of the state legislature and in the US Senate. He attended the University of Georgia but did not finish, being kicked out for fighting. In the years leading up to the Civil War, he became a strong secessionist and was a member of the Provisional Confederate Congress. Jefferson Davis selected Toombs as the Confederacy's first secretary of state, a position he held for a brief time, becoming a brigadier general in July 1861. Under his leadership at Sharpsburg during the Antietam Campaign, Toombs's Brigade distinguished itself by holding "Burnside's Bridge" against 4-to-1 odds. He resigned shortly afterward and ran an unsuccessful bid for the senate. Named adjutant for the Georgia Militia, Toombs served in the Atlanta Campaign. Fleeing the country immediately after the end of the war to avoid arrest, he later returned and resumed the practice of law. Toombs was an acquaintance of William Delony's. Toombs never applied for a presidential pardon and died an unreconstructed Rebel.

Twiggs: John D. Twiggs was major, then lieutenant colonel of the 1st South Carolina Cavalry. The unit joined Hampton's Brigade in November 1862.

Vallandingham: Clement L. Vallandingham was a Presbyterian, a member of the House of Representatives, and a leader of the Democratic Party in 1860. As the leader of the "Peace Democrats," also known as the "Butternuts" and "Copperheads," Vallandingham opposed Lincoln and his views of slavery. After numerous speeches against "King Lincoln," Vallandingham was arrested on 5 May 1863 for violating General Order No. 38, which stated that declaring sympathies for the enemy would not be tolerated. Tried and convicted by a military court, he was ordered deported and sent to the Confederacy on 19 May. Sent to Wilmington, North Carolina, by Confederate authorities who were suspicious of his intentions and actions, he eventually made his way through the Union blockade to Canada and returned to Ohio in 1864.

Venable: Charles Scott Venable (1827–1900) was a professor of mathematics at the University of Virginia prior to the Civil War. When war broke out, he served in the 2nd South Carolina Infantry until spring 1862, when he joined General Lee's staff, serving on it until the end of the war.

Vincent, Strong: Strong Vincent was the lieutenant colonel of the 83rd Pennsylvania Infantry. He was killed at Gettysburg leading his brigade while defending Little Round Top.

B. H. W. Benjamin H. Watkins [Wadkins] enlisted in the First Georgia Infantry in March 1861. He transferred to Co. I, Cobb's Georgia Legion Cavalry, as a sergeant on 14 February 1862. He was paroled at Greensboro, North Carolina, on 26 April 1865.

Waldburg/Walburg, Mr.: George (M. or W.) Waldburg (Walburg, as spelled in correspondence) was a major planter outside of Liberty, Georgia, on St. Catherine's Island. His operation was one of the first commercial successes of the new cotton gins with long-staple cotton.

Walters, Fred: Fred W. Walters was a bugler in Co. C, Cobb's Georgia Legion Cavalry. He enlisted 1 August 1861 in Athens and became the chief bugler of the legion on 1 December 1862. He was wounded in the action at Dispatch Station,

Virginia, on 28 June 1862. He disappears from the record following his being sent to obtain a horse in September 1864.

Ware, Annie: She is unidentifiable.

Ware, Nick: Nicholas Crawford Ware (1835–1863), from Wilkes County, Georgia, enlisted as a private in Ritch's Company, Co. B, Georgia Troopers, Cobb's Georgia Legion Cavalry, in March 1862. In January 1863, he transferred to Co. H of the legion cavalry. He was killed in June 1863 during the fighting at Brandy Station.

Washborne, Mrs.: Probably Cornelia Washborne (1839–1918), wife of Henry K. Washborne. Henry was from Oconee County, Georgia, and served as second lieutenant and then captain in the 22nd Georgia Battalion of Heavy Artillery. Cornelia applied for a Confederate widow's pension in 1904 and again in 1905. Both requests were turned down without cause.

Wayne, Henry: Henry Constantine Wayne (1815–1883) was Georgia's Confederate adjutant and inspector-general for much of the war. Prior to the Civil War, Wayne led Jefferson Davis's expedition to the Middle East to purchase camels for Davis's ill-fated attempt to introduce them to the US Southwest when Davis was secretary of war. He saw brief action in Georgia, commanding at Ball's Ferry during Sherman's March to the Sea.

White, S. G.: Samuel G. White of the Salem community outside of Milledgeville was one of the three delegates representing Baldwin County at the Georgia Secession Convention. In 1861, T. R. R. Cobb appointed him surgeon of Cobb's Legion Infantry. He remained in that position until he resigned in October 1862 following the Maryland Campaign.

White, Mrs.: There are too many possibilities for "Mrs White" to determine who she was and her involvement with the Delonys.

Whitehead, Charlie: Charles Lowndes Whitehead (1835–1866) was from Richmond County, Georgia. Having previous military experience in Nicaragua, he enlisted in 1861 in Co. E, 4th Georgia Infantry, as major. He was wounded in the arm at Sharpsburg in 1862. Whitehead then served as captain on the staff of General A. R. Wright until 1864 when he was sent back to Georgia as colonel in charge of the Georgia state militia. He was a Presbyterian and died in Burke County, Georgia.

Williams: Gilbert William Martin Williams was from Johnsons Station, McIntosh County, Georgia, in 1860 when he represented his county in the Georgia House of Representatives. Williams was a delegate to the Georgia Secession Convention in Milledgeville in January 1861, where he voted "YES" for the state's secession. He later served as colonel of the 47th Georgia Infantry.

Williams, Thomas: Thomas C. Williams was a farmer from Jackson County, Georgia, prior to the war. He enlisted as a lieutenant in Co. C, Cobb's Georgia Legion Cavalry, on 1 August 1861, in Athens. He was promoted to captain in April 1862. Williams spent most of 1864 in the hospital and was retired to the Invalid Corps at Macon on 15 November 1864. Following the war, he returned to Jackson County and resumed his farming. He was married and died in the 1880s.

Willie: William Gaston Delony Jr. (2 September 1860–21 September 1871). "Little Willie" was Will's and Rosa's fourth child.

Willingham: "Old" Willingham is Willis Willingham of Oglethorpe County, Georgia. He was a delegate to the Georgia Secession Convention in Milledgeville in January 1861. He voted "NO" on the prospects of secession.

Wimpy : John A. Wimpy, also known as "J. A. W.," enlisted as a sergeant in Co. C, Cobb's Georgia Legion Cavalry, on 14 August 1861, in Athens. He was elected lieutenant on 28 December 1862 and resigned on 7 October 1863 due to disability.

Winston: Col. John Anthony Winston (1812–1871) served in both the US House of Representatives from Alabama and in the US Senate, where he served for ten years. Winston served as Alabama governor from 1853 to 1857. During the early part of the Civil War, Colonel Winston commanded the 8th Alabama Infantry. Although not very well liked by his men, he served with competence during the Peninsula Campaign and Seven Days' Battles. Following the war, he again tried entering politics.

Wright: Gilbert J. Wright enlisted as first lieutenant in Captain Lawton's Company, Co. D, Cobb's Georgia Legion Cavalry, in November 1861. From Albany, Georgia, he was promoted to captain of Co. D, Dougherty Hussars, in May 1862. He was promoted to major in July 1863 when William Delony was promoted to lieutenant colonel of the legion cavalry. In October 1863, Wright became colonel of Cobb's Georgia Legion Cavalry.

Yancey: Benjamin Cudworth Yancey was from Fulton County, Georgia. He enlisted as captain of Co. B, Fulton Dragoons, Cobb's Georgia Legion Cavalry, on 14 August 1861 in Atlanta. He was appointed major on 15 November 1861 and resigned on 23 May 1862. Following the war he farmed and practiced law in Clarke and Floyd counties. He married twice prior to the war and died in Floyd County, Georgia, in 1891.

Young, B.: William Benjamin Young was 24 when he enlisted as a corporal in Co. A, Cobb's Georgia Legion Cavalry on 17 August 1861 in Augusta. By the early summer of 1862, he was lieutenant and then promoted to captain on 8 August

1862. He was captured at Ely's Ford on 29 February 1864 and sent to Fort Delaware. He was released on 10 June 1865. Young married following the war and died in 1898 in Columbus County, Georgia.

Young, P. M. B.: Pierce Manning Butler Young (1836–1896) from Spartanburg, South Carolina, and Bartow County, Georgia, was a cadet at West Point when the war broke out. He resigned a few months short of graduating from the academy in March 1861 and headed South to join the Confederate forces, rising from a second lieutenant to major general by the end of the war. Thomas R. R. Cobb made him adjutant of Cobb's Georgia Legion in 1861, becoming lieutenant colonel of Cobb's Georgia Legion Cavalry in November 1861. Gen. Wade Hampton cited him for "remarkable gallantry" during the Antietam Campaign where he was wounded at South Mountain. He was promoted to colonel in November 1862, then to brigadier general in September 1863. Sent to Georgia in November to procure more troops and remounts, Young became active in opposing Sherman's advance from Atlanta to Savannah. Following the war, he became a planter and congressman and entered the US diplomatic service, serving in Russia, Guatemala, and Honduras.

From this day to the ending of the world,
But we in it shall be remembered—
We few, we happy few, we band of brothers;
For he to-day that sheds his blood with me
Shall be my brother.

—Shakespeare

Bibliography

Andrew, Rod, Jr. *Wade Hampton: Confederate Warrior to Southern Redeemer*. Chapel Hill: University of North Carolina Press, 2008.

Barringer, Sheridan R. *Fighting for General Lee: Confederate General Rufus Barringer and the North Carolina Cavalry Brigade*. El Dorado Hills, CA: Savas Beatie, 2016.

Beers, Henry Putney. *The Confederacy: A Guide to the Archives of the Government of the Confederate States of America*. Washington, DC: National Archives and Records Administration, 1986.

Blackford, W. W. *War Years with Jeb Stuart*. New York: Charles Scribner's Sons, 1945.

Boney, F. Nash. *A Pictorial History of the University of Georgia*. Athens: University of Georgia Press, 1984.

Brooks, Victor. *The Fredericksburg Campaign, October 1862–January 1863*. Conshohocken, PA: Combined Publishing, 2000.

Brown, Kent Masterson. *Retreat from Gettysburg*. Chapel Hill: University of North Carolina Press, 2005.

Bryan, T. Conn. *Confederate Georgia*. Athens: University of Georgia Press, 1953.

Cannan, John. *The Antietam Campaign: August–September 1862*. Conshohocken, PA: Combined Publishing, 1994.

Catalogue of Trustees and Alumni and of the Matriculates of the University of Georgia, Athens, Georgia. E. D. Stone Press, 1906.

Cisco, Walter Brian. *Wade Hampton: Confederate Warrior, Conservative Statesman*. Washington, DC: Brassey's, Inc., 2004.

"Civil War in Loudoun Valley: The Cavalry Battles of Aldie, Middleburg, and Upperville, June 1863." Report prepared by Cultural Resources GIS of the National Park Service, 2004.

Clark, John Elwood, Jr. *Railroads in the Civil War: The Impact of Management on Victory and Defeat*. Baton Rouge: Louisiana State University Press, 2004.

Clemens, Thomas G. *The Maryland Campaign of September 1862. Vol. I: South Mountain*. El Dorado Hills, CA: Savas Beatie, 2010.

_____. *The Maryland Campaign of September 1862. Vol. II: Antietam*. El Dorado Hills, CA: Savas Beatie, 2012.

Coffman, Richard M. *Going Back the Way They Came: The Phillips Georgia Legion Cavalry Battalion*. Macon, GA: Mercer University Press, 2011.

Coleman, Kenneth. *Confederate Athens*. Athens: University of Georgia Press, 1967.

———. *Athens 1861–1865: As Seen Through Letters in the University of Georgia Libraries*. Athens: University of Georgia Press, 1969.

The Counties of the State of Georgia. Savannah, GA: The Georgia Society, 1974.

Crouch, Richard E. *Brandy Station: A Battle Like None Other*. Westminster, MD: Willow Bend Books, 2002.

Curran, Thomas F. *Soldiers of Peace: Civil War Pacifism and the Post War Radical Peace Movement*. New York: Fordham University Press, 2003.

Davis, Stephen and William A. Richards. "An Atlantan Goes to War: The Civil War Letters of Maj. Zachariah A. Rice, C.S.A." *Atlanta History* (Spring 1992) 20–39.

Dowley, Clifford. *Lee*. Boston: Little Brown and Company, 1965.

Elder, Angela Esco. "A Community of Condolences." Unpublished paper. Athens: University of Georgia Department of History, 2012.

The Fredericksburg Campaign: Decision on the Rappahannock. Edited by Gary W. Gallagher. Chapel Hill: University of North Carolina Press, 1995.

Freehling, William W. *The Road to Disunion: Vol. II: Secessionists Triumphant.* New York: Oxford University Press, 2007.

Freeman, Douglas Southall. *Lee's Lieutenants: A Study in Command.* New York: Scribner, 1998.

―――. *R. E. Lee.* Vol. 3. New York: Charles Scribner's Sons, 1935.

Gagnon, Michael. *Transition to an Industrial South: Athens, Georgia, 1830–1870.* Baton Rouge: Louisiana State University Press, 2012.

Gallagher, Gary W. "Robert E. Lee and His High Command." In *The Great Courses.* Chantilly, VA: The Teaching Company, 2004.

Galloway, Tammy Harden. *Dear Old Roswell: The Civil War Letters of the King Family of Roswell, Georgia.* Macon, GA: Mercer University Press, 2003.

Hanging Rock Rebel: Lt. John Blue's War in West Virginia & the Shenandoah Valley. Edited by Dan Oates. Shippensburg, PA: Bird Street Press, 1994.

Harrington, Hugh T. *Civil War Milledgeville: Tales from the Confederate Capital of Georgia.* Charleston, SC: The History Press, 2005.

Hartley, Chris J. *Stuart's Tarheels: James B. Gordon and His North Carolina Cavalry in the Civil War.* Jefferson, NC: McFarland & Company, 2011.

Hartwig, D. Scott. *To Antietam Creek: The Maryland Campaign of September 1862.* Baltimore, MD: Johns Hopkins University Press, 2012.

Henderson, William D. *The Road to Bristol Station: Campaigning with Lee and Meade, August 1–October 2.* Lynchburg, VA: H. E. Howard, 1987.

Hill, Benjamin H., Jr. *Senator Benjamin H. Hill of Georgia: His Life, Speeches and Writings.* Atlanta: H. C. Hudgins & Company, 1891.

Holden, Frank A. *History of Athens and Clarke County.* Athens, GA: Legal Profession of Athens, 1923.

Holland, Lynwood M. *Pierce M. B. Young: The Warwick of the South.* Athens: University of Georgia Press, 1964.

Hopkins, Donald A. *The Little Jeff: The Jeff Davis Legion, Cavalry, Army of Northern Virginia.* Shippensburg, PA: White Mane Books, 1999.

Howard, Wiley C. *Sketch of Cobb Legion Cavalry and Some Incidents and Scenes Remembered.* Clearwater, SC: Eastern Digital Resources, 2007.

Hull, Augustus Longstreet. *Annals of Athens, Georgia, 1801–1901.* Athens, GA: Banner Job Office, 1906.

Hynads, Ernest C. *Antebellum Athens and Clarke County, Georgia.* Athens: University of Georgia Press, 1974.

Klein, Maury. *Days of Defiance: Sumter, Secession, and the Coming of the Civil War.* New York: Alfred A. Knopf, 1997.

Krick, Robert K. *Civil War Weather in Virginia.* Tuscaloosa: University of Alabama Press, 2007.

―――. *Staff Officers in Gray: A Biographical Register of the Staff Officers in the Army of Northern Virginia.* Chapel Hill: University of North Carolina Press, 2003.

Latty, John W. *The Gallant Little 7th: A History of the 7th Georgia Cavalry Regiment.* Wilmington, NC: Broadfoot Publishing Company, 2004.

Longacre, Edward G. *Custer and His Wolverines: The Michigan Cavalry Brigade, 1861–1865*. Conshohocken, PA: Combined Books, 1997.

———. *Gentleman and Soldier: The Extraordinary Life of General Wade Hampton*. Nashville, TN: Rutledge Hill Press, 2003.

Marshall, Charlotte Thomas. *Oconee Hill Cemetery of Athens, Georgia*, Vol. 1. Athens, GA: Athens Historical Society, 2009.

McCarter, William. *My Life in the Irish Brigade*. Campbell, CA: Savas Publishing Co., 1996.

McCash, William B. *Thomas R. R. Cobb: The Making of a Southern Nationalist*. Macon, GA: Mercer University Press, 2004.

Mesic, Harriet Bey. *Cobb's Legion Cavalry*. Jefferson, NC: McFarland and Co., 2009.

Morrell, I. W. *Directory of the City of Savannah for the Year 1850*. Savannah, GA: David H. Galloway, 1849.

O'Reilly, Francis Augustin. *The Fredericksburg Campaign: Winter War on the Rappahannock*. Baton Rouge: Louisiana State University Press, 2003.

Pickerill, William N. *History of the Third Indiana Cavalry*. Indianapolis, IN: 1906.

———. "Quebec School House." *Valley Register* (8 April 1898).

Poss, Faye Stone. *The Southern Watchman, Athens, Georgia: Civil War Home Front Coverage, 1861–1865*. Snellville, GA: Private Printing, 2008.

Rable, George C. *Fredericksburg! Fredericksburg!* Chapel Hill: University of North Carolina Press, 2002.

Reddick, Marguerite. *Camden's Challenge: A History of Camden County, Georgia*. Camden, GA: Camden County Historical Commission, 1976.

Rea, D. B. "Cavalry Incidents of the Maryland Campaign." *Maine Bugle* 2 (1895): 117–23.

Reed, Thomas. *The History of the University of Georgia*. Athens: University of Georgia Press, 1949.

Reese, Timothy J. *Sealed with Their Lives: The Battle for Crampton's Gap, Burkittsville, Maryland, September 14, 1862*. Baltimore, MD: Butternut and Blue, 1998.

Rhea, Gordon C. "'The Hottest Place I Ever Was In': The Battle of Haw's Shop, May 28, 1864." *North & South* 4 (April 2001): 42–57.

Sauers, Richard A. *"A Succession of Honorable Victories": The Burnside Expedition in North Carolina*. Dayton, OH: Morningside House, 1996.

Scroggins, Mark. *Robert Toombs: The Civil Wars of a United States Senator and Confederate General*. Jefferson, NC: McFarland & Co., 2011.

Sears, Stephen. *Chancellorsville*. New York: Houghton Mifflin, 1996.

———. *To the Gates of Richmond: The Peninsula Campaign*. New York: Mariner Books, 2001.

Settles, Thomas M. *John Bankhead Magruder: A Military Reappraisal*. Baton Rouge: Louisiana State University Press, 2009.

Sherwood, Adiel. *A Gazetteer of Georgia: Containing a Particular Description of the State: Its Resources, Counties, Towns, Villages, and Whatever Is Usual in Statistical Works*. Atlanta: J. Richards, 1860.

Sifakis, Stewart. *Compendium of the Confederate Armies: North Carolina*. New York: Facts on File, 1992.

———. *Compendium of the Confederate Armies: South Carolina and Georgia*. New York: Facts on File, 1995.

———. *Who Was Who in the Civil War*. New York: Facts On File Publications, 1988.

Smedlund, William S. *Camp Fires of Georgia Troops, 1861–1865*. Lithonia, GA: Kennesaw Mountain Press, 1994.

Southern Historical Society Papers. Millwood, New York: Kraus Reprint Co., 1977.

Stackpole, Edward J. *Chancellorsville: Lee's Greatest Battle*. Harrisburg, PA: The Stackpole Company, 1958.

Stegeman, John F. *These Men She Gave*. Athens: University of Georgia Press, 1964.

Sullivan, Buddy. *Early Days of the Georgia Tidewater: The Story of McIntosh County and Sapelo*. McIntosh, GA: McIntosh County Board of Commissioners, 1990.

The Tangible Past in Athens, Georgia. Edited by Charlotte Thomas Marshall. Athens, GA: Private Printing, 2014.

Thomas, Emory M. *Bold Dragoon: The Life of J. E. B. Stuart*. New York: Harper & Row, 1986.

———. *Robert E. Lee: A Biography*. New York: W. W. Norton and Co., 1995.

Thomas, Frances Taliaferro. *A Portrait of Historic Athens & Clarke County*. Athens: University of Georgia Press, 2009.

Voccelle, James T. *History of Camden County, Georgia*. Kingsland, GA: Southeastern Georgian, 1914.

Warner, Ezra J. *Generals in Gray: Lives of the Confederate Commanders*. Baton Rouge: Louisiana State University Press, 1995.

Wells, Edward L. *Hampton & His Cavalry in '64*. Richmond, VA: B. F. Johnson Publishing Co., 1899.

Wittenberg, Eric J. *One of Custer's Wolverines: The Civil War Letters of Brevet Brigadier General James H. Kidd, 6th Michigan Cavalry*. Kent, OH: Kent State University Press, 2000.

Wittenberg, Eric J. and Daniel T. Davis. Out Flew the Sabres: The Battle of Brandy Station, June 9, 1863. Ed Dorado Hills, CA: Savas Beatie, 2016.

Woodward, Harold R., Jr. *For Home and Honor: The Story of Madison County, Virginia, During the War Between the States, 1861–1865*. Private Printing, nd.

Collections

N. J. Brooks Papers. Kennesaw Mountain National Battlefield Park Archives, Kennesaw, GA.

Carson Family Papers. Lane Library, Armstrong State University, Savannah, GA.

Carson Family Papers. Hargrett Rare Book & Manuscript Library, University of Georgia, Athens, GA.

T. R. R. Cobb Papers. Hargrett Rare Book & Manuscript Library, University of Georgia, Athens, GA.

William G. Delony Papers. Hargrett Rare Book & Manuscript Library, University of Georgia, Athens, GA.

Robert T. Hubard Memoirs. William R. Perkins Library, Duke University, Durham, NC.

James K. Munnerlyn Papers. Southern Historical Collection, University of North Carolina at Chapel Hill.

F. W. Walter Letters. Private Collection.

Nathan B. Webb Journals. William L. Clements Library, University of Michigan, Ann Arbor, MI.

Gilbert J. Wright Letters. Private Collection.

Newspapers

Augusta (Georgia) *Chronicle*

Augusta (Georgia) *Daily Chronicle & Sentinel*

Augusta (Georgia) *Daily Morning News*
Banner: Athens, GA
Daily Chronicle & Sentinel: Augusta, GA
Daily Constitutionalist: Augusta, GA
The Daily Journal: Wilmington, NC
Daily Morning News: Augusta, GA
Georgian: Savannah, GA
Macon Daily Telegraph: Macon, GA
Southern Banner: Athens, GA
Southern Watchman: Athens, GA
Valley Register

Journals
Atlanta Journal.
The Georgia Historical Quarterly.

Government Records
Confederate States of America Records. "C.S. Secretary of War," M437, Roll 24, NARS.
War of the Rebellion: Official Records of the Union and Confederate Armies. Harrisburg, PA: The
 National Historical Society, 1971.

Websites
www.ancestry.com
www.brandystationfoundation.com
www.fold3.com
www.HMdb.org

Index

Butler, Matthew Calbraith, 174, 177–78, 228, 269, 270, 271
Butler's Brigade, 270, 275

Caenah, Thomas, 18
Camak, Helen Smith Finley, 73
Camfield, Caleb Halstead (Holly), 128, 147, 153
Camp Birdie (VA), 108n2
Camp Caroline (VA), 96
Camp Clover (VA), 95
Camp Cobb (VA), 53–54
Camp Disappointment (VA), 70, 62
Camp Hardtimes (VA), 114
Camp Hunter (VA), 91, 99–103
Camp Marion (VA), 58–59, 89–90
Camp Meadow (VA), 117, 120, 121–22, 124, 127
Camp Mud Hole (VA), 58
Camp Randolph (NC), 93
Camp Rapidan (VA), 160
Camp Tom (VA), 148–49
Camp Washington (VA), 55–56, 57, 70
Carlton, Henry Hull, 247, 249
Carlton, Joseph Barnett, 79, 80, 197
Carolinas Campaign, 48n
Carson, Gordon Cubbedge, 286
Carter, Bennett H., 226
Carter's Mill, 116
Catherine (Delony slave/cook), 34, 186, 264
Cavalry Brigade, 2
Champion, Marcia, 17
Chancellorsville (VA), battle of, 193–94. *See also* Chancellorsville Campaign
Chancellorsville Campaign, 193–94, 205n19, 216
Channing, W. H., 283, 294–95
Chapman, George, 272, 274, 275
Charles II, 5n11
Charleston (SC), 245
Cheeseborough, John W., 246, 248
Chickahominy River, 95, 110–11, 116, 142, 234
Chickamauga (TN/GA), 245, 271; battle of, 267n59
chimney corner patriots, 3, 230n36
church ball, 213
Church, Alonzo A., 219
Church, Ester (Mrs.), 32
Church, William Lee (Willie), 97, 102–3, 109, 121, 125, 128, 133, 137, 218–20, 212, 213, 227, 232, 233, 251, 265, 273, 274–75, 280, 292–93
Clanton, James Luke (Young), 164–65, 169–70, 220, 227–28
Clark, John Bullock, Sr., 205
Clark, T. H., 175, 176

Clarke County (GA); secessionist sentiment in, 38–39; organization of, 39n16
Cobb, Howell, 53, 54, 38, 98, 122, 132, 133, 139–40, 149, 162n1, 181, 256
Cobb, John Addison, 85, 256
Cobb, Marion, 52, 74, 76, 282, 292
Cobb, Mary Ann, 43
Cobb, Thomas Reader Rootes, 2, 3, 9–10, 25, 31, 37n9, 39–41, 78, 98, 102–3, 104, 120, 129, 139, 154, 158, 159, 168, 185, 289; on cavalry going to Hampton, 108; commanding the cavalry, 110; on condition of his legion, 62–63. *See also* Cobb's Legion, organization of; correspondence of, 43, 46, 47–48, 52–62, 68, 70–71, 82n12, 89n1, 93–98, 105n49, 106, 108, 109–10, 114–18, 120n36, 148–49, 157n23, 159n1, 161–62, 164n14, 170n17; on Davis, 118; death of, 108n2, 182–83; on Delony, 53, 57, 62, 98, 106, 108, 112–16, 120n36, 149, 162; Delony's feelings toward, 3, 82, 127; desiring to remain with his cavalry, 159n1; on Hampton, 118; issuing whiskey rations, 117; on Jackson, 161–62; military correspondence of, 112–13; new recruits for, 96–97; officers and, 94, 107, 162; preparing legion for war, 42–46. *See also* Cobb's Legion ; promotion of, 162, 170, 181; pushing for secession, 38; reception of, 155; selecting second-in-command, 54–55 ; visiting Delony, 157n23; winter service for, 155
Cobb's (Georgia) Brigade, 53, 93, 133n39, 162n11, 183, 246–47
Cobb's (Georgia) Brigade Infantry, 111n10, 162n1, 173
Cobb's (Georgia) Legion, 114–15, 142, 173, 270 ; in battle, 112–14, 129–30, 131, 145–48, 152–53, 163–64; battle flag of, 283; at Brandy Station, 226–29; at Camp Meadow, 121–22, 124, 127; at Camp Washington. 55–56, 57, 70; at Camp Hunter, 91, 99–103; at Camp Marion, 58–59, 89–90; at Camp Randolph, 93; captains dissatisfied in, 125; cavalry of, 1–2, 43–48, 91–97, 108, 110, 116. *See also* Georgia 9th Cavalry Regiment; Cobb's pride in, 53; compliments for, 117–18; condition of, 62–63; Delony commanding, 174–75 (*see also* Delony, William Gaston, in command); destroying railroads, 113, 114, 115, 161; drilling of, 89n1, 94, 99; eastward movement from Martinsburg, 162; first military excursion, 60; at Gettysburg, 237–38; Hampton's command of, 117; Howard's account of, 52; illness in, 54, 58–60, 69; infantry of, 93–94, 96; at Jack's Shop, 273; lacking saddles and guns, 96–97;

at Little Washington, 164–65, 169–70, 172; losses of, 60, 90, 130, 131, 147, 226, 227, 234, 238, 276; in the Loudoun Valley, 221–23; military prowess of, 174; at Occoquan, 175–77; officers in, 60–62, 70; organization of, 95–98, 107, 108, 125, 126–27; picket duty for, 70, 83, 114, 116–18, 122, 124, 127, 133, 136, 142, 149, 166, 201, 268; recruiting for, 89, 90–91, 135, 191; recuperating from Gettysburg Campaign, 243–44; reporting to Stuart, 124–25; reputation of, 229–30; reunited at Camp Tom, 148–49; skirmishes of, following Gettysburg, 242; splitting of, 192; near Stevensburg (VA), 189–91; transferring to Georgia, prospects for, 159n1, 161–62, 166, 168, 171, 179, 181; Union gunboats and, 116; at Upperville (VA), 232–35; at Williamsburg, 55–56

Cobb's (Georgia) Legion Cavalry, 1, 47, 48n, 145, 148, 189, 160, 190–91; 1st Squadron, 97; 3rd Squadron, 97; 4th Squadron, 97; at Brandy Station, 217–22; Company A, 97; Company B, 97; Company C (Cobb's Legion), 97. See also Cobb's Legion listings; Delony's Company; Company E, 97; Company F, 97; Company H, 91, 97; Company I, 97; Company K, 192; Company L, 192; Company Q, 242; at full strength, 192; losses of, 220; retreating after Gettysburg, 241

Cobb's Legion Cavalry: A History and Roster of the Ninth Georgia Volunteers in the Civil War (Mesic), 2
cockfighting, 30–31
Coffman, Richard, 2
Colquitt, Alfred Holt, 57
Confederate States of America, 41, 42n30
Connor, Daniel A., 295
Constitutional Union Party, 38
Cook, Ferdinand Frances, 195
Cotton Planters Convention, 49
Cowles, William Henry Harrison, 163
Crawford, Martin J., 180
Crumley, William Macon, 119
CSS Arkansas, 138
CSS Georgia, 92–93n9
CSS Virginia, 92
Culpeper (VA), 189–91, 220, 228, 229, 241–42, 247, 278
Culpeper Court House (VA), 194, 213, 217, 240, 297
Custer, George, 236–37, 272, 281
Custer's Brigade, 272
Custis, Martha, 111n11

Dabney, Chriswell, 218n6
Daniel, T. M., 297

Daugherty Hussars, 191n8
David, John White, 165
Davies, Henry, 271–72, 277
Davies' Brigade, 273, 276–77
Davis, Jefferson, 43, 55, 93n12, 101, 118, 123, 209n25, 240–41, 245, 258
Day, J. W., 243n29
Dean, Charles (N. or W.), 247
Dearing, William P., 130
Deloney, Elizabeth (Eliza) Bolling, 4, 5n9, 7n19
Deloney, Henry, 4
Deloney, John, 4
Deloney, Louis Henry, 4
Deloney, Maria O. Baird, 5, 6, 16, 37
Deloney, Martha A., 5, 16
Deloney, Martha M., 4
Deloney, Martha R. Montfort, 4
Deloney, Rebecca Bradnax, 4
Deloney, Robert James, 4, 5
Deloney, Robert James, Jr., 5
Deloney, William (William's grandfather), 4
Delony, Eliza Huguenin (William and Rosa's daughter), 11, 21–24, 27–30, 36
Delony, Maria, 281, 298
Delony, Martha, 9, 37, 187, 281
Delony, Martha Roberta, 259n57, 282n12
Delony, Robert (Bob), 30–31, 66, 120, 131, 135, 137, 167, 168, 181, 201–2, 203, 206, 212, 281, 282n12, 292
Delony, Rosa (William and Rosa's granddaughter), 286
Delony, Rosa Eugenia (William and Rosa's daughter), 32, 34, 36, 64, 72, 73, 74, 76, 80–84, 86, 88, 103–4, 118, 139, 156–57, 183, 185, 195, 198, 211, 214–15, 251, 260, 284, 285–86
Delony, Rosa Eugenia Huguenin (William's wife), vii, 5; ancestors of, 4, 5–6; battle flag presented to, 298–99; on cockfighting, 30–31; on William's coming war service, 42; death of, 285; on defeat at Fredericksburg, 184; dreams of, 17–18; early adult years of, 11; early years of 6–7; handling family finances, 65, 76–77, 136, 138, 150, 166, 184, 225, 234, 264–65, 266; household problems of, 186–87; household work of, 65–66, 73, 80–81; on house preparations, 24, 25; letters of, vii–viii, xiv–xv, 3, 11, 16–20, 23–24, 26–35, 48–49, 63–68, 73–74, 76–77, 79–82, 84, 118–19, 123–24, 131–32, 136–37, 183–88, 195–98, 256–57; letters to, after William's death, 287–99; marriage of, 9–10, 14; neuralgia of, 208, 210; on officers, 82, 195, 196–97; pregnancy of, 259, 264, 280, 282; relationship with father, 9–10; supporting Confederate cause, 92; on the war, 187–88;

Richmond Hussars (Company A and Company I, Cobb's Legion Cavalry), 44–45, 46, 53, 97, 109, 129, 165n15, 169, 172, 190–91, 221, 227, 248, 284
Ritch, Jeremiah E., 66, 94, 102, 107, 121, 125, 129, 169, 172, 209, 213, 217, 220, 226, 233
Roanoke Island (NC), 92
Robertson, Beverly Holcombe, 135, 144, 222
Robertson's Brigade, 144, 145–46, 222, 223
Roman Legion, 43n
Roper, Joel Cole, 214
Rosser, Thomas Lafayette, 162, 180, 244, 246
Roswell Troopers (Company E, Cobb's Legion Cavalry), 97
Rutherford, John Cobb (Johnny), 57, 95, 114, 115, 159, 161, 166

Salter, Thomas W., 124, 149, 250
Sarah (Delony slave), 22, 186, 210
Scammon, Eliakim, 145
Scammon's Brigades, 145
Scott, James, 4–5
scurvy, 230
Second Manassas Campaign, 143–44
Seddon, James, 93n12
Sequestration Act, 63
Seven Days' campaign, 131n38
Seven Pines (Fair Oaks; VA), battle of, 98, 105
Sharpsburg (MD), 148, 152, 158, 163
sharpshooters, 162–64, 176, 220–22, 226, 277
Shenandoah Valley, 216
Shields, P. B., 281, 294, 295
Sibley, Henry Josiah, 207, 209
Sigel, Franz, 175
Siler, Jesse W., 163
Simmons, Moses S., 226
Sketch of Cobb Legion Cavalry and Some Incidents and Scenes Remembered (Howard), 2
Sledge, James A., 25, 26, 32, 56, 215, 256, 262
smallpox, vaccination for, 183
Smith, C. F., 100n46
Smith, George, 29
Smith, Hoke, 108n2
Smith, Thomas H., 248
South; railroad system of, 92n7; states of, seceding, 41, 42
South Carolina, military units of; 1st Cavalry, 142n2, 175, 177, 217, 227, 263, 264, 270 ; 2nd Cavalry, 142, 145, 163, 174–76, 217, 228, 267, 270, 275–76; 4th Cavalry Battalion, 142
Sparta, Edgeworth Bird, 18
Special Orders (Army of Northern Virginia); No. 104, 192; No. 183, 142
Spotsylvania Court House (VA), battle of, 48n
Stagg, Peter, 271–72

Stanton, Edwin M., 278n34
Stanton Hospital, 278, 280–81, 283–84, 294–95, 299–300
Steel, Leigh Hull, 12n6
Steele, Michael D., 12n6
Stephens, Alexander, 38
Stephens, Linton, 38
Stoneman, George, 192, 193–94
Stovall, Pleasant, 280
Stovall, Thomas P., 44–45, 52, 53, 55, 57, 59, 83, 97, 103, 105, 107, 121, 126
Stovall's Company, 52, 59
stragglers, 158
Stuart, J. E. B., viii, 48n, 113, 133, 137, 148, 149, 158, 159n1, 166, 167, 172–75, 211, 223, 232, 245, 272–73; abolishing Company Q, 242; at Brandy Station, 217, 220 ; building force, 216; on Cobb's Legion, 117–18; commanding Army of Northern Virginia cavalry, 142–45, 270; criticism of, 124–25, 135, 160, 231, 244–46; near Culpeper, 245; at Dumfries, 177–180; Delony and, 129–30, 170, 175; favoritism of, 141, 181, 269; at Gaines' Cross Roads, 163–64; at Gettysburg, 237; glory ride of, 236–37; grand reviews for, 128, 208, 212, 216–17; hosting balls, 144–45; on Hampton, 174; Hampton transferred to, 108; increasing his forces, 211, 214; at Jack's Shop, 273, 276, 278; leading Hampton's Cavalry, 238; in the Loudoun Valley, 222–23; at Mechanicsville, 110–12; at Occoquan, 177–78; organization by, 137, 244; other officers and, 155, 175; on Young, 140
Stuart's Brigade, 135, 220–21
Stuart's Cavalry, 110, 111, 114, 162, 163, 173, 192, 230n35, 242, 278
Stuart's Tarheels: James B. Gordon and His North Carolina Cavalry in the Civil War (Hartley), 2
St. Vitus Dance (Sydenham's chorea), 136
Sulphur Springs (VA), 148

Taylor, Elizabeth Bolling, 36n4
Taylor, Jane Henrietta Burke, 32
Taylor, Richard Delony Bolling (Dick), 7, 66, 131, 186, 187, 200, 207, 260
Taylor, Robert G. (elder), 6–7
Taylor, Robert G. (younger), 7, 36, 206
Taylor, Thomas, 7
Temperance Society, 57
Texas Brigade, 111
Thomas, Ella, 18
Thomas, Emory, 244
Thomas, George, 267n59